Those in the Light, Those in the Dark,

Volume 1

Those in the Light, Those in the Dark,

Volume I

Deborah Lenz

iUniverse, Inc.
Bloomington

Those in the Light, Those in the Dark, Volume I

iUniverse books may be ordered through booksellers or by contacting:

iUniverse
1663 Liberty Drive
Bloomington, IN 47403
www.iuniverse.com
1-800-Authors (1-800-288-4677)

ISBN: 978-1-4401-8243-3 (pbk)
ISBN: 978-1-4401-8244-0 (clth)
ISBN: 978-1-4401-8245-7 (ebk)

Printed in the United States of America

iUniverse rev. date:05/20/2011

Dedication

Dedicated to my Mother, Athena, Joseph, baby James, the twins, to my Family, The Allegiance, to Giovanni and his music that kept me inspired to go on even when everything else was hopeless, to all Soulmates, Soul Energies and to all Life Forces . . . wherever they may be.

To Zeus and the others involved. To Spanky the cat who saw it all and Anje, my Rottweiler, the best bodyguard . . . ever.

To Black Beauty and White Allegiance for their protection against the Forces . . . to the few who helped and believed us during all of the bizarre things that happened.

And finally, last but not least, to my Soulmate, for without him none of this could have been possible.

Preface

I pick up my car phone and ring my chauffeur who is already waiting up front for directions. I tell him that we are going for a long, long ride today. We pull out and he enters the interstate with great ease. He drives White Allegiance, my white ultra stretch limousine, just the way I like it to be driven. Of course, White Allegiance commands the road and all look to her beauty. We headed northeast.

My mind automatically goes to the reason that I am here today, the reason that I came back to this life and all that has happened to me. It will always be there . . . strong . . . firm . . . and as real as this very moment.

I pick up the phone again and take a deep breath. I ring my chauffeur and say, "Let's go home. You know the way."

"Yes, Deborah. I'll take you home," he replies.

Oh, how I remember it all so well! It started such a long, long time ago. How can you possibly understand any of it without understanding the beginning? Yes . . . my Soulmate and I were there too. What is so amazing is the similarity between us, even today. Of course, that is because we are still the same two people that we were then. I look out the window and, yes, White Allegiance is awesome . . . but then, so is my Soulmate . . . and so am I. And you will be too when you are done reading this.

THIS IS A TRUE STORY

. . . and the characters are real people. With the exception of Frederick and Deborah Lenz, the character's names have been changed to protect those in the Light.

.

CHAPTER ONE

I knew from the very beginning I was going to do what I ended up doing. I came to earth at rapid speed and entered at what would be the creation of life for me. I recall being in the womb and it seemed to take forever to be born. Where I had come from the time was much different. Finally, I was born. My biological mother had very beautiful features and my biological father was quite handsome but neither one of them were ever what you would call my parents or family. I was barely attended to by them. I had however, my spiritual Family, which was my real and true Family. We were all from Olympus and the heavens and had done many things together for millenniums.

I was never attached to my parents or any other person. I constantly had my own Family by having the Allegiance with me. The Allegiance was the Family with the Creator, all of those in pure White Light. I kept to myself and listened to what my Family told me. As I grew, so did my Powers. I found no challenges here and was very bored. I preferred to stay outside all of the time. Where we lived, there were endless fields of wildflowers and so many tiger lilies. I loved to lie down in these fields and look up to the heavens.

My Family changed my metabolic structure and brought recall to my desire to go home with them. Athena called me Daughter and attended to me much of the time. She would run her hands through my long hair and I would sit next to her. One day my biological mother came looking for me and it was apparent that she could not see Athena. I realized that I was not human but merely in a human body. I was only three years old then but from that point on I was never the same. I listened to Athena, who told me many stories. I especially wanted to hear one of her stories again and again.

"He is here on the planet too," she would say. "He is the only one like you Daughter," she would say with such importance. "You must be aware that the world will not understand all that you will do but never ever give of you to the world."

I wanted to know more about this one who was like me. I knew I saw Light and I knew about Darkness. I could locate things by thoughts and energy. I could move things and understand how they moved. Athena told me to never tell anyone about these things. She told me that I was in a place where people were not evolved in anything. They sleep here and try to avoid their responsibilities, she would say. As time went by I saw this and tried to stay to myself. Everything I saw I knew already. Nothing was a surprise to me. It was as if I had been here again and again. My physical body was flooded with energy and the more energy I reflected, the more irritated people felt around me. Because of my age no one looked at me and they blamed everyone or everything around them, when I was the one causing these energies. I was not noticed, in fact, I was left out of everything and kept from everyone.

If it had not been for the Allegiance, I would have never survived my childhood because being here was a constant struggle with such negativity. I held onto my Family for dear life. They continued to prepare me for what was about to come. I had more than visions. I could extend myself to the level my Family was at and still go through the functions here. No one saw it, no one was aware of any of it. I knew I was not of this world because I could completely transform to other levels, changing my body during these transformations. It was very hard to be here, so very hard. Athena stayed with me, guarded me and protected me along with many others from this realm. They could not come back into the human body because their vibrations were so high that a human body would malfunction and burn up. There was no loneliness as long as they were there. Athena spoke of the Creator and I remembered this as strongly as if the Creator was right there in front of me. Only Love, Truth and constant Protection came from the Creator. It made me smile. Except for being on the earth, I felt that all was as it needed to be. I constantly had overflowing Love with me. If only you could have felt all of this, you could have understood that the Creator is the only source of Love, not human beings. It just didn't feel right to be on this earth though. I would listen to people's conversations and hear nothing but primitive thoughts being expressed and very animalistic behaviors. People wallowed in being irresponsible and tried to manipulate everything. People were covered in Darkness. There was no Light here. No one had Light. I wanted to go home.

Athena told me that I could not go home yet, that I had a very important purpose here and that I had to stay. I asked her if someone else could do this job.

"Daughter," she would say, "No one can do this but you. We will always be there to help you and no matter how it seems you will have our help."

Yet the more I saw the more I wanted to leave. I saw hate, anger, violence, manipulation, lies and devastation again and again. I saw families appearing to be the perfect family, yet I saw only tolerance from the children as the parents enforced what appeared to be love.

Wait, I thought, until the children wake up and in years to come they will. That will be when the parents say, where did we go wrong? I saw everyone receive constant opportunities to wake up yet they refused. Around the age of four, the Allegiance pulled me from my biological family. You will say that my parents just separated and divorced. Who do you think caused that? I was automatically using very evolved systems and I had so many close calls that I almost got caught. The reason the Allegiance pulled me out was because if I had been caught I would have been locked up, experimented on or they would have had to take me back home. My preference looking back on it now would have been to take me back home but Athena told me I'd just have to come back again. I couldn't understand one thing. Why me? Why couldn't someone else do what it was I had to do? This was the only thing that sparked my curiosity. It was intensely empty as a child if I went near anything of the human realm. There was only the Allegiance to hold me and love me. Again and again I was reminded that I could not become attached to anything of the earth realm.

At four years of age I was beyond my years and yet had to endure the childhood surroundings. As I grew I was increasingly isolated. I was awkward and did not fit in. I began to strongly be pulled to my Soulmate. I knew he was out there somewhere and I felt him more at night. I knew it was him and Athena just smiled when I asked if this was the one special person like me. I could go on if he was there and I could barely wait to meet him again someday. Why was he here? Why did he come back? Sometimes I would forget myself and alter things around people. They would refuse to acknowledge it and ignore what they had seen. As I grew I was constantly hungry and noticed that when I tried to merge with my Family I used up a great deal of energy. Years later it would be called levitation and astroprojection.

I felt so drawn to him, my other half, my reflection, my Soulmate. It was deep beyond my heart that I felt this desire, this pull. It was deep in my soul, I was sure he could levitate and astroproject as I did because he came to me and spoke to my heart. He was real and did exist. I knew it but I felt that he pushed away feelings for me. By five, no one in the earth realm loved me or cared whatsoever about me. It had really been this way from birth but there were a few moments of weakness from time to time and crumbs of bread or kindness momentarily thrown my way. Since I was surrounded by Darkness and people wallowing in it, I presented a great fear to them being so filled with Light. When people were mean to me I would pull away and call to Athena.

"Athena, take me to him, quickly!" I cried. I did not want to be here, anywhere on this planet but if I had to stay, I wanted to go to my Soulmate. People were mean and ugly and very cruel to me. All this did was push me closer to my Family. I knew that my Soulmate had to be going through many of the same things. There were many days that I could not cope with everyone's negativity and Athena would take her hand and in a circular motion she would make a circle of energy around my face and I would fall into a very deep sleep.

Those were the nights when the tears fell from my eyes and the longing to go home with the Allegiance was more than I could bear.

The Olympians did things to remind me of who I was. All of them loved me and I loved them as well. Athena, Awesome Goddess was closest to my heart. So much love came from her and from me as I embraced her deepest of all. So you see, my Family was different but I had one too and would always have them. Beyond Athena was our Creator, without whom there would have never been Athena or anyone else. In school I was horribly picked on in hand-me-down rags and laughed at. I would look at these children and say to myself, someday they will need me. Someday they will remember the White Light, the Awesome Creator and leave their Dark ways. I had compassion for them. They were lost, I thought. I gathered all of them in my thoughts and released them back to the Creator asking that they be allowed again to remember the Awesome White Light.

I used to daydream out of the classroom window. I was so bored. I never wanted to go home to my earthbound home setting. I was very scrawny and never had enough to eat. I had very hard chores to do but at least they were mostly outside and that is where I needed to be. Athena would keep me company and when you are used to her, even chores are fun. I had to carry many heavy buckets of ashes from the furnace each day and the long walk to the back of this house was far. Athena would help carry these buckets with me. It seemed like I was having fun even doing chores and it made others angry. No matter what I did, I never complained or tried to get out of what I was told to do. I knew Athena would help me and it gave me the opportunity to talk freely to her. Sometimes Zeus would come by and I did not like him one bit.

I would grab a hold of Athena's beautiful gown and hide behind her. Zeus would rant and rave and Athena would say, "Be gone with you Zeus." He would mumble as he sped off, turning into a burst of light going everywhere.

"Why am I so afraid of him, Mother?" I asked.

"Oh Daughter, some day you will confront him and you will know why." She said soothingly.

"Will I war him?" I asked her.

"Yes Daughter but you will win and wake Zeus back up to the memory of Love."

"Love for whom?" I asked.

"For you, Daughter," she said.

"Why me?" I asked again.

"Because you are his daughter too." Athena said, looking at me and holding me tightly. She always smelled of flowers and incense. It was hard to describe it but it identified her even when I could not see her.

At times when I was at school I would be daydreaming out of the window and she would dance past, making me laugh out loud and I would get punished by my teacher. She always made me smile. It was impossible to concentrate and everything in school I already knew. My nickname was know-it-all and I always had an answer to everything.

I don't think I ever realized to what extent I was different. It seemed to be a difference that no one wanted to be near but Athena said it was because everyone was so Dark. She told me that the day would come when people would come to me in great numbers to hear the Truth. I thought Athena was just saying that to make me feel better. I saw how children were torn apart by the things they were forced to believe. Then I saw how they would be attached to everything but the Creator. No one talked of this. Even the adults were caught up in their levels of Darkness. For instance, it always surprised me that their best friend was their mother or sister or childhood acquaintance. How odd that they did not call the Creator their best friend. How could anyone be better than the Creator? I could never imagine anything being better than the Creator. From time to time the Creator would embrace me so strongly that I would be filled with so much Light and energy that I never wanted anything else. Athena was Awesome as Mom but never as Awesome as the Creator. Nothing could compare to this. Didn't anyone here remember the Creator?

As I grew, Athena helped to numb the events of my childhood. I was so far beyond my childhood and very ready to leave it. I still remained constantly hungry. It was a horrible feeling. I never had much to eat but no matter what, I never felt full. I was not loved by anyone here. The human race didn't know much about love or the true meaning of it. All they could do was smother and manipulate you. It was filled with control and artificial ingredients. I had real Love and there wasn't any way I'd ever give it up, for the Creator was the Ultimate Love. If it had not been for the Allegiance, I would have been pulled out. I was so used to Athena that I behaved similarly. I didn't know any different.

"Why don't people accept me, Athena?" I asked one day as she sat by me in a field filled with tiger lilies.

"Because, Daughter, you mirror their energy back to them. You read their minds, their hearts and their souls. You tell everyone like it really is. It is not well that you speak of these things, you know. You must be still and observe. The day will come when you shall speak of great things."

"Can anyone see you, Mother?" I asked her.

"Only if I choose it but some will see me in the years to come because they will be close to you, Daughter," she said holding me

Since I had Athena, the Angels and all of the other Olympians, I was very secure. I wondered why I could see them and no one else could. Whenever I even came close to becoming attached to anyone but them, I was gracefully pulled away. Athena would once again remind me that I could not become attached to anything of the earth realm. I had to stay focused. I had a purpose she continued to tell me about.

She told me many stories about this one who was like me. He will be a leader and the most powerful man in the world. People will not recognize him as he will be cloaked and his full powers were yet to come. As he is like you, no one will ever be able to connect with him but you. She told me, "He is from our realm as you are, Daughter. Already he comes to you automatically on the soul level. You receive him without even being fully aware of this. Soulmates do this automatically."

I saw children and how programmed they were. I would be teased and laughed at but I understood why. It never bothered me and I released them to the Awesome White Light of the Creator. When

Athena and I spoke, I would always say, "Yes Mother, I remember. I do not have to learn, just remember." She would smile.

You must understand that having Athena for a Mother made all biological mothers look very primitive. I would watch how they would suppress their children and be so messed up over their own lives that they would take it out on their children. I was taken to a Catholic church where I saw the okay on sinning. You sin and then confess and some man in a long robe okay's it with their God. I was so bored in church that I would scan everyone. I would "see" that they were having affairs or carrying on with great deception, thinking that they were safe and well hidden. I recall a man staring at me one Sunday and he told me to stop staring at him. I wasn't but there was that mirroring effect working full time.

I looked at him intensely and said, "If you don't want anyone knowing you're cheating on your wife, you certainly shouldn't be staring at me." He lifted his hand to hit me but Athena dashed in and intervened. He never came back. He also never knew what hit him.

It bothered everyone that I so accepted everything done to me. If I had extra chores I did them and did not complain, in fact, I appeared happy about it all. Of course I was happy, I had the Allegiance with me. Unlike other children, I was never left alone by them. It was very dangerous, Athena would say. Darkness was searching for me because it knew I was going to change things. They didn't dare come near me with Mom and the rest of the Allegiance around. Can you understand now how special my life was?

Whenever Zeus came around I called out to Athena. I did not like him one bit. I knew by Athena's stories that he was not comfortable with me. All in all, I was not going to be open to him. He never stayed long, though, which was well for all of us. He seemed to command authority, except from Athena.

As the years went by, I was constantly saturated in the White Light and Sacred Teachings began to come to me. I didn't realize the magnitude of these Teachings at the time but Athena told me that the day would come when I would teach these things. She also told me the stories of the Olympians and how they left these myths behind. After all, they could make mankind believe whatever they wanted them to, playing games on them because when given a choice, man chose Darkness.

To everyone reading this, it would appear that I had had a very horrible childhood. I suffered horrible ear infections that lasted months and months, year after year. The one thing I could not handle about being here was my body being defective. Anything wrong with my head especially caused severe imbalances, which affected my powers. Since no one attended to me and I did not complain, by the time I could no longer physically function, things like ear infections were severely out of control. My ability to tolerate pain was incredible. All I had to do was astroproject leaving my body when the pain was too great. No matter how sick I was, I still had to do my chores. If I did not do my chores, I received severe punishment. Remember, though, with the projection of the Allegiance I endured. I still did not complain.

After my biological parents had separated, my father lived with his brother's wife, who had separated from her husband. My biological father never acknowledged me on any level but the so-called stepmother harbored a great hatred for being forced to raise me. I was not a bad child, good child or an anything child. I just didn't exist on any level except as a functioning robot that did endless chores and had punishments that were taken out on me from this stepmother's Dark ugly evil. She was the epitome of evil. What made this worse was the fact that she was a nurse who could see medical problems all along but she chose to ignore them. Athena in her rage stepped in and intervened as much as possible. My constant hunger was the symptom of a medical problem, yet year after year it was ignored. I would be so hungry that I would tremble severely and be ice cold. I ate many of my meals outside alone because I was told I was too ugly to be present at the dinner table. Remember though that being outside allowed me the freedom to be with Athena and everyone else from the Allegiance.

Years later, many years later, long after it was too late, it would be discovered that I had had such severely low blood sugar that all through my childhood I had been going in and out of comas and only by the grace of the Allegiance was I kept from dying. On one such occasion, I called out to the Creator and cried that I could not bear such horrible feelings any longer. All of a sudden a great wall of White Light embraced me and I felt the Creator hold me. I would be okay that day and for many days to come.

You must understand that I did not take on these events but merely went through them, detached and unresponsive to all involved. I did speak of them though with the Creator, Athena and the Angels that kept me. I was kept by them in such a beauty that in one moment all would be forgotten of these earthly matters. There was always inner peace, inner beauty and the outpouring of White Light all around me. The fact that I had intense powers and used up so much energy completely changed my metabolic system. This affected my blood sugar also. There were many nights I was not allowed to have any dinner and I would be dreadfully sick all night. It was on one of these nights I was so sick that by morning I could barely walk.

Athena told me I should eat some almond candies in a jar there on the counter close by me. I told her I would be severely punished but she told me that I was so ill that I would die if I did not. So I ate one, then two, three and so on. All of a sudden I felt stronger and I ate every one. I could not believe how quickly I had felt better.

"You are sick, Daughter, from not having enough food. Listen to me, I will keep you," Athena said embracing me like the loving Mother that she was.

For eating those candies I was severely beaten by the stepmother's daughter. She too was as evil as her mother. Athena held onto me and as much as I was beaten, I could not feel a thing. I must tell you, she went after both of them big time. The stepmother seemed to know how important food was for me, so it was one of the things she used as punishment. I would be on a timer and if I was one second over from completing a chore, I would be denied my dinner or other meals. You have to know I did my chores as quickly as possible but could not live up to her laws. I would have severe bouts of fatigue and become so exhausted that I could not stand up. You could see how sick I was with this blood sugar problem and it was the one place she used her evil the most. She made the biological father construct a belt to hit me with. She called it a cat of nine tails. He hit me, often and hard.

Athena in despair decided to intervene so I would not die. "How Mother," I asked, "will you do this?"

"It is easy, Daughter. I will provide you with the means to get food and we will walk and I will show you how I will do this." She stated casually.

Now Athena was not in a solid body so I thought to myself, how is she going to provide me with food? When the stepmother made me go to the corner store, which was a bit of a walk, Athena went with me.

"Mother," I would say, "I am so hungry I cannot walk."

Then Athena in all of her splendor performed her wonderful powers. I still laugh at this even today. As people came out of the corner store, she created a windstorm so powerful they would lose a dollar or a couple of quarters and Athena would tell me what to buy. Someone had to help me.

"Will they miss that dollar, Athena?" I would ask her.

"No, Daughter, I have programmed their minds to forget that they ever even had it." And so Athena kept me alive.

No one told me what was wrong with me, not even Athena but she did tell me that the stepmother wanted me dead. Athena had me put these little snacks in a jar and hide them. How can you not adore her? She was incredible and still is even today. I loved her more than you can imagine and I will always love her. I could go on and on about this and all that happened day in and day out but there was a great turning point about to come.

I was so sick and had such horrible ear problems that my eyes would just tear and tear. The school nurse could not understand why I was being sent to school so sick. I was constantly sick and constantly sent to school sick. The stepmother, who was a nurse, made it apparent that she knew exactly what she was doing.

You don't violate that which Athena has claimed as hers without great retribution. Believe me, even Athena reached her limit with the stepmother and declared war. I am not sure exactly when this war was declared but one day the stepmother announced that when I was beaten I didn't react right. So I would be beaten extra until I would cry but little did evil stepmother realize whom she was messing with. I didn't cry no matter how much I was beaten, because Athena protected me. Between the cat of nine tails and a large wooden spoon, I should have been screaming but the White Light protected me.

You know how Athena made those wind storms? Well, she had many other abilities that came in handy for the events that followed. I didn't have a running chance with starving, hard chores, beatings and bad ear infections. The only chance I ever had came from the Creator, Olympians and Angels. They all literally had to hang onto me around the clock. If you don't yet believe this, there is plenty yet to tell you which will truly convince you.

Athena was so beautiful and she saw me that way too but on one horrible day the stepmother and her daughter shaved my head as a punishment. They laughed and laughed at me, making me go to school that way, where everyone laughed and made horrible jokes about me. I had always had long hair but after this event I vowed to never let anyone touch my hair again. It took so long to grow but they still continued to chop it all off. Only when I finally left this place could I let it grow.

Another time I was locked in the basement and forced to remain seated on the basement steps. The floor was dirt and there were spider webs all over. I had to sit there for hours and it was often used as a punishment for not getting the chores done fast enough. On one such occasion, while sitting in this pitch black damp basement, a spider jumped on me and started crawling up my leg, then another and another. I could not move, I was so paralyzed by this. I tried to hold perfectly still for hours while these spiders crawled all over me.

"Oh Family, protect me." I plead in my mind. "Athena help me." She rushed in and sat on the stairs with me and held me. Can you imagine big black spiders crawling all over your body and you're forced to sit there and take it?

"Oh Daughter, you are so of purpose. What is happening cannot continue. I forbid it. Great evil shall fall upon the stepmother, her daughter and the biological father."

She reminded me of how Darkness would use anything or anyone to try to end me. "When a special one comes to a great purpose, Darkness is always there waiting in hunger to devour Light. That is why, Daughter, you have been so protected. We will never leave you, no matter what happens. We love you."

I cried in her arms for what seemed like forever. Finally, on this very bad, stormy day it became the beginning of my downhill battle my downhill battle, for as I was forced to do the chores this day, I had a precognitive flash of being hit by lightning. It was moments later that the stepmother told me to wash the dishes and for the first time ever I resisted. The lightning was very severe and I just knew I was going to be hit. It did not do any good to protest, as she would force me and she did. The lightning did hit, coming through the water and struck me instantly. I became nauseous, shaking all over and feeling as if I were on fire. I grabbed the front of the sink and as my legs gave way, I could not see, my eyes were temporarily blinded. I called out that I had been hit by lightning and the stepmother responded, "Do the dishes!"

I couldn't do them. I couldn't see them. I remember tears falling down my face. Oh Creator take me, please take me. I don't want to live anymore. I didn't dare let the stepmother see my tears but the Allegiance did and they began the wheels of motion to get me out of this environment. Was all of this worth ending up with my Soulmate? I had hardly had the time to think about him. It was finally going to change and the Allegiance reassured me of this.

To the public, no one ever knew what the father, the stepmother and her daughter ever did to me. Most never even knew I had been born but the schools that I went to knew I existed. Small things, like drawings for Christmas gifts at school, were terrible for me because the stepmother wouldn't even buy a fifty cent present for the name I had drawn. I'd try to get out of the gift drawings but someone got my name and I had to get someone's name as well. I would end up wrapping up some old puzzle that had been thrown out and had belonged to someone else, with pieces missing from it. I had to use newspaper, bits of string or an old paper bag because I had no real wrapping paper or tape and I didn't dare ask for any.

Two years in a row I drew the same name and this poor boy had to get these dreadfully broken puzzles from me. He didn't complain. He somehow knew and spared me the embarrassment. For the few of the stepmother's friends who did know I existed, she would put on these birthday parties where she invited people and made me go through opening the presents and then sent me to my room. When everyone left she returned all the presents. This happened for Christmas as well. Her evil was beyond my understanding.

Finally, I had dishes to wash one night, stacks of dishes from a party the stepmother had. It was late, very late but I had to stay hidden until everyone left. I couldn't do it you know, stay awake and do all those dishes. I fell asleep over the sink and had to stay up almost all night. I overslept in the morning and had no breakfast. By the time I realized I was not getting any, the stepmother would not let me go back upstairs so I could get one of my hidden snacks. She made me walk to school that day on an open highway. It was about three miles to the school. Cars were speeding by so fast that they threw me into the sticker bushes. I was forced to walk in them to keep from getting hit by big trucks and cars. It took almost four hours to get there. I was dehydrated so badly and I must have looked horrible because after that I was removed from the stepmother's house, never to return.

My Family embraced me and even Zeus smiled.

CHAPTER TWO

I was almost thirteen years old when I was taken out of the stepmother's house hold and put into a home. It was different and I was no longer beaten. I was teased though and made to do chores but not nearly as many as the stepmother had made me do. Since no one ever loved me but the Allegiance, this new place really had little impact on me. There are many things I do not speak of. Mostly it would be a waste of time. What really ever mattered here was my purpose, which the Allegiance would not let me forget. I thought intensely about my Soulmate and wondered if he had lost me in this move.

I had meals now, real meals with a better balance but I probably needed different food. Either way, at least my plate was full and I would feel a little better. Finally too, my hair started to grow. I was able to get more sleep at night and my severe and constant starvation state changed. I was now only hungry a few times throughout the day.

The lack of food for all those years, though, had made me so ill that it left permanent damage. Athena changed and became more calm but still spoke at great length about the Dark Force and how it would use new tactics to try to reach me. I already knew what she was talking about but she brought many things to the forefront. Darkness didn't wait for an appointment, it always showed up uninvited. The older I became, the more it needed to make sure I did not accomplish my mission.

"It must really be important," I said to Athena one day. "I mean, really important."

"It is, Daughter, more than you can ever imagine," she said. "If Darkness takes you, you will die."

I had a little bedroom and I really liked it. It was so small you could barely move around in it. There was a large window, which looked out over a porch roof and a large pine tree that embraced the porch so far up that its branches were like large steps. I now saw another way to leave this room.

Two of the children in this family were nasty and ugly and they would tease, steal and lie constantly. They would sneak into my room and break things, steal things and they were never reprimanded for any of it. Their parents just let them do this. I came to this family with nothing but a box of old clothes. I never had any toys or keepsakes but I did protest the violations that they allowed their children to inflict. They would just walk into my room, even while I was changing my clothes. They were only a few years younger than me, so it was not as if they were unaware of what they were doing. It was so bad that it would be a game to them for hours and hours each day, bursting in on me and grabbing things, throwing things or doing whatever they could do to destroy anything I had. They would punch me and slap me and I was not allowed to respond back. This was more than unbearable. How could I live like this?

"Athena," I said, "Fix these little brats."

She laughed and said "You know, Daughter, I have not done children in so long that it brings a laugh to me. I suppose a few skinned knees should slow them down and a few good bike spills should make them too sore to bother you for a bit of time." Leave it to Mom to do her little fry jobs. It was kind of funny.

One evening a few days later Athena visited me again. "We have little time left, Daughter, before the Dark Force will locate you and try to alter your direction. We must spend much time together," she said so concerned. No matter what, I knew Athena was right and that all else had little importance.

Athena fried these little brats and their complaints from bike wrecks grew. Skinned knees, elbows and scratches only lasted a couple of days. It slowed them down but did not stop them. School was so boring and the only private time I had with Athena was late at night, after everyone else was asleep. At first I would just open my window and sit out on the porch roof.

"Athena, I have all of the Teachings," I said.

"Yes, Daughter, I know but the Dark Force knows that you have something very special and they must stop you. You are in more danger the older you get. You are becoming such a beautiful young woman. There will be desires and passions blooming in you. This Dark Force will do anything to violate these things. You are so innocent and naive in this human body," she said so concerned. The moonlight on Athena's gown sparkled and her face glowed. There was always a flood of White Light around both of us.

I had no desires toward boys. I just wanted to meet my Soulmate. I knew the Dark Force did not want Soulmates together. How did I know this? I just knew it. It was like everything else I knew. I just had Total Knowingness of all things.

It was very hard to watch the adults live in a constant state of denial. The second they would get a small clue to anything, they would pull back, and blame or give credit to whatever their minds could come up with. Why? They were lazy, irresponsible and preferring to on their own. No one had any recollection from another lifetime as to how to do anything. Quickly go buy books, ask people or do something but remember, if the garden fails they will have something to blame it on. If it is successful though, they will take all of the credit. This is a cycle that the human race plays out. All along, when people get a second of Knowingness they give it away. That is what I call giving your power away. I lived on a planet with idiots. No wonder my Family kept with me constantly. Surely I would have checked out without them being there. There would be no reasoning with anyone because all of their answers were a collection of everyone else's thoughts. Talk about frustration, I remained as much to myself as possible once again. I could not speak the language of anyone, it was so filled with nothing that made sense. When I would ask, where this conversation was coming from, no one could really answer the question. I must have really been different because nowhere could I find anyone with real thoughts of their own. No one had any idea where most of their ideas even came from. They also did not see anything wrong with this.

It was not a shock when I asked when my birthday was and no one knew. The stepmother and biological father never bothered to find out. Athena told me that the Dark Force used things like birthdays to try and do astrological charts to determine the best tactics to use on someone. If they couldn't get your birthday, they would try to locate those around you to determine what their birth signs were. After all, what was attracted to you had some significance.

It was all right on schedule my whole entire life. It was no mistake that no one knew when I was born. You could say, well how could they not know? Easy, if you have been with me since page one. I knew that the Dark Force did not have full Knowingness because if it did, no one would have survived such terror of the souls. That meant that mankind still had a chance and as long as there was a chance, hope would always be there. How many parents didn't even know their child's birthday? I was glad that I had had idiots for biological parents and relatives because even after all of the evil they tried to do to me, Darkness itself still could not penetrate their minds to locate my actual birth date. This must have frustrated Darkness to no end. Since I was in isolation, there was no one around me to even do any astrological charts.

It amazed me how children gave so much power to their powerless families and relatives. Only when family members were bonded to the Creator did a true connection take place. How often was this, since no one knew the Creator? I had to go to church only to see more lost people giving their power away and actually thinking things would change. They all bought this and they would cling to it. That right there told Darkness where their weakness was. So Darkness intervened and caused change and of course they gave praise to some god. Never once did anyone get clarity as to who was making these changes. If Darkness really wanted a soul, it would really clean things up so that that person would further be convinced in some god. All of these were illusions, really good illusions. Then came the bottoming out, devastation and blame to this god. I couldn't take it, watching this week after week. Churches were organized traps to make you further give your power away. It was truly amazing how no one really knew the Creator.

My hair grew and grew and I must tell you, Athena liked this. "After all," she would say, "it was most intolerable for a Goddess to have short hair."

I continued to go through the motions of doing what I had to do but my time with my Soulmate and the Allegiance was more and more precious. As you can see, everything that happened in my life had an important purpose. There were no mistakes and all of it had to go the way it went. I felt like I was born an adult, doing a crash course on how to save the planet.

Where I lived was an old barn and lots of acres of land. There was so much space that you could get lost in these fields. I craved to be alone so I could speak freely to my Family. It no longer took forever to do my chores and my energy seemed to be better. Even though my diet was high in starch, it was still a great improvement from the stepmother's starvation ritual. It was so hard to stay inside, even in the middle of winter. It seemed as if this room was perfect for the nighttime getaways.

"Oh, Athena, it is nearly impossible to be without my Soulmate. When shall I meet him?" I would ask her.

"Daughter, some things I am unable to tell you even though I know the answer," she would tell me more than once.

"I know that I will meet him and at times I can barely contain myself. Can you tell me nothing about him?" I asked her.

"Daughter, truly this human body makes you vulnerable and naive," she responded.

"It slows me down Mother, so very much. Am I the only one who knows of this?" I asked her so curious.

"There are only a handful with some Knowingness but only you and your Soulmate are of great Knowingness. Such is the magnitude of both of you," she said always reaching out to hold me.

I had something to look forward to no matter what happened. Every time I would see a classmate get a spark of Knowingness, someone would continue to try to put it out. The stronger ones lasted only a little longer before surrendering to this force as well. I wanted to reach out and ask them, "Why do you give your power away?"

I remembered my Soulmate more and more. I also noticed how Athena would pull back from time to time if our conversations about him became very intense. I was clear and sure about everything but him. I knew that the Allegiance kept certain things from me because I was not to know of them yet. The invasion of my bedroom continued and it was still a daily thing. Athena needed to really fry these boys once and for all. Thank goodness Mom had that gentle touch, because other entities could have hurt these boys. Athena decided to do dreams on them and that lasted for a long time. You cannot violate at any age without some lesson coming back your way. Athena only gave them as much as was needed and no harm was ever done. How beautifully and graciously Athena handled things. She always held me and loved me. I always felt so honored to have this experience. Can you imagine having such experiences?

The outside world was constantly amazed at how secure I was. How filled with direction I was. I walked like I had so much confidence. I walked like Athena. There was definitely something inside me that glowed. It wasn't something that I was conscious of. That is what kept Athena on guard all of the time. It was also something that the Dark Force was searching for. Although I spent a lot of time with Athena, I spent more time with the Creator. All of my thoughts were directed there. All my answers came from there. My very being was from the Creator. All Knowingness came from there

It was clear to see why no one got answers, especially the ones they wanted. They were all talking to Darkness, claiming it was their god. Everyone was so empty and lost. When I would suggest that maybe another way was needed, they would cling even tighter to this Darkness. If you cannot get clarity with anything, then how do you know whom you are talking to? I don't know was always their answer. Still, they would complain about how bad their lives were. As time went by, I knew that my purpose was very important because I was getting constant reminders from the Allegiance. Something was about to happen and my precognitive states were always right.

"What is it, Athena?" I asked her one night.

"The Dark Force has searched long for you and they are getting very close. You must keep all of the Teachings stored in your soul.

Nothing can be written down. You have been moved to this location for a reason," she said.

"Does this mean that I will have to leave?" I asked, very concerned.

"No but someone will be sent to try to take you away." She replied.

I liked this tiny room and the endless fields that I could get lost in. The lightning storms were very violent though, so much so that the lights would often blow out and the phone would go down. It was on one such day I wandered off to talk to my Family. I felt so much better these days but I still had that hunger from time to time. I turned around after I had gone through many fields and saw that the house was very far away. I had never gone this far but it was so wonderful. There was a small creek and wild onions all over. It smelled wonderful with all of the wildflowers too. I dropped to the ground and called to my Family. Today the Angels came and in a circle embraced me. There was something odd in how things felt and the Angels turned quickly in their circle so that their backs were to me.

"What is it, Family? What is it?" I asked. I looked up and saw it moments before it hit me.

I do not know how long I was out but the sun was setting when I woke. I had been hit by lightning again. My Family was still gathered closely around. I could not believe I was struck again. Why? It made no sense to me. I would have died if my Family had not been there to protect me.

Zeus had not come by that often and when I asked Athena if he was gone for good, she smiled and said, "Zeus? Daughter, we can never get rid of him! He will be there when he is supposed to be. Once you have been born into the Kingdom of Olympus you never lose your status. You will always be his daughter."

"Well, Mother, I do not like him and this is that. Be gone with him," I said.

Athena laughed and laughed as she reached out to hug me. "The blood runs thick," she said.

The two brats were finally back to the teasing and violating my space again, so Athena decided to take the last and final step. She appeared to them and when they saw her, they never again came near me.

I had a few friends in school. I guess you could call them friends. I wasn't really close to anyone and didn't want to be. I could not really communicate with any of these girls. I was in high school just ending my sophomore year when everything changed in my life. I was allowed to double date and one of the girls in school had a boyfriend who had a friend that went on the double date with me. This girlfriend from school was just using this guy and he decided he wanted to go out with me. To show you what idiots I had for so-called parents, they accepted this boy because he was able to put on a good front for them. They could not see his game. He was the type of boy that they would approve of. I looked at this picture and it made me sick. It was now only two months from my sixteenth birthday. I did not want to go out with this boy but he was driven to call and come over and he would not stop. My Teachings told me that I had to connect to something from him and so I agreed to one date alone. I could not stand him but I knew on a soul level that he would take me to someone I needed to meet. I had to ask Athena to intervene when this guy tried to put his hands all over me. We drove around on some back roads and all of a sudden I felt someone just a short distance away. As we came around a corner, there he was in the pouring down rain trying to change a tire. "Stop!" I yelled.

"So you know Jimmy?" this guy asked me.

"No I don't but help him," I said quite insistently.

"He lives down the road from me. I know who he is," this guy said in a nasty way. I knew he didn't like him. I jumped out and walked up to Jimmy. He looked at me and I looked at him. It was instant that our energies merged together. I recognized him from another time. He recognized me. It was love we felt for each other right then and there. He was like a Greek Adonis, tall, dark and handsome beyond anything I had ever seen. I was frozen in the rain staring at him. He kept smiling at me. Then he said in a whisper, "We are Soulmates." I could not speak. I was frozen. He asked me for my phone number. I could barely remember it. He took my number and he gave me his. The guy who was supposed to be my date got mad and drove off.

"Don't worry," Jimmy said. "I'll take you home." I knew he was going to take me home and many other places. I was in love. He was in love and there was no turning back.

"Oh Athena! I cannot walk or think or function," I said to her in a smiling voice.

Athena responded, "Daughter, it is well of you to know him."

"I have met someone like me, Mother. He speaks like me and understands me. We don't even have to speak and we each know what each other is thinking. It is like us, Mother. I can barely contain myself. Where did he come from? I am so excited," I said to her as I danced around with such excitement.

"Daughter, he is like you but not like you," Athena said with hesitation in her voice.

"He knows about Olympus and he has powers too," I told Athena.

Athena sat me down and said, "Love him, Daughter, with all of your heart. Embrace him and tell him many things. There is great danger for both of you. Your guard is down, Daughter. The Dark Force will be able to find you if your guard is down."

I became serious as I saw tears in Athena's eyes. "Mother, oh Mother, I love you so. Why do you cry?" I asked her. I had never seen Athena sad before. I was so surprised and not sure what I should do. I held her and sat with her for a very long time.

"It is ancient times that we are now talking about, Mother," I said. She nodded yes.

"He was from Olympus, wasn't he?" I asked. Athena nodded again, yes. "He was a son of Zeus once upon a time," I added. "Yes, Daughter," Athena said but she added, "He was cast out and abandoned. Great Darkness fell over him and he battled the Darkness for so very long alone. He became a great warrior and protector. He came back in this life to protect you!"

"Athena, he said that we are Soulmates but I know that he is not my Soulmate. He is a Soul Energy. Why does he think that I am his Soulmate?" I asked her.

"He has saved you many times from your Soulmate," Athena said.

"Mother," I hesitated."Why would I have needed to be saved from my Soulmate?"

"Daughter, not all times have been well with your Soulmate," she responded

"I know we have battled as all Soulmates do but surely I can handle my own Soulmate," I said to her, very alarmed.

"Remember I told you that there were things I could not tell you?" Athena said. "Well, your Soulmate is very powerful like you but sometimes we need help in Soulmate matters."

I calmed down and thought about what she had said. "But I love Jimmy as though I have known him forever. He feels the same way about me. We must have had many lifetimes together, Mother," I said to Athena.

"He will need you, Daughter, to help him in this lifetime," Athena said reassuringly to me.

"Then he is not here this time to protect me from my Soulmate?" I asked.

"No Daughter, but he is here to protect you from other things. He loves you dearly and has waited many lifetimes to find you again. Love him and tell him of things," Athena concluded.

I did love Jimmy and he called me so many times. The family I lived with disapproved of him. Of course, because I had broken my usual behavior and was showing a happy attitude and appearance they had never seen in me before. They could not get clarity about anything, no less what was good for me. Remember the human race cannot handle love, happiness, or anything positive. Now I am speaking of real love, happiness and positive energy from the Creator. Only at that level is real love possible. Since no one knew the Creator, no one had love.

For the first time ever, I snuck out of my window and down this pine tree to meet Jimmy at the end of the lane. We could not stop talking, kissing and holding each other. We constantly missed each other something terrible. We clung to each other as though it might be our last time together. He constantly picked me white and pink wild roses. We had picnics and lay down under the stars. It was right for him to hold me and love me. We counted the minutes and hours before we could see each other again. The family that I lived with decided not to let me see him again. It did not matter to me, I continued to slip out each night to see him. We were nearly the same age. We would look into each other's eyes and smile. It was beyond love and time. It had purpose, meaning, it was necessary. He still proclaimed himself to be my Soulmate. I let him. I let him embrace me as I had never been embraced before. He was so familiar and he told me that he had remembered other lifetimes with me.

"We have traveled through time and space, Deb. I know it," he would say. He seemed so old for his age. "I shall never meet anyone like you again," he said so sadly one day.

"There is pain in your heart," I said to him.

"Yes and when I hold you I never want to let you go. Someone will come though and take you away from me," he said barely able to get the words out.

"No!" I protested. "Jimmy, no one will take me away from you. They can't. I won't let them. I love you. I desire you." I told him as tears started pouring out of my eyes.

"I hear you," he said, "but I know that this will happen. I just know it. I am always right about things. I am like you, Deb." I could not stop crying.

We had been together for months, day in and out and he was sensing someone taking me away. He held me but he never let go of these feelings. No matter what I did or said, from that point on, he held me tighter, knowing that he was going to lose me. I just kept reassuring him that I would never leave him. We spoke of the Gods and Goddesses and he had not recalled that Zeus had been his father.

Jimmy and I traveled through many lifetimes as we lay out under the stars. I needed him so very much. I could not lose him, I just couldn't. No one in a human body had ever shared so much with me. Our love was deeper than we even realized. How could anything separate us? I was his and I no longer cared if I ever met my Soulmate. I didn't need my Soulmate. Jimmy was as close to being my Soulmate as possible. I could not lose him. I wanted to spend the rest of this life with him. Whenever I tried to make plans he would now say to just take it one day at a time.

"You never know," He continued to tell me.

"No," I would say, "we will never be separated. Stop thinking our time is running out."

Athena always spoke to me about the mission I had to do here on the earth. "Why couldn't Jimmy be part of it?" I asked her. "He is part of it but cannot be there for the rest of his life or yours," she told me.

"Athena, I will do my mission here once I know what it is but if I have no one on the earth to love me I will die inside. Please help me," I said crying to her. "I can't let him go. Won't Darkness take him now that he has been with me?"

"Indeed it will but it will kill you, Daughter, if it finds you with him. He is not strong enough to lay down his life for you again. Not in this life," she said.

"Oh, Creator," I screamed, "I will do any mission here but after loving him so deeply, how will I go on without him?" I cried. "I cannot, I will not. I would rather die than lose him."

Athena spoke, "Daughter, he will die if he stays with you and on some level he knows this. You must let him go." How was I to go on? I didn't want my Soulmate anymore. I didn't care to ever meet him. I saw Jimmy and we talked of all of this. We cried in each other's arms and loved each other as much as we could.

"Jimmy," I said, "I will never let you go. No matter how much time goes by I will love you. I will love you forever. No one will ever take your place."

He cried and in his gentle manner he embraced me. "Our time is short," he said, barely able to get the words out.

"Can't we stop it?" I begged him.

"No," he said, "I must battle the Dark Force, Deb." I saw in all of these months how it played out in his life, constantly trying to destroy him, putting blocks up all over to make him struggle and suffer so badly. It was trying to do him in.

"If I stay with you too long, Deb, they will locate you," he told me so seriously.

"Then we can fight it together. It's been after me my whole life." I declared. If we battle it together, we will be stronger," I said to him

26

with a new energy in me. "Do you think that anyone will ever love me like you do?" I asked as tears fell down my face. He took me into his arms and held me.

"Oh, what am I going to do with you?" he said.

I had found something on this earth that was like me. I was willing to do anything to have it. Jimmy asked me one evening if I would be willing to sell my soul to the Dark Force.

"I am not afraid of the Dark Force. I am not afraid of any Force. We have the Allegiance, Jimmy and they love you too," I told him. "Be gone with this Dark Force."

We knew as the summer ended and fall came that we would not see each other by Christmas. The snow would fall and I would stand alone. He knew that great struggles were coming and that he had to do it all alone. He was the warrior and one of the sons of Zeus. He had battled again and again. He would never risk losing me by allowing danger to touch me. We were pure and innocent and untouched by mankind and its Darkness. Instead, we were on levels way beyond mankind, the human race and our battles were of Forces so evolved that we had little help on this earth. Our battles were ancient, yet renewed by the Dark Force still trying to hang onto its paradise. It hunted for empty souls, lost souls and vulnerable souls. Where would Jimmy end up and would he make it? I knew from the Teachings that Divine Order had to be kept and nothing could alter this.

In sadness, I held my head down as Jimmy took both of my hands into his. "I cannot touch you anymore," he said. "They will grab us if we ever lie down together again. They will observe our nakedness and beauty. They will feel our innocence and love in our souls. They will bring forward demons to devour us." Tears fell down his face onto my hands.

"I love you," I said, choked up inside. "I love you."

He pulled away and I grabbed him, screaming to him, "No Jimmy! I can't make it. I can't live without you. If you are my Soulmate as you say, you can't walk away from me and abandon me." He grabbed me and promised that we would always be able to find each other. All we had to do was think of each other and we would know where we were. He had to go and turned to leave.

"No!" I cried out again. "Hold me, kiss me one more time, just one more time," I said as I stood there with my arms open to him. He turned and rushed into them embracing me longer than we had ever embraced. We wanted to be frozen in time but our tears had met and we were flooded in sorrow. We both finally knew now that our love was not meant to be.

CHAPTER THREE

I never did recover from the loss of Jimmy. I could not forget his presence, his essence, his life force. I knew that there would never be anyone like him again.

I walked out to the fields in the cold of winter, so worn out that I could not cry anymore. Athena held me and loved me as did all of my Family but it was never the same. Just like when I was hit by lightning, you cannot go back and change it. It was done and the cold hard truth hit me like a solid wall of helplessness. I could not go on without him. Even, just even, if I could, where was I to go on to? I did not want this mission or anything else. My whole life I had been raised by a Family that no one could see, feel or understand.

Why did Jimmy have to battle the Dark Force alone? I could have helped him. Someone could have intervened from the Allegiance. Athena held me and spoke. "Daughter, you must go on now!"

"No!" I yelled at her. "No!"

"Daughter," she said, "If you do not go on you will be pulled out."

"Then let me be pulled out. I don't care. It is not like before. Before, I never knew of this kind of love. I cannot go on, knowing I will never have it again," I said to her.

"What about your Soulmate?" she said.

"What about him? I suppose he will love me as much or more? I don't believe so. I just don't believe it," I said crying.

Athena began to weep. "The Dark Force will win, Daughter. If you give up they will take Jimmy too. You must fight, you must, so many are counting on you."

"Oh, yes, good old mankind is counting on me. I just can't believe this, Athena. I am born knowing everything so that no matter where I go or what I do I can never be comfortable or content because I know it all," I screamed.

Athena responded, saying so sadly, "If only I could tell you what is ahead of you."

"Yes Mother, if only, but you can't. The Creator won't tell me, no one will tell me because I am denied this Knowingness. Why Mother, because I will want to check out?" I said, so upset.

"Daughter," Athena said.

"No, do not say any more," I yelled at her. "I want to be left alone. Leave me, all of you. The whole Family leave me. Why stay because it's so wonderful? Right. Then why don't you all come forward and take human bodies? If I do not belong here, then what am I doing here?" I was so upset I was shaking and of course, do you think I could have any privacy? No! Zeus has to show up.

"And what do you want?" I yelled at him.

He yelled back at me, decreeing, "I will not allow such behaviors."

"Oh really?" I said to him. "And just who do you think you are?"

He started to stir up a storm and I would liked to have called it one big temper tantrum. Athena raced to me and shielded me. "Daughter, run! You shall be struck," she said to me in a whisper.

I started to run for dear life and as sure as anything, lead fingers himself started striking the old lightning bolts around. No wonder this house I lived in had so many lightening rods on it. Zeus attempted to shove Athena out of the way so he could get to me but she raised her arm and he came to a halt.

"I shall deal with you another time," he said to Athena. "And as for her, I will get this insubordinate child later as well," he roared.

"You will not touch her, Zeus!" Athena finalized with her splendid tone of voice.

As usual old Pops burst into light beams and disappeared. Can you believe this? I can't! It all hit one thought after another. I'm on a planet full of idiots and I have a Family playing Star Wars. I'm wanted by the Dark Force but I'm so fixed in the White Light that the Allegiance made sure I could never get out. I'm in a dream. That's it! I just did not wake up yet.

The phone rang and it was Jimmy. My heart was pounding with excitement. "Deb," he said, "I just wanted to talk to you."

"Jimmy how are you? I miss you so much," I said to him.

"I am okay", he said. I knew as soon as he said this that he was not okay, in fact, I knew he was calling me because he was in trouble.

"Can you come and get me?" I pleaded with him.

"No," he said, "I don't have a car."

"Please, Jimmy. Please try to come by tonight," I said in a whisper so no one in the house could hear me.

"I'll try," he said, and hung up. It had been weeks since we last saw each other.

I waited until midnight but he did not show. I climbed out my window and ran down the long lane to the road. I could feel Jimmy was close. I sat down on the stone pillars that outlined the driveway. Then in the moonlight, in the freezing cold, I stood up and saw him walking up the road. I raced to his open arms and held my love. My soul had been once again filled and nourished by his touch. The longing and waiting was now over. We went to the barn and laid down on some hay. Our cold hands became warm. Our bodies warmed each other. He told me he had walked all these miles to get to me, which were many. He just needed to hold me, feel me, love me. He looked tired but it was as if he had just returned from some battle.

"They are winning, Deb," he told me.

"The Dark Force?" I asked.

"Yes. Remember all our talks about it? I need you, Deb and you need me." He spoke with such intensity I could not bear it. I started crying because I knew I would not see him for a long time after this night. Once again, we could automatically read each other.

"Don't cry, Deb," he said, holding me so close.

"But Jimmy, I can't bear you going through this all alone. Please let me be a part of it. I will battle with you. We have the whole Allegiance to help us," I said.

"No matter what I do, trouble follows me and battles me. I am so tired of the fight," he said.

"What can I do?" I cried to him.

"Just love me, be there," he said so sadly. He knew what was coming. I did too, and no matter what we wanted, things were going to go the way they were. I knew that no one could change his or her journey. If it were possible, Athena would have helped me change mine. Only members of the human race think that they can change these things. They base this on their egos and their intense need to have more *power. While Jimmy lay there embracing me, Athena's words came to my mind. Words like, the Dark* Force will win if I didn't do my mission here on the planet. Fight, Daughter, fight, her words came into my mind. Athena's words that the Dark Force would take Jimmy kept coming into my mind again and again too. I had to stop this. I would not give up. If the Dark Force thought that it was going to win, it had another thing coming. I had to fight.

His warm big arms so strong and firm would soon let go of me. He would have to battle this Force alone but no matter where he would be, I would be there too, in his heart and soul. He stood up, pulling me up alongside his of body. He had the most beautiful smile ever. He could go now and I would be okay. We walked out to the road, knowing that it would be a long, long time before we would see each other again. We were silent and held each other's hand, gently squeezing our fingers from time to time, reaffirming our closeness. It was beyond love. It was bonded to the Creator because if it took the rest of my life I was going to fight this Force. I knew that I was stronger than Jimmy in many ways because I had been raised by a Family that dealt with this Force. If some of the Dark Force is in human form and some in a form considered supernatural, then in order to battle it you would have to know both Forces to be successful. One of the reasons the Dark Force was so powerful was because there wasn't anyone able to battle it completely. The human race is so ignorant as to how to keep this Force out of their lives.

Jimmy held me. "I love you," He said.

"I love you," I said back to him. He smiled and turned away. "I'll always be there for you," I said in his direction.

He turned momentarily and said, "I will always be there for you too." Then he became a shadow that disappeared over the ridge.

I didn't cry but stood even stronger because a large dark cloud descended over my head and I knew the battle had begun. I spoke clearly and out loud, "I release you Dark Force back to the Awesome White Light of the Creator, where you will remember Love, Truth, and Protection." At once a beam of White Light raced to the center of this dark cloud and dispersed it. I knew that cloud had fled only to re-gather for a bigger battle yet to come but for now, the White Light had heard and responded and I knew that it always would. I had all of Jimmy's love letters to cherish.

The situation living with this family started to deteriorate quickly. I just withdrew even more. These people had no idea what I was about. They didn't want to know. They just wanted me to do my chores and not get out of line.

When I saw Athena I rushed to her, holding her dearly. "I love him so much Mother," I said.

"I know Daughter," she said, so glad to see me.

"I will battle, Mother, I will!" I told her as we both smiled.

"The Creator has you, Daughter, as the Creator has all of us," she said. The human race will continue to be doomed as long as they continue on with their evil. They are all twisted and turned around in the wrong way." Athena said.

"It amazes me, Mother," I said, "that what is Darkest, they actually think is their god or going in the direction of their god. They actually treat their god like it is human and even thinks like them. Can you imagine saying things like the Creator took it away or gave them something? Oh yes, and they blame their god and label their god with human words and behaviors. This is so funny. They put their god in religion. This one religion actually thinks it's very defective because it has decided you get lost and then you have to be saved and they tell you how to be saved. They speak about my brother Jesus in this religion. They do not tell the truth about Jesus and they even think he is their God. Since you can never leave the Creator or get lost, why would they make this silly ritual? My brother would never participate in such silliness however, Darkness would. It is sad that they are so asleep. Darkness has always wanted the females repressed because Mother, always we see it clearer than the males. This world is male dominated. They also are prejudiced against skin color. How funny! Can you imagine such silliness? It is lower here than the animal kingdom. The males here want to be a god and they cheat and commit violations. They are so sick that they have convinced the human race that they are ruled by their male anatomy. This is their excuse to violate further and the females put up with this. They claim it is a scientific fact".

Athena laughed and said, "Yes Daughter, they claim that their stick is their rod and all things are ruled by the rod." We laughed so about this because it made man look so primitive that other species looked more evolved.

"Why, even Zeus thinks the lightning rod has power," I laughed, continuing on with Athena.

"Where do you think the word came from, Daughter?" Athena said, laughing now so hard that the whole Family was in hysterics.

All of a sudden I became dead serious. "Mother, why is it so strong in me, that we have laughed like this in Olympus. It is past life I recall here." I spoke so focused.

Athena was so roaring with laughter now that all she could say was "Yes, Daughter, but haven't we been laughing about his rod for millenniums?"

I started to laugh but realized I had to run or I would be late for school. "Daughter," Athena yelled as I sped off. "You do not need school, you need to teach them."

In the next moment the laughter behind me burst apart and was gone. I had to do another reality check to make sure that this was not all a dream. As soon as I got to the school bus, everyone was staring at me. Sure I had my warrior armor on, but, was it that bright? Apparently so. By the time I got to school, everyone was either moving closer to me or further away. Obviously you could see the Dark versus Light. All of a sudden I was an overnight star. Let me point out how this is really sad, that the human race is so lost that one spark of Light gives instant hope. I had more than one spark. I was charged to the max because after all, I had been hit two times by lightning. It was so dreadful to take those two strikes. What was it supposed to do, jumpstart me?

At lunchtime all of these girls gathered around outside and asked what was new. What was new, I thought. I responded by saying, "Everything is new!" You would think that I had had some major makeover and everyone was staring.

"Talk to us, Deborah," one girl said. They all acted as though I had something important to say and I guess I did. Each day we all got together and as the months went by so did the school year. Everyone came to me with all of their problems and they were very confident that I could solve them. They all wanted to get to the final conclusion of the problem and not do any searching or understanding as to why it had happened to begin with. You could see why they never got anywhere. Everyone was lazy. It always came back to everyone being irresponsible again and again. The adults were no better, in fact they not only were irresponsible but if you hinted to them that that was apparent, they would become nasty and ugly.

"Athena, get me off this planet," I demanded.

"Daughter, you know I cannot," she said.

"It is so repressed here," I said to her. "People are deliberately in it."

I thought of Jimmy as the school year ended. I knew that he was not okay. I knew that ugly black warriors were after him. It was probably for loving me or worse yet, maybe it was our very own Soulmates causing such war. My love was as strong as ever. He was my eternal flame, my reflector, my breath of air. Oh how I loved this man. I did not lose him but merely had hope of a greater magnitude to go on. Just knowing he was somewhere on the planet had a calming effect on me. He had stopped the many exits I probably would have tried. No, I know I would have tried. If it had not been for Jimmy I would not still be here today. His spirit, his life force was the driving factor that pushed me forward, that kept me here. What people didn't realize is that the Dark Force was after everyone. It's just that some of us walked around with our high beams on constantly.

This brings me to my first experience with driving. It was incredible! You'd have idiots that drove with high beams on constantly. These were rude, asleep, behind the wheel types. It was obvious that they could not see and needed more light, because in spite of your flashing them or piercing their eyes with your high beams, they refused to lower theirs. What can you do? Obviously the Dark Force doesn't want you to see. Do you really think that they miss a trick? I've seen what they do to cars and trucks. Even if this person deliberately keeps their high beams on, they are merely allowing the Dark Force to notice them more. You see rude people walk around in one of the vibrations that the Dark Force plants in them. So as they keep track of their inductees, there goes one more on the road to their heaven. The next time you pass the high beam blaster, remember where his travel is headed. By the way, do you know any rude people? Now you know who has them.

There are also the losers who stay in the passing lane. They are really trying to stop the flow of harmony. They force you to pass on the right side. They are trying to stop the Light. Don't worry, their lives are so in the Darkness that there is no hope for the "accident causer" unless they wake up fast and move over. Some might say that they just forgot to move back over to the other lane. You don't forget when someone driving behind you is laying on the horn or flashing their lights for you to get over. What's your excuse? As for me, if I encounter this I just send beams of energy which force you back over into the right lane and on the right track, whether you want to be or not. If you come near me, you go in the Light or flee. I do not put up with the other Force.

Some of the girls in school ended up pregnant in their senior year. They came to me for advice about this. I was shocked!

"Athena," I said, "they want advice on pregnancy, abortion, marriage."

"Then tell them, Daughter, what you know." She said to me, very confident that I could handle it all.

At first I did not want to say a word, but with much persistence I sat them down and began to speak. "Now you have never heard what I'm about to say, and never will again but rest assured, you will know for sure what to do once and for all," I said to them as their faces started to show a glimmer of hope. "Here is what I know," I said and began to tell them.

"First of all, a woman in Light cannot carry a baby in Dark."

"How can a baby be in Dark?" one girl asked, upset.

"Listen to me or walk from here. You have come here for Love, Light and Truth. Be still or leave," I said firmly. Here they go again, trying to rush to the final conclusion of their problem or what they perceive as a problem. You see I don't believe in mistakes. "Now I will start again. Do not stay if you feel you cannot handle this. Please hold your questions until I am done. Let me begin now without further delay. As I started to say, a woman in Light cannot carry a baby in Dark. You first have to understand that souls enter and leave the body. Darkness needs to be explained here. Why is it that the human race perceives Darkness as total hell? There are levels of Darkness and there are levels of Light. Let me start with Darkness. All of you are asleep in certain areas, which means, you are in the Dark. Now, as you remember, the more you wake from your sleep and see the Light, such as right now, I can read your minds. You are saying no Dark should be allowed. You do not mean this or the whole human race would be gone."

"Let me go on." I said a bit impatiently. "Only a woman in Dark can carry a baby in Dark. If this occurs, she will feel comfortable in her body and not reject it. She may not like it but the actual state of her physical body will not reject it. A soul in Darkness can only enter into a woman in Darkness. If it tries to enter a woman in Light, it will be in for the battle of its life. Some souls try to go into Light before they are supposed to. A soul in Darkness does well to stay in its own realm until it is time to go into Light. It is not easy staying in Light after a long time in Dark. Allow this and do not interfere. "

"Yes, I see the look on your faces. Did you honestly think we are born, die and go to heaven living happily ever after? We have many lives. This too, I can validate for you when we have another time. For now we are on another topic. "

I thought carefully before I spoke. I wanted to very sure they understood. "It is possible to have a whole family in Darkness and they think that they are in Light. The difference is in Darkness you think you're in Light. In Light, you know you're in Light. The Soul knows, the human race thinks! Can the father of a baby be in Light and the mother of the baby be in Dark? Yes but will the baby be in Light? No, Dark can only carry Dark. It is the mother who determines if the baby is carried. Now let's turn this around. If the father is in Darkness and the mother is in Light, can she carry a baby in Dark? No. Light can only carry Light. Remember Dark can only carry Dark. Let's say a mother in Light conceives a child in Darkness. The drive in her to terminate the pregnancy is so overwhelming that it consumes her every thought until it is ended. The soul inside her may be so strong that it tries to pull its own mother into Darkness. Can this happen? Only if the mother is in Dark to begin with. She may be in the illusion that she's in the Light. If this soul realizes it cannot change this mother, it will usually exit on its own. Thus we have what is called a miscarriage. If a soul comes into a mother in Light but it is ready to transfer from Darkness to Light, there will be a battle in this transference but it still could make it. The pregnancy, however, might be labeled dangerous, difficult or very hard on the mother and baby the whole term. Just by the way the pregnancy goes, I know what the situation is. Of course, you will probably go to a doctor and hear all kinds of other things. If this soul is transferring while in the mother, there are special things both need to do to make this easier. Your doctor will know nothing about this. Darkness is so good at giving you the illusion of Light. "

"A mother in Light with a soul in Light is called an easy, happy, wonderful pregnancy. The more in Light, the fewer symptoms pregnancy can give. Light gives you clarity and if you know your situation you will recognize all things. Remember, a difficult pregnancy is a mother in Light with a soul in Dark trying to transfer over to Light. "

"A mother in Dark with a soul in Dark is bearable and tolerable." I went on. "The pregnancy ending in abortion or miscarriage is a mother in Light with a soul in Dark. A mother in Dark will never conceive a soul in Light."

The group of girls was not shocked or alarmed by all that I had said because it made total and complete sense. It touched their souls so much they did not want me to stop. "Deborah," one girl said with such a look on her face. "How do you know all of this?"

"My question to you is, how is it you all forgot this? I've always known this," I told them.

"Do you know everything?" she asked me.

"Yes and all of you can know everything too," I told them.

"I have a question," another girl asked. "Okay, now that we are all trying to figure out what we are in, Dark or Light, what happens if we want to change what we're in? Can we?"

"First of all, trying is a word like the word thinking, so you would be in Darkness speaking this. Your terminologies help you recognize where you are at. Also, you are really speaking for you but are using the terminology "we" as though all of you are thinking the same. Each one of you has your own uniqueness, therefore your sentence of, "We are all trying to figure out what we are in, Dark or Light," would not be appropriate. Unless you have Total Knowingness and can see all things, you should not assume ever that everyone is thinking like you. I can tell you right now, that there are eight different situations right here in front of me. I will answer your question though.

If you are in Darkness right now and are asking, can you go into the Light, yes, but when you're born in Darkness and then go to Light, you will have a stronger battle with Darkness than someone in Light, born in Light. What this means is the one in Light has had the resource of the Creator all along, whereas one in Dark merely forgot that and is now able to grab back hold of the Creator. You may both have the same war but the one in Light, has had the remembrance of the Creator longer. Darkness hates Light, so it tends to try to go around it first, rather than taking on a direct battle. "

"If you are pregnant in Darkness carrying a baby in Dark, your baby is still going to be born in Darkness even if you desire to go into Light. You then will begin the transfer to your baby once it is born. It is never hopeless because the second it is, Darkness has thrown you an illusion and you bought it. Believe me, it costs to stay in Darkness. It costs to stay in Light. You will see this as we go along."

This girl was in Darkness but so loved her baby also in Darkness, which her love put the desire to go back to Light in her so strong that she began to transfer this to her baby so it could meet again the Awesome Force of the Creator the second it was born. And so it was well received and understood all that I had said. There was so much to say. I could have talked forever but it was enough for them to hear in one day.

They all needed to understand how to get into Light and stay there, so that would be the next topic once we came together again. There were terminologies used with these different types of pregnancies and I was going to also tell them of this.

Athena had listened in and was dancing about, waiting anxiously for all to leave. "Daughter most awesome Daughter, you were wonderful!" she burst out saying.

I smiled and said, "Athena, this is a lot of energy right now swirling about me from so much teaching here."

"Daughter," she said, reaching out to take my hands, "It is your Light that has allowed them to wake from such a deep sleep.

"Next you'll be telling me that I'm the princess charming here to wake up the prince," I said to her but she looked at me ready to say something and then stopped. "I know, I just hit upon something in reference to my Soulmate, right? Right? Come on, answer me, Mother," I said, very demanding to her.

"Daughter, be still or you will wake up the Forces," she said back to me.

"What are you up to?" I asked her. She would not say, and trying to get her to tell what she could not, was like being glad to see Zeus on one of his big entrances! Speaking of Mr. Big Boy, he must have heard us because as sure as the clouds separated, Pops dropped in.

"Why does she make fun of me?" he asked Athena.

"Because," I said, "you are most primitive."

Athena looked at Zeus and Zeus yelled, "If I wanted you to talk I would have commanded it, woman!"

"Oh so now I am woman? I have a name, Zeus!" I said. "You should know that!" I continued. "Do you think that your big entrances scare me? Lose it, Zeus! I fear not of you. You are like a big hot air balloon."

By now of course Athena was positioning herself in front of me because Zeus was ready to strike. Seething and near foaming at the mouth, he yelled to Athena, "Shut the woman up or I will do it myself."

"Oh be still, Zeus! She is no coward. She has inherited from both of us. You would not love her if she were weak. Now be still yourself and be gone," Athena said, tall and straight in the aggressive pose.

I started laughing behind her long white gown and she cloaked me so he would not come back at us. "Oh, let the old buzzard fly," I said in a whisper.

"Daughter," Athena said, "Do not provoke him. It is not well to war with him today."

CHAPTER FOUR

Without hope, the human race was doomed and that was it. Did you ever see someone with a good dose of hope? There is no stopping them. I could not contain myself with Zeus. It just came out of me. Mr. Immortal, trying to do his male thing. I should give myself a good dose of hope that he should change. Maybe I did get a jumpstart from those lightning strikes. Just about then I heard chuckles from the heavens.

"You are able to do things that others cannot. You have systems which are unlike anyone else on the planet," Athena said.

"Yes and I struck you," Zeus echoed.

I somehow knew that I had stepped into his line of fire. Athena in her majestic way sat down next to me. "You know how much you are like us. You are able to do things that others cannot. You have systems which are unlike anyone else on the planet," she said.

"Except for my Soulmate, I know." I said back to her.

I knew that the Dark Force consisted of those you could not see and those you could. There were Dark masters walking on the planet right now. They were cloaked in Darkness the same way we were cloaked in Light. There was such a delicate balance between the Forces. It was imperative that the White Light prevailed. I stood up tall and once again the warrior came forward in me. Yes, I would battle and somewhere along the way my Soulmate would help.

The girls from school and I got together again the way we had when I first started to tell of my Knowingness to the girls. They had so many questions. They wanted to know about the Creator and how to get into the Light and stay there. I could barely believe that I had had such an impact on them. It was only just beginning and little did

I know then to what magnitude it would all become. I had to be careful not to overwhelm them. I was incredibly sensitive to their souls and knew when each one had had enough. So I began to speak of the Creator. They all sat down, crossing their legs and leaning on their elbows.

I stood before them, smiling and so filled with the White Light. I knew that the very words I would speak now and forever would touch and embrace their souls for eternity. The silent, etheric crowd stood in the background glowing. It was as if thousands of crystals were being touched by the sun's rays and rainbows collided with each other all over the place. The girls were totally unaware of this and could not see any of it. I thought to myself how much the human race was missing. I also knew that Darkness even in the size of one grain of sand would prevent anyone from seeing these things. Your soul had to be pure in all things and so fixed and bonded to the Creator that nothing could pull you out. There was so much to say and I knew that my whole life would be teaching that which no one could find anywhere. These Teachings were sacred and untouched by the human race. I had to be careful to keep them that way too.

I began to tell them that the Creator was the most Awesome and that we were all attached to the Creator like a bungee cord. The Creator would always be Love, Protection and Truth. Surely you need nothing else. No matter how much you might stretch the bungee cord you would never get away, it would always go back to the Creator. No matter what you did it would still return you. Darkness goes back, Light goes back, all go back. You have religion on this earth, which uses the word god, however, their god is not the Creator. You never need to be found, saved, reborn, re-registered, or reinstated with the Creator, I know.

The girls looked at me in amazement. I knew also that whatever I said today would have to carry them through the rest of this life because I would never see any of them again. The most important of all things was to stay bonded to the Awesome White Light. We had to watch all of our terminologies because even the word god triggered negativity, guilt, rejection, words like sin, not good enough, falling short of, needing to be cleaned and so on. By using the word

Creator it held open the doors of acceptance for it had a pure sense of introduction and safety. After all, perhaps they now had hope, a chance to really be in the real White Light. What kind of idiot could give a person such an ugly interpretation of their god? This particular religious trip was, you're dirty. God's clean, so wash up but no matter how much you wash you can never be clean enough. My final comment to all of this: "Your god is master of something but certainly not Light".

I saw the glimmer of hope in each one of these girls. It was as if they were being flooded by the touch of the Creator. It brought tears to my eyes because I was finally into this mission and seeing it right there in front of me, alive, changing, accepting and it was all tangible. I watched the ill thoughts leave all of their minds like waiting rooms ready to be filled with the real thing.

I was driven to do that which I had been so prepared for as a baby. Don't tell me that babies are innocent, naive and vulnerable. They are brilliant and in most cases it's the parents who are idiots. The only vulnerability the baby has is its size. It is born with Knowingness and the parents snuff it out as fast as they can. Again and again, they smother the baby until its Knowingness goes back to sleep. So then begins the battle as the baby struggles to stay awake even with the odds so stacked against it. It is a dreadful sight to see. You all wonder why your children in your eyes are so messed up. What is happening to the youth today? Please read on and maybe you'll wake up too.

The Creator is simple. Man is complicated. Complicated is a Dark word. It represents an almost impossible conclusion. You can't find the beginning or end unless it leaves the complicated state of being. Listen to what I say. Terminologies determine where the soul is. If you can recognize where the word comes from, you can recognize where you are. The Creator is simple, clear and complete. If you remember the Creator, your life will take on simple, clear and complete. The Creator gives Truth, Love and Protection. There is nothing more that you need. The Creator is not human, only people living on the planet earth are human. You cannot bring in things from other dimensions and use human techniques on them. Human beings can't break the cloaking devices that these higher life forces use. Let's face it, all those egotistical losers can't tap into this and never will. All higher entities have cloaking devices, all of them.

The girls sat so still listening to me in total amazement because they knew I spoke the Truth. They had such a connection in their souls. It was simple. I told them to be in the White Light. You needed only to say the exact words I spoke. It would be instant too. All you needed to do was release yourself to the White Light of the Creator. Could it really be that easy? Yes, but how long would you stay in it before you slipped back out again?

One girl looked at me and said, "You mean you don't stay in the White Light?"

I said, "No, if you don't know how. Who has told you how?"

She said, "No one," And then all of the girls agreed that no one had ever spoken like this and that it was so easy to understand.

I continued on, "In order to stay in the White Light you have to understand Darkness. Did you honestly think that you could go back to the White Light without the Dark Force trying to follow you and stop you?"

The girls looked confused. "You mean we have to take the Dark Force with us?" one girl asked.

"Indirectly, yes!" I said.

"I thought that we were supposed to stay away from Darkness," another girl commented.

"And who told you this?" I asked.

"Well everyone, I guess," she said.

"Now," I said to them all, "you will know the Truth about it all. All things must be released back to the Awesome White Light, especially Darkness. There are two Forces here on the planet. Light and Dark. The Grey zone is Darkness. The Grey zone would be those who continue to go toward both Forces. They don't trust the Light but won't give up the Dark. They are power-dominated and continue to feel power, which is generated by the Dark Force. They walk around convinced that they are superior but when they come to a crossroad, they are the biggest of cowards. They take lies and twist them to their truth. The Dark Force, however, claims lies. You expect the Darkness to give you lies. They can afford to because they give you illusionary truth. They have the power to call it what it is whereas the Light Force has Truth.

You should always release the Dark Force to the White Light and Love of the Creator. This will ensure that you will have an easier path and definitely a safe one. The last thing you need is Darkness all over you. The Dark Force wants what you have if you're heading back to the Light. Once you are securely in the White Light you need to make sure you do not leave it. That is the hard part. Unless you are born with the guarantee that you can't get out, you will have to stay focused your whole life. Believe me, you will become stronger as time goes by. So you release Darkness to the Awesome Love and White Light of the Creator. After all, it is the only place that it can find Love again, Truth and Protection.

There is one religion in which I have heard them often say, "Get behind me, Satan." Do you know how ugly and cruel these religious people are? They have big egos and big power trips. My brother Jesus would have never dealt with this Dark ugliness. Yes, you all look at me in wonder. Yes, Jesus is my brother. I stand strong and bonded to the Creator. I release this one they call Satan to the Awesome Love and White Light of our Creator. All things go home. Do you honestly think that you as human beings can generate love? Never! But with the generator of the Creator in a constant flow of Love, you will create the bridge to express Love and be Loved."

Things were clicking with all of the girls because they, in their own ways, were starting to put on their armor. It is called, "Honor all things." Send forth the Love you generate from the Creator to those who so desperately need love. Who better to send home, than the Dark Force? It is denied Truth, Love and Protection. How Dark do you think it can stay in the Creator's Light?

"Wow, Deborah," one girl said, "I have never heard it put so beautifully and simply."

"You are all in the White Light because Darkness cannot come near me and you even questioned yourselves as to which Force you might be in." I said. All of them lifted their hearts and I could see tears fill their eyes.

"I don't have to hate anymore," a beautiful girl said. She stood up and embraced me. "I want to thank you. No one has ever made me see it so clearly."

"You never hated but merely tried to as a defense," I told her.

Another girl stood up and then all of them came forward and reached out to me. "You really are filled completely with love. It is pouring out of your soul. We can all feel it," she said and the others agreed. "Where do you come from, Deborah?" one asked.

"From the Creator," I said. "Let's go on, there is much to tell you," I added. "Remember I was going to tell you more about terminologies in reference to pregnancies? Let's talk about all of that. Remember I spoke about the different types of pregnancy? Light to Light, Dark to Dark, mother in Light, baby in Dark, mother in Dark, baby in Light and mother in Light with a baby in the transference over to Light stage.

All of the different pregnancies have different physical conditions and terminologies. Light to Light would feel great, positive, elated, internally peaceful. There would be a great bond. It would be hard for Darkness to pursue this combination. Dark to Dark would feel comfortable and after all, Darkness won't pursue what it already has. There would not be any real joy or dislike but in many cases, it reactivates the mother's instincts to nurture and protect and may very well begin her journey back to Light. A mother in Light with a baby in Dark? This situation is one where you have a good loving person all of a sudden needing an abortion. The guilt that is put on her destroys plenty. She cannot carry this baby but at the same time, society condemns her and destroys her life. She is so filled with guilt that she usually ends up plummeting deep into Darkness, which means Darkness has accomplished its job. Just because of his ignorance, the human race suffers. It is also like, what they put on their god, too.

It is sad for the woman in Light with the baby in Dark. She is driven to such despair to end it all and yet she herself cannot even truly tell you why. However, if she can speak to this soul and release it to the White Light of the Creator and awaken its sleep long before it's born, it can begin the transference over to Light.

A mother in Dark cannot conceive a baby in Light because of her vibration. There are so many combinations such as multiple births and the lack of being able to conceive. Each has its own set of energies and terminologies. Everything has this, a reason, purpose and terminologies to go with it. When a woman says she does not want the pregnancy, it is because it is a soul in Dark. She can use all of the excuses possible but I tell you that there is only one reason.

Now you release yourself to the Awesome White Light and Love of the Creator. There is only one Creator with White Light. Why White Light? Because if you release yourself to the Light, it tells Darkness that you have not identified Creator. After all, the Dark Force has Light too, so they will give you the illusions of Light.

Strobe lights, flash lights, headlights and so on. When you say White Light, it tells Darkness that you are with the Creator. You are also reminding Darkness of the Creator and thus helping it to get back home. It is going to get real sick of hearing about the Creator if you continue to do this. It will lose interest in you and go elsewhere. The minute you release yourself to the Creator, you are immediately in the White Light, Love and Protection. Nothing can touch you unless you step out of this. All negativity will pull you out. All things that are negative will do this. Even if you are in the White Light, you can slip out of it in a moment's notice. Your terminologies will do it and your thinking. What you think can be tapped into outside of the White Light. Sure you will have negative thoughts but they must be protected too. Once these thoughts are in the White Light, clarity will help transfer them over to positive. Something else you need to say is, "Creator, I ask that you protect all of our conversation so that nothing can tap into it. I release all of my conversation to you, Creator, in the White Light and Love of your Awesome Force."

"Some of the terminologies for a mother in Light with a baby in Light would be what?" I decided to let the girls respond.

One girl raised her hand and said "Happy."

"Yes," I answered her back. "What about Dark to Dark?"

Another girl raised her hand and said, "It's okay. Nothing great being pregnant."

I agreed with her. "How about a mother in Light, with a baby in Dark?" I asked.

Another girl spoke. "I have to get rid of this."

"Very good," I told her. "Now what about a mother in Light, the baby is transferring out of the Dark to Light? " I asked them all. Almost all of them at the same time said "Come on baby, you can do it!"

"Yes," I said, "Because the mother would be encouraging, sending energy and Light towards her baby," I concluded.

"Must we end?" they all said.

"We have been here long enough. All that has needed to be said, I have said. There is a point when the soul is filled with much remembrance and you can only handle so much," I concluded.

I was looking forward to seeing Athena. We all said our goodbyes and school was finally over with for good. I missed Jimmy so much and I longed to see him. I just knew that he was not okay. I just felt him and knew it.

"Oh, Athena, I do so love you," I told her. "I miss being with the Allegiance on your level. I don't forget it, either."

"You are a great teacher, Daughter," she said to me.

"Great, Mother is basking in the sun next to the Greek columns in Olympus," I said resting my head on her knee. "I want so to tell you of what lies ahead. It saddens me at times watching your limitations in this body. It holds you up and causes pain. If someone else could have come to do this mission we would have chosen another," she said so lovingly.

"Mother," I asked her, concerned. "Will there be great pain ahead for me because of this body?"

"Yes Daughter, more than you can bear and because you are able to handle things at a greater magnitude, you will not be able to gauge your limit. There is nothing we can do and we cannot change it. You lie on the fine line of the etheric body and the human body. That is why you are able to see what you see."

"Athena, hold me. I do not want to go on," I said, as I had a real sense of what was about to come. "Is this pain far in the future?" I asked her.

"No, Daughter, but we will be with you," she said.

"Is anything going to happen to Jimmy?" I asked her, hoping that she would say no, many things will happen to him but no, he is not going to die. He has the blood of Zeus in him. He is a warrior. Zeus may be intolerable but he does have his moments. I have seen them and as much as he rants and raves, he does love him and he loves you," she said firmly.

"That shall be the day when he comes without insult," I told her.

It was deep, that which was coming. I did not want to leave Athena's side so I did not. I fell asleep in her arms and she draped me in her refinement. I did not make it to the house that night and so war hit me as this family accused me of doing great wrong. School was over and I was given two weeks to get a job. I had a job, a big job. Did they mean that I should go out into man's world because it certainly was not a woman's world. Two weeks came and went and I was forbidden to leave the house or use the phone or function. No job, no social life either. I could not do this. Eventually I was told to pack my things and leave. Where was I to go? How was I to live? My life was over. I was alone and now I was abandoned by these human ways to even function on the planet. Athena rushed to me and held me.

"Oh Mother help me, I know not what to do," I cried.

"Daughter, listen to me. We shall not abandon you. Great evils have entered this house. You must leave it now. We will go to a place where we can gather," she said to me, so concerned.

I picked up my love letters from Jimmy and put them against my heart. I will go to him, I thought. Yes, I will go to him. I put my things in my car and went to start it. They had pulled off a part so the car would not start. I went back into the house and world war three broke out. They now forbid me to leave. I had graduated. I was seventeen and I was supposed to get a full-time job as a minor. No one would hire a minor when they could hire an adult. I was leaving and that was it. I lived out in the country where there wasn't any city to even look for a job. It wasn't as if I had never worked. I had worked all through school, part time at a hospital. Now part time wasn't good enough.

I did leave that day after much war. I did not have any money and there was no going back. That was it. I was alone, homeless and soon I'd be starving if something had not intervened. I drove to the town Jimmy was in and called him. He told me to come over and meet him at this road. Things were not okay at his home and he would have to sneak me into his room. When I saw him, I could see the toll that the Dark Force had put on him. He looked tired and stressed but he still smiled and held me. Oh, how I had missed him. I felt my body totally relax in his arms but I felt tension all through his. Something was so very wrong. He told me that I could only stay a couple of days because if I was caught there, it would be more than he could handle. He would have to sneak me in at night and sneak me out in the early morning. I could not do this and yet I had to rest. It was clear that Jimmy had changed and there was now a distance between us. I knew that he could not cope with this Force, battling it all alone. I tried to talk to him but he closed up, something he would have never done before.

"I love you, Jimmy," I told him and he smiled in a way that did not have the depth that it had had in the past. "Is it that you don't love my anymore?" I asked him.

He grabbed me and held me tightly. "I will always love you. Always." He said to me.

We were two souls that kept coming together but could not stay together. I realized that we had been separated too long and that the Dark Force was winning. I talked to him but it did not seem to matter. He was so distant and consumed by the stress. Once again, I reassured him that I would always love him and that nothing would end that. I could not stay after two nights and so I had to drive away. I needed to spend time with my Family and be still. I drove deep into the woods and spent several days in the wilderness. It was there that much clarity came and all of the direction I needed. My whole life had been carefully planned and guided by the Allegiance. I knew that there were no mistakes and that all things had Divine Order to them. I knew that none of us could change our destinies and no matter what I thought or felt, it was all going to go the way it had to go. Athena stood by my side, the Angels stood by my side and the most important of all, the Creator embraced me in the Awesome White Light. I was not alone but after seeing Jimmy, there was such a sadness in my heart for him. He had changed so much that it seemed as if he was in a trance.

"It is a program from the Dark Force," Athena said."They are slowly trying to gain control of him."

"Athena, what can I do?" I asked her.

"Just love him and remember your purpose," she said.

I sat there surrounded by nature, which was truly inspiring. What a gorgeous world with all of its plants, animals and weather. I sat back and looked up at the sky. That was where I truly wanted to be, outside, in the Heavens and far from this mission. I could not forget the way Jimmy was. It was very intense to see him so changed. I felt compelled to save him from this. I felt sure of my abilities to battle this Force, but I did not feel well about my Soulmate. Why hadn't he come forward yet?

I woke to Athena holding me in her arms. If I was really supposed to be here on this earth, then why was I constantly reminded of my etheric body? Would that not have been removed from my memory? Perhaps it was left there to remind me never to come back to this planet. I was here to take my Soulmate back home. I knew it. So I just find my Soulmate and do it. How hard could it be? Meanwhile, I would teach those that desired to know.

"Oh Daughter," Athena said with a great pause. "If only I could tell you of things to come."

I looked at her, trusting so that she knew all. "If only you could tell me, then I would want to check out," I said, knowing what was ahead by her intensity.

She looked at me with such a stare. It must have been very close for her to have such concern in her eyes. "Okay, Mother, what lies ahead is horrible. Right? I mean, you can at least answer yes or no. That way it can confirm what I feel." I said to her, not really needing an answer. I would have definitely checked out if I had known then what I know today. I could have never guessed in a million lifetimes the dread and horror that was going to come. It was so beyond the beyond that no mortal human being could have ever survived it all.

The most I could ask for was that the Allegiance hold onto me and love me beyond any human mortal realm. I was driven to go on because I knew on some level that I was helping Jimmy but there had to be more that I could do.

I was much in the etheric realm holding onto Athena when from nowhere, a bolt of lightning hit me again. I was dazed and hurting something awful. Had I not been holding onto Athena, I would have died right then and there. "Was it Zeus, Athena?" I asked her, huddled up in a ball of energy.

"Yes," she replied.

"Show yourself Zeus, coward that you are. What's the matter, aren't you big enough yet?" I screamed at him. He did not return after that for a very long time. I had to go on and prepare myself for the battle.

How sad everyone was. Step out of man's realm and go back to the Creator. People were all blind, deaf and dumb. I stayed for a short time with a girl who was pregnant. Her baby was one of those babies transferring over to Light. You could see the struggle in her eyes. She was in Light though and the baby was more in Dark than Light. There is that fine line from Dark to Light, such as, the human body to the etheric body. I was more etheric than human but human enough to have the substance of the human body. That was why I was able to see things in the etheric world. When an etheric body tries to go back into a human body, it virtually cannot be completely human. Its vibrations are so high that there is a negative charge that is created by the human body to stop the full absorption to the human state.

There was great danger for this baby if it was separated from its mother at birth. There was always a period of danger brought on by any transference, as Darkness was hovering over that soul waiting to see if it could frighten it enough to surrender. Long ago, back in what you would call the old days, women had babies and those babies were tied to them. There was less danger for those babies because Darkness would have had to take on the mothers as well. It wasn't until doctors stepped in that evil had an easy ride. What women have lost is their full Knowingness of childbirth that they have always had. Through the years, they have allowed men to take over and that shut down their abilities to Know.

How long was it before a woman was allowed to be a doctor? You might sit there and start claiming how your doctor did this and that and how your baby wouldn't even be here today without your doctor. I say to you that you are as lost as the rest. If you set yourself up for the doctor, you will create medical conditions for the doctor to further claim more of your power. dear reader, these are the facts.

This girl delivered her baby, who was not very strong, but the baby boy was holding his own. Here comes the evil, she wanted to keep her baby with her but the nurse said no, it goes to the nursery. I knew by the evil of the nurse that Darkness would claim this soul back. Nurses are trained to lie and cover up a doctor's mistakes. This is evil. There was not even a grain of compassion for this baby. This nurse was evil to the max. I felt in the hall a great demon hovering over the nursery, waiting for this soul to become so afraid that it would surrender to the demon and thus it did. The baby stopped breathing. Without the mother's knowledge, her baby was removed from the hospital. She was told it died. She was so distraught that she could not even respond. She knew the Dark Force had taken her baby back. I say to you if anyone covers up and lies for a doctor, that person is Dark and evil. There were plenty of cover-ups.

After a week, the baby was returned, black as coal in both feet and hands. It had been neglected and since no one checked on the baby, it had been without oxygen for five minutes or more. This tiny baby had been claimed by the demon that was now living in it. Of course, the baby stopped breathing when this thing entered it, taking all of the baby's life force from it. The hospital could not handle the situation so it shipped the baby to another hospital. That baby was terrified as this thing came for it. It couldn't tell anyone and it was not strong enough to battle it. Imagine the terror as this thing took over. Yes, the baby knew. As I have said before, the only thing vulnerable about a baby is its size.

I could not stop this demon because the hospital would not let me in. I had to stand there and watch it all, unable to intervene. I felt that baby's terror and pain. For the rest of its life it would have to battle this demon. It was sad and the mother was devastated. She finally got to hold her baby again and in all senses it had died because it felt horrible and when this little boy opened his eyes, they were as dead as shark eyes. You could see and feel this demon.

As the years would go on for her, she would have her life destroyed, being blamed for her little boy's monstrous behaviors. Eventually he would end up trying to kill her and many other people. The demon always knew when to repress itself so all blame could go on the mother. After all, she could not prove the real reason her son was so violent and disturbed. He would end up lying and claiming horrible things that his mother had done, when she had done none of what this boy said. The boy would eventually be removed from her home and put into another great evil called social services. It would end up costing this mother everything and as for her son, he hated her and had nothing to do with her. All of this happened because one nurse would not allow a mother to hold her baby when it was born. Of course she was only following hospital policy.

There is always someone to blame something on. The planet was so infected with evil that it did force some doctors to be decent in their practice but nearly all doctors were deep into the Dark Force, practicing ugly, negligent, butchering medicine. Hysterectomies were a big deal and many doctors needed to power trip the female. What better way than to rip out her insides and make her sterile. There were only a few great evils on the planet that caused a chain reaction effect for everyone. One of the great evils are doctors. As Athena put it, many of these doctors had past lives in the medieval times as black magic practitioners who slaughtered people and tried desperately to be god. If you knew the truth about doctors, you would stop going to them. There aren't many who are good but the good ones can be found if you search.

I met up with Athena dancing about the clouds. "Mother, come down here now! Always you are about, so elegant and strong. Why don't you just take me with you?" I said to her. She immediately came to my side. I knew she would dash in if I even hinted that I wanted to check out. "Okay, Athena, I'll stay on the planet," I reassured her.

She smiled and said, "Daughter, I am proud of you. Be it whatever you may do, I shall always love you. Your beauty is of great desire."

At that, I burst into laughter saying, "My, what is of great desire? Honestly Mother, you bring to me much happiness." She stood proud and continued on, "I have decided Daughter to tell of things I should not but I will not tell of it all. You need to stay focused and your etheric body keeps you from being on the earth strong. You concluded that you were here to get your Soulmate and that is exactly true."

"So we are going to talk about him?" I asked.

"Yes, because he is very powerful like you," she said.

"I know Athena, Soulmates are opposites, so if I'm in Light, he is . . ." I hesitated, "Oh Athena, he is in Dark! I never thought about it. He is in Dark at the magnitude that I am in Light," I said with the realization of what my mission would be.

"Daughter, you are in Light deepest of all," Athena reaffirmed. "Meaning? He is deepest in the Dark?" I asked her. Why even ask her when I knew it, as soon as I said it. Oh great, I've got a Soulmate who was going to be a handful. Surely I would have the ability to wake up my Prince Charming. If I could not do it, I wouldn't be here. Honestly, how hard could it be? After all, I had made it this far and I had seen plenty of Darkness. I'm sure he was on the etheric level as much as I was. I would just do my mission and go home. I was confident of it all. Athena and I talked by the wildflowers and small waterfalls. Oh, it so reminded us both of another time and journey. I loved her and always would. Where would I be without the Allegiance, all of them?

CHAPTER FIVE

Athena and I talked for hours and she told me things that she said she was not supposed to but being so much like her, she saw what she would have done and saw me doing the same thing, checking out. I needed to go deep into my memory banks and bring forward a greater strength and understanding of the Dark Force. Sure I understood it but if I had to deal with the deepest of all levels of Darkness, then I would have to deal with the violent danger of it all as well. Believe me, that power was more than any human being could handle and once again, all was reaffirmed that I was not one hundred percent human. I couldn't be and still be able to handle great wizards, masters and all of the others in bodies or out. I sensed great trickery and thievery present in this Force. In all of time, know this, the right woman can handle the right man no matter how difficult. I was the right woman for my Soulmate and I was sure that I could handle him, no matter how difficult it would be. How bad could it be? Athena jumped in and together we said, "Very bad!" and we laughed and laughed. "He's just a man and all men can be handled by the right woman," we both said with great conclusion.

I was alone again but what of it. I could always see where everyone had come from and where they were going. I was so bored and wondered how many men were on the planet like Jimmy. There could not be many because I would have sensed it. Athena had told me that my physical was my weakness and that it would slow me down. It was imperative that the Dark Force know as little as possible about me and that I be very careful not to let anyone know anything. She told me a doctor could destroy me if he had my very life in his hands. Many doctors practiced the Dark arts on their patients. I knew this because I had seen this my whole life. No one ever took me to doctors but people around me went. I saw and heard how messed up they became as they were inducted on a soul level to these Forces.

"Dread, Daughter, that you should ever have to go to a doctor," Athena said. Here she was once again trying to prepare me, I just knew it.

I knew the Angels used vibration language and thus I could identify with them. The planet earth did not know of this language and so in its history, its inhabitants once again tried to put Angels into their levels of comprehension.

There was one Angel in particular that had been with Athena and me for quite some time. Finally, one day when Athena departed he came forward to speak. The only way I can describe him to you is that he reminded me of silk. I can only say that he had substance similar to Athena but he was definitely a delivery entity, carrier of bad news. How much worse could it get? I was so floored by his message I could not find a response. He embraced me as I fell to my knees, quite ready to hang on to him and depart with him.

"Are you sure you're right?" I asked him.

"Oh yes," he replied.

I thought that I must have fallen asleep because I was in denial so bad but I knew I was very much awake, too awake, and too immortal. I was now searching as fast as I could to find a way to be more human, more mortal, so I could be cancelled out of this mission. This Angel not only told me of the mission but several more.

"So this is it, you just leave your message and go?" I asked.

"I will remain close by for now," he said, appearing calm and sedate.

I said to him, "I guess you'll have to hold me up," as my legs began to collapse again. "I can see it now. I have to return a fleet of Angels who have fallen into the Dark?" I started laughing, almost hysterically and thought the Creator has had a nervous breakdown. I would have like to have said, Creator, there has been a big mistake but deep in my soul I was truly kidding myself. Why did all of this seem so familiar? If I had had my etheric body it might not have sounded so impossible. How in the world was I going to do this? Someone must have snapped. I've got the wrong job. That's it, they just made one huge mistake. I would have liked to have said, "Aren't I a little young?"

To the Allegiance, age held no merit. You get a mission, you do the job. Do you think the Creator would pick and choose who gets what? Never. We enter with the package, sort of like tools that we need for each life but tools get lost or left behind or replaced. What starts out complete gets altered from birth, meaning the destiny remains the same but the tools to go through life may be altered. You still have to go through this life but if someone took your hammer you'll have to use something else. All of this only applies if you are born one hundred percent human. Those born of etheric energy have different systems and are here on missions. There are those in the Dark of etheric energy too. When you are on a mission, you have Knowingness but the Allegiance keeps things from you until you need certain knowledge. It is done deliberately so you cannot alter anything. This is done so gracefully you do not even realize it.

Likeness handles likeness. That is perhaps, except in the case of me. In order for me to handle a fleet of Angels, I'd have to be one. The fact that they're fallen would mean I'd be in the Light because the job was to rescue them. Right? I can see it now. Okay, everybody, line up, you're going back to the Creator. I suppose my electric drill ought to drill some sense into them. Don't ever tell me the Creator doesn't have a sense of humor. I'm back in hysterics again. This is too much! I'd like to also say that many religions will say their god won't give them any more than they can handle. This is not so because if you lose some tools along the way, you're not going to be able to fix a swinging door that's off its hinge that keeps hitting you in the head. Imagine a god that takes back a perfect plan because you lost a screwdriver. Get real.

You're born with all you need. You are the one that doesn't stay bonded to the White Light. Do you think your god is going to step in, as if god steps in and hands you another screwdriver? No! What the Creator does is give you Protection, Love and Truth. It's in this that you find a way to fix that door. You have to become creative with that which the Creator gives you. I could just see the orders coming in, five million hammers by Tuesday. Your god would have to work overtime. You might say to me that your destiny is different from the next person's. No! All destinies are the same, to go back to the White Light. It is your journey that is different, not your destiny. Remember, we are born with the tools to take that journey so that we may all reach our destinies.

You may also be in a continuation of a previous journey. It is like that baby who had that demon waiting for it. The demon and baby still had things to do or it could not have reclaimed it. To give you an example, that baby would have chosen a mother who would have had the birth at home or some other circumstance where the mother would have been able to hang onto her baby. Most of you would say how horrible and I would say that this baby merely merged with an entity that had been its father time and time again in previous lives. What was needed to be was and no one could have changed that baby's journey. It was even set up that I could not intervene.

"Well Athena, you have known about this Angel thing all along." I said to her.

"Daughter be that as it is, I could not speak of this until the time was right," she said.

"But what about my Soulmate? I mean when will I have time to reconnect if I have this mission with the Angels? I know that I came back for him but there shall hardly be a moment left," I told her becoming upset. "Honestly Athena, have they all flipped up there?
"

She laughed saying, "Daughter you speak from time to time using mortal terminologies. How funny. The only flipping we do is when our challengers battle us."

"You know what I mean. Must all my phrases be in Olympian dialect? Surely the mortal realm will never understand me," I said to her and quick was her come back.

"Daughter, Awesome entity named Deborah, Love flows from your soul and Light forever embraces you. Spirited Daughter of wisdom and war, be that of your Mother, go forward with the breath of future, the power of flight and be so directed with our Creator, that all shall remember the source, the Awesome White Light." She stepped forward, spun around in a circle and burst into beams of Light.

Thank you Mother, I said clearly to myself. The Creator is always the same and the tools are always the same but the journeys are different. All I needed to do was get the mission finished and I would have time for my Soulmate. Just do what I had to do. Wouldn't you know it I'd get a mission the size of Mount Olympus. I knew that each one of us was born with something after us and something to run to. In other words the thing chasing us was the Force to make us go on, to live, to push us forward so we would not quit. If mankind decided to give up, what was chasing him would catch up. In all, there was a safe haven and if you knew where that was you could stop and rest. Thus comes the statement I need a breather, a vacation, a rejuvenation, a rest, and so the soul goes to the safe haven. Harm comes when you rest too long and the pursuing Force catches up. If it gets you, it merely tries to throw you off your course. At that point you would say things such as, boy I feel like I'm out of synch, things feel off, the timing isn't right. All that has occurred is that someone has been resting too long and they need to go on. This can happen in relationships, lunch breaks, stop lights, anywhere. So if you are thinking or speaking these particular things, know the reason why. There are plenty of terminologies that go with all situations.

It is funny that I should see Jimmy again nearly a year later. He hugged me so long I could have fallen asleep in his arms. I was so elated. Oh how my soul needed to touch his. We promised to keep in touch and never lose each other.

"I need a rest Deb," he said and as soon as he said this I knew where it was coming from.

"You have to balance yourself," I told him. "If you push forward too soon, you'll be in precognition and you'll get into a state of exhaustion. Then you'll have to rest but if you rest too long, the pursuing Force will catch up."

"What" he said smiling? "What did you just say?" he said as he burst into laughter.

"Jimmy, you of all people know that we are born with something pursuing us and something we can run to that is a safe haven." I said.

"Yes," he said, "we know what pursues me." We both laughed.

"Yes and it pursues me too," I said. Time was short and we talked as if we would run out of time to finish all we had to say. He was tired looking but that smile, that big, beautiful smile, always got to me. He now took on a new feeling to me. He was gorgeous and so sensuous. That childhood sweetheart had turned into a man. I thought to myself, look out Allegiance. Your little entity down here is wanting to do some very mortal things. I will never forget this meeting because I truly could have walked away from my Soulmate, mission and everything else that day to go off with him for eternity. Being around Jimmy was so wonderful. No matter what he did, it didn't matter. His soul just touched mine with a gentleness no other could ever do. I was sure of this and I could claim this sureness because it was pure Light. Be sure of one thing reader, the White Light never changes. It is pure, consistent and always there. You need only to reach out to it. It will always greet you, embrace you and hold onto you as long as you stay.

Athena and I spoke again about doctors, how dangerous they were, especially to someone like me. For me, they were the chasing force. The few I had encountered so far could not control themselves around me. There was some immediate connection they were aware of on a level, which you might call psychic. Later in my life more would be revealed about this Darkness that doctors held and the danger that so many of them caused their patients. I had systems unlike others and for a doctor to touch me I would have to hide these things. The few I had encountered had displayed obsessive behaviors towards me, wanting to dissect me like some untouchable specimen that had the key to life. It amazed me that a doctor wanted to be paid for his services but needed to use me to gain a better perspective on his own private life. When I insisted that I be paid for my services, that was, of course, another story. After all, most doctors feel that they are superior to everyone. I could not help it if doctors felt like idiots around me. Athena was right about them wanting to be the old wizard. They set you up to get sick, then keep you sick so they can continue to get rich from you playing victim. I do not want to tell you the fate of most doctors but I will as time goes by. Athena had spoke of three major Dark Forces in the planet and medical was one of them. Later I will get into the other two.

Jimmy stayed in my mind for the months to come and all I kept seeing was our next meeting, his gorgeous smile and that intense pulling right into his heart. I cannot fully tell you what his mere presence on the planet had done for me. My days were filled with anticipation of Jimmy and we would call each other from time to time. I would encourage him and he would touch my soul.

I started to get the name of a cult deprogrammer because I kept meeting people in Darkness and helping them literally to see the Light. These people had had their fill of strobe lights, black lights, flashlights and so on. Every time I spoke, it taught someone, somewhere, something. You cannot imagine how many people had lost their hammers along the way.

Small groups of people started to gather for classes and everyone was changed by what I said. I spoke of the Creator and the beginning of life as I knew of it. What was so amazing is everyone's reaction to how simple everything was. That is because the Creator is not complicated, the human race is, so it can trap its victims and keep them from their Knowingness. What I said made all religion look very different. Everyone concluded that the Dark Force ran religions.

Once you remembered the Creator you woke up to seeing things completely different. They worshiped some sort of god but certainly not the Creator. Once someone remembered the Creator, so then did their Knowingness come to them? One woman told everyone that for years she was raised in such heavy religion that she truly was convinced that she would never be worthy of god. She loved her husband who had another religion but their families battled over their marriage, children and each other. Her husband was a lost sinner her family said and unless he was saved he was doomed. What a sick, sick, religion. Her husband could not take the abuse her family continued to play out. It created devastating effects on their intimate life and eventually they separated. This woman was so distraught that she severed all ties to her family and had planned to try and get her husband back. It was ten long years of such pain which all came from religion. In the end, he was killed in an accident on his way to reconcile with her. Her family said that god had punished him and he would face his maker and be judged. They even tried to convince her that god had taken him away.

There we are again back to a god who gave things and took things away. What was even more ill was that people actually believed this and when asked how they felt about it, all they would say is that it was not for them to question god but fear god. They all believed that they were going to be judged. All of this was exactly how the Dark Force worked. Gives you the dream and then takes it away. So go ahead and blame your god.

The Angel of Silk came to observe me more often and it occurred to me that I was being watched constantly. Athena said he watched me because the great war was about to start. All I kept thinking was what about my Soulmate. I would never have time to even find him. It never once came to me that he might locate me first and keep watch over me.

The Angel of Silk spoke only in vibration language as I have said and it is very hard to explain this to you. On a smaller level it would be similar to you thinking about someone calling you, then your phone rings and it's the person you were thinking about. Vibration language does not need sound.

As much as I missed Jimmy, the pull to my Soulmate was becoming stronger and stronger. I found myself wandering in thought to him. Athena was there but no longer constantly. I was in the company of this Angel and it was tense at times. It was as if he knew not how to respond to me and he would even bump into me. Now if you do not believe in Angels I can promise you they do exist. Angels like to brush past your shoulder and it feels as though someone was standing right there momentarily. Very similar to the statement, "I could swear something just went past me," but as you turn there is nothing. Now that I've made you aware of this you will recognize that feeling. Only Angels do this, not other entities. Other entities approach you differently and your terminologies are different. All of this is to help you identify what is coming and going. Remember the statement, "I feel as if something just went past me." It is terminology to help you identify an Angel is present. Have you been touched by an Angel?

Now you know. You still don't believe this? Then ask an Angel to touch you. It is as clear and as simple as that. Go ahead and test this.

At first it startled me that Zeus would appear out of nowhere. My defenses went up immediately but before I could call for Athena he was directly in front of me. I braced myself for war but he did not fight me. He merely stood by me for several moments and then dissipated. What was that all about? What, no battle?

I continued to talk to groups of people. It was so hard on everyone trying to recognize their troubles because they had lived so long in it all. Again and again all of these heavy religious terminologies continued to be in their language. If you speak it, you're in it. Words like sin and judgment were so heavy in their vibrations. What idiot decided that we sin because it certainly wasn't the Creator. If the Creator made you perfect then how could you be so defective? If you believe you have defects, you bought someone's program. I guarantee you that you're not in the remembrance of the Creator.

It was truly amazing to see people come out of the traps as well. They themselves could not believe how easy this whole process was that I was teaching. No one anywhere had this. I constantly reminded each of them that their journeys were all different but their destinies were all the same. No matter how Dark things might be, your destiny could never change. We all were headed toward the White Light. Many problems were so severe because everyone was at a complete loss. Everyone had similar stories. Their marriages were bad or if their marriages were fine their kids were out of control.

Many had children that just went Dark overnight. Remember what I said about conception and the kind of mother carrying a certain kind of soul. Also remember the baby taken by the Dark entity at birth? A child that goes Dark overnight is abducted by the Dark Force. A child that battles for a long time is desperately clinging to the White Light. If you would only wake up you could see this. Parents are not responsible for their children's own journeys except in the guidance of these little beings. As a parent you guide them, hopefully in the White Light. However you're probably only now realizing you've been in the Dark Force for quite some time. All souls respond to the White Light of the Creator. It melts down the battle Darkness challenges you to. Many children turn on their parents because the parents shut down their Knowingness. These children have had to battle to keep their Knowingness from birth but most give up the fight a few years into life. Of course you have reacted to my saying you are not responsible for the journeys your children must go through. Let me explain what this means. Each soul must do its own journey. You, as a parent, cannot, change your child's journey. You guide them and in guiding them, you make them aware of their surroundings and help them to remember the White Light. They are only vulnerable in their size. All children are born brilliant. While guiding them you share the living experiences but you must allow them to go in their own journey. A good example is a parent who wants her child to grow up to be a lawyer but the child has to be a police officer. The argument comes as the parents interfere with the child's journey. The child, on a soul level, knows he has to save his Soulmate and unless he's a police officer he won't be in the right place at the right time. Your child may not be aware of this on the conscious level.

As people came for understanding, they left with the knowledge of how to change it. They had never viewed it the way I put it and they had hope for the first time ever.

I needed to find my Soulmate and I could not stop the pull to him. I loved him clearly and freely. From the moment a baby is born, they begin their journey back to their Soulmate too. The one who is in the White Light is responsible for the one who is in Darkness. In the Soulmate relationship, one is always in the White Light and the other is always in the Dark.

We all have only one Soulmate, however, not everyone meets his or hers in every life. Since we have many lives, we are still connected but many end up with a soul energy that is a good friend, good past life connection and so on. Soul energies have also been our great heroes of past lives. They were the ones that made us smile, loved us no matter what. Although the soul energy is wonderful, it is not the Soulmate. The Soulmate makes your heart beat, your mind melt and your soul move. They make you feel to such depths that you could die for them and yet, at the same time, kill them. They splash you with rain while they smile like the sun. They throw you away and then run to you hanging on for dear life. They are cold and then hot. When they think about losing you they are in such despair that they can't go on without you. They will go against all beliefs and defend you to the world, yet face to face have confrontations while all along screaming and raging and then in the next moment, kissing you so passionately that they totally forget everything else. They force you, move you, take you and then plummet into a deep disbelief that they are doing any of this. They hate you for even thinking thoughts when they don't want you to, yet hold a bouquet of flowers behind their backs ready to romance you.

In all and all, it is so bizarre that you may say, is it worth it? Oh, yes! They are the love song. They fill up every void holding you tighter than your body can imagine. They fit perfectly into all parts of you. They are always and always more. Nothing can replace them, take them or lend them elsewhere. They are the other half of your soul. Once linked together the fit is complete. The bonding to the Creator can be no greater, for when Soulmates link, it is the key that turns the lock. As they go through the door they return to the beginning knowing that there will never be an end. Soul energies must move over when the Soulmate claims you and they do so usually with a great fight.

Jimmy felt that I was his Soulmate. Yes, I loved him greatly but never as I knew that I would love my Soulmate and he would love me. No one could replace that or really ever come close to that. Jimmy would always be special because of our connection but I knew the day would come when we would say goodbye forever. It seemed that no matter what, timing was always off for him and me. Another year went by and we met again but this time he looked very bad and it was clear that his battle with Darkness was lost. He was deep in the wells of evil. He could not climb out. It had taken control of him and had absorbed him completely. He looked at me and a deep chill ran through me. I was afraid and he looked as if he was going to take control of me.

"Jimmy," I said, "Snap out of it. It's me, Deborah, I love you. Remember we go way back."

He looked more intensely at me. "Yes, Deborah of course I know you," he said sarcastically. "You are scaring me, Jimmy," I said.

"Why would I do something like that?" he said back to me.

We went to a Tahitian restaurant and torches were burning all around us with Tahitian music playing in the background. It was very hypnotic and I felt as if I was being pulled back into a past life as Jimmy began to hold my hands. It was in a past life with him where he took control and had me as he pleased. I felt strongly to leave but he said that we could at least have our dinner and drink before we said goodbye. Somehow he knew that we were never going to see each other again. There was a part of him playing out this Dark role on me and my resistance excited him. No matter what I said, I could not get him back, he was that taken over by this Force. "Drink up," he said again and again.

The room began to spin and I said that I was dizzy. All of a sudden, down I went and Jimmy lifted me up in his arms and carried me out. He took me to his house and laid me on his bed. I could not move. I had been heavily sedated and my speech was of no use.

He was black and demonic as he pleasured himself. My soul held me unconscious as this occurred. My mind held onto the thoughts that Jimmy thought I was his Soulmate. In terminologies, thinking was mankind, Knowing was the Creator. If he had even said, I know you are not my Soulmate, he would have still been in the White Light. Instead, he would keep saying "I think" and so he was not. Believe me you will know when the Soulmate has arrived. You won't be thinking anything. Your legs will probably start shaking and you will lose total control. Oh you'll be terrified, yet allow yourself to be opened wide up for whatever they may present. You won't have a choice in this. It was Jimmy's terminologies that identified where he was at.

I woke in the early morning and he was asleep next to me. He had used up so much energy fighting my Light and he had taken his pleasures as far as he could. I wanted to cry but I understood the Darkness and knew it was too late for him. He woke moments after I tried to get up.

"Don't go Deb," he said. Our time was up no matter what. I felt ripped apart by the way it used to be and how horrible it had all ended. I needed to leave with the very best of all of our love. I had to find the beauty and walk with that forever in my heart. Jimmy was the only, earth, walking person that had loved me, held me and shared with me. We had the best of times. I needed to leave while I could hold the tears back. There was no returning. Sadness flooded my heart so much that I wept as I slipped out of the door anyway. Even Jimmy knew that there was no future. I closed the front door and stood there only a moment. All of a sudden, I turned and Jimmy had his face pressed up against the window. He put his hand to the glass beckoning me to put my hand to his. Tears flooded his eyes.

"I love you Deb," he screamed.

I looked away and started walking. When I got to the end of the driveway, I turned around. He had his hands to his chest and he had fallen to the floor. Something had been put in my drink to drug me. I would have never been that sedate. I drove away almost unable to see from the tears. The change in Jimmy was apparent but one small ray of Light was still there. That ray of Light brought forward the tears and pain momentarily. It all reminded me of that baby boy taken over by that demon. It was so sad. I kept wondering if I could have helped but we both knew that every time we tried to come together something always interfered.

Athena stayed with me for a very long time that day. I did not feel the same way anymore. I had done all I could to help people. I had so loved Jimmy and sent him into the Awesome White Light. I didn't think it mattered any longer if I helped anyone. I didn't want to bother with anything. Athena in her majestic beauty cloaked me with her energy and I stayed very close to her for what seemed like forever.

"You need a break Daughter. You have reached out to help hundreds of people for so long. You need time to relax now," she said.

"I don't care anymore. I don't know how it all could have come down to this. We aren't going to see each other ever again," I cried.

"I know you are sad and your heart does ache but your Soulmate is there in this world waiting for you," she said.

A wave of loss kept coming over me. I felt the Dark winning and could do nothing to stop it. Jimmy was taken into it all so intensely and in a moment's notice his eyes were consumed with a possession. I could do nothing. I could say nothing that would ever make a difference. Where was I to go in my life?

Athena kept coming back to me as time passed but I was very sick and could not tend to anything. Had I lost such a part of me? Had all of this had such an impact on me? I had bouts of crying and overwhelming sadness. It wasn't me and it felt like something was trying to take over me. As the months went by I battled my sickness to the point of no longer being able to function at any other task. Athena told me that a great evil was trying to take me. Jimmy was not my Soulmate. How could he have had such an impact on me? This body of mine was never something I truly understood, in fact it was a weakness as Athena had often said.

I was so sick, I could not just lie there and die. I went to a doctor, which was a place Athena forbid me to go. If I thought losing Jimmy was hard, to be told I was pregnant was probably the most devastating thing I could have ever heard. No wonder I was so sick. I cried so hard knowing I was in Light and this baby was in the Dark. I began to release this baby into the Light but I was so sick it was obvious something was terribly wrong. I became determined to prove that my Teachings were wrong. I'd find some way to hang onto this baby. Athena told me that my Teachings were right and that I could not carry this baby much longer. "Athena how can I change this?" I asked her.

"You cannot!" she said firmly.

I knew that this baby was not in the transference state either. "Oh baby James you are not going to make it. Oh Creator, help me to go through this." All through my life I had always had the Angels and their Awesome Presence. I knew beyond all things, that they were all there to help baby James back to the Light. It was understandable but painfully sad. You have to know how much I loved Jimmy in spite of everything. He never knew about baby James. I cried, of course and the void was devastating. I sort of did not know how to get back to myself. I guess it was that mother, nurturing thing. I still felt his soul, I still felt the tearing apart. Another time baby James, another time, I kept telling him. There remained a haunting and desperation from time to time from him. Every year the spirit of baby James still comes back to me strongly and the desire to be born is well within him.

I continued to teach people who just kept coming my way. Once again, I taught how we needed to identify ourselves to Darkness. If Darkness knew we were Protected by the Creator and that we sent it back home, we not only were honoring it but it kept out of our journeys. I cannot tell you how many times Darkness came to me just outside my energy field so it could go back home. It would say, "Where do we go? No one sends us home." Come on people, get a clue here. Those in the Light are responsible to help those in the dark remember the Light and you know by now that I'm not talking about headlights either. Everyone complained about how miserable things were but once again many did nothing to change it.

This world had such a control issue and sexual one. Who gave the male dominance over the female? A male always loses a piece of his soul every time he has a physical relationship with a female. It is in this loss that creates possibilities for a soul to enter upon conception. The energy has to be there in the female for the soul entering to make it and thus creation can begin. I'm sure you never looked at it this way but I have always known this. It also has to do with the reason seduction plays out. If a female continues to have male soul energy within her she will carry a boy. It depends on who she is within a relationship. It alerts a male entity that you would be willing to carry it if it decides to be born. Certain females can only carry boys, some can only carry girls. Forget about the medical field, they know not of such things. Remember too, it would be too messy for doctors to have to deal with other possibilities. Don't worry though, except for the rare exceptions, doctors are at the bottom of the list for possible enlightenment.

People liked what I said and how it had an immediate impact on them. It was sad that I was the only one knowing about these things. I was so far beyond their levels and it was becoming incredibly lonely as time went by. Little by little, this loneliness turned into an inner peace that slowly came upon me. I felt calm and relaxed as the months went by. This internal peace made quite a statement when, to my surprise, I discovered I was four months pregnant. There was not one clue that this could be. After being so sick with baby James, I never expected that any pregnancy could be so wonderful.

Athena did not come by me all during my pregnancy, which I found surprising. There seemed to be a major reason why but she did not tell me. I sensed that it had to do with another time for her and a baby boy. Years to come I would find out that what I had sensed was right. Light gave birth to Light and my son was born so content and at peace. There wasn't any way he was going to be put back to sleep or shut down. There would be no fist clenching or arm folding across his chest to try to protect his soul. I welcomed to the world my awesome baby! I knew I would fully honor him and he would fully honor me. Why? The White Light is constantly in a state of Honor. I was the keeper of this tiny entity's body, mind and spirit. The only thing vulnerable about him was his size.

Remember, Light always honors Light. Light always honors all things.

CHAPTER SIX

The days of seeing Athena dwindled. She did not like the lack of full attention from me and she did not care for the baby stages or being interrupted. I did notice though, that she would come immediately if it involved Soulmate related things. Her joy was to be my Mother but her job seemed to be my Soulmate. Since she was with me all during my childhood, my Soulmate must have had the need for some assistance as well. Athena wanted to bask in the sun while someone did her nails and toes. To this day, I still have this habit of nail doing, except I do my own. I realized how many things she affected in me. All of those goddess type qualities. Be gone with those unkempt mortals, she would always say. She said that these things she gave me my Soulmate needed to see as well.

The whole Family kept me out of the caught up, book read, small-minded existence of the human race. Most people really believed that they could not express their Knowingness without being knocked down by society. Again and again, no one had the courage. Jimmy tried but even he couldn't battle it. It goes back to what I said about the Dark you can see and the Dark you cannot see. When it came to courage though, the amount of strength the female had when it came to safety of her baby even made Darkness take a second look. Darkness uses seduction as a tool to trap you but it has always been well aware that it could be trapped by the female and her power of motherhood.

Even Darkness dreads the battle with a mother protecting her young. So the female is stronger and her ability to override society and its traps are greater. When the female sets up the den, keep out means keep out. In times of trauma, the female can take on more Darkness than a blackout in the whole entire world. Males just look at this as the female is out of control, over exaggerating, fickle, emotional. Hello? Wake up males. The female has to be stronger as she is the carrier of life. Your seed means nothing if she cannot carry it. Could Jimmy have won his battle with Darkness if he had been a female? The chances of winning or maintaining would have been greater. Females that do not have children are not as prone to that intense motherhood protect force but still the female is stronger. Once you have a baby you do hold that extra power if you use it.

Darkness walks all over the males. This is easy. They are in a perpetual state of pms, penis male syndrome. Yes, males have pms. You didn't know that, did you? One thought from Darkness and they are falling out of Light. It is a twisted world that allows a male to excuse his behavior because he has to exercise his anatomy. Not only has this become a condition but, the female allows it. The female and male have the same drives in the physical relationship. Females have allowed society to convince them otherwise.

If you want to say that science says differently, well you don't want me to tell you what science is. I'll tell you anyway. Science is the state of allowing the illusion to become reality. I could do many classes on this and prove to you again and again that I am correct in all of this. As I tell you things, I cannot give you all of the Teachings but only some of them. Much cannot be written, it must be merely listened to. Why? Because someone would try to violate it.

Let's go to passion. Only when you are bonded to the Creator can you have passion. On the human level you have sex. There is a big difference here. A male in passion is so awesome and so overdue that most females can't even phantom this. Sex is the human race, passion is the Creator. Imagine having passion instead. The male then is at the highest level that he could ever be in, in all areas of his life. Passion fills him in his mental, emotional, physical, spiritual and intellectual realms. These are the five basic energies we continually use. Can you have sex and passion at the same time? No. Why? Because passion belongs to the Creator and sex belongs to the human race. Once you are doing passion, it isn't just the act of love but the zest and love for all things. Sex is sex. Can you have sex in your intellect? No, but you can have passion.

Now you're going to wonder what is the meaning of passion as I see it. Passion is the total experience of Pure White Light filling your soul. In other words, it is the highest connection with the Creator while in the human body. As you see it, hear it, smell it, taste it, it is the soul's craving and need. Sure, you have Light in all souls but imagine waves of Pure White Light untouched or even viewed by Darkness, surging into you, filling you beyond your most awesome thoughts and dreams. A good dose of passion soothes the soul. It is mandatory to have and can only be experienced by being bonded to the Creator. Note too that the Creator is constant and forever. By the way, have you had any passion lately? Another difference is that sex ends and the memory of it fades. Passion continues to generate passion. If you say to me that you have had sex but it too continued in your thoughts, I'd say it was plain lust in the first place. Lust is a human vibration and is one of Darkness's favorite charms. Lust is the termination of all desires and the immediate demand of fulfillment. Ugh! Had any lust lately?

So there is much to say. You need to listen to what words you speak and recognize where you are. Where is most of the planet? Certainly not in passion, because lust feeds sex and passion feeds the soul.

The Angel of Silk was still there but new Angels came and for now Zeus was busy. All he seemed to be good for was the lightning strikes. Isn't it funny that, even out of their earth bodies, they all still had personalities. What does that tell you? Even among the Angels each was different. The Angel of Silk was incredibly sensitive and appearing a bit shy. So this should tell you that you don't need the body for expression or personality. Oh, should we bring up science again? No! Let us move on.

You need to begin to see that there are certain terminologies for the human race versus the Creator. When you use the words with Creator, your vibration is higher. When you use the words with the human race, it is lower. Someone is going to say but it is all just words. Yes but since we have to identify where you are, you have to use language as the source. Okay, I will say, do you then speak vibration language to me? I will hear it, understand it and we can do away with this language that the planet uses. On a simple level, positive words are the Creator's words, negative words belong to the human race and their primitive levels. Darkness is negative, White Light is positive. Something to think about as you wait for more.

It was clear that Athena being gone left me feeling a bit in the longing state for her. When I was a baby and child, she was always there for me. She was so protective of me and always that beauty and grace as she cared little whom she might run into or what circumstances might have met her face to face. You can imagine how I got so used to her. Clearly it was too intense right now. She was within reach but preferred to stay at a distance. The timing for her to come back was years away.

Angels graced me with their presence instead. Would you believe that one was a brat? He would continually tease people. I never knew any other name better suited than the Joker. Joker and Silk never got along. Joker was doing apprenticeship to be more in Light. It was clear somewhere in time he had been working for the other Force. The jokes he played on people were unreal. Joker was quite good for not having a solid body if you wanted to view all of his deeds. He was good at putting thoughts into people's minds. Things like going to a restaurant and making someone forget to screw on the ketchup lid or salt lid. Things like that. He only went after grumpy sour pusses that needed to be cheered up. Most of the time they did not react well to a lap full of ketchup or their meal drenched in salt. Once in a while though, he would accomplish his mission and one soul would remember their sense of humor, lighten up and look at their life. Most though, would scream at the waiter, "You idiot, how could you forget to put the lid on?" Of course the waiter had had this negligence erased from his memory. Here comes the terminology for this one. I could have sworn I put the lid on, I could swear I did. Maybe Joker was around. Can these things be allowed? Yes, if it is to help someone remember Light.

The Angels were constantly on guard to all vibrations coming and going. They seemed to be looking for something specific, like Athena she was looking for something specific. For her it was my Soulmate. Since my mission was to take the Fallen Angels back to the Light, I was waiting for them to show up. I guess the ones in Light were guarding me. Why couldn't the Angels guarding me take their own back home? Why in the world was I needed? This was hard for me to believe. It was just me. So I had Knowingness and taught things that no one had ever read or seen before.

Oh well, I still had my Soulmate on my mind. Where Soulmates are concerned, although they are total opposites, they also have things in common. How often do you hear parents tell their children to Love the Creator first. They don't see the parents doing it so why should they Okay, you might say, it is all a little too radical for you. Fine, let's see how radical it gets in the Dark Force. That's okay because you haven't finished reading all of this. Perhaps you'll see things differently when it becomes more intense. I still kept wondering if there had been some mistake but I knew that there was no such thing as mistakes. Divine Order would not allow that. Perhaps they needed someone in a human body because it required substance.

Remember that girl that had the baby taken over by the demon. She had to endure this baby trying to kill her, burn her, burn down their apartments again and again. This boy stabbed people, robbed, set fires, poisoned people, twisted things, lied and set people up for harm and sickness. Worst of all, there was no control or therapy that worked to stop him. Of course, this demon controlled this little boy. By the age of twelve he had been removed, blaming his mother for everything and so did everyone else. These demons look for kids when they are vulnerable.

Believe me saying it's a little radical to talk about the Creator is one big regret for the parents who end up losing a child to a demon. The older a child is when taken over the better its chances are to break free. As for this woman, she only had moments with her son in the Light but this soul craved evil and this entity knew it. They fed each other's energy. When parents are at the end, where do they turn? They don't want to believe that these things are really going on. After all, they can blame someone, somewhere, but does it ever change? Remember this, there is no positive with the human race, only with the Creator. You are in illusions that you are happy and that's why it doesn't stay with you. You are in illusions that these Forces don not exist. You are in illusions so deeply that you actually believe another human being could do so much trauma to another's soul. Any human being cannot generate that much power. You may be bonded to the

Creator and happy but you may have Soulmate problems and that is a completely different matter. When in Soulmate energy you may swing from happy to sad but I will talk about that later.

People continued to call me begging for help. There was so much depression and a good medical diagnosis for all patients. Doctors, yes one of the big evils as Athena put it. I began to date doctors, which was the true beginning of my career as a Cult Deprogrammer. It became more incredible than I could have ever expected. I was about to unveil one of the biggest evils that many doctors were doing. They were malpracticing using cult teachings on patients for practice so they could get better at their abilities. It was done in a way completely unaware to anyone. They had fraud rings going where they could set patients up and send them in a circle of medical despair and trickery.

It was a brilliant plan for the doctors to get rich doing nothing. When a patient came, one doctor would send them to his friend and so on. The patient never got better but had to pay for five or six referrals. Of course, trying to prove this was impossible, that was until me. I was dating a doctor who let it slip when he thought that he was heading to the altar with me. I had seen how little he did and how much money he was able to collect from all of his unsuspecting victims. The phrase, *a license to kill* was incomplete, it was a license to kill or anything else. These people were being taken for every cent. Meanwhile the doctors pretended to be so caring and concerned. He would laugh over dinner with me and replay the whole thing with each victim day after day. I asked him how many doctors were in on this.

"Why, all of us but no one is ever going to admit it and it is impossible to prove. Besides these patients are asking for it on some level," he would say. All fell prey to this regardless of their age or illness. Why was it in careers that if you messed up, you were fired, yet the bulletproof systems of doctors exempted them from all things? It was a fraudulent set up from day one. It was a guarantee for a free ride once in. Any doctor that has this superiority attitude is Dark. Any doctor that lies and cheats the patient is Dark. They don't know more than you, you have merely forgotten it all. If you could for one moment realize the full magnitude of the fraud, you'll stop going and find one of those rare, in the Light doctors. Oh, they are still out there but it is truly rare. Since the human race will still manifest sickness, then the need will still be there for the doctor. At first I thought that perhaps there might be hundreds of doctors doing this but as time went by it turned out to be thousands.

It is important to realize the devastation that children can have on your life if they become possessed or taken over. Possession is the abduction of the soul. Taken over means that there is may still be a chance for the return of that child. You must fully be able to recognize the entity that has taken over the child and all of the programs that this entity has put there or you will virtually be unable to pull the child out of it. When I say recognize, I mean call it by name, know where it's been and where it's going and so on. You must be aware of its cleverness.

An example I give is this girl kept two bracelets from a master on the planet, which kept her connected to him. She could not shake her deep connections but of course some deprogrammer claimed to have cleansed her. Yet there are no deprogrammers as complete or as thorough as I am. These entities are clever and can give you great illusions. They use techniques that are on timers. They will plant something that will surface years later. I can tell you if this will happen as I see it but you yourself can also see it.

Remember the woman whose baby was taken over and became so evil that it nearly destroyed her life? He grew to be monstrous and yet I tell you this woman's heart and soul was of gold, Light and deep love. Society branded her and this evil child made sure he played everyone to the max as the poor victim. His goal was to destroy her no matter what he had to do. It would have been best for this baby to have exited but its destiny was not as such. You can only know of such horror if you yourself have ever had such a situation. There are many of you out there at wit's ends for answers. Believe me society knows nothing. It knows nothing. Experiences continue to be told with never a solution.

There is only one Truth, one answer and one solution. I speak of the Creator, not other terminologies with religious connections. Who are you talking to, people? Where are you? Do you know yourselves? You think you know. That is not good enough to "think." You have to "know" for sure. How are these children being abducted if you are connected to the Creator? You aren't! Go ahead, continue on, and nothing but confusion will be present.

The group of people with the highest abductions is what you might refer to as the upper class, middle class yuppie types. They are by far the easiest group to get to. You know, the clinical, sanitized, uptight perfect yuppies. They don't have passion, they have clinical sex, like an office visit on a timer. It had better be with great control and done as well as their starched shirt collars and their neat folded clothes in their drawers. After all we don't want one hair out of place. They are so fixed in their superiority, that Darkness has a set, set of rules. If you have tunnel vision you are under the roof of Darkness. An open mind is a lot harder to control. A strong will is hard to break but a yuppie is a loser.

Children in general hate these kinds of parents. They raise their kids from books and what time frame society says that the child should be in. There is no room for the child to break free of the stress of all of this. Not only is it all programmed but the Dark Force has a guarantee that the souls they take from this group will stay with them their whole life. This is just another form of brainwashing. Notice that all through the ages rebels were locked away. The ones who spoke up were jailed. No wonder most of the heroes died off. We live in a world of shut downs and brain controlled laws. Why was there no justice, because to begin with there wasn't any. You have all sold yourselves short, given up, and given in. Or are there a few of you left that are still saying, no way? Bravo to you then! Get up, fight, you can't lose if you play to win. There is no negative if you play positive. Your soul will cooperate, I guarantee you. Of course, the war will be great. You'll put doctors out of business and they will do their best to keep you playing sick, make you sick or insist you're crazy in the head. Notice how society kills the heroes and locks away the truth. Oh yes, let's get back to that funny god that takes things and gives things. What an ego. I'm glad the Creator is top of the line. Once again I ask you, who are you giving your power away to? Who do you call god? Go ahead, argue with me because that tells me there is still some fight in you and hope that you will awaken.

Time and time again students came to me without ever being told about me through any advertisement. All of them had unusual stories of how they found me. Always the classes were filled with Angels that no one ever saw but me. I had to repeat many things constantly but slowly they began to see the Light, the real Light. Finally they were able to let go of these negative programs and go back to the Creator. Most will say just let things go. Oh really, do you know who's out there ready to pick up your extra baggage?

One person said to me "Must I watch every little thing?"

Hello! See how irresponsible people are. Is it your baggage? Why would you want someone going through your things? Here comes their answer, because I don't need it anymore. Oh really! Are you sure? If you don't need it, why are you letting anyone or anything go through it? Why are you not sending it back to the Creator, your safety deposit box? By not sending to the Creator, you are notifying Darkness you are not done. Perhaps that is why you continue to do the repeat syndrome. You have never thought about it like this, have you? I know where your baggage is.

Many of my students could not get enough of the classes, they were starving all of the time. Little was allowed to be written down. It was because no one was allowed to copy, take or reproduce any of it. The soul had to be the main carrier of this knowledge and believe me their souls were just fine with all of this. There were answers for everything. The answers were immediate too. Nowhere did they find such fulfillment and it was instant. All of the negative programs had created so much tartar on their souls and once they were aware of this, the enlightenment began to reveal itself. Again and again they received their own validation. They began to get back their memories, their identities and it belonged to each of them, not me. I didn't have to convince them, change them or give each one something different.

The Creator is the same for all. Can you imagine fully understanding everything? Wow, this is what they received and it was easy, clear and immediate. Where did this come from? I was born with it. I have always known. What was so amazing was the simplicity of it all. The Creator is not complicated, the human race is. You must understand too that many were not ready to give up their Darkness so the classes did not attract them.

The Angel of Silk was so proper and well mannered that it was a pleasure to be in his presence. I missed Athena's rushing in and taking over. It was adorable how she did this. She never really took over but merely acted out like she did.

Did Zeus really strike me? No, but I had systems which collided with his, sort of like two batteries being forced together. I did not know how involved Zeus really was until much later. He really was not the big bad boy he wanted everyone to believe he was. He still had that fair haired, fair skinned, major iron pumper look. Athena was darker, with darker features. Now you're saying they aren't in bodies but I tell you the vibration of these things even in the etheric form. As I have said, you tend to keep the same likeness again and again. None could cover the elegance of Athena. It irked her to no end when stupid mortals acted like she visited them or channeled through her.

"Oh how stupid," she would say. "Like I'd come to the mortal realm for what? Because someone needed to have importance surrounding them while using me? Nothing was of more disgrace than unkempt mortal women spraying themselves with cheap perfume pretending to be some reincarnation of a goddess. Then these mortals use the loose terminology of Angels, this is an Angel, that is an Angel and so on. Angels are not children or good people. What a boring primitive planet," she would conclude.

"Daughter," she would say to me, "Come let us bask in the sun, dip into the pool, arch our splendid feet and let our reflections upon the water send gold through our hair. "

"Athena," I'd say, "You are most persuasive."

"Daughter, you do not belong in this realm," she would say laughing.

Yes, to have no cares in the world would be great. Oh the temptation to just leave and not come back was great. Yes, Awesome Athena was greatly missed by me and how I loved her more dearly than words could ever say. Athena, come back to me, I silently thought. The Angel of Silk was quite curious by my vibration. I spooked him as I lunged forward saying, "I'm just thinking about my Mother."

How good was this Angel going to be in a major crisis? I was beginning to feel like I had to take care of him. Danger was definitely close by but for the life of me I could not see it. That meant that it was Soulmate related. The Soulmate had a way of causing major problems without even being there. It was amazing how many people actually thought that their Soulmate was a child of theirs, or relative or even the same sex as them. There were also those who thought that the Soulmate was a wonderful friend of theirs. That wonderful friend was what I called a soul energy, not Soulmate. It was amazing how ignorant most people were about their Soulmate. They all usually concluded that it was an easy, happily ever after relationship. How could that possibly be if one is always in the Light and one is always in the Dark? People shunned that part about the Dark. More illusions. I wanted to just finish this mission, get my Soulmate and leave. Yes, I wanted to bask in the sun with Athena.

I tell you that you need to desire passion, not sex. You want to know, not think. You want Light, not Dark. You want Truth, not illusions. You want to recognize what you are in and what you are saying. If you have children do you know where they are or where they tell you they are? Can you tell if they will be abducted? Are you stuck in programs? Of course you are. Now I can just hear someone saying that this is all too spooky. Fine, then stay where you are but don't come running to me when you decide that the fear of staying where you are is greater than the fear of what I am saying now. The waiting line for your type is already much too long.

Motherhood for me was the most fabulous thing that could have ever happened. It was so private and special. My son was so precious to me and very enlightened. His inner Knowingness just poured from his soul and, yes, he too had the Dark Force nearby. It is always nearby but you know how much you can't stand me telling you this. It's like that starched shirt collar. Get real! Life is not stiff and someone needs to put a wrinkle in this life style somewhere.

Athena always said, these yuppie types had major hang ups about their identity. She would laugh and say, with their clothes off they even looked the same, all boring and uptight. The females of this kind had fixations about their bodies so bad that they might as well have stayed in a bath of lard soap for life. Athena would laugh saying, how these women found themselves to be constantly dirty. Uptight yuppie females were worse than the men. They were so fake but mainly insecure as all and loved to power trip another female. They females were ruled by one thing but I will not use the word Athena used. I shall leave it to your imagination.

I guess we would have to say doctors are yuppies, nearly all of them. Most of the nurses are evil and there are no exceptions if they will lie for a doctor. Notice, they will say that they don't have a choice because they would be fired. Another sell out. Any job that forces you to lie, participate in mutilations or death, is evil. Get a clue. You are evil if you are able to claim this. There are no exceptions. I continued to date doctors but to my horror they were not only ripping their patients off but they were having them abducted by these masters, wizards, etc. that they worshiped. These doctors knew full well what they were doing and it was great recruiting after all. If you are sick who can be clear about things. Of course, these doctors could corner you into the mental problem department if you gave them any grief. It is a doctor's safe haven to claim you are mentally ill.

Imagine anyone having such power over you to destroy your whole life because some evil doctor might get caught with his evil deeds. There has never been a doctor yet that could keep his identity from me or behave properly without sensing my knowing what he was up to. It's like I have radar and he has just been caught breaking the law.

Finding a good doctor is as hard as seeing Athena but it can be done. It is sad to say that it will cost you dearly to find this. There is nothing more disturbing than hearing someone say my doctor is great. Then why is your daughter so deathly sick? Well we don't know, she's been on antibiotics for a whole year and now she has stomach problems all of the time. Antibiotics for a whole year? No doctor in their right mind would put a child on powerful antibiotics for a whole year because she started out with a cold. I bet it cost a lot to be permanently messed up. The conclusion is that the doctor never really knew what was ever wrong but since he was one of those old family doctors he would never run the risk of being sued. This girl is now so stripped inside and she is ruined for life.

Remember what I said about a career that guarantees you full power on anything or anyone? They make you sick, you stay sick and they get disgustingly rich off of your pain. If you knew how little they really knew you, you would cringe. In all of my research, I discovered hundreds of thousands of malpracticing doctors with a guarantee to continue with it all. A license to slaughter, maim and kill with no remorse or guilt. If cornered, their final comments were, "Well, people asked for it."

I could not believe how many twisted teachings these doctors used on their patients. The reason most acted like a god is because of their power over their patients. Even for those who had won a battle against a doctor, they have had to go through such degradation on top of everything else.

There are so many things to say but I will move on, telling you only to walk from any Dark in your life but you must make sure it is Dark. Remember that there is no clarity unless you release yourself to the Awesome White Light of the Creator. Once again, you may argue that you are already there. I talk to god a lot, you might say. Be still and listen, you need to show Darkness where you are at. If it knows that you are with the Creator it will leave you. You are responsible to send it back to the Creator by releasing all Darkness to the Awesome White Light. I must continue to tell you this because you must do this to protect yourself. Is it too much trouble to say you might think? If so you have no idea how much trouble is coming. How can you wake up and have no connection to the Creator? I can also hear some of you saying that you are connected but you call your Creator another name. There we go again. Does Darkness know whom you are talking to? If it's another name, I can bet they know how to play this one with all of their illusion to make you think you're at the top, with the top. Your ego gets in your way.

Does it matter what you are calling the Creator? Yes. Especially if it's that god with hell and brimstone. This religion is based on the human race and their interpretation of god. Darkness knows all about this and has a good time running you around and around. Even Darkness sees how sick and disturbing this religion is. There are many religions and all are interpretations of the human race. Why do people question this kind of god? Because their souls are craving the true Creator and this god thing is not right. Instead of being able to come forward with their truth, they are knocked down, shut down, or they walk. If they walk they are shunned by all they know. Once again, I tell you it takes great courage to stand up for what you know is Truth. They then will say to you, god has punished you.

I was truly floored when the Angel of Silk rushed in and stood towering over me. What in the world was this? He spoke. "Deity Deborah, great danger bestows itself upon you. Be still as I cloak you."

I sat down and it seemed like hours before I could move. It reminded me of two ships passing in the night, not friendly ships either. Great fear was present that each might find out about the other. Waves of energy hit me right through his White cloaking device Angel of Silk used. "It is him?" I asked.

"Deity, be still, he will locate you," he spoke in a whisper.

"Of course he will locate me. That's why I came back," I told Angel of Silk.

"It is too soon. There is great danger, I cannot let harm come to you," he said to me cloaking me even greater.

"Harm? Be still yourself. I am not of this mortal realm. I am that of my Mother and carry upon me wisdom of great depth. Be removed at once or I shall use upon you my powers, Deity called Angel," I stood up saying very loudly.

"If, Deity Deborah, I let you show yourself you will be hurt. Yes, you have systems which eventually will surface to battle this one," he said very concerned, "but now is not the correct time."

Somehow what he said touched upon my soul and I knew he was right. I sat back down feeling shocked and bewildered at all of this. My Soulmate was there, right there next to me cloaked himself but he was in black and carried the sword of death. I was so shocked that Angel of Silk stayed next to me long after my Soulmate left. What hit me so hard was what my mission was.

"Angel of Silk, speak to me that of which I must do," I demanded of him.

"Did you see him?" he asked.

"Of course I saw him. He is, you know, he is . . ." I stuttered. I could not get the words out, I would never get the words out. There had to have been some terrible mistake. It could not have been him. I must be filling in for someone else. "What is wrong with everyone?" I yelled as I lifted my head to the sky. "It can't be," I screamed. I fell to the ground in such despair that Angel of Silk held me. "There must be some mistake Angel of Silk, there has to be. Do you know who he is? Of course you know, everyone knows. Tell me there is some mistake," I cried out.

"Athena," I screamed. "Athena," I screamed even louder. Athena came forward but she stood at a distance. I tried to rush to her but Silk held me back. "What are you doing? Let me go at once!" I yelled pulling free. "Mother," I cried running to Athena. Just as I got to her she raised her hand to stop me. "Mother what are you doing?" I asked.

She turned her head from me and spoke. "Daughter, you do not want to know of me now."

"Mother," I said as tears poured down my face. "I will always want to know of you. Be gone of this despair you bestow upon me. I am that of you, Mother. No one of all Deities has put upon me such love. You cannot turn from my presence now."

"But I must Daughter," she said softly.

"I command different Mother. Do not turn from me," I demanded.

She started to cry. "It pains me Daughter that I must depart from you," she said.

It occurred to me that it was because of my Soulmate she spoke this."Mother," I said, collecting myself, "is it because of him that you speak so to me?"

"Yes," she responded.

"I must come upon my mind and put things in order so that I am of understanding. Mother stay and tell me of the story of this," I said reaching out my hand to her. Finally, she lifted her hand to me grabbing me and holding me tighter than ever. I cried so from the depths of my soul. Oh how I loved her. She wept so and would not let go of me for a very long time.

"Daughter, let us not speak of this now. It is not worth the discord it could present," she said to me and I agreed with her. Nothing was worth grief between us, not anything or anyone. The Angel of Silk stood in the background looking somewhat sadly at us as if he too wanted to be so loved. I could not believe how wonderful it was to see Athena after all of this time. "I must go Daughter," she said after many hours.

"Be close to me Mother," I said.

"I will always be within a whisper's call, my Daughter," she said as she collected herself and burst into sparks of Light.

"Angel of Silk, come upon this vibration and embrace it. You too may feel the Love and Light of this," I said beckoning him forward. He looked so surprised but came forward as if he were gliding on wind. For another day all of this could be but for now, I loved my son more dearly every day and my Mother, Awesome Athena.

CHAPTER SEVEN

Athena coming to see me was wonderful but I could not believe that this Soulmate of mine was so Dark. The sword of death was the symbol lying over his force field. It is recognized by only certain entities. Few can see this but I saw it clearly. There was great trouble in all of this. I carried upon me the symbol of Love. Yes we were opposites but it was beyond all that I could have ever imagined. I could not believe that this was real. No wonder Angel of Silk was there. He did come through in that crisis. He was so incredibly gentle and powerful. I felt close to him and saw his tremendous strength. He was so big that he towered over me twice my height. He told me that my Soulmate would come close again and that if he did not cloak me I might be killed. My Soulmate had great systems similar to what you would call bionics. Even though I was told I had this too, I was not near the level he had when he passed by me. Angel of Silk told me I was in the beginning stages of activation. I suppose that theory about Zeus jumpstarting me might have had some truth to it after all. I could not settle myself to such things as who my Soulmate was. As much as I knew that there was no mistake, I had no avenue to relieve this unsettling feeling. I could not get this out of my head. Where was I to go with all of it?

I was so elated that Athena was still there. Something was underlying between my Soulmate and her. She was hiding something from me or keeping something for later. There seemed to be an unsettling energy that followed me from this point on. No matter what I did it would not let go. It was similar to a dark shadow lurking in the background. You could feel it and I could see it. My students constantly asked if an entity was present or if we were being watched by someone.

Although I had been affected by my Soulmate, I was sure that he too had been affected by me. I felt as if I were being tracked. It was high tech for the planet earth but it was very familiar to me. I had felt this many times before and I had known all of this again and again. It was now rehearsal time. All I had really known about myself in this life was that I had great Knowingness, I had very advanced telepathic powers and of course the mission. It was a bit hard to grasp that I had systems like my Soulmate. I just wanted to be a regular human being and live like all the rest, in a perpetual state of denial. What is Deborah requesting to be, an idiot like the rest of the planet? No, because I knew that, rare as it may be, there were people who did know plenty but they were living in fear.

Fear by the way, all fear, is a learned vibration. It is something that the soul has in storage. You cannot fear that which you have not done. Just because you do not remember it, doesn't mean it won't surface. All this means is that you'll be afraid but you won't know why. Would you like to know why? Denying your fear does not make it go away. It will crave to be understood and fear will collect more fear. Its purpose is to be remembered and it will drive you crazy if allowed to be ignored. It will become your deepest nightmare. Fear makes you paralyzed. Fear stops all states of Knowingness and replays its vibration until it is resolved. It is a past life vibration and you are stuck in past life with anything you fear. Remember, you cannot fear that which your soul has not come upon. This word fear has held everyone in such a state of despair for what seems like forever. If you fear it, you did it and it then owns you.

It is so funny to hear the word imagine. Yes, you imagined it. The soul does not imagine. Your inability to deal with what your soul is telling you creates the word, imagine. There is no such thing. You are playing out fragmented memories. Just like the words, make believe. It is impossible for the soul to make believe but once again you cannot handle what you need to know so you close down and use words like imagine, make believe, etc. All fear is a learned vibration that is stored in your soul! The only time fear is mandatory, is in the state of

Soulmates. At this time, fear is a gauging mechanism that Soulmates use to identify past. This is the only time it is acceptable because the Soulmates cannot dismiss it. Soulmates are unlike anything you could ever imagine. When Soulmates do fear, they are also doing recovery. It is all too much for you to understand right now but it won't be as we go along.

Let me say though, if you wish to stay asleep put this down. If you desire to know, read on, but if you desire your Soulmate read between the lines. I cannot tell you all of what I teach. As I have said, it would be violated if written down. This might lead to confusion for most but if you really desire to know, you will pursue this further.

The classes grew and people just could not stay away. Always everyone wanted to see things like Angels, Athena, Zeus, Jesus, and anyone that was out of the human body. People that had entities inside them were being violated from within by whatever entity had them. There is no situation that an entity has the privilege or right to invade a human body. I do not care if they appear to be for the good. That is all it is, an appearance. There is no good that comes from an entity that crams itself into the molecular structure of the human body. There are no exceptions.

Channelers are in violation as well and those who channel through them are being violated. The human structure is not of that of a channeler. Just because you cannot see it, does not mean it is not there. Wake up! You have been stuck in this low vibration of denial again and again. Believe me, if I can see it, it is there!

As these classes went on and the more awake people became the more they were able to see things that they never dreamed possible. This brings me to another word, dream. A dream is that of the soul trying to give you a full truth that you cannot deal with on the conscious level. When you awake you cannot recall the whole dream, just parts of it. You will have the parts necessary to bring that truth forward in the future. To remember the whole dream would be hard to cope with. The times that you do remember the whole dream it is related to your Soulmate. Is this always true? Yes. The Soulmate is the most fragile relationship ever. Information about the Soulmates must be revealed regardless of how much you resist. Since you are opposites you may have a hard time coping and need to know things that you cannot cope with on the conscious level. Your dreams are safe and usually most will say, "Oh well, it was just a dream, it wasn't real." The human race is best known for states of denial.

If you think that being married or having a companion cancels out the Soulmate, you are wrong. Nothing cancels out the Soulmate. You may never meet them physically in this life but believe me they are there walking alongside of you somewhere. You may be taking the pill to relieve the headache that they have. The relationship with Soulmates is so fragile that one small thing can send them into space so fast and far from each other that it will take lifetimes to find each other again. Although you never lose each other by the identical sound your souls vibrate, you will experience the ripping and tearing apart until your next meeting. You will still feel his or her soul vibrating but you will not be able to locate each other. What is truly sad is that all suicides are Soulmates unable to make it in this life. They conclude to suicide because it is hopeless and they will not reconnect unless they are both out of the physical body. They are so devastated inside that usually no one can stop it, however there is a way to if you know the dynamics of Soulmates. Once the two are gone, they reconnect in their etheric bodies. It may sound quick and simple but it is very complicated.

Nothing could ever drive someone to kill themselves but the Soulmate. One will pull the other out. This has happened again and again and I have even been with the one when the other has killed themselves. The wrenching is so traumatic that the mind flat lines and the other might as well be dead. To find your other half is so innocent and pure but also so dangerous and emotional. One may be mad that you did not find them sooner. The other may be mad that you found them at all. In a moment's notice all may be forgotten and love rushes forward or more pain or whatever the two must do to work it out, play it out and reconnect.

There is so much to say about Soulmates but again I cannot reveal all in writing. It is so intimate and sacred. You must also be ready for this. You may ask me how you will know if you are ready. You won't wonder or think about it, you will know you're ready.

Remember, think is the human race, know is the Creator. I was born knowing the situation of all Soulmates and where they are. You might say to me, then why do you not tell me where mine is? Soulmate is the closest you will ever come to the full return of the Creator. You must know this sacred destiny.

Fear in the human race is past life. Fear in Soulmate is necessary. You actually go into an altered state when they tune into you or they are nearby. You feel the pulling right inside your chest and are compelled forward even if you are dragging your feet. You must go, you have to go and all else loses its hold. The power in this is beyond the human mind. It is not a human experience. It belongs to the Creator and the both of you. It is the ultimate bonding. It is the return back to the Creator. Are you ready to meet your Soulmate knowing all of this? I will gladly tell you how to find your Soulmate if you are ready. Someone has to help you. No one on this planet knows this. By just understanding your Soulmate, helps you understand who you are and why you are like you are. Again and again I tell you that you must be bonded to the Creator to even handle this. I must stop now and let you digest all of this.

I flew up out of my bed as I heard my name called. "Who is it?" I asked. As I cleared my eyes and mind of sleep I realized that it wasn't my name but my vibration that was being beckoned. It was him. Oh no, he had located me and panic hit me. Get your bearings, it is energy, he knows not where you are. All that came to mind was this man with dark hair and a warrior type robe in black searching for me with great anger in his eyes. The sword appeared and then disappeared. My heart was pounding so hard I thought that it was going to jump right out of my chest. I got up but knew immediately that I was being scanned big time. How far could he be? Oh how Dark I felt he was. I shivered intensely as I knew he would be displeased to find me. Okay Deborah, collect yourself. Just tell him to take a hike. Yeah, Right! I was going to tell Mr. Big Boy to take a hike. The energy somewhat reminded me of Zeus. At least I knew Zeus would always go away but somehow I knew my Soulmate was not going anywhere. Fear, well let me tell you it was beyond fear. Terror? It was beyond terror. What was I to do, wait it out?

I finally fell asleep again and it seemed so deep I could not wake. The Angel of Silk rushed in, "Deity Deborah wake. There is great danger!" he said rushing around me.

"No," I mumbled, "it is love, Angel of Silk. I love him."

"No!" he screamed at me. "He is abducting you!"

That was all I needed to hear to wake up faster than you could imagine. For the Angel of Silk to scream it had to be an emergency. I felt my arms and legs. They had been touched. I felt naked and stripped down. I clutched my covers and held my arms. He was trying to pull me into the Dark Force. It was illusions he was using just like these cult leaders were using, but where the Soulmate was concerned, it had the "ultimate" pull. If I thought that I was shook before, I was truly in shock now. The seduction he was using was such a violation. I was being drawn into it and forced deeper into sleep so I could not resist. I sat back and could not comprehend this power. The Angel of Silk had saved me.

"It is not enough," Angel of Silk told me. "more Angels must come as he gains in strength."

"You mean it gets worse?" I asked.

"Soon I will not be able to cloak you alone. He will penetrate my energy field and he will take you."

"Is this for real? I mean, I'm in a dream, right? The kind of dream you only get bits and pieces to?" I said, desperately trying to rewrite history. I started to feel funny and I began to tell Angel of Silk that I must go to him. It became a chant. Rushing to Angel of Silk's cries were three more Angels.

"Get used to it," Angel of Silk said. "Many more are coming." The Angels huddled around each other speaking in another language but I had to know what they were saying, so I tried to tune in. If I had all of this bionic power then I should have been able to understand it but I could not. Maybe I needed another jumpstart from Zeus. I had things to do and these Angels needed to just stay out of my way.

I resolved myself to thinking it was all just one big melodramatic play. Imagine having four males, angelical males hanging out all over you. I could not even take a shower without them around. They would not listen to me for anything. I could not corner them because they were transparent with little substance. I could nt outsmart them because they never left my side. In all they were making me nervous. I could see them and kept thinking I would run into them, but they moved like lightning. Gee, there's that word, Zeus would say. Maybe they were related to Pops. I tried to take what they were doing very serious but it was hysterical.

"Come on," I told them, "I can't believe things are happening." They were very serious. "Why didn't females come?" I asked Angel of Silk who by now was my favorite.

"No females!" he said strong and firm

I'd like to know why but he turned from me never mentioning it again and I didn't either. There was a reason and I would ask Athena the next time I saw her. In the daytime, my Soulmate did not bother me, by but night was a whole different thing. The Angels were on alert big time as if some huge alien ship was about to land. Honestly, it was a show every night. Every time they sensed something I jumped sky high thinking I was in trouble.

"Can't a lady ever get a good night's sleep?" I finally yelled out after months of this Angel routine night after night.

I heard one of the Angels say among themselves, "Doesn't she know?" I perked up. What don't I know? I thought.

"Excuse me gentlemen, what is it I don't know yet?" I asked them. They jumped to attention like security guards. "I heard what you said," I announced as they stood there looking as if they were caught with their hands in the cookie jar. All I can tell you is how it looked. I knew that they were keeping secrets from me. They refused to speak. "Okay, I'll call, Athena," I yelled out.

Athena came rushing in. "Daughter, what is it?"

"Mother, these four have secrets about me and I demand to know them." The Angels bowed down to Athena but then you know she always commanded full acknowledgment when she makes her entrances. They moved back far enough to be out of listening range and Athena sat upon my bed. It was girl talk now. I cuddled up next to her waiting to hear all of these secrets the Angels had been keeping from me. "Well, Mother?" I said anxiously waiting.

"I can speak of some of this, I cannot speak of all of it," she said. "You are different Daughter, very different."

"I know this," I responded back to her.

"No Daughter, you do not know yet how powerful you are. You do not know how unique you are," she said so serious.

"Mother you are scaring me," I said to her with full attention.

"Your Soulmate Daughter, he is not of this world," she added.

"Okay, I know this now. He is like a wizard, something like that? " I asked trying to forget what I had seen.

"Daughter, what is your job?" she asked.

"To take the Fallen Angels home, then get my Soulmate and go home," I said.

"You know that it is not quite like that. You must take the most powerful of them and the rest will follow," she said with some hidden message.

"Okay, I understand. It makes the job easier. So when I get this done I can then focus on my Soulmate?" I asked her in a hurry to get this finished.

"Daughter you are not ready to hear these words I hold back from you," she said in a way that reaffirmed that I did not want to hear one more thing.

"Mother, let's forget it all and enjoy our time," I said quickly. I was in this Soulmate thing and it was very apparent it would consume me if I didn't focus on the mission I had. When she left, the Angels moved back in to nearly suffocate me and so I was stuck with all four over me.

As the months passed, I would have these horrifying dreams. Always the same type of dream. He carried the sword of death. He was after me and meant to do me in. Okay, so we had some past life issues and it could be solved probably quite quickly. Almost all of the cults did the same things. I'd like to say that my definition of cult is, anything that takes you from the White Light. That meant anything from addictions to obsessions and so on. It did not narrow it down to just the over-inflated male egos.

Those males who did have large cult followings all did the same thing. One of the biggest things was having their sexual appetites fulfilled by as many women as they could use. Going into some heavy religions did allow them to justify this and allow them to feel no remorse for such degradation and that is exactly what it really is. Any female who sleeps with some master, leader, religious fanatic is asking to sell a piece of her soul. Believe me, none of you will ever mean anything to these kinds of men. The more they can use you, the less of a soul you have. You allow it because you want to be important, you want to be a star, you want to prove yourself and surrender yourself in hopes you will be the one he wants and you can have an easy ride. You do not love, you are a user as much as the master is. You feed each other's evil and you are not innocent or naive. If you loved the Creator, you would never allow such things. I tell you that you do know what you are doing but you will continue to deny and put the responsibility elsewhere.

Males only think of one thing. It is their eternal excuse to cheat and violate, constantly. They always end up thinking about what is really important when it is too late. Even then, very few are devastated by the departure of their mate. They go back to the pms and blame it on the fact that they can't help it. This is what has destroyed most of the planet. Many a woman has been destroyed by this but not the man. Every woman I have ever met has had the same drives as a man, they were just so severely bottled up and repressed. As I have said, these masters, wizards, and so on, always violate the female followers sexually.

You must understand that the Creator is the same for all. There are no divisions of any kind. If you look at how religion has divided the human race, you can see what I am saying. If it does not bring everyone to the same place, all the history or books written on religion mean nothing. As you know there are so many divisions that it is never going to change. You must also see that the Creator is for all life forces, not just the planet earth. You may say that you have to do a certain religion but you cannot understand why. I will ask you certain questions to help you identify your terminologies. You may be stuck in a past life, you may need to connect with certain people or you may be in Soulmate. If you must do religion, remember, you will buy into it or give your power away unless you are bonded to the Creator first. Many of your Soulmates may still be in religion and you're being pulled into that direction. Religion can be a tool or a trap but you must be protected before you do anything. Do not buy into anything. Ask the Creator first that which you should do.

You may say to me, "Can I be bonded to the Creator and bonded to religion at the same time?" No, you can only be bonded to the Creator because Religion is an experience here on earth. It may be something that you have to go through but remember the Creator is always and forever. You do not take your religion with you when you leave this world. If you are reacting to what I am saying you have given your power away to whatever it is that is triggering you. All I will say to this is that you have deposits of power all over and someone else is in charge of it.

As time went by, baby James came back desperate to be born without realizing that Jimmy was gone and that was who he needed as a father. He was in a different dimension and unable to comprehend where I was. It was heart breaking as I felt his soul's desperation and his inability to break free of where he was. Jimmy had fallen deeper into the Dark Force and baby James did not realize that as time passed, a Darker Force was on him than when he had been first conceived. After a couple of weeks, he did dispense his energy.

I could no longer live in the area I was in because these masters of Darkness were beginning to lose their followers. It was because of me and they were getting very upset with trying to get information on me that they could use to take me down. I was also interfering with their students, like all of those doctors who were paying their large tuitions so these masters could live upper class. To conclude, I was affecting things and that was not okay with them.

Now not only did I have to battle these cults, I had to deal with the rest of the human idiots who had great ideas on how to terminate these masters. They also had what they called the best rescues to get people out. Their ideas of rescues would be done with the exact practices these cults promoted. Rush in, grab the victim against their will, start some stupid deprogramming and get rid of the brainwashing. Look at this picture, total failure. Anyone who has ever had this done to them has never been de-programmed. They still have within them a reactivation program that could surface at any given time. Also many of these masters want you just as you're dying, so they give you the illusion that all is done and gone.

You would be amazed at how many people are going with these leaders. Many of you right now will say that you don't want to hear it. Oh well, more irresponsible people. Darkness will never let go as long as you continue to live in a state of denial. Let me tell you one thing you can count on. These Dark masters never lose. They have mastered many things but mastering the human race even an idiot could do because you continue to play out the same old thing. Few are strong enough to overcome such Forces but I know that you are out there, battling and probably very much alone. You may feel like giving up but release yourself to the Awesome Creator and I know that you will feel rejuvenation immediately. Exhaustion comes from the human race. Rejuvenation comes from the Creator. Again and again I will say to you, stop giving your power away.

Many of the things I taught stayed with the students but each being on their own journey had their own special hurdles to jump. Some were dealing with very Dark Forces and others had easier journeys. It was truly amazing how they began to feel that they had a purpose, a value, a direction. You cannot imagine how wonderful it was to see someone grab a hold of the Creator. For me, there was nothing greater or more rewarding. It would not matter if only one in a million turned to the Creator. It would be well worth it.

Do you remember the three great evils? Doctors are one of them and so are attorneys. As I dealt with these cults, I found attorneys just as involved as doctors. They supported these leaders and paid large sums of money for their tuition as well. I would see again and again as they would take the truth of a case and start the process of one lie after another. Even when you think that justice is done, it is not. Justice is based only on one side, winning. It might have started out based on other things but it is based on twisted truth in the end. You need to realize that there is no justice and never will be. Justice is the restoration of how things originally were. This is impossible to have because as time goes by the vibration of things change.

By bonding to the Creator, you have an internal peace and Knowingness that allows you to see things clearly. Nearly every attorney is the follower of a system based on manmade laws. Many laws go back so long ago, and women have never allowed to participate in this system. The biggest enslavement of all time has been the female. People can talk about all kinds of prejudice but it is the female who has been enslaved by this and still is. They are the carriers of life yet it is the male that has gained control of all aspects of the female's life. Nearly every female has been abducted by the male ego.

It has always amazed me that the Creator is Perfect and has made you Perfect, yet you spend your whole life claiming defects or excuses to continue to invalidate this. Once again, the terminologies kick in. I am not perfect. Everyone makes mistakes. I will keep trying to get it right. One negative after another. You are created perfect, so where is all of this coming from? You cannot change Divine Order. Your life has been perfectly on schedule since your first breath. You were designed perfectly to go through this life without defects or lack of anything to accomplish that which you must. Not only does it feel terrible to continue on with all of this negative, it goes against what you truly desire. No matter where you are right this very moment, you are exactly where you need to be or you would not be there. The human race has a very strange idea about what they call perfect. Hasn't anyone seen how this imperfect world cancels out Creator? You cannot flash back and forth. Haven't I told you that that is the gray zone. Has anything in your life ever been perfect?

Oh, by the way, who started the belief that we are so messed up? People are not sorry, they cry this out when they have been caught or forced to do some part of their journey that they do not understand. Sorry? Do not tell me you're sorry. Are you trying to discredit, terminate or get rid of something you have done? First, if you are bonded to the Creator, you would see Divine Order. You would understand what was going on and you would never be in the position to have to say you are sorry. Different degrees of this would be, regret, remorse, and so on. I will never be sorry because I have such a Perfect Creator that I know there are no mistakes. Are you doing mistakes? If so, I know where you are.

The Darkness continued to seek me out. The more I spoke, the more intrigued they became. It needed to shut me up because I was so effective. People were not allowing abductions and brainwashing as easily as they had been in the past. This was not okay with these cult leaders. Since I viewed cults as anything that took you from the White Light that meant nearly everything was cult related. These cult leaders wanted that cult power. I just spread it out all over the place naming things they felt were not cult related at all. Of course, cult deprogrammers claimed success with whomever they had abducted from the cults. They wanted nothing to do with me. As I said before, these deprogrammers were using abduction tactics themselves and psychological theories to get rid of the brainwashing. Were any of these people bonded to the Creator? No. Also, you cannot take someone until they have completed the reason that they are there to begin with. If someone goes against their will, they still have more to do and need to stay where they are.

It came upon me by a strange circumstance that happened one afternoon. A fire truck some miles away came blaring by with full sirens on. Pain shot through my ears so badly that I fell to my knees holding my hands over my ears. There was so much pain in my head and I yelled out repeatedly as I tried to get back up. Both of my ears had searing pains in them long after the fire truck had left. I knew that something was terribly wrong. My whole life I had had a great sensitivity to sound but something was now very different. When I took a shower, the sound from the water coming out was as loud as Niagara Falls. I had to cover both of my ears with my hands to keep the sharp pains from being so unbearable. This continued for weeks until finally I had to go to a doctor. Yes, Athena had said more than once, dread Daughter that you should ever have to go to a doctor. I kept hearing her words over and over again. You may be asking yourself, then why was I dating doctors? It will reveal itself as time goes by.

The doctor hooked me up to the necessary equipment. He turns around and starts yelling, "Is this some kind of joke?" I had no idea what he was talking about. "You're deaf and have been your whole life," he said angry for me wasting his time. I looked at him and told him I could hear just fine. He charged me extra for wasting his time. I cannot tell you enough how evil doctors are. By now you should know, only seek out those in the Light. Stop making excuses for them. It's like police officers who keep saying that they are only human. When they strap on a gun and have power over you, they are no longer just human. They have taken on a level greater than human by having such power over the rest.

I went to another doctor who told me once again that I was deaf. When I asked him to explain how it was that I could hear him, he sarcastically said that I was reading his lips. If this was true, then why did I speak clearly? Deaf people cannot sound out words like someone who hears them. No one could tell me why I could hear hearts beating, sounds coming or going at great distances as well. No one could tell me anything. The sensitivity to sound only increased. It became so intense I could not sleep at night. Eventually the sharp pains decreased but my hearing became greater and greater as time went by. I had been told that I had systems and I wondered if this was part of it. All of those ear infections as a child only deteriorated any hearing I might have had but these doctors kept saying that I had never had any hearing levels at all. Eventually I adjusted to this intensity but it never left me.

More people connected with me, desperate for help. Many had spent their life savings trying to find help and doctors and lawyers took that money too. Their lives were so filled with stress and desperation. Why did they come to me? What I taught not only made sense, it connected them back to their souls. The whole point of what I taught was to get one to remember the Creator, to bond and find clarity in their journey. How many things have happened which could have been prevented, everything negative, everything Dark.

CHAPTER EIGHT

There were so many things that I could not tell you and you have to know, that knowing where everyone's Soulmate was, did weigh heavily upon me at times. Time and time again I could have intervened, but those in the White Light cannot step in and change one's journey. It was never for me to do and you are never supposed to give your power away to anything or anyone! Only the Creator gets your power so you can be recharged again and again. To help you understand this you could view the Creator as one big battery recharger and the more you use your battery the more you need to be recharged.

Besides my mission with the Fallen Angels, I had the mission with my Soulmate and the mission to teach the Knowingness. I could teach and find my Soulmate but this Angel thing was something I could not get a grip on. I kept running scenarios through my mind. I would have visuals of what they would look like or what they would be wearing. Or maybe they weren't in form. I was exhausted searching this one out, so I decided to forget about it as long as it seemed like I still had time. What I did not know at the time was that these Fallen Angels were there right from my birth but they were with my Soulmate.

I went on seeing people and helping them as much as I could. I recalled one very precious soul named Steve who so badly wanted to take his life. I asked him where this was coming from. He found this interesting because if he could find that, then he would have power over it. He had been in therapy for years and it was always the same old story. Go on medication, find the money to pay the shrink who was as lost as you and take weeks, months and years to do the family scene.

Isn't the family what had caused it all along? When are you all going to see that only the Creator has the Truth? You cannot trust the human race with anything, ever. By attending all of those shrink sessions he had given his power away to a system that had failed him. By the time he had found me he was moments away from taking his life.

Now in order to terminate your life you are affecting your soul and humans cannot get into your soul. This belongs to the Creator and of course, Soulmates are involved here. Human beings can only affect your mental, intellectual, physical and emotional realms. Now the wrenching to exit is not coming from the Creator. Creator does not wrench you, but Soulmate does. Since suicide affects the soul and the state it is in, only Soulmate and matters of Soulmates play out here. Once again the human race will blame it on everything but the real reason.

Since Steve had gone so long without knowing the reasons why he wanted to die, it was crucial to reach him before his Soulmate killed herself. She was now powerful enough to pull him out because he was so worn out. He was broke and disgusted with the games that the doctors had played with him for so many years. Where was he supposed to turn? Within five minutes, I had him looking at the whole picture. It was simple and easy to see. In ten minutes he was talking about the Creator. Then I told him that he had only ever really had two choices in life. Go through life in the Dark or go through life in the Light because either way he was going through it. As I have always seen it, he had been so caught up in the choice mode and I continued to tell him. The Creator is simple, clear and easy to comprehend.

Anything coming from the Creator is always the same. Steve had not remembered any of this. His eyes lit up and the reconnecting began his recovery. He needed to understand his relationship with his Soulmate and that would come next after he had some private time to feel the Love and Light again. No matter what, you may forget this but your soul never does. Remember too, that no matter where you are right this minute or what you've been through, your soul is immediate.

Steve could not stop thinking about what we had talked about. He was shocked at how fast he was seeing the Truth about everything. Then he fell into the regret mode that started to send him back towards the old programs he had bought for years. What was important was that he go right back into the Knowingness state. If he remained too long in those old programs, he would have been right back where he was when I met him. As you go back to the Creator, it is a process which each has to go through at their own pace. Sometimes you may be so starved for this connection that you rush into it. Then you may realize how long you have been separated and you may be overwhelmed by guilt, remorse and regret. These are all human levels. The last thing Steve needed was to feel this.

He spoke of the severe religious upbringing where he could never have his own ideas of what his family called god. He recalled as a child the longing to be with god privately. When he questioned his family about god, he always a lack of worth. Deep inside, Steve closed up and died as that small child.

Once again, I say to you that this is not the Creator I know. The human race continues to worship gods, each other, or anything that keeps them from responsibility. It is the total history of the human race. Steve just could not believe all of this religious manipulation he saw his family and others playing out. He went through the motions as he starved year in and year out for that private relationship with the Creator. This left him so empty and feeling so worthless that death was only a matter of time.

At the other side of the spectrum was his Soulmate who had grown up feeling Steve's negativity. It was so intense for her and made no sense her whole life. She had no reason to feel such devastation but it prevented her from taking all of the steps to success that constantly came her way. This built a tower that would eventually fall and hit her all at once. When she bottomed out everyone came at her for ruining her own life.

Steve was raised so negative that he never had anything to ruin. Steve's Soulmate became so suicidal that Steve even felt an increase to do in himself. He was so unaware of her but as I made him see this, he then connected many past events to her as well. Things like the big dreams he had that were really opportunities she had but was too afraid to take. He had all of the dreams while she had all of the negativity. As he looked back, he could relate all of the times that he unconsciously tried to give her the dreams. He kept telling me how he had so often tried to throw these dreams away but actually he was sending them to her. All she ever wanted was one dream, just one, and it never came. Everything was so clinical in her life. Steve's dreams had never reached her because the Dark Force intervened, so when she finally plummeted to such depths of despair, it was no shock that she felt her only avenue was suicide.

Steve needed to understand why he had the parents he had and the upbringing he had gone through. Remember in chapter one what I said about needing the genealogy from the biological father and mother? You cannot be born unless there is an agreement to enter. You have to have certain features for each life and we tend to do similar features again and again. As Steve and I talked, he began to see parallels in his life that also started to make sense and sense was something he needed badly. We were so busy talking that he had completely forgotten that he had come to see me because he wanted to commit suicide. All of a sudden, that was put on the back burner. He no longer had time for it. His Knowingness was starting to come back to him and everything I said fell right into place. "This is Awesome, Deborah," he said reaching out to me with tears in his eyes. I smiled and he saw my silence in that moment, as one soul rekindling another.

There was so much Steve remembered as the days unfolded. I have always said that you do not need to learn, you need only to remember. Steve understood his Soulmate now and himself by what he had taken on from her and what he had given to her. They had not even met in this life yet and he was putting this all together. He needed to understand the whole thing. As he changed, it forced her to change and he began to release her to the White Light of the Creator. On a soul level they spoke and the fear of never connecting began to fade. You see, her dream, the one she struggled to have, was to find Steve and for the first time ever she was finding him on levels she had never known possible. A reason to go on, to live, filled her and Steve began his journey back to her on levels that were not visible to others.

Remember, all matters that affect the soul are Soulmate related. All matters that affect the mind are human related. The ultimate trauma to Soulmates is the direction of suicide. Remember, human beings do not hold the power to move the soul, force it out of the body, or anything else. You cannot be the reason one commits suicide although many are blamed for this. The soul belongs to the Creator. The Soul is never affected by the human race. Even Darkness cannot affect it but the mind can buy into the illusions that Darkness gives you and this power is so strong that you will believe whatever they send your way. Soulmates do soul related things. Suicide is viewed by the human race as bad. Suicide with Soulmates is a last attempt to reconnect. Many suicides would not take place if one could remember that Soulmates never lose each other.

I do not care what excuse you want to use in reference to what I have said. I do not care what age or situation you want to line up as the reason. In every case of suicide I can tell you where both Soulmates are and how the one pulls the other out usually quite quickly. It is like Steve and his Soulmate. Once they reconnected on the spiritual level, they had found each other again. Suicide was no longer necessary. If you say to me that they did not really connect because they had not really seen each other in person, then I tell you that you are asleep and stuck in programs. One of the biggest traps the human race is stuck in is the need to have things on the visual level only. It is what you cannot see that continues to run your life, program you, and keep you on your small little levels. The Dark Force knows this and gets away with so much. By only dealing with the visual, you have left out the power of all the other senses. If one sense is missing when you interpret something, you will never get the clarity of anything. Remember too, just because you cannot see it, does not mean it is not there.

I had the opportunity to see my biological mother one more time and so I did. I had not seen her since I was very little and this connection was not well. She had never really been my mother so it was very awkward for her. She was filled with guilt and had gone on some religious trek to find relief from all the programs she herself had bought her whole life. She was so far from the Creator, clinging to this being born again and having all of her sins washed away. Here we go again with negative programs. If the Creator made you and Divine Order cannot be changed, what is sin? My biological mother never sinned. She may have been stuck in the primitive levels of the human race but even she could not escape Divine Order. She could not change her journey anymore than I could have changed mine.

I told her that no one had known when I was born and she reacted to this. It was clear that she was hiding something and then like some religious ritual, she did this confession thing. She told me that my birth certificate was not correct and that I had been born after the date on it. I asked her when and she only said that the month I was born was correct. We go back to Darkness trying to locate you through your birth date. I would now always be safe from this intrusion. So the biological mother gets this big burden of guilt off of her when indeed it was the best thing that she ever could have done for me.

If she had had her Knowingness, she would have seen the Light in all of this. Instead, she hung onto suffering, guilt, and lies versus honor, success and the Creator. I was glad that she had done what she did and it validated Darkness's frustrations over the years to locate this. It seemed as though the biological mother had truly forgotten not only my birth date but that I had ever really existed. This was very good because for the rest of my life I could be assured that no one would ever have this information, including me.

For now, there was so much to do and I was well into the battle with Darkness as I continued to help people. Every time I had to rescue someone, I had to deal with all of the Darkness that was lingering over them. Because of my intense hearing abilities, I was able to locate things quickly and it helped with getting people out of their situations as safely as possible.

As time went on, Jimmy's life just became Darker and Darker and this meant that if baby James was ever to be born, he would have to be carried by a woman in Dark. The Angels kept guard like some big event was about to show up and they didn't even know where, when, or how. You could barely breathe there was so much tension in the air. Forget this Soulmate thing I thought to myself. With this much stress it was not going to be worth it. You cannot wish it away though and if it is in your journey you will do it whether you want to or not. It all took me back to the start of this life, how I knew that all I had gone through had been a preparation for what was about to come. Remember I was in isolation for years and I accepted that because it was well explained to me. I had no birth date, which saved me a great deal of trauma from the Dark Force. You need to remember that this is their main key to access abduction or elimination of people.

Now you cannot panic because you gave some astrologer your birth date but you did open doors to stir up things. There is one sure way to protect yourself if Darkness has been alerted, just release yourself to the Awesome White Light of the Creator and ask for Protection. If you look at how much is sacred, the human race just invites Darkness in. You are asking for it.

Time did go by and we all waited for some connection or attack but nothing came. The Angels said that my Soulmate had accessed my knowing of what he was going to do next, so it was changed. No one seemed to know what the next move was and so it lingered on.

One of the striking features that I had was this huge mane of hair. It was so thick people envied me for it. After that childhood event, my hair was never cut and it grew to my waist. You have to know Athena was in her glory over this. I saw so little of her now. There was some big secret that her realm knew about but refused to tell me. It had to be very big for Athena not to tell me. She had held firm on keeping it from me. What could be so terrible?

I went on with what I did best, which was help people. It was no shock to discover children in many of these cults. I am sure to most, it would come as a shock that these parents could not deal with their children being violated and they did not want them back. Can you imagine this? Where then was I supposed to put these children? Oh you might say social services, another big evil on the planet. That is the last place you put them. After an experience like they have been through, it is best to find someone related or someone who could love them. Social services runs on the same level as the cult deprogrammers who run in and abduct people. Rare is it that there is a good foster home. There are many good people out there who want to be parents but the social services system causes stress on them that tends to make them quit and give up. There are so many things to say which will truly shock you but you need to hear it. It is time for the cycles of destruction to be stopped and you will never get it if you do not wake up.

It was a devastating experience as three Angels of Darkness rushed towards my energy field while the Angels in Light were guarding me. They collided with each other as Angel of Silk and the others tried to protect me. I looked at these Angels and they were not only Dark but they were cloaked in black. What was so shocking to me was that I knew who they were, what their names were and that they had arrived to take me. I was shaking so badly but I held onto Angel of Silk who hovered around me.

"It is Nawbay, Seakept and Kayborg, Angel of Silk," I whispered to him.

"Deity Deborah, be very still," he whispered back. These three were trouble and they were guarding my Soulmate? That was it, I concluded. My Soulmate would have to go on without me because I could not deal with any of this. No one could deal with this, human or not. As the Angels battled they were making high pitched noises that were shooting into my ears. I fell as the pain hit me and tears flooded my face.

"Oh Creator, come upon us all and take us home," I cried.

They were fighting frantically and moving as fast as lightening. Then, as quick as it started, was as quick as it stopped and all returned to their own space. To tell you I was afraid would be putting it mildly. I was so upset I became sick. How was it that I knew the names of those three? Had we battled before? Oh how their names had rushed so right into my heart. I knew them well but I could not remember from where. If my Soulmate was involved with them I would never want to know him. Angel of Silk made me feel as if I were bathing in a warm bubble bath that smelled like lavender. It was his way of trying to calm me down. It did calm me down but what he said did not.

"The battle has begun, Deity Deborah and you must go through it," he said as sensitive to the situation as he could.

I looked at him so intensely. "What?" I said to him, as we both knew that I had heard him quite clearly.

"You are upset because you do not see what is coming," he responded.

"I don't see what is coming? Oh, I see what is coming. Do you see this? " I said pointing to my body. "How can I do anything stuck in this? " I further said.

"If you didn't need your body you would have had our bodies instead," he spoke back to me so confident that I could do this job.

"They will fry me, burn me, disintegrate me, Angel of Silk," I said holding my own.

"They will not. They fear you," he said trying to make me see it all.

"They fear me? Those monstrous Dark Angels fear me? I have to laugh at that, Angel of Silk," I concluded with a giggle.

"I speak the Truth, Deity Deborah. I speak only the Truth," he finished and turned from me.

All that kept running through my head was that all fear was a learned vibration. Oh that was about as comforting as a good dose of precognition, something I did not want anything to do with either. He was not worth it, this Soulmate. I could see myself being stuck in Soulmate forever. Oh great! Had everything taken on a whole new perspective? For a second I questioned if my Soulmate was even in a human body but I knew as soon as I thought that, that he would have to be. Soulmates are constantly in the same likeness so that they can connect. I knew all this but it did not get rid of this feeling of dread. I thought of Athena. Yes, I would call Athena so that I could try to get it out of her, all that I must do. I knew that Athena had the answers but once again, she would not speak.

"Mother, I demand it of you." I said to her.

She became very sad and took me into her arms. You cannot imagine how much I loved her. "Daughter, I cannot come back. Maybe someday but as it looks now, I may never be able to come back. Some day we will both be in the same realms. When that happens, we will laugh and look upon these days as silly. If I tell you what I know, you will never stay in your body. You will find a way to leave. I know this and I believe that you know this too. Trust me Daughter, precious Daughter. I love you so and you represent a part of me that no one else could ever be. From now until forever, you will always be my Daughter," she said so filled with completion.

"Mother, where will you go?" I asked her.

"I go to Olympus, the playgrounds of the heavens. If there is the slightest chance that I can come back, I will. We are not sure how all of this will turn out yet. You see, there are even things held back from us. I do know how all things are to go, but will they? You have all of my wisdom, Daughter and you will make war something fierce. Remember this, you must find your Soulmate and bring him back to the White Light. We will all be doomed if you fail," she said collecting herself and bursting into Light beams.

I stood there and in a second all was still. Even the Angels had told me again and again that I had to do this. I did not cry when Athena left because we had shared our love and if I never saw her again in this life, I would surely see her in Olympus. I did not feel sad, I just felt like I had an impossible mission. The Creator and I talked and the Creator said the same thing. Now the Angels could joke around and Athena could speak of how she wanted to do things but when the Creator spoke, that was it. I would not even question it, it was so solid, correct, and confirmed. So guess what, I had to get my Soulmate. I had to put aside everything no matter how traumatic and do what the Creator said. I went to bed saying, get the Soulmate, and I woke up saying, get the Soulmate. Athena was no longer going to be even coming back for Soulmate reasons.

I went on and Angel of Silk stayed by my side. All the Angels were on constant guard especially after that attack. The days of loving my Soulmate in the unseen realm left me. I was only concerned with getting him back to the White Light now. In all, I could not stand him upsetting so much. I could not stand him period and the more I thought about it, the more firm I became in getting this over with as soon as possible. Maybe, just maybe, this part of the mission would change.

So I waited for this and went on with the rescues and teachings. I did very well until the night came. Nighttime has always been a favorite time for Darkness. Most human beings were more vulnerable at night. For me they were tired and they had to rely on headlights and other forms of lighting to see. Nearly everyone has a vulnerable part of them that is in the Dark. Many are scared of a big deep forest at night. Remember the Dark you can see and the Dark you can't? Why is it so hard for you to see this? It brings to the surface something that triggers you. Lighten up!

In time, you will see all of this. Can you see that no one sends Darkness back home to the Creator? It does not have the knowledge to do this. It is up to everyone in the White Light to do this. Can you tell me a better way to straighten out things? No, you cannot. Perhaps there is no one left in the White Light, so the planet is doomed? Come on, I know you are out there. I know the White Light is just waiting to shine through. All negativity belongs to the human race. All positive belongs to the Creator. Go ahead and challenge me on this. I will once again tell you, go to the Creator. It is okay if you are negative. Maybe you need to be or maybe you have a good dose of Soulmate. Either way you will eventually go to positive.

Remember this too, you only think that you have choices. You will go through your journey in Light or Dark. Human beings do not possess the power to rearrange their journeys. You can barely get it together. How in the world are you going to alter anything? Let us view Creator like a vehicle. Creator is supposed to be an automatic, not a stick shift. The human race is a stick shift. The soul automatically wants to return to the Creator but many people are so divided. Is all well with your soul? Your answer should always be yes because that belongs to the Creator. Remember what I said about people trying to put god into the actions and reactions as they would see it? Creator does not play out all of these small things that the human race finds so catastrophic.

Like Steve, many come searching out a way to understand the Soulmate relationship. What you need to realize is that you have been in the Soulmate relationship all along. Once again, you need to really see that this relationship does not have to be together as you view together, face to face. In order to be enlightened, you must be open to all levels. It is like your senses. Just because you cannot hear something doesn't mean that there isn't any sound. Let us say that there is a room filled with people and only one person sees something. Does the majority rule? Because most did not see it you all discredit the one who did? This is your lovely human race filled to the brim with invalidating the minority. Guess what everyone, you are the ones who can't see. There are so many levels. It would truly shock you sleepy heads.

Just like Soulmates, there are so many levels that I cannot tell you about. If you cannot even deal with small levels, how in the world are you going to handle anything big? What is so funny too, is how most of you want to be something big, important, noticed and what do you do? You invalidate what truly makes you awesome. Did you think the Creator took away all of these levels? Not the Creator I know. Why was I able to bring these levels forward in all who came to me? Because those that reconnected to the Creator found that all that they had been told, they never had to begin with. Who told them? Was it you? If it can be thought, it has been, still is, and will be. Oh how you may anger yourself over such things. Good! That means there is still fire in you and hope that you will see. Notice that when anything unidentified happens, you are changed. It does not have to be flying either. How many of you are married to an unidentified object? Just because I told you about Soulmate doesn't mean you jump up, leave your spouse and go looking for yours. Great disaster awaits you if you do. If, on the other hand, your unidentified object is beyond being identified, that is another story. Your spouse is not your best friend. If you are saying that, I will ask you where then is Creator? When Creator is Best your spouse would be what? If your spouse is a karmic lesson, you would be using other terminology. I will get into this later. Creator is your Best Friend, always.

Life went on and my son grew with a gentle and loving nature. He was surrounded by many things and viewed them with great clarity. How could he not, he had the Creator?

Now I looked forward to my Soulmate with dread. Dread is in all Soulmate relationships but at the same tim, there is great joy. Once again I tell you Soulmates do things and speak in Soulmate terminologies only. The word dread in the human race would be past life, fear, etc. What is negative in the human race may be positive with Soulmates. Remember if you think you know where your Soulmate is, you do not. Think is the human race, know is the soul, the Creator.

Believe me there is no thinking when it comes to the Soulmate. You know that you know when you meet them. I had already met mine and it was more intense not having seen him in person. Here it comes again, about what you can and cannot see. Must I send you your Soulmate the way I was sent mine? I guarantee you, you will believe in the realm you cannot see. Be calm though because I will not send you your Soulmate, it is between you and the Creator. All I will ever do is send you back to the Creator by releasing you in Love. Nothing good came from my Soulmate. Jimmy was gone because of him, baby James was forever caught in his realm, Athena could not come back and there was a great deal more that I cannot speak of. Oh, if only I had known then what I know now. Could I have changed any of it? No, because none of us can change Divine Order.

As much as I could not stand my Soulmate, he had the other half of me and I'm sure he was thinking the same thing. Let me interject that think, in Soulmate, is Soulmate terminology as well. In other words, when dealing with Soulmate, you are forever in Soulmate terminology no matter what you say. To help you understand this, let's say you know your Soulmate. Whenever you communicate, be it in person or other levels, you are speaking Soulmate terminologies. When you then speak to anyone else, you may be in a past life, a karmic lesson but you are in a whole different energy. You may be in the present state just talking to someone you know but you are not in Soulmate until you go back to thoughts or any other connections to them. I would love to tell you all and all of it at once but it would overload your abilities to comprehend. This is why I continue to give you parts of this throughout. It may be hard for you to get the whole picture because I cannot reveal all of the Teachings. I tell you that this is a sacred, delicate relationship with Soulmates. You may say that it does not sound like it. There you go again, not hearing all of the sound. Oh well, I guess you will have to ask the Creator.

Darkness was getting quite perturbed with me. After all, I was going around speaking of things that would free people. I also had the one thing that all Darkness did not have, the knowledge of their Soulmates. It was almost how they viewed astrology, that invasion of one's most private and intimate self. They themselves felt that their

Soulmates could view them in the same way. Soulmate was major trouble for Darkness. Soulmate is the only meltdown that Darkness could not control. Can Soulmates be in Darkness together? No, one must always be in Light while the other is in Dark. I've already told you that the one in Light is responsible for bringing the one in Dark back home.

Now can you better see what I am saying to you? Just sit back and relax. You are exactly where you need to be this very moment. Remember I said that there is great dread, but joy also? Think of this as your Soulmate goes back to the Light. There is the joy and dread just melts away. For now, I was in dread but someday there would be joy. Was it okay to be in dread, only in Soulmate.

I did not think of Jimmy that much anymore but he had played a very big role in the direction that my life went. I knew things were very bad for him and all I could do was release him back to the Awesome Creator. You may ask me if that was enough. Is that enough for you?

The one thing that had always been curious to me was why was not there any female Angels? That struck me very odd. Of course, Angel of Silk had had a fit over me even asking some years back. It certainly seemed like such a male thing.

Along the way we had taken a little kitten we eventually named Spanky. She played such funny roles as well. I could not stand shorthaired cats and as Spanky grew, she ended up longhaired. The rest of that litter was shorthaired so where Spanky came up with so much hair was beyond me. She went everywhere we did with no protest. She could tear up everything and do that full blown up hair act. I will tell you pets can make you react even when you want to ignore them. Often we were laughing so hard over her behaviors that it lifted the serious moments.

Spanky did not like the Dark Force and she would attack anyone in it. Animals sense this very strongly. Never underestimate your animal's reaction to things. As Spanky grew she bonded to my son. She always slept above the pillow with him adorning herself as ruler of the throne. She was such a little spitfire. My son would make it known where he was to sleep and Spanky would make it known as well. In the end she always slipped out from his grip the second he fell asleep and placed herself above him. She seldom left his side. She was like a mother guarding her young. If you needed someone to play with, she was always ready morning, noon and night.

I loved this little cat something fierce. It was such a necessary part of our lives. Whenever there was a lot going on all you'd have to do was look at Spanky to see the approach of Darkness. She would go ballistic when no one else could see anything except for me. Animals are so advanced in this area. What you may ask here is if animals have Soulmates too. Yes they do and in time even Spanky ends up meeting hers.

So, you are not going to go run out and get a divorce or leave your love for your Soulmate. Why, because you are already attached and perhaps you are not going to encounter them in this life, face to face anyway. You need to realize that Soulmate is beyond marriage. What you need to do is stay right where you are. If it needs to change, it will. If you have felt that this is all too intense, then let me tell you that this is nothing next to what is about to come. I say to you again, there is so much I cannot tell you. What I do tell you is that you have never ever needed anything but the Creator. It is Creator who has put you on your journey. It is Creator who will tug on your bungee cord and pull you back when you have gone too far. Close your eyes and allow yourself to feel this. Stop fighting that which you cannot change.

CHAPTER NINE

Once in a while memories of Athena would fill me with a smile. She was such a beautiful Entity. I felt as though I might see her again someday. Once in a while Zeus would present himself but it was only for a few seconds. Although the Angels remained, they had let their guard down. So much time had gone by and Nawbay, Seakept and Kayborg had not returned. At the time, I could not recall where I had met them but I was sure that it was not of this world. You cannot imagine Darkness that condensed. I felt strongly that I was being watched but there was a certain element of peace allowed. I knew that Darkness only gave the illusion of retreat. When it came to surrendering, they had an endless lot of energy to keep right on going. There was always plotting and scheming every hour of the day. Sometimes at night I would wake up realizing I had been touched, yet, not touched. I felt an intense loneliness within my Soulmate but I did not want to know him anymore. I had always been bonded to the Creator so much so, that I did not move until I heard what was next. People would say how ridiculous this was because we had a brain and the ability to use it. Again and again when these people came up against a crossroad they would fold, fall apart and get out of it by going into the blame system. It was always someone else's fault that their life was so messed up. I had no idea to what extent I had had any real impact on anyone but they were out there, wanting to do something for me and eventually the day would come that they could.

To me it was hard to believe that people wanted to make their lives so miserable. How far was I willing to go to help them? Whatever it took, I would say again and again. You must also realize that some people must remain in whatever level of Light or Dark they are in.

118

Can you help? Yes, by releasing them back to the Creator. This is truly honoring them but the second you decide to pick and choose who you want to release, you are power tripping the Light. Darkness will be alerted to this vibration because you are not really releasing anything. You have put it into the human level and it's not really Light, it's manipulation now. Can you see how much you invite into your space? I ask you, to whom are you talking?

So many children wanted to know about this god who was judging and holding things from them. You can see why they could not deal with this because their souls were telling them something different. Many saw great deception and disappointment with this god. What idiot decided that this god got mad and disciplined you? Once again, it's not the Creator I know. Can you see how the human race has turned some gods into humans? Imagine this god at Seven Eleven having his morning coffee. Do you know how big his coffee cup would have to be? These children were starving on every level. I could see small rays of hope being smothered by someone always in authority. Hope is the continuation of the soul seeking Truth. Kindness invites hope. One of the reasons that the human race wanted to play god is because in their small, unenlightened minds they thought that they could make all of the rules. After all, anything goes when you are god. Oh, really? Notice in history how man always had these confrontations with god. Where were the women?

By now you should realize that I cannot understand your god or gods, as it seems like one big control issue. One day a lady came to see me and what was supposed to be a class turned into a confrontation. She tried to put her religion into what I was saying. She hated the happy, positive energy I felt when I spoke of the Creator. "You are supposed to fear god!" she screamed at me.

I must tell you, to have a confrontation with me, is most unadvisable. All of a sudden she was out of control carrying on with one religious phrase after another. I knew that the Angels were going to jump in if she went too far and sure as anything, they rushed in and knocked her over. Instead of shocking her, she became so ugly that she started screaming that Satan had me. I could not contain myself when she said this and I started laughing. It was clear that something had a hold of her and I had fueled doubt and fear in her. What was really going on was that she had a heavy past life with some god and had been greatly fooled by the Dark Force. Fearing god and speaking of Satan along with the anger, made it clear to me. Too bad, she could not see this. Her journey was very hard but she had been given the opportunity with me, to rebound and she let her Darkness consume her.

The more people I helped the more Darkness I stirred up. Was I afraid? I never felt fear because I had the Allegiance with me constantly. Remember, all fear is past life and I was not in any past life. This woman kept saying I was supposed to fear god.

I could see that the children were going to grow up and be so starved that they would turn Darker and Darker as time went on. Again, I would notice their souls trying to connect with mine and their parents would shut them up. If in the parent's eyes, they thought that their children were going in directions they could not control, they would yank them away from such things. If these parents can't even get clarity about themselves just what is that they were yanking their children from? This cycle had to be broken and someone had to do it. Whatever it took, I kept saying and so my direction became dealing with any and all situations.

Many could not pay for help whether it was to be rescued or talked to or even to attend classes. No one was ever turned away. Even those sent by the Dark Force could not return to it because the classes were so effective. Besides, when given a choice to remain in Darkness or find their Soulmate, they all chose their Soulmate, thus you can see the power of the Soulmate. Whenever I was in what you might call an impossible situation with Darkness, I would start talking about their other half. You see even Darkness wanted that perfect relationship, the ultimate relationship, the Soulmate. I could count on this to bail me out every time. I did not need manpower, weapons or anything except this. It worked on all of these masters of Darkness, including the ones you could not see. In order to keep everyone safe, I had to code everything so that no one outside of the safety net would know what anything meant. This was not dangerous for me but for those trying to leave Darkness, it was. What is familiar to you is hard to let go of unless you are sure of where you will end up. Too many have interpreted leaving Darkness for Light as another form of Darkness. After all, if you have been away from the Creator long enough, it is a sleepy re-acquaintance. It continued to be one traumatic case after another and I was always able to turn it around. The only people who could not be helped were those who were intensely in Darkness.

The Creator had told me often that my body would be my weakness. If I was ever overcome or went down and Darkness tried to take me, I would probably die. The more you are bonded, the less you can cope with the vibration of Darkness. It is important that all of you be bonded in all areas in your life. The closer that you can be to the Creator, the more serene your life will be. The only exception is of course, the Soulmate. That is because one is always in Darkness, one is always in Light as I have already told you. You will have to deal with your Soulmate sooner or later. Let me tell you this. Soulmates are one soul, divided in half. One half is female, one half is male, one sees the Light side, one sees the Dark side. Now imagine putting both sides of something together. You would have a total perspective on everything. While exchanging this knowledge you would have a completion and a balance as well. The one in Light does have the power to pull on the one in Dark and vice versa. Soulmates can never be both males or both females.

Many who are gay will refer to someone they love of the same sex as their Soulmate. This is not so. It is a soul energy but not the Soulmate. You may ask me then, why are people gay? Soulmates enter together and exit together. Now you may be saying that you do not know anything about this, so how could that be? Once again, I tell you, there is much that you cannot see. If you were not in a physical body you would understand this better.

Remember I said that Soulmates have their own frequencies. It is in this that they pull each other together, lifetime after lifetime. As one exits, the other is pulled out. As for timing, that varies depending on what body you are in. In the human body many Soulmates that are bonded exit within a year or two of each other, so the Soulmates reconnect and return to the Creator. During this time they are no longer divided by anything, including which sex they are. It is a rejuvenation time until they are ready to reenter again. Also, during this time they may switch polarities yet still be in the form of when they first divided. If you have always been female then this is the form you have maintained, therefore your Soulmate has always been male. If you switch polarities and you reenter the human body, you will return gay. You cannot return polarities back until you exit again and bond back to the Creator.

Now you might ask why would Soulmates do this? If a previous life has been traumatic, they may switch roles to help each other deal with these traumas. It is not until they take the human body that they realize what has happened. In order to fit in with the human race they deal with denial, hiding, escape, fear and trauma. All of their wanting to change the way they are will never work. It isn't that being gay is right or wrong, it is very hard to do in the human body. Gay people do not meet their Soulmates as long as they are gay. What is intended to help the Soulmates, turns out to be even more traumatic. It is easier for the female to be gay than the male. This is because she plays many roles throughout her life, more so than the male. Remember that all things need to be released to the Awesome White Light of the Creator. If you are triggered by gay people, you have an issue with this. If you are triggered by anything that is what you have an issue with it. Of course, you know by now that Soulmates must trigger each other as it is part of their reconnecting.

Now what does it mean if you are not in Soulmate and you are triggered? You are doing a karmic lesson. A karmic lesson is nothing more than an incomplete state of Knowingness. I teach you that you want to turn karmic into caramel.

Each job I took I never knew how or where it would end up. Everything had to be so private and coded so that no one could be located. The most important thing was that one not reactivate the Dark Force once free from this energy. I had to move a lot because it was a challenge to keep everything as private as it needed to be.

When I needed better clarity of course I asked the Creator. Many of these cult masters searched for something that they could hold over someone. Who wants some private secret revealed? Once they had this, there was no end to what they could make someone do. As

I have told you, their main source of support came from doctors, attorneys and of course all of the bored executives who wanted to play in the untested waters. I can hear some of you saying, "That's not my doctor." But I say, there goes those statements with absolutely no clarity to back it up. If one wants to play god, they had better have a flawless chart. Watch what you defend or protect. I can tell you, you will lose and your protection is about as powerful as a kite on a windy day, all over the place. What do kites do in the end? They come crashing down. After all of this, do you honestly think that I would ever count on my own protection? Why aren't you with the Creator? I know you have things to do first. Is that why you are always last?

Many wonderful soul energies came into the picture. You may say that these were just friends. Anyone can make a friend, few can find a soul energy. Unless you have ever had one, you'll never understand. The bond between soul energies is like a long, long journey and you finally find each other. You are so elated and rekindle the past looking forward to the future. You are as close as close can be and you share a loyalty like nothing else. It is well with your soul to find a soul energy.

The only time and I emphasize this strongly, that a soul energy becomes a karmic lesson, is when the Soulmate begins to lay claim on you. The disruption between two soul energies can come apart in minutes. Many a soul energy relationship has been destroyed by a Soulmate only testing the mate and doing nothing more. Beware of the deep bonded relationship blowing sky high. Terminologies in this would be: what happened, we were so close, I cannot believe she would just walk out after all we have been through, I'll never find anyone like her again. These are just a few of the terminologies that you would use. You are right, though you will never find anyone like her again. Now, you may blame this relationship for breaking up on other reasons. I will tell you the only thing that can separate the power of soul energies is the Soulmate.

Get this and get this clear. Look back on this soul energy relationship that you might have lost. Chances are, the Soulmate has already left and your soul energy is asking what happened. Unless the Soulmate is claiming you to reconnect, they were merely checking out your space and energy. They may have felt your intense bonding to this soul energy and felt threatened.

Now are you concluding that this Soulmate thing is a real pain? Welcome to Soulmate. It is more of a pain than you can ever imagine unless you are in it. It's worth all of the risks and after all they have your favorite painkiller. The cause and cure scenario. Where do you think that that statement I'm damned if I do and damned if I don't came from? Someone had a dose of Soulmate. Now you know that they went and blamed it on something else. The human race gets an A plus for giving their power away and never getting clarity. I guess that it must go back to that coffee your god has in the morning. You know that god with that big cup. If you think that cup is big, you should see the size of your Soulmate's cup. So why bother with the Soulmate then, if it is like this? In time you will see as I tell you more.

I had a lot of soul energies even though they were rare to find. Perhaps they all needed to come together in this life to help me with this mission. There were many cults designed with the male masters having harems of women in illusions that they were good students. All that these masters have ever had was a severe case of penis male syndrome (PMS). Then you take the cults that were labeled other things like alcoholics, overeaters, drug addicts, violence seekers, obsessions and many more things too numerous to mention. Remember anything that takes you from the White Light is a cult.

The finances to rescue became more and more difficult to find. By the time many had reached a point of desperation, they had already exhausted all resources. Someone had to rescue them. Just watch, I'd probably have to rescue my own Soulmate and as soon as I said this, I was directed elsewhere. Let him rescue himself. What would be totally unacceptable is if he turned out to be a doctor. Can you imagine this? Mom would have a fit. Remember her saying, beware Daughter, that you should ever need a doctor. Oh, I would beware all right. Just thinking about it gave me the chills.

Now let us talk about karma. As I have said, a karmic lesson is nothing more than an incomplete state of Knowingness. What primitive told you that you have to do karmic lessons? Where do you get your Knowingness, it comes from the Creator. So if you have an incomplete state, where do you go? You would be shocked at how many people told me that they were in karma and had to do these lessons. Well go ahead then but those of us bonded to the Creator will be busy enjoying ourselves. How many times must I tell you that you send everything back to the Creator? If you lack for anything, you bought that illusion because you were created whole, complete and to say you lack says the Creator messed up. You do not need to do karma because it is a trap. You release all to the Creator. I know you have a problem with this but stay with me and I can guarantee you will. How do I know this? Remember, I have Knowingness. As I have told you too, we are all born with something that pursues us and something we run to. Review your life and see if you can find this. From the time we are born we have this. I give you much to think about, don't I?

I was startled as I woke from such a dream. Kayborg stood over me with the sword of death that I had seen over my Soulmate. I was so shook up, I cried out for Angel of Silk. "Come to me now," I yelled to him. He rushed in before I had even finished my sentence. "Angel of Silk, I saw the sword of death and it was pointed at me," I cried as he gave me great comfort.

"Deity Deborah it was not a dream," he responded back.

"It was real? " I asked him.

"He was here," he said.

"Do you mean you let him march on in here and do this to me?" I cried even louder.

"If he had come upon you to hurt you, we would have intervened," he said reassuring me.

"Kayborg wants to kill me!" I yelled out.

"Deity Deborah, what is the meaning behind all of this?" Angel of Silk asked me.

"He wants to kill my Soulmate and then me?" I asked.

"No! Look at all of this," he said to me quite insistent.

The Knowingness rushed into me even though I was half-asleep. The sword of death did not belong to my Soulmate, it belonged to Kayborg. Kayborg was going to kill my Soulmate and he had no idea that this sword was even there. Here I was thinking that my Soulmate wanted to kill me. Wait one minute, I thought. I am not going to let this get me weak in the heart. Be gone with this Soulmate, Athena would say or would she? No, she would tell me that I had to get him back to the White Light. Great, he is in big trouble and I'm in trouble because of him. What a pain all of this was. I decided I would find a way to get him back to the Light with as little contact as possible. I had enough to do without this ridiculous situation. As confirmation, I heard all of the Angels yell "Right!"

Most of the human race does not realize that there are Angels of Darkness too, so this image of Angels being all good is not correct. What kind of Angels do you call to? Angels have Soulmates too.

Everything was wonderful until Soulmate entered my mind. I kept teaching people and every time we got on the topic of Soulmates it just stirred mine up. Waves of dread would just hit me something awful. I tried to ignore it and for the most part, it did leave me on the surface. Those who were awake enough to realize the trap of karma decided to release it to the Creator and it was no longer that incomplete state. Could it be that quick and easy? Is not the Creator immediate? Are you not the one who delays? Do you see what I'm saying? Delay is the human race. Immediate is always Creator. Note too, that you delay so much so that you come incredibly close to running out of time. Oh yes, that is when you yell to your god saying, help me, and guess what? You wait and wait. Oh well, if you would just call to the Creator you would have immediate results. Your soul knows that the Creator is immediate. It tries to send you there but you keep intervening on your small primitive levels. Here comes that statement, god let me down, so you wait and wait and wait.

Oh well, how many times must I tell you to go to the Creator? There are so many statements made about your god. How about the statement, revenge is mine says the Lord. Just the word revenge is negative and filled with a threat. The Creator does not do revenge. That is something created by the Dark Force. Just who is this lord, certainly not Creator. This lord entity sure is doing and saying a lot of Dark things. Creator is Love and Love is Love. There is no manipulation or negativity with Love. Oh yes, some idiot somewhere decided to put their negative two cents into it and added some hell and brimstone.

This is just another control issue. Don't you love the statement, "it's for your own good"? Excuse me, for the good of who?

I guess I just cannot get a grasp on why everyone is so lost when it is looking them straight in the face. Is it your ego that has made you so stupid? Honestly, can't you see all of this Darkness in that which you give your power away to? The ego is supposed to be nothing more than a bridge of expression to what the soul is trying to tell the mind. That is it, period. Where is your ego? Is it stuck with your pms? Oh well, it is hardly worth the time to deal with you if you comprehend so little. Okay, let us move on.

Now to conclude with the karmic lessons, release these to the Creator and all clarity will come. You can have a good time with the rest of us while these idiots worship some god that is too busy drinking his Seven Eleven coffee to answer your cries for help. Do you know what is so silly here? These people that are so used to never hearing an answer or getting results will question the Creator and Creator's validity. They are so used to believing that it is in god's time, like god does time. I guess some of these gods do really do time, sort of like prisoners. Does not this say that you are so used to the Dark that you can't even see the Truth if it hits you in the head? Oh, it is going to hit you in the head and everywhere else. Do you know what? Some of you like the attention, the abuse. You are in the battle zone people. It costs to be in Darkness, it costs to be in Light. Check this one out, god is free and does not cost anything. Oh really? The price you pay for staying bonded to the Creator is high. You see you have to give up all of your Darkness and since you own yourself that is hard to do for most. All people who claim to own themselves are what I call mini false gods. You are bonded to an attitude. That attitude is ugly. You are a loser and a low life, you are an "it." You have worn out and blown out your egos. I doubt you will ever be repaired though, you cannot see past yourself long enough. Do you know any, its?

For the more positive few who mingle among the Dark crowd, it is a full time battle to stay bonded. This majority Dark crowd is jealous and needs to break you on a daily basis because you threaten them. You are the kind of person with a sigh saying, "Here it comes again."

It has probably done some damage on your health by now. Do you use the terminology, "it's eating away at me"? Do you see that I have a terminology for everything and that every terminology identifies where you are?

Many people became very angry with me and they would walk away only to show up sometime later more angry for leaving. You need to listen to what I say here. You cannot wake up any sooner than you are supposed to. Stop using terminologies of regret for not having done it sooner if this is the case. Allow the Creator to show you the perfect schedule that you have always been on.

There is something else I need to make you aware of. Do not expect your Knowingness for you to turn around and violate it. I promise you that Divine Order reigns here and all will be pulled from your mind. You will become a babbling idiot and in this life never have another chance. Many have come to class to tape or twist what I teach then try to sell it. All that have done this speak funny now as Divine Order intervened and pulled it all from their minds. In doing things like this, your soul goes back to a deep, deep sleep. Know this, if you do violation, Divine Order will shut you down. Even the mere thought of violation will do this. I know that a lot of what I tell you may trigger many questions. You are only getting some of the Teachings and by now, you know why. You may also notice that I repeat many things again and again. There is a reason for this.

Our wonderful Spanky was such a little terrorist but when it came to danger she was a real guard cat. I did not think that a cat could be so good at such a specialty. The second she went into her aggressive position and her pupils became big, we knew danger was lurking about. She would scratch and claw up anyone who came near my son or me. She went everywhere we went even on the rescues. Since she loved to find cubbies, she started to travel around in a backpack. One day I was doing a large class in a big hotel when all of a sudden the backpack started moving across the stage. You should have seen the look on everyone's face. I had completely forgotten that she was with us and thought that she had been left in the room. All of the nonbelievers momentarily shifted over to the other side. What a character she was.

So many hundreds of times she left a lasting impression. Good old Spanky saw it all.

Do you know that saying, "nothing ever lasts forever"? Whoever came up with this must not have known the Creator. Many people tested me with things like that and every time I knew the answer. What was so hysterical was that they all had had the answers too but they decided they wanted to be god and landed in the pitch black. Oh how hard they had tried and nothing ever worked. After a while you can even see to what levels they had left the Creator. I was doing quite well managing the Soulmate thoughts until night. It was on a hot summer night that brought me to such memory. I had fallen asleep with all of the windows open. The moonlight flooded the room as I peacefully fell asleep. Some hours later I stirred to the sound of a cello playing. The music was so painful as it became louder. I rose and walked to my window. I searched for where it was coming from but it seemed to be all over me.

"I am the cello, you are the flute and the Angels are the orchestra," he said in a whisper.

"Soulmate?" I asked.

The wind stirred as if to answer me. The cello cried out in pain piercing my heart. The flute gently climbed trying to uplift the cello. You could hear the Angels singing in the background. Tears fell down my face. I reached out to the wind. I did love him somewhere, somehow.

The cello said, "Do not abandon me. I am sorry that I left you behind. I always loved you but I was blinded by that which I could not see. I am dying for what I did. Love me, please love me."

The flute responded, "I love you, don't leave me, please don't leave me."

The cello spoke again, "Forgive me, I never meant to hurt you. I did not see."

"Please don't go. We can make it right," the flute said.

The Angels concluded as the cello ended. I fell to my knees clinging to the windowpane. My soul wrenched me. I did not want to remember him so and love him so but I was drawn to him with such a force, I could not control it. You will never know such pain until it comes upon you. All else will fall to the side and will be as nothing next to this. I looked at the moonbeams and I knew that somewhere out there he could see this too. If that was all that connected us at that very moment, then let my love touch the beams and let them find him. I became the cello taking his pain while mine was overwhelming. I sent my love on the notes of the flute and somewhere, somehow, I promised to find him no matter what. How could I return him to the Light without reclaiming him, holding him and sharing the pain?

As Dark as he was, was as Light as I was. How could he see without even a ray of Light? Oh, that you should ever come upon Soulmate, you will need the Creator's constant veil of gentle Love. Why must Soulmates do things in such opposite extremes? You do not want to know all there is in this ultimate destiny. You must search your own soul and go that which your path makes you. There is nothing by chance, I promise you this. There are no mistakes. You see or you do not see but either way you will go through your life.

I found myself crying for the whole human race as I saw all of the pain. This was pain that belonged here on the earth, not with the Creator. I cried for all of those who suffered. I asked the Creator to shield those who truly wanted to find the Truth. I asked the Creator to send an Angel to each one who needed to see, that they may feel the touch of this Awesome Force. I cried for all of the Soulmates and right at that moment, I heard the Creator tell me that all would be done and to go forward and speak. As always, the Creator was instant.

I cannot tell you how much Love flooded me. It was endless and everyone wanted it. So many were filled to the brim with so much regret. Again I spoke that you cannot go back and change that which your journey will not allow. I heard people speak about all of their flaws. So many negatives and as usual, within moments I made them see and see they did. One man said that he wanted the Creator to Love him as much as I was Loved. Are you worthy and I am not, he thought?

"I am willing to do, whatever it takes. I love the Creator because the Creator started my very soul. The Creator has Loved me with such an Eternal Flame that I could do no other. You merely forgot but your flame burns bright," I told him.

"Are you sure?" he asked.

"As sure as the Light comes upon me and fills my force," I concluded.

The cello came again and the tears filled my eyes. Would I be too late? Somehow, I sensed this from him. It went from not even wanting to see him, to an urgency to embrace him. My soul was starving for him. I knew that nothing could ever fill this void but him. It was clear that something very big definitely stood in our way. It was Dark and heavy. Between the tears, I went on and the more classes I did the more I felt as though it was somehow helping my Soulmate. After all, you can never get enough Light.

If I needed to be side tracked, I got a visit from Zeus. The two of us could get more battling done in a few seconds than most could do in a lifetime. What was the purpose of him occasionally dropping in? I am sure it was to try to irritate me. Maybe he thought with Athena gone he could overpower me. Like Mother, like Daughter and that's what Zeus got every time. I felt that somewhere deep, deep inside, Zeus must have loved me. It was clear that people could not grasp that once they released themselves to the Creator, they were there. The constant cranky complaints about how it felt, only delayed their bonding. What many wanted was an easy ticket. After years and years of tartar on them, they expected Creator to clean it off instantly. You clean your own tartar. Once again, they kept reverting to the behaviors they had for their god. Is the human race lazy or what? Is god the cleaner? I do not think god does domestics. Now I will tell you direct, Creator does not do domestics, ever. You do and you are responsible for this.

The cello played again and pain came upon my heart. Tears filled my eyes and each tear began to fall. I felt his pain and felt his Darkness. For a moment I felt him reaching out to me and then he pulled back.

"Would she want me," I heard him say and the pains of the cello went on.

Where were the Angels? I thought. Then as gentle as a breeze, I heard their chorus and they were the orchestra and I was the flute again. No matter how it looked, I knew that all would be fine.

CHAPTER TEN

Word got around so much so, that I could not keep up with all of the calls. The fascination grew over my Teachings. I pointed out one of the ways to locate where your Soulmate was. First you needed to determine how much discord was in your life. You could find this out by the terminologies you used. If you spoke certain words, it meant that you would be geographically thousands of miles away from each other. The more powerful you were connected, the closer you would move towards one another. Before they knew it, many were coming to their own conclusions and right on the very location of their own Soulmates. Did terminology tell you everything? Yes, but it was a little more complex than just terminologies. You would have to recognize everything that indeed I was there to tell you, if you really wanted to know. The fact that it was so easy to see once you could relate it, made it at times almost unbelievable. Everyone was so used to their god being so complicated.

Complicated is a human condition. Simple is the Creator. Light is the Creator. Immediate is the Creator. I would not have to keep repeating this if it was easy to grasp. The more in Light you go the more of the battle with Dark you can see. This is why you must release all Darkness back to the Love and Light of the Creator. Remember once again that it costs to be in Light and it costs to be in Dark. You will pay the price.

Now here comes those crabby kinds saying how disgusting all of this was. God is free? Nothing is free, nothing! We are up against energies and the price for staying bonded to the White Light is a fulltime job. Are you ready to wake up?

You have a lot of power you gave away to collect. I can promise you, those that you gave it to will not surrender it back to you easily. After all it's been a nice Dark ride taking all the power you so nicely gave them. Oh, so you say that you didn't realize it? Yes, you did on some level and you allowed it on some level. Now go take all of your power back.

How? Here we go again. Release yourself to the Awesome White Light and Love of the Creator. Then release whomever it is that you have to deal with. If you say to me that you cannot do that, then I will say that you are Darker than they are. How dare I? You mean after all they have done to you, you have to release them? What a pompous arrogant power trip you are on if you conclude this. How dare you conclude the state of their souls! Are you god? Do you think you are god? Walk from me and do not come back until you are ready to honor all things.

One person said to me that they felt so badly about another person that they honestly couldn't release them and mean it. Here we go again. Did I tell you to mean it? I told you to say the words. Where did this, "mean what you say", come from? Say the words, I do not care if you scream it, say the words. Do you see all of the attached conditions added on to everything? Do you know how easy it was to say the words after this was clear? Everyone was actually saying that they released all to the Creator. It felt so good to do this.

Another thing I found interesting was how people had to go somewhere to pray. Was this something that had a location or condition? Did you have to get ready to do this? How silly all of this was. Are you not bonded and in the state of conversation twenty-four hours a day? Why must you stop everything and go pray? Where are you going? Why are there so many conditions on prayer? Honestly how do you do it? I guess it is because your god is complicated or something.

You really should get to know the Creator. You don't even have to put on your Sunday best or wash your hands and face. The Creator will never find anything dirty about you because you were made Perfect and you're perfectly on schedule as well. Hard to believe? Hard is the human race. Easy is the Creator. I would say you need to lighten up and have some fun. Oh well, I will wait until you feel you've earned it. The rest of us have been paid in full by the Creator so we don't have to earn it. Can you see where you are? Come on, let go of this earn it idea. You've been long enough without that Awesome Creator's Love. It is your birthright to have and cherish the Creator's love forever.

One of the problems people going into the Light had, was their ability to see how much they wouldn't let go of. It's either all or nothing because the in-between was the gray zone and that was Darkness. By seeing what they could not let go of, they could also see how much Darkness was in their lives. Anything you hang onto is in the Dark. If it is not with the Creator then where is it, with you, small mortal being that you are? You will not find me hanging on to anything. No way, I will not let Darkness into my space. All things go to the Creator, all things. Not even one small thing is left out. Is this too much trouble for you? Or is it too much work? Okay, stay where you are.

The Darkness by now was determined to find a way to put an end to me and so it became their goal to do this. They came together and in an arena I was only one small speck of Light but no matter how dense their Darkness grew, I walked on and spoke on. The Creator said that all would be fine. I knew Kayborg, Seakept and Nawbay would be back. I knew that many surprises awaited everyone too. The only surprise I would ever encounter would be Soulmate. I never did know to what degree he had known about me until much later.

Thoughts of Jimmy faded and I seldom thought about him. I must tell you again that when a thought of someone comes into your head they are sending it. When you take it upon yourself to think a thought to them, you are in the state to send. You would be amazed to know how many people do pick up and send thoughts all day but never bother to get confirmation on it. Weeks later they may be talking and realize that they were both thinking about each other at that very moment they were sending and receiving.

A lady came to see me very upset and somehow needing to prove me wrong about her situation. I had told her over the phone that she had an issue with god. I had only talked to her a few minutes but I knew by her terminologies that she had a past life, a negative past life involving a god. I told her to sit down and I would help her. What I would not do was give her all of the answers. I first asked her what bothered her the most. She said that she could not stand god. I asked her how strong this feeling was. She said that she hated god. Now we were making progress. What else bothered her greatly to the level of how she felt about god. The reason for this was to align all of the energies that were of the same vibration. She proceeded to say she hated houses with fences around them. They reminded her of prisons. "I am afraid of big cats like lions." I asked her if that was all. "I hate god. I hate god," she repeated over and over.

Although you may say that there is next to nothing in this brief conversation let me show you where it went. After she said these things she looked at me and asked me what it all meant.

"Are you ready to hear it?" I asked her.

"Yes, yes," she said.

Remember, fear is past life and there was a fear of cats. She mentioned the hatred for god several times, which meant it was strong. The most interesting thing came from the fences. Fences were meant to keep you in or out. I asked her which would it be for her. Inside, she said very sure of all of it. Where had she been with big cats that such fear was present? I started to ask specifics about these cats. It was clearly long in her past. After all, when would it have been that she could have had such contact with lions? I asked her where the cats were and what had they done to her. She said that she believed that they were in an arena and that she had been eaten alive. Seconds later it hit her in a complete memory. She said that she had been sacrificed to these animals and just before she died she yelled out to god to save her.

"God didn't save me," she said angrily, but then turned around and looked at me. She just about kicked herself for being such an idiot. "You mean I've been hating god all these years for nothing?" she asked me.

I just smiled and she checked her watch. In less than four minutes, it had come together, lifted from her heart, returned to her soul and she went back to the Creator from there. She asked me how she could keep this released without it coming back. I then asked her if she was really with the Creator or some god. She glowed and said that it was Creator and if she ever doubted herself she would remember how being with the Creator felt.

Did I tell her why she had this fear? No, she located it. All I did was line up all of the same energies, the same vibrations coming from this fear. You see, all fear collects the data, which is causing it. That is why, when you do not stop and review this, it grows into a full-blown problem and in some cases even panic. If you can recognize that all fear is a learned vibration of the past, you can get a better grip on it if it comes into your life. The only time fear, which is from past life, is related to precognition, which is future, is when they are related.

Let me give you an example. Let us say you have to go into a sky rise and when you get there, standing at the bottom you are afraid and it becomes impossible to do. I would make you talk it out. You can't you go in, because you are afraid. Why are you afraid? You do not know why you are afraid. What will happen if you go in? It fear it will collapse on you and you'll die. You begin to actually talk out the fear. Where is this coming from? After talking it out it is concluded that back in the 1940s a building collapsed and killed you. Since you had never been in a sky rise in your present life, there should have never been any fear. Remember, fear comes from a past life experience. What you do not know in your present life cannot be a source of fear.

Since I can only give you part of the Teachings, I must leave out many details but this is to give you an idea of fear related to precognition. Sometimes there are more complications, such as if it is Soulmate related or there are several past lives involved.

One day I asked the Creator why the Olympians had been sent to me in the beginning of this life. Creator, with this forever ongoing sense of humor told me that the mission was related to Olympus and that I needed to reawaken certain entities in this life to that energy. Besides, Creator said, I would have been so bored without them and weren't they great entertainment. Creator told me again that if I ever fell and the Dark Force took me, I would begin my death and once activated there would be no stopping it. This all remained with me strongly.

Of course there were all of those boring skeptics out there that had about as much knowingness as a clump of dirt. Also, the real hate marchers trying to gain control of anything and everything never bothered to understand what they hated. Again and again they tried to come into my space. Let me tell you that it is most unadvisable to do where I am concerned. It was time to call in their Soulmates and every time I did, they had more problems than they ever thought possible. To say they were left in the dust was putting it gently. They became what I called mud people. Let me tell you there are a lot of of mud people. Thus comes the terminology, "a rebel without a cause".

Can you see how there is terminology for everything? All you have to do is recognize the terminology to understand where things are and where they are going. Do you want to step into someone's karmic lesson? If you are not aware of terminologies you will be. In fact, you are probably aware more than you realize but no one has ever pointed it out to you like this. When you have the Creator you have an internally warm feeling inside. You are content, you see the perfectness of life, the abundance of the Knowingness, you are Awesome. Then you see the idiot, the fool. Yes the fool on the hill. Do you honestly think a fool would do valley? His ego would not allow it. Have you seen any fools lately

Let us move into, why are there other races of people? If you have read this far you should be saying that it is necessary to match the Soulmates. Get a clue! Soulmates continue to match up. Do you think your Soulmate can be green and you pink? How is he or she going to locate you if you are a different color? It is a great evil that the human race does the racist thing. Do you think anyone can change it? No, so stop being brain dead. Are Soulmates ever different races? Only if they are that race together. Once you leave your etheric body and come into this unnatural human body, it is hard enough to make it, no less try to locate your beeper, the Soulmate. Wake up and stop goofing off. No matter what race you are, you have the same ability to be bonded. The planet has too many excuses to keep it in Darkness. Once again all of us bonded to the Creator will be out enjoying life while you, stuck in the human race types, can stay miserable.

Let me remind you again, do not attempt to violate Divine Order. Do not attempt to use it or anything but honor it. If you do, your mind will be scrambled like a computer virus. Can you imagine what an idiot looks like with the virus? Do not think that the Creator and the Allegiance, that which is the Family of the Creator, will put up or tolerate violators? Do you want the wrath of Zeus on you, or how about a few Dark Angels after you? I have seen this happen and once scrambled, you are done for this life and perhaps several more. I know your Soulmate is not going to be too happy about his idiot Soulmate. It is really very clear, either you get re-bonded to the Creator or you stay a primitive in the human race.

It was incredibly hard to deal with the suicide types close to the end. In most cases these were the real emergencies and when these calls came in at all hours of the night, it was usually help them then or they would be checked out by morning. If one of the Soulmates had already taken their life, it was nearly impossible to hang onto the other. In this situation it was mandatory to bring forward a soul energy and get the bonding in them with Creator as soon as possible. They also needed to understand the Soulmate relationship. It is almost like being attached to a big cord. Once out of the body the Soulmate in this form can pull the one out in the human form very easily. Can you intervene? Yes in most cases but sometimes it is too late. Remember I told you that a human being could not be responsible for matters of the soul. As much as one adds all of the programs to a suicide, I can prove to you again and again that it is a Soulmate matter.

Do you know how much quiet is out there over suicides? The same levels of quiet are with females and babies that do not make it. Why are so many Dark souls coming back in? If human an beings would not interfere with pregnancies, they wouldn't. If all were bonded to the Creator we would not have so many problems.

Can you believe some idiot said that it would be too boring if everyone was in the Light? Here we go again. How many times have I said that one of the Soulmates must be in the Dark, while the other is in Light? Now, do you wonder why I keep repeating myself? It never ends.

Another example is, someone coming down with a cold or so they thought. I said to them why take this on? It was clear that there was no Soulmate struggle in this woman's energy field, so there wasn't any reason to do this cold. I told her to release it to the White Light of the Creator. Oh, she went on to say that the best policy was to just put it all out there and let it go the way the universe wants it. Check out these words, policy and universe, Dark and Dark. Policy is a human word and universe leaves it wide open for any entity to take control.

Another common conclusion is, ask that what you need comes forward. Are you going to get the clarity as to what is coming forward? Is it illusions to make you think that it is always what you need? Will it be protected? I promise you that whatever you put out there will come back even Darker. Go ahead and give your power away. Oh by the way, at that level, universe, you are going to lose most of who you are. Once again, watch your terminologies.

What I taught made sense but it allowed every person to get the clarity they needed on their own journeys. Many wanted to give their power to me. All they were really doing was transferring it around. I would not allow it and some even left because I refused to allow this. You see all they wanted was to be irresponsible and lazy. They wanted me to tell them what to do. A few even tried to con me into it by telling me how great I was and how they needed to study under me. Under me? Ego plays here and although it appears to be a humbling ego, it is as big as ever. Do not get under me because I will not put up with it. You lazy kinds might as well join the mud people. I am sure you can get them to tell you what to do.

As time went by, more and more things became coded and cloaked. Darkness had forever to put a contract out on anyone so letting your guard down would have been very unadvisable. Again and again most could not pay the expenses that it took to help them. Many very grateful people donated stop off places and anything else they could do to help, they did. Without these people helping, many would have not made it. Can children commit suicide over the Soulmate? All suicide is Soulmate no matter what age. Parents can take these children to one doctor after another. You can even postpone things by drugging them up. Unless there is intervention along the way, they usually end up dying or living a devastated life. The thing that puts you to sleep from the Creator is also the thing that wakes you back up. I can locate this immediately because it is the most outstanding stress on you.

Love, it was deep in my soul and yearning to come out for my Soulmate but a soul energy came forward among all of the others and so my Soulmate would have to wait. As soon as this relationship had started, out of the Dark came a call from Jimmy. I was floored because he was the last person I would have ever expected to hear from. It was clear that he had missed me greatly and that things had gone progressively worse for him. I really did not want to stir up old memories but he did.

Now Jimmy was not my Soulmate but what was so interesting was how he came forward the second I had found someone new. Remember that the Soulmate was be triggered to come forward when they felt jealous or threatened by you being with someone else. I recognized immediately that he had been set up to play Soulmate and I did not buy into it. I told him that we could not see each other or talk anymore. I hung up and forgot about it all but he called again the next day and the day after that and so on. I could not get rid of him. It was a bit haunting. I had loved him so and it ended. I saw it through as best I could. I went forward but he went backwards. The more I turned him down the more he seemed driven to come forward. My new relationship was an intensely strained one as a result.

Enough was enough and finally I agreed to meet Jimmy and tell him. I knew the second I saw that gorgeous smile I was in deep trouble. You of course would say I was still in love and you would be right. I looked into those gorgeous brown eyes only to get lost in his heart again. I must tell you that he was something out of a romance novel. As much as I tried to turn away, my knees were shaking so badly, I could not. My heart was pounding so hard with excitement I thought that he could see it through my blouse. He ran his hands up the inside of my arms. He kissed me on the neck and of course, that changed my plans completely. We were re-bonded and as soul energies go, it was once again great. I thought that he would break my heart all over again but I did not care. We talked and laughed and carried on like two little kids. Much I will leave to your imagination. Oh what a man, what a God from Olympus, oh what trouble was heading both of our ways. We could not help it though, we couldn't get apart from our touches. Love, but love that could never be and I thought that I was rid of this man.

Athena had warned me that our love would stir up the Dark Force. I was so drawn to him but he was pulled to me and the Light saturated his soul until he started crying from starvation of the Creator. "Oh Creator help us," I said silently but I knew that no help would come because once again our love was not meant to be. Do you understand that you cannot have that which is not in your journey? He left days later in the moonlight. Yes the moonlight, where I had heard the cello. Oh the pain of that cello stayed with me. "Good bye Jimmy," I said to myself. There were more important things to do than rejoice in our brief interlude.

My Soulmate was so deep and sad. Such an emptiness hit me in the months that followed from him. Where was he? How close was he? He must have been very near. Many nights I would wake up startled knowing that I had been touched, yet not touched. Where would I be when I finally met him?

More and more people came to me ready to check out. Those that had been on drugs for depression were so altered that they could not even comprehend what I was saying. I had to embrace them and return them back to the Creator myself. Why didn't these doctors have the truth of this? They were in Darkness. Notice that the doctors in Light speak terminologies in the Light. Even in the most fatalistic diagnosis, they will still give you Hope. Remember, Hope is the continuation of the soul seeking Truth. All illness is Darkness no matter how major or how minor. Sometimes illness is played out in Soulmates because the human body is the Soulmate's biggest trap.

People bonded to the Creator have illness only because the human body decays. Remember too, that you are trading excellent health with Creator for ill health with Darkness then it does not go. There is no such thing as excellent health. There will always be certain bodies that may appear in better health than others. All and all the body must go in its cycle and it will. The rate of decline may be quickened by your negativity. You may also activate long sleeping illness when you bond back to the Light. To give you an example, there are shields that all levels of Darkness use. When you remain in a frozen state of Darkness you may also freeze up any pending illness. When you let go and take the Light, your guard comes down, releasing these illnesses that you have been harboring for years. During these years, all of the sickness has continued in that frozen state to grow but it has not surfaced to the diagnosis stage yet. Terminologies for this would be, he was fine and just up and died, she was in such great health and went for a checkup only to find out she's dying.

Now you are thinking you are not going to go to the Light because you are afraid to activate illness. Here is how you prevent this. When you go to the Light, you release all of you every time. The reason this activation for illness only hits some is because they're going to the Creator in bits and pieces. Creator wants all of you. Do not leave your parts lying around to be vulnerable to illness or for that fact, do not leave anything vulnerable. Darkness will have a field day with your parts. Just say, I release myself to the White Light and Love of the Creator. The word myself identifies all of me. You would be surprised at what people release. I run into everyone's jumbled up messes constantly. You do too but you just have not been so aware of it yet. If you are going back to the Creator do it all, not the gray zone act.

A doctor is the last place that you go with Knowingness on any level. They are so deep in the sleep that they will try and try to fit you into some syndrome until you finally buy into it and there goes everything. Sickness does not affect your soul. You may have bought some illusion that it does but it does not. Your soul belongs to the Creator and again I tell you this. People will say that they have done what they have to learn. Learn is the human race, Know is the Creator. Why are you trying to learn what you already know? All that has ever happened is that you fell asleep to your Knowingness. Why is it that no one ever learns? They do the same thing over and over and over again.

My heart broke when Spanky slipped out of the car on a trip. We searched days for her and after two weeks, we finally gave up. Oh, the tears came as she was such a part of our lives. I can tell you it broke my son's heart. She had jumped out with her collar and leash on and what were the odds of her getting caught on something. We continued on our trip and six weeks later we started back. As we got to the location again where she had jumped out, I drove to the exact spot. To our shock there sat Spanky. Someone had apparently unhooked her leash. She had this look on her face as if she was fed up with waiting and what had taken us so long. I was so happy. The experience did not even affect her. Good old Spanky sure did entertain us. I have to tell you there is nothing like a pet, especially the ones with defiant personalities. Oh how we loved this cat.

Life went on and always more people needing help. Many had no idea what I even did. People would just say, "Call her, I can't explain what she does. All I know is that it works." How could you explain what I did? No one anywhere was doing anything like me. Some astrologers became angry because they thought that I was telling people to stay away from them. How many times have I said that you must do your journey but being bonded to the Creator gives you clarity and you will also be doing your journey in Light.

As I said before, perhaps you need to do religion. Then do it but with the Creator. If you need to do astrology then do it, with the Creator. Remember it does not mean it is right or wrong. It means it is Light or Dark. Oh people, what I say helps your journey. Why do you think that you are in what you are in? You have to do it.

In all of the Dark masters I had to run across, there was one who stood out from all of the rest. He called himself Zen Master Rama. He was the most powerful and greatest of all wizards. Now dealing with this one was always tricky because he was a pro beyond pro as a magician. I however could match his games. Rama could not fool me but was he ever so good at fooling everyone else. He was a creator of dreams, sender of dreams and destroyer of dreams. He was the only one that caused close calls and they came way too often. I did not like any job related to him. I nicknamed him Rombo. He was constantly assigning himself to whatever level made him look bigger. So he was whatever he decided and you worshiped that or got fried. Now being fried by Rombo was long and painful. It would last the duration of your life and take every penny you could ever make. There was no situation impossible for him and all situations were impossible for you if he was involved.

With no exceptions, all who fell into his trap never got out, never. The man was so evolved that he even surprised himself. To him, life was one big show and he was the star. He would set the stage and you were expected to participate. If you made one wrong move or mistake, you paid and you paid big time. To get tangled up with him would indeed have been dangerous. All rescues involving someone from his cult took a great deal of planning. Next to any and all cult leaders, Rombo was millenniums beyond everyone. Perhaps I should say everyone except for me. For in me, Zen Master Rama had finally met his match.

CHAPTER ELEVEN

If you ever stop to listen to people, you can see how stuck in past life they are. Most of it is religion oriented. Why? It takes real effort to move forward. It takes being responsible and most prefer to let someone else carry the weight. When you bond with the Creator you are no longer stuck anywhere. You are able to see the Truth of all things. All through time many have invested big time into their beliefs and they don't want someone coming along and upsetting things.

I tell you to be bonded to the Creator so that you have clarity of what you are doing. Then again, why have clarity when you can get some god to be responsible for all of your mess-ups. I guess the bottom line is that you have not had enough yet. I can tell you, people trying to come out of Rombo's force had had enough. No matter how much I deprogrammed them, he had a backup for a backup in all of his programs. You could not get out of it and it never ended. My time to each individual was ten times as long because the man was beyond clever.

The thing you need to realize is as you wake up, you are going to see more Darkness. What you need to see also, is that it has been there all along. Now the change comes as you become more and more aware. Do not let it upset you or get the better of you. First of all the second that happens you are giving your power away to it. You must stay bonded and try to remember that all is where it needs to be. Who has been around to help Darkness go to the Light? Ask yourself this. Also, weren't you in the sleepy state, another form of Darkness until you woke up? Here is another thing to think about. If Darkness is so bad then what were you doing there? Now that you are waking up why does it bother you so much? There will be plenty who will put all of this down and say that they cannot deal with it. There will also be those that cannot get enough. Remember too, that there are those that touch and those that change. Which one are you?

Another thing that comes up is thinking that you are an idiot for not knowing the things I've talked about. The idiot is someone who continues to get one opportunity after another for enlightenment and professes to be enlightened while knowing nothing. Someone who has been asleep to keep their Knowingness safe until it is time, is indeed a different story. These are people with a purpose, with a mission. That which is sacred must be kept safe until the time is right. It goes back to Divine Order. Are you power tripping Divine Order if you feel you should have awakened sooner? Be still, be at peace, and calm down. Some missions require a greater rest, for they are difficult missions.

Remember too, you are not all mortal. The soul is immortal and you have one. Do not forget this part of yourself by trying to shove your soul into mortal. Terminology of someone who recognizes this would say, when I die my soul leaves, the only thing of me that continues on, immortal, is my soul. It is okay to claim this realm as it is Truth. Do not let your mortal become so heavy that you sleep-coat the soul again. Are you mortal? For a time, yes, and you are immortal forever. As long as you have any body, anywhere, it will be some kind of mortal frame but you always carry that immortal soul. To help you focus, just remember that this shell over our soul is temporary and even if you live to be one hundred, you will shed it.

What you must do where I am concerned is stay detached from me. I am doing my mission and giving you things to help you but there is so much I have left out that you need not concern yourself with. Being overwhelmed, will set you back. I have given you many opportunities here. There are those who may start giving their opinions about me and reviewing what I have said.

Let me tell you that never in a million years will you now or ever begin to understand me. You need to understand who you are! I promise you, there is plenty you can discover about yourself. You need to be able to trust especially because it is broken constantly and most just accept it and go on. As long as you play forgiveness you continue to invite violations. Never forgive that which had to take place. If you had been releasing the person who violates, you would see no reason to forgive. Trust in the Creator. Do not trust anything else, trust no one but do honor them.

Now someone is going to say this is ridiculous. You will tell me how you trust your friend or your husband. You are playing victim as well as getting victimized then. Now here is how you trust once someone is bonded to the Creator. When you both have the same answers about something that you know is from the Creator, you are bonded in trust with Creator. Even if you interject a slight difference as long as you both understand. Just remember someone out of control may be a liar just as equal to someone in control. Behavior does not produce trust. Time does not build trust. Trust is a Dark program just hanging out there waiting for you to take it on. Do not put out trust and don't ever expect to receive it. You can share through Creator. People lean on this trust me thing, way too much. A lot of egos can't deal with this, they want to be babysat.

Now let's look at all of the traps. Trust is violated and violated and makes you play victim. Victim requires attention and attention comes in the form of, trust me. The cycle never ends. Don't do it. It is sad to say that I saw many suffer horribly, clinging to fragmented brainwashing. There has never really been anyone able to help these people but me. Experience in deprogramming does not help.

By the time you could even get out of your own problems to recognize, where are you with the Creator? The Creator gives you the Knowingness. Everyone runs to someone, something or they run in circles trying to find human based answers. The Dark Force knows where you are. You make it so easy for them. You are like mice in a cage and they are the cats ready to play. Their games are lethal and remember this, they never let you go. Only the bonding to the Creator breaks this power. Remember also, everyone is born running from something and running to something.

How about running to the Creator? Maybe you are afraid that you will run so hard you'll knock the Creator over. Trust me, you are not going to run the Creator over. Notice I used the word trust. Why? Because the Creator told me you aren't big enough. Go ahead and prove me wrong. So I am concluding now that we will both get the same answers from the Creator, thus we can both trust. This is how it works. It brings you closer to the Creator and your sharing is wonderful. Do we both agree that we are not big enough to knock the Creator over? This one was easy to see.

There are millions of people in cults that live a nine to five lifestyle and do not even know that they are in one. How many of you are reacting to this? The great denial should kick in here. I can hear this and in the next sentence you're complaining how Dark your life is. How often are things pointed out to you and you still cannot see them? Perhaps you need to read more.

In all of the cults I dealt with, which involved large groups under the reign of one leader, no one matched the Zen Master Rama. No one anywhere had ever given me such a Dark and evil feeling. This was a Darkness so intense and powerful that it made me cringe.

The women coming out of this evil were severely altered after being subjected to an intense level of degradation and it was so traumatic that recovery was nearly impossible. What was done to these women was the ultimate violation. This man would take the most intimate part of each woman and at the most vulnerable state he would pull on their souls, attempting to claim them while having sex. The women were not any good to him unless they could be brought to such vulnerability. He did not do well with those who resisted, fought him and had a will of iron. Those kinds had to be subjected to worse violence and more degradation. They had to be exposed and embarrassed beyond any level of tolerance. The humiliation levels were devastating. These were not the typical cult practices that I had encountered in the past. Sure these others did sexual violations but not at the levels of this man. He craved the abduction of the soul. It was as if he could not continue unless there were more who could surrender their souls. It was as if it were his only source of nourishment.

There was something very different about Rama. I had to laugh at the name because of its other meanings. Talk about a severe case of pms. There was great dread in me where he was concerned. As much as I kept trying to treat it as one more cult situation, it did not fit. Even other cult leaders dreaded this man.

Everything was affected by those I helped out of this power. Where he was concerned, no one got out and no one could break his hold. If they even tried, they would suffer great punishment. Of course, that meant me as well.

Much of what I told you about the Dark you can see and not see applies here. Again and again, it is so important to recognize that what you can't see is very valid. One way to recognize this at times is the feeling one gets when this kind of Darkness is present. When it is very active you can feel it. It's so unsettling and you don't feel good. Terminologies when it is present would be, there is something in the air, it feels dangerous, I sense bad is coming, can you feel this and who has bad energy here? More would be, I do not want to be here, it feels creepy, it's going to be a bad day today, I can feel it, things feel off, I felt fine until I got here and so on. These are just some of the terminologies to alert you. For all things, I could give you so many terminologies but these are the most common used when this unseen Dark Force is present. Of course, the human race blames all of this on other things. You will never see things unless you are willing to wake up to it. If you have used some of the terminologies I have mentioned above, that Force was present. The more bonded to the Creator, the more aware you are. I cannot tell you enough how this is the most important of all things.

Rama had just as much power in both of these realms. To the best of my knowledge I was not aware that he had targeted me for a later date. I tried to stay clear of this man but over and over people from his cult kept calling me. On some level it seemed as though he was deliberately setting all of this up. The rate of calls was too overwhelming to just conclude that it was all coincidental. You know how I would view the word coincidental.

The levels of trauma and fear in the women from Rama's cult was overwhelming. They were so far gone and so eliminated in their minds. No one understood what they had been through except for me. He was so thorough that no one could break his hold but I could. He had an invincible plan and knew that he could play the human race for all it was worth because humans only dealt with rules and laws created by man. These rules and laws were designed with so many flaws that it has allowed Darkness to get away with everything. A good terminology for this would be, "he gets away with murder". There has to be crooked lawyers to defend such Darkness and crooked judges keep ruining people's lives. Why is this allowed? Because the majority are in Darkness and Darkness keeps reflecting Darkness. What a situation the world is in. Can it change? Of course it can but not until people begin to wake up. Do not be overwhelmed to see how really Dark it is when you wake up. You cannot imagine any of it from how I've seen it. Yes it's bad, it's Dark, but remember, Light always changes things. Darkness gives you the illusion of change but leaves you waiting forever.

Rama knew that he could do anything and get away with it because he was dealing with idiots. After leaving his cult, trying to make people believe you was impossible. In other words if one tried to get help, they would have to alter their story or leave much of it out. Doctors are not trained to care or understand. There were no books to reference on Forces like this. This left someone open for more trauma. If one program were left undiscovered, that would be what kept them attached to the mind control.

What is amazing is how idiots can't get things clear so they need you to play victim so they can research what puzzles them. Now take someone who needs help coming out of any cult. What is out there? Idiots using you as experiments to build research so they think they are qualified. Rama knew that this was what these doctors, researchers, etc., were doing. All he had to do was plant programs that no book or experiment could ever find to guarantee his success. Do you know how easy this is? All he had to do was pick programs in the Darkness that you could not see. Remember, again, that Darkness that you cannot see. He knew too that no one could describe what he or she could not see or understand. Trying to make anyone believe you would be impossible, that is except where I was concerned.

There were men as well who came out of Rama's cult completely destroyed. He did not do to the men what he did to the women though. For the females it was the destruction of their womanhood. He had an obsession with smell and it was a tracking device to determine which souls were vibrating at a higher frequency. These women were singled out and set aside for a slower, more vicious program of degradation. To give you an example, people that are sick have chemical changes in their bodies that create a different odor. A healthy body smells different. None of these women were ever aware of this. Certain foods created odors as well so he would demand specific diets to enhance the smell he needed. He made women use certain scents. Without getting graphic, this scent was mandatory for a certain place on the female body. This was also the sacrificial place where your soul would be pulled out. If the scent was correct the release of the soul would be easy. After all, he did not want any problems. That is one of the reasons everything was reinforced again and again. Follow the program or do the punishment. Many were punished not realizing the reason why. When meeting Rama, he would target one area immediately if you were female. Males made good servants but the females carried the power. We all give off a certain essence. Many of my soul energies were males and as such, warriors. I had a large group of wonderful soul energies and many were involved with some of these cult situations.

I had not thought so strongly of my Soulmate after the last time I heard the cello. It was so heart wrenching that it only brought tears to me. I did not want to cry any more. If I had to cry, then let me cry with him together in his arms.

Always the dreaded phone call from someone in Rama's group would come. If I said no, I knew they would be doomed forever. I knew that no one ever got completely out. As much as I deprogrammed them there would always be one more program to surface at that moment or much later. There were constant relapses and countless hours of conversation. All came out broken in all areas of their lives. Imagine such evil and nowhere to go for help. Most could not speak right and I had to tell them what had happened. It was the worse violation I had ever seen and he was growing in power. He was using techniques so ancient and yet high tech that it was impossible to catch him. Yes, I know you are going to say, until me. That is right, however, I was only one person with hundreds of needs rapidly turning into thousands. He had taken all of their resources and their needs were overwhelming. The ones who he felt he could drain for the rest of their lives he put under contract, meaning they had to send every cent they made. Others were forced to do degradation for the rest of their lives. Either way, each person paid and paid. If someone did not meet the quota everyone suffered. They all had to do humiliation while he took and took. The fear in these people was beyond any word to describe it.

Angel of Silk remained along with all of the other Angels but it seemed as though, all were quite confident that I could handle things. I, on the other hand, could not see why everyone was so confident. It did seem as though ever finding my Soulmate was going to be impossible.

I saw no life for myself with such a need to help all of these people. It was clear that no one wanted to be involved and no one cared enough to make a difference. It came down to how selfish everyone was. It was just fine for me to give up my life. After all, the excuse the human race used was that I was the only one who could do the job. Perhaps you can better see why Athena, Zeus and all of the Angels were there in the beginning of my life. I had a super human mission with no help from this human race. My soul energies did all they could but it didn't even make a dent. Rama was abducting souls faster than I could keep up. Why me? Why did I have to deal with this man? Calling out to Athena would do no good because somehow, she was connected to this man. Maybe someday the secret would be revealed. It came to me in my brief moments of peace, that it was best to walk from all of this because I could not do it but I was driven and compelled with such a power, that it was like a Soulmate pull. I had no time for Soulmate. I had no time for anything.

All through history, it was always the male pms that blamed the female. Although the males needed the females, they needed to own them as well. Notice too, when a man could not deal with himself, it was always the female that provoked him. This was especially true with matters related to the physical. All through history wars were fought over men unable to control their lust. The female was always blamed for this evil and became a prisoner to it. If you look back on history you will see this again and again. You may ask, why did she become a prisoner to this? The simple answer is because she is the carrier of life, which forces her to participate in the sexual act to provide life.

Thus comes the terminology, *"it's woman's work"*. The original division between man and woman came from the Soulmate relationships.

Three major problems that have continued on the planet all through history have been the lack of being bonded to the Creator, the human race in battle and of course the domination of the physical relationships. More wars have been fought over a woman than have been written. War is Dark and evil no matter what the circumstances. What made the males become so Dark with their pms? As the females tried to reclaim their power it started to threaten the males. The more they reclaimed the more it threatened. This problem goes back to the beginning of time. Religion made it worse. Just take the Adam and Eve story. Once again, the man keeps going on with the blame system on the woman. Just stick the whole situation on some god. Talk about keeping one enslaved.

Rama thing was way out of control and the more I had to deal with anything associated with him the more I detested him. He hit these students of his so hard that he had a safe proof program, guaranteeing that no one would ever expose him. He had a short fuse and the wrath of Con. When he got angry a major tidal wave was in the making, the Richter scale was over eight and everyone was ducking down trying to become invisible. It was rather easy. Go along with the program or get fried. Anyone in his path got it. Anyone not in his path got it and so there was nowhere to go.

Everyone had to be put on hold as there wasn't enough of me to handle those outside of Rama. It was very upsetting to those I could not reach. I could not send them to anyone because there was not anyone who did what I did. They all had to stay bonded to the Creator. That was the bottom line and for many this was quite a test. People finally had to stay in Dark or go to Light. As many times as I have said, go to the Creator, many really did not do it.

You need to remember too that there was a reason these students were with Rama. As I have said, all is where it needs to be. No matter how it appears, you cannot see the whole picture. Some people are attracted to things that you may view as negative. Remember that they are doing their journeys and you need to honor all things. For me it was Soulmate related with Rama but it did not reveal itself enough. Sure, I was fed-up with this man but he could not have triggered terminology like this if it was not Soulmate connected.

One night after a very long day I fell into a deep, deep sleep. I was not easily aroused but I heard a male voice calling out my name. "Yes, what is it?" I said, not sure that it was reaching anyone.

"Daughter, that is but is not, you have thought of me and I have come to speak to you," this male voice said so proper and clear.

I turned so fast that I fell out of bed staring up in shock. I thought to myself I am overworked and still asleep. I am just major exhausted and I am hearing things. I searched frantically as that huge face leaned down and looked deep into my eyes. "Thor?" I said looking unsure.

"It is I, Daughter that is but is not."He said in such a soft gentle voice.

Oh it was wonderful hearing the Olympian dialect. I immediately thought of Athena. "Thor? I have not seen you in ages," I told him as my guard came down. He smiled this great big smile from this huge head and gigantic body.

"I came because you called for me," he said.

"I did? When did I do that?" I asked him.

"In your sleep you called out," he responded and added "You are so in danger by this Entity."

"Of course you would know him," I said very glad to see him. "I thought that everyone had abandoned me up there. It is so hard being here Thor. It gets so lonely." I said sadly.

"I know it is but I have come to tell you that no matter how bad it gets, we are there for you. Do not think we would ever abandon you. It is such a big mission for one so little," he said hugging me.

"You are so gentle," I said smiling. He made me feel like a small little person completely safe in the arms of such a strong powerful giant. We talked of times so long ago and how he took me in once and raised me as his daughter. We both loved Athena. He told me that some day she would return and that he knew this.

"You cannot imagine how much I have missed her," I told him.

"I know how much because no one has ever been so loved by her and you truly are her Daughter," he said.

"Thor you have been the only father I've ever known," I reassured him as I sensed he wanted and needed to hear this.

"Just remember, that of your Mother, you are too," he said leaving.

I swear people just dropped in as quickly as they left. I needed to be leisured from time to time. I certainly was not going to get any of that from here.

We had to move a lot as the thought of Rama finding out about me was very dangerous. I knew about the scanning and activation energy. All you had to do was think his name and he could locate you. You see I too could do this and I taught others how to do this as well. Most could not do it as good but it could still be done. One of my main concerns was his ability to pick up my location through someone else's thoughts of me. I continued to keep as private as possible but I knew that it was only a matter of time. I knew Thor was telling me this without actually saying it.

I watched Rama students deteriorate even though I stayed on top of things. I knew that this was Soulmate related and the thought of a two for one was about as deadly as it could be. He had one Soulmate, which forced the other to seek out their whereabouts. Now I am only speaking of the Soulmates that were to connect in this lifetime.

Although his front was this self-created Zen system it was rather odd that so many of his students were displaying Soulmate energy. I have to tell you that I did not want to be involved with this man on any level especially if it was going to drag me into anything related to Soulmates. I was not able to stomach Rama's energy because it was so Dark and violent. He was the Darkest of all Dark on this earth. With great dread I sensed so much trouble coming. In spite of all of the warning signs, I could not once again change my journey any more than anyone else could. Human beings love to give themselves credit for all of the decisions they have made in their lives. I tell you all was going to go the way it had to anyway. Where was the Creator in all of this? You guessed it, right where the Creator always was.

As students of Rama's fell by the way side they were so severely punished that it left permanent scars. There was not any way anyone could live up to such tough regiments. He wanted to make sure that they received little sleep and that they did everything perfect. After all, Rama would say, you never knew if it might be your last day on the planet. It was mandatory to have everything in perfect order. The females were always treated differently. They were potential sexual contacts, and he had no desire to have a relationship with them. He had one thing on his mind and that was it. Rama had to gain in power and that power was only obtainable through the female orgasm. The man was a low vibration for sure.

It was imperative that everyone keep what I did confidential especially when it came to the rescues. The whole point of being safe was to keep everything private. Once trust was broken it was impossible to fix. The human race has its own interpretation of trust but where I was with trust was always the Creator. Once the privacy and trust were broken there would be no reconnecting or any further help. Most kept everything as confidential as possible but every once in a while some pompous loser would become jealous and try to make trouble. This usually came in the form of trying to sell what I taught. Sometimes they were hired by cult leaders to try to put a stop to me. Always they searched for the techniques I used but I always kept something from everyone. I have not named all of these other cult leaders for a reason. Know that there are many reasons behind everything that I do. As I attempted to move further from Rama the closer he moved towards me. He knew that someone was taking his people and he felt a challenge like never before.

There was little time to hear the cello and the thoughts of Athena ever coming back eventually left me. I was so busy helping the lost, homeless and violated, that I gave up all Soulmate thoughts and realized that even that was gone. There wasn't any way I could ever just go off and find him. I was too committed and dedicated to what I had to do. I had my soul energies and we cared so for each other. As long as I did not hear a cello or flute I was fine.

What did not come as a surprise was students coming to me after horrendous experiences with other cult deprogrammers. Some of these people were using the same techniques that the cult leaders were using and in fact stirring up more problems. I needed to remain out of the public in order to be effective. I never had any desire to be known and recognized. If you found me then you were connecting to what you needed. I had a voice mail number in Colorado but I was seldom there. Because I always collected my messages from afar, I was nearly impossible to find. Anyone who did locate me had to search at great length.

Repeatedly, Rama came into the picture. I was seeing things in his students that they were not even aware of. Some of them were numb because they had been terrorized. Rama was not a stupid man, he was brilliant and even that was an understatement. The areas he lacked in were the areas I did not. This was where I was brilliant.

Something strange was happening to me as I walked into an office and totally erased all of their computer disks. I was not even aware of this until everyone started screaming. Then they looked up at me while I announced that I did not do it. It is amazing that no one believes in these kinds of things but boy are they quick to accuse the first thing that might be the cause. What was even more astonishing was that the computers all started to work again when I walked out. I was acutely aware that I was being scanned big time by Rama. Although I had covered my bases to ensure safety, he was somehow alerted to my presence. There was no doubt that I appeared to be the ultimate challenge to him. I detested him as his rape of the heart was beyond any mortal realm. It ensured all would go with him when he exited the planet. Who could rescue anyone from something like this, no one unless they understood what this really was. The more his disgusting energy tried to locate me the more I put up higher levels of protection.

My metabolic system was changing rapidly and I knew that this mission, the big one, was about to begin. Angel of Silk was close and reassured me I could do it. Although I kept denying it, I was displaying Soulmate energy. It only took one person to tell Rama what he thought I was about. Rama only needed to tap into this person's mind to pull out this information. How many times have I talked about the power you cannot see? Rama knew as well as I did that from a legal aspect you could not prove any of these levels. What do you expect, as I have said, a planet full of idiots? What is so amazing is that if it serves the human race they will integrate some of this unseen power. Such as, yes, there are Angels, yet they will discredit things like Athena and Zeus and say that was just a myth. When will the human race stop announcing how stupid they are? What is all of this based on, science? Remember what I said about science. So let us conclude that Angels are not a myth but Greek mythology is. Oh well, the point has been made. What runs the human race? pms. Here is something to think about. Some male doctor came up with pms for women. What actually took place was his pms needed someone to blame so he mirrored his own problem out there and women took it on.

I knew that the battle with Rama was only a matter of time, something I was running out of. I had the Angels, the Olympians, but greatest of all, I had the Creator. I had been raised in preparation of this. Even though I did not know how bad it would get, I did know all would be looking out for me in the heavens. There was no reason to think that I could stop him any more than he could stop me. War had been declared somewhere in time. Divine Order would prevail and Soulmates would make it someday, somehow.

CHAPTER TWELVE

Our precious little Spanky continued to be the best guard cat ever. If any animal was ever born for the job she was. No matter how tired I was or how sound asleep I was, she woke me to anything Dark coming our way. She was so cute, and oh how she could kick up a storm. Nighttime was her romping hours and she could make more messes than you could imagine. If she needed a playmate she would jump on our beds and bite our feet. You could never catch her to reprimand her because she was so fast. There was always the greeting when one of us came home and the cuddling and loving could always be counted on.

The war had begun but I was so busy I did not realize just when he had declared it. It came as a direct hit to me with one of his energy fields. I was hit so hard I nearly fell over. It was very familiar but I could not quite place it. He was Dark and filled with an intense evil. I felt as though death passed right next to me. The sword of death came to my mind of course. Athena had told me as a young girl that my Soulmate would be a great leader and the most powerful man on the earth. Of course, I was trying to correlate things when he hit me again and this time I did fall over. Dread filled me as my memory of this evil began to come back. I recalled many past lives and all of them filled with his violating and degrading women as well as other Dark evil things.

I realized that this was so dangerous that I would not and could not do this mission. I concluded that it was done and over with for me. I would not do this and that was final. I felt sick and as if I could not get enough showers. I felt as though I had been tapped into and touched. He was reliving a rape of me and every vivid detail was being played out in front of me. He was so disgusting I had to turn away.

Some students asked me one day if they could call the Creator, God. I asked them if we were we talking about the same thing. Did everyone understand that we needed Darkness to understand, where we were. How much is this ignored? Constantly. Most never even recognized this need. Except for the Soulmate, our great exception, it is a full time job dealing with Darkness. Sure, Soulmates deal with it but other factors play here. The great bonding with Soulmates may take more than crazy glue. It can get so hot with Soulmates that they need their own refrigerating unit. So can you call Creator god?

Darkness has found so many ways to give you the illusion that you are with the big god, that you need to fine tune this. Remember there is the Dark Force. This Force has everything from the Darkest of Dark to the lightest of sleepy heads. There are Angels in Dark, Olympians in Dark and Soulmates. So, if you want to call Creator God, then say God Force, so the Dark Force knows which Force you are in. I release all things to the Awesome White Light and Love of the God Force. Don't worry, all will know where you are, especially the Dark. You are always in one Force or the other. Now say it and watch the effects it has.

You are probably going to wonder why I have not mentioned this before. It is all I can do to get you to the Creator with the clarity that you are actually there. Can you call the Creator anything else but God Force? No, not if you want Darkness to recognize where you are. Since you are with a Force anyway, which one do you want to be with? You can rest assured that I will find you and I will not even have to look. I can scan all things and I am the best there is at this. I promise too, that if you test me on this, I will reveal a whole lot more than you may be re ady to know.

I went on steering clear of Rama big time. Besides being a violator, he thought he had a magnet the size of the planet. All would eventually be sucked into his vacuum of hell. Females would be scanned for sexual tolerance and levels of resistance. Males were just scanned for pms and regardless of the size of their anatomy, Rama was the greatest and all the rest fell to the wayside. Do as you are told or fry. What was it like to be fried? It could hurt very badly or just a little. Either way he always had that back up for that back up. He was obsessed with the female orgasm and it did not matter what the female thought. You either get to it or get fried. Believe me there was no mercy.

Can you believe that there are actual idiots on the planet that believe that some of these men come back so evolved that sex is their only great high. Hello low lives, they are not great! They anoint themselves great masters and you become their slaves. Since when does the penis run the planet? Someone gave their power away somewhere. You never needed the penis, you needed the passion coming only from the God Force. With passion the lovemaking surpasses any individual organ. If the penis runs the planet, what are you, the sink-hole? Come on, wake up, the war between male and female has gone on long enough! All parts of the body are beautiful. Is it the size of the organ? No! It is the size of the bonding to the God Force. You would be surprised at how big things look from that perspective.

I guess you could see why Rama wanted me removed. I told it like it was, fearless as all when I did. Only the Soulmate thing showed signs of wearing and stress. I was being sucked into the vacuum of hell with no hope of connecting to him and yet I was unable to break the spell. Even though I had given up, he apparently had not because I could feel him still from time to time. I thought this mission with Rama was the reason I had to go into this vacuum. I also felt the Soulmate pull in the same direction, so even dragging my feet, I was going. I did resist hard and strong but to no success nor did I get the chance to change the journey.

How often have you viewed the fool on the hill? They praise all of their accomplishments. They make all of their own choices that by the way, are always right or so they think, while you are looked down on for making all of the wrong choices! Excuse me, Divine Order again. You have not got enough brains to make the wrong choices. Sorry, that that mini-god concept is only a concept. Wake up and stop being so primitive, people! The fool could never do valley because his ego would not let him. Must I repeat myself again and again? There is a reason that accidents happen. When you do not listen to what your soul is saying it will create a way to stop you because you are heading in a direction that is trying to take you off of your journey.

All accidents happen when you are trying to alter this. This includes Soulmates as well. If two Soulmates are supposed to meet and one is fighting it so much so that it will stop their connecting, an accident will take place.

Divine Order will not allow you to slip off the path. If you refuse to listen to what your soul is saying, then you are going to get this experience. The soul will try to prevent this by giving you ample warning. Again and again one always wants to know, why me? What did I do to deserve this? How could this have happened to me?

Here is another good one. How could god let this happen to me? God? Your soul is programmed on a journey and if you are going to blow it, you are going to get it. If people would start listening to the God Force, you would hear what you were deaf to. The only time outside of this would be Soulmates refusing to connect in spite of hearing the God Force. Usually they end up getting it big time, as Soulmates do things very big. They cannot help it as the body traps a lot of their vibrations. Soulmates tend to explode in all areas of their lives.

To say that there was some exploding between Rama and me was putting it mildly. He kept doing things to people that they could not prove. It goes back to the Dark you cannot see. He used plenty of this. It was a guaranteed, foolproof way to manipulate the life out of the human race. If what you can only see can be held accountable and not the unseen, realize this, the world is going to hell because the unseen is winning. I have the ability to do the unseen too but nothing will help you do it without the God Force. I know, for many it is hard to say Creator. Just remember to put Force after the word God. All energy creates a force. Release all those old programs of yours to the Awesome Love and Light of the God Force. Bravo! I actually felt some of you do it. Repeat many times that which I have said. Some people are very sleepy and need to hear it again and again.

There was no reason for such degradation on women from Rama. He had more than a severe case of pms. He had the spandex pms, stretching things to the maximum. The more he stretched things the more I displayed Light. He was not going to drag me into the Dark, no matter what. Did I have a limit? Not according to the God Force. No matter what it took, I would say again and again. Dread came upon me often from this man, sort of like a flu heading your way and you have to build yourself up to fight it. Leave me alone, I kept saying. Why could not he just leave me alone? Some of this degradation I cannot even tell you, it is so horrible. When a woman has been touched like this, she seldom regains all of her power again. I could see that he gleefully loved this! He could see with disgust I could not stand him. It was so Soulmate that I cringed. It could not be him. He could not be my Soulmate, never! I had to get a grip on things. Sure, we had things in common but with severe differences. He claimed that he did not believe in Soulmates. You see, he wanted to get as many orgasms as possible and having his Soulmate nearby might cause problems. In his mind it never occurred to him that she might not want him. Disgust turned into an intense repulsiveness. Rama was an assaulting low life.

Of course no one talked about Rama this way and got away with it but I did. I was sure that he was keeping score. Like I said, even if you weren't in his path you got it. Just the mere fact that I was born was reason enough to eliminate me. I never had to do anything except exist. I was a threat no matter what. Those that were in his group were messed up enough but the ones who did not even know that they had been targeted were really in trouble. In this area there were hundreds of thousands of lost souls. You cannot imagine some of these techniques used to abduct you. The level of Darkness Rama was at was lacking a word that would substantially cover it. I kept thinking of ways to get out of it all. Down deep inside I knew that there was the mission but I had made up my mind that I was not going to do it. In fact, I packed up and even drove away. Just a short drive down the road I heard the wrenching sound of that cello and tears poured from my eyes. I kept going against all of the signs to stop and turn around. I refused to listen to my soul. Look at the picture. I knew that Rama was going to toy with me. I sensed his evil trying to abduct my soul. I knew that he would never stop. I knew that I would lose everything if I stayed and did this mission. I saw that all of my soul energies were in great danger and they would suffer too. The further I drove the worse it got

Then it happened. My car engine blew with no warning. I had a very good Volvo, which was in wonderful condition. Volvos just do not blow engines. It was too clear what had happened and I was forced to turn back. Then his words came, "thought you were going to get away did you?" He was worse than a bad case of poison ivy, breaking out all over. He would send such strong thoughts that you would be saturated in them.

Do you remember what I said about sending and receiving thoughts? You can send a thought to someone who tells you days later that they received it. Now let us go one step further. You send an even stronger thought and this person goes so far as to pick up the phone and call you right away. When you go one step further, you actually do what the person is sending and then confirm it. How about going yet another step? How about sending so intensely that you are overloaded to the point of fear. Remember, all fear is a past life from somewhere. He loved sending, to the point of scaring the life out of you. Tell me how then, are you supposed to make him stop? Yes, release yourself to the God Force. The true battle playing here between the God Force and Dark Force was one on one. For me, it was the Soulmate that made me remain.

What comes next is so devastating that it is all I can do to write it, even ten years later. I have not given you a timeframe on things but this event I am about to tell you happened in 1987. After my car broke down and I was forced to go to Colorado, I met a woman named Lois. It was only a matter of days before my life was to take a turn for the worse. Little did I know that Lois and her daughter not only knew of Rama but one of his students as well. Did they know who I was? No, but you will understand as I go on.

I woke to a day of more Rama and his scanning. He seemed to be very happy on this particular day. It was a happiness similar to one having had a successful hunt, with very little resistance from the prey. I suspected he had set a trap and was anticipating that I would just fall right into it. Being aware of this and very cautious of his ways, I proceeded with great awareness on this day. I watched everything and still I did not see what was coming. I was taking a bus downtown when all of a sudden, as if right on schedule, the bus slammed on its brakes to avoid hitting a car that had just dashed right out in front of it. I flew out of my seat, hitting my head on the roof of the bus and ricocheted down one of the steel poles. It was hard to explain how I felt. My mind began to go into broken thoughts and it was increasingly harder to concentrate. I knew that I was hurt and needed help. By the time I made it home, my vision was leaving me and the light bothered my eyes something awful.

I saw Lois and her daughter as I was leaving to see a doctor that they both knew. As the hours passed I became more disoriented and it was increasingly harder to stand. I was at the office of Dr. Chris Nada. My vision was now so bad I could not even make out the nurses' faces or much of anything else. I was taken into a room to wait but I was so dizzy I was falling all over. The only thing I knew when this doctor said hello was that it was Rama's voice. I was shocked thinking that Rama had somehow traded places with this doctor. I could not make out his face and the more I heard him speak, the more distressed I became. This be the ultimate abduction, I thought. He stood in front of me and it seemed like it was Rama but it was this doctor all mixed up together. What in the world was going on? I had covered all my bases and yet he was standing right in front of me. I could not make out his face. His hair was dark and his voice was identical right down to the emphasis on certain words. His mannerisms were identical too. My vision was so blurry and I pulled away from this doctor, or was it Rama, or both. He told me that I needed to be in the hospital. He did not like me and he too pulled away. I had such an intense feeling, but it was and it was not. I swear I was in front of Rama. The more this doctor talked, the more I knew I was in a trap with no way to get out. Rama had set up the bus accident. Even meeting Lois was a set up and now this doctor. My thoughts kept scrambling and I had a very bad headache.

Dr. Chris, as I soon thought of him to separate his image from Rama, called an ambulance and I was admitted to the hospital. I had no way out of the bed as he put the guardrails up. I could not stand up straight anyway. I lay in bed and tried to think clear. A nurse came in and asked me if I wanted to call anyone like my mother. Right, I needed a phone for Athena. I told her no, that I had already called for my Mother. After the nurse left I called out to Athena.

"Mother, oh do I need you now," I said softly.

"I am here, Daughter. I am back," she said.

"Athena, you are really here?" I asked.

"Yes, Daughter, the time has come for me to stay with you," she said smiling.

"Mother for how long can you be with me?" I asked expecting her to say just a few hours.

"I shall be with you for many years," she said quite pleased about the whole thing.

"Years!" I wanted to jump for joy as I tried to shout it out to the world. My head hurt way too much to move very fast. "Oh I must be in a great deal of trouble if I have you for years Mother," I said very slowly.

"Daughter, you are in the biggest of all trouble. You did not listen to your soul. You were almost killed by the one," she said with a sense of discipline in her voice.

"Yes we both know who the one is. I could not listen, Mother. He is so Dark and evil. I cannot stand him. I know that my soul was even screaming out to me but I turned with great defiance from it. I cannot believe that you are here. Can you really stay? " I asked her so filled with anticipation.

"Daughter, that of your Mother, a great Dark evil looms above you. Only you can battle him. Only you can make him remember love and that is what you must do, no matter what!" she told me so strongly.

"I detest him. I detest him beyond all things. I will never love this man," I told her.

"Daughter, you have no choice. His Darkness is so powerful here on this earth that he will destroy earth itself. Love is the only thing that can melt him down," she said.

"Mother, I would rather die than deal with him. Why me, why? It is related to my Soulmate, isn't it? " I said quite sure of the answer. "You have only one Soulmate. We all only have one Soulmate," she said.

I interrupted her, "Are you saying Rama is it? Is that why I just got cracked in the head?" I said, getting more and more out of control.

"Daughter, listen to me," Athena started to say but I interrupted her again.

"Until my last dying breath I will never love him, never," I yelled as the tears fell.

"Did I say that he was it?" Athena said trying to settle me.

"It's what you didn't say, Mother!" I cried, desperate to make this all go away.

"Did I say he was your Soulmate?" she responded back.

"No, but . . ." I trailed off.

"No buts about it. You will have to convince him that you are and you will know when you'll have to do this," she said very softly as if the Dark Force could hear us.

"Mother, why is Chris identical to Rama?" I asked her.

"There is that which I can tell you and that which I cannot," she concluded.

Oh she concluded all right something similar to a Zen principle. Although Athena did not say very much my concern was for what she was not saying. The head injury did nothing except confuse me. I knew that Athena knew and I was afraid that she felt that I could not cope. I could not see and it was impossible to get a clear visual on Chris. He asked me not to call him doctor as he said that he could not stand that. He was very sarcastic with me right from the start. He had a terrible attitude and it was clear that he could not stand me. I was so sad as the realization hit me that at a time when I needed to know, my head was spinning. I could not understand why Chris was so much that of Rama. Athena stayed on my bed as I drifted off. It was sad all right, that all of my tuning in was temporarily down. Chris had such a bad attitude where I was concerned that it went above and beyond reason. I was a threat to him and it only baffled me. He told me that I had better go out of my way to thank everyone, since they had given me extra attention when I had first entered his office. I looked at him with a frown.

"That's their job," I said to him. He did not like my response.

"You were quite a bit of trouble for us," he said very ugly.

"What do you mean trouble? I just sat there," I retorted.

"Yeah, right," he said even uglier. It was clear he was triggered.

He told me that I needed to stay in the hospital longer but I refused to stay. He knew I wanted to leave but he did not come back to release me. I tried to sit up but could barely deal with balancing myself. I felt like I had a head the size of a basketball. I could not get the bedrails down and so I just had to lie there.

Of course, I cried, as everything seemed to be happening to me while the Darkness appeared to be winning. The tears poured from my soul this time. He was here, he had arrived and I detested him. The man did not have one ounce of compassion in him. He was cold and cruel. He was just like Rama. I cannot tell you how badly I felt but it was as if the entire purpose for my ever being born had been all for nothing.

I thought about my love with Jimmy and how much it had meant to me. There were two others that I had loved as well. They, like Jimmy, were gone. People had come and gone from me like leaves blowing along in the wind. It was as if all was moving along and I had to stay behind. Yes, so that I could be Rama's playmate. He made the games, the rules and the victories. I was like a mouse in a cage waiting for the kill. I was in such pain physically and the pain inside reached out to touch that pain. Oh, had I been played and used. Here was Chris, of all things a doctor, the one thing I could not deal with. I was so floored I could not cope. I could not even find the words to speak. I went inside of myself and saw no purpose to go on. Where was all of the going with this man? He was identical to the Darkest man on the planet.

I turned to Athena and she looked at me with such concern, "Daughter all is not as it appears."

"Like that is going to comfort me, Mother," I said completely exhausted. "There is no future anymore. What is this with Chris that he hates me so? He just cannot stand me. There is neither rhyme nor reason for this."

"Daughter, look at something here. Is he not just like this one who calls himself Rama? There is a reason for it," Athena said.

"Oh there is a reason for it all right. All males have a severe case of pms," I said so loudly that a nurse walked in asking who I was talking to. "Where is this Dr. Nada?" I said, avoiding her question.

"He left already," she said.

"He left when he knew that I needed to be discharged?" I asked with a touch of the same sarcasm Chris had used on me.

"Can I get you anything?" she asked me.

"Yes put the rails down, I want to get up," I demanded.

"Dr. Nada said we couldn't do that because you'd fall out of bed," she said making sure that she followed his instructions.

"Look, I'm not going to fall out of bed. Just put one rail down and I'll ring to get up when I'm ready," I said pleading with her.

I talked her into it because she did put one rail down. As soon as she left I tried to sit up. I was so dizzy that I could not hold my balance and down I went onto the floor. He was right, I would fall out of bed. How dare he be right on anything. Now I really was detesting him the way I detested Rama. Let the two of them have each other, I grumbled, as I crawled back onto the bed and fell asleep holding Athena.

The next day was awful. He refused to let me go home. I must tell you that I was not ready but I could not stand to have him in authority over me. I concluded that I did not want to see him ever again as well. For what point did he keep me, for the point of devastating me?

I felt like I was living in a movie. Well at least I had my beautiful son and Athena. I realized that people my whole life had been affected by me. I did not even have to say anything and they reacted. I never saw to what degree. I was just trying to do what I was supposed to do. The one time I refused to listen to my soul, I got hit and I knew that it was Soulmate related. A lot of good that did. I thought that I was at the bottom. Boy did I have a ways to fall.

I managed to get a nurse to help me take a shower but the ordeal was too much. I nearly blacked out and it was very traumatic. My body would not cooperate. My memory was impaired and my headache was severe. I was determined to leave and asked the nurse not to say anything that would stop me from going. Finally, Chris marched in.

"I am ready to go," I demanded.

"Not today," he said. "Oh really? Why not?" I demanded further.

"Because it's too soon," He said to me.

"I got up and took a shower," I said very sarcastically.

"Yes and it damn near killed you," He responded. "Who said it almost killed me?" I asked.

"I said it and you continue to try and tell me that things are not as I'm saying they are," He said very pompous.

I burst into tears and he tried to remain in power but he lost it and melted down. "Okay, if you are better tomorrow I'll let you go but you will have to sign a release which will say that it is against my better judgment," he said, walking out.

Oh, against his better judgment, right, his better judgment. Mr. Know It All. I had to give him credit on knowing I had fallen out of bed and I was definitely not ready to leave the hospital. I really was not in any condition for much of anything but I did not want to see Chris again. The great, meeting with my Soulmate would never happen. What a disappointment. Everything was over for me. It just kept coming to my mind and I was unable to grasp anything with clarity.

The next day Chris arrives and tells me that he knows the very best doctor in the world and that he is going to send me to him. "He will straighten you out," he said very happily.

"I thought time was the best healer of a head injury," I stated.

"Yes it is but you seem to have problems elsewhere," he said in his usual sarcastic voice.

"Problems? How do you conclude this? Is it because I cannot stand to be in a hospital or around you? " I said, holding my own level of sarcasm.

"Look, I'm going to set you up so you can prepare to meet him. His name is Dr. Lenz, Dr. Frederick Lenz.

A cold chill ran through me. Where had I heard that name before? My memory could not recall it. I guess the look on my face alerted Chris.

"Have you heard the name before?" he asked.

"I don't know. It is familiar but I can't place it," I said, very sure that I had heard of it but it was beyond me to remember from where.

"He's very well known," Chris stated.

"Yes but I don't go to doctors," I said back to him.

"Perhaps I am opening a whole new door for you," he said, very elated.

"A new door for me? I think not, I don't go to doctors," I said, trying to make it very clear to him.

"Well, you will go to Dr. Lenz," he concluded.

Can you believe this? I will go to Dr. Lenz. Who in the world was Dr. Lenz? He had to be a neurologist, after all, I had a head injury. I put myself together waiting for Lois's daughter, Joan to pick me up. When she got to the hospital, she and Chris talked. He told her that we needed to get me started on a tape he was holding in his hand. I thought to myself it is one of those self-help tapes and I spoke out saying I did not need it.

Chris said, "You can't see Dr. Lenz unless you listen to this first."

I did not respond as I immediately saw this Dr. Lenz as thinking that he was so important, that you couldn't get an appointment until initiation. What a nut he must be. Chris just glowed every time he spoke his name. Of course, with blurry vision I could not read the tape label but I took it right there at the hospital and Joan took me to one of Lois's apartments to stay. I lay down and threw the tape on the floor. My head was hurting so badly but Chris had not given me anything for the pain. How odd I thought. It was as if I was deliberately kept in pain. I called the office and asked him why I did not get any help with the pain and bad headaches.

Out of the dead blue Chris says, "Heal yourself. You are so far above everyone else. Heal yourself," and he hung up.

I could not believe it. What in the world was he talking about? I was left holding the phone completely baffled as to what I had just heard. I then called back. When he answered the phone I demanded to know what in the world he was talking about. He said that he knew that I had not listened to the tape and he would have nothing further to do with me until I did. He instructed me to fill the bathtub with warm water, get in and listen to the tape. He then hung up. I could not understand why I had to listen to this while in a bathtub. Perhaps the warm water might do me some good and Chris was so demanding that I did what he said. It was odd as I turned on the tape because it was Chris's voice, so I stopped the tape and tried to relax in the water. I called him again and waited for his call back. I tried the tape again but it did not seem to want to play. When Chris called back, I asked him why he had given me a tape of him. He told me it was not his voice that it was Dr. Lenz. I could not help but hear exact voice similarities and he said that he had studied with Dr. Lenz for so long that he sounded so much like him. It was weird all right and it did not feel good, any of this. What kind of doctor passes out tapes before you can get a referral to them?

I warmed the bath water again and this time instead of fast forwarding past this music, I decided to do what Chris had asked. I got so relaxed I nearly drifted off once again, almost forgetting about the tape. So I turned it on and closed my eyes. There was music and then the voice, "This is Zen Master Rama." I went ballistic when I heard that and tried frantically to get out of the water but Rama was there all over me forcing me to stay where I was. I started to fight the energy field he had put around me. The tape was the initiation tape to abduct your soul. I could not believe it and my fight pushed him to the limit and he tried to drown me.

"You will surrender. You will listen to this," he kept saying again and again. I was gasping for air and choking on water. His violence was awful and he kept saying do what I say or die. I fought and fought. I knew what this tape did to people but I was losing ground as my head was hurting beyond anything I had ever felt. He was drowning me and I could not get up. The tape continued in the background as I battled his grip. I was using every last ounce of energy but I was losing the battle. He had set the trap that he was so sure I would fall into and now he had me.

"Go ahead and fight. I never lose," he yelled at me.

Oh God Force I called. Quick, I have to call the Force. I was turning blue and I knew he would win. As I called out to the God

Force, suddenly I came bursting through the water gasping for air. Rama backed off and fled. My front door was wide open. I was shaking so badly. I could not calm down. Oh God Force, help me. Chris was one of Rama's students. I could not believe the connection. He was one of those doctors who practiced cult teachings on his patients. It went back to years ago when I told you about it, doctors like these. The pieces were all coming together and I was left realizing that Rama was coming back for something far greater.

CHAPTER THIRTEEN

I could not sleep after Rama's attack. I knew that he would be coming back. Oh how I wanted to be free of him. Did it matter about Chris, no, not in the least. Why should Chris matter after what he had done to me. I had managed to outmaneuver all of Rama's tricks and here Chris just hands me over to him and does it with a sarcasm like he is at the top and I'm nothing. How long had I battled Rama? Years and everything was completely blown up in a few short minutes. I could have said that Chris was brainwashed but he did not quite fit the normal picture. He got off on what he did. He empowered the brainwashing as it satisfied his soul and he turned it around to try to brainwash me, knowing full well what he was doing. He had this nonchalant attitude of superiority unlike anything I had ever seen. He displayed how perfect he was in his ego and put me down.

I had not just been disobedient to the doctor's orders, I had now been completely abducted by Rama. Rama was so angry because I had only heard his voice for a few seconds on the tape but in his mind it was a tease to him. The initiation had been started and needed it to be completed.

Oh how everything had changed in only a moment's notice. I had no life. Chris had just pulled it from me. He took the breath right out of me and there was no way out. The head injury made it so difficult and impossible to get clarity. I was more than injured. I was now wide open and vulnerable beyond comprehension. Oh God Force, how was I going to get out? There was no way out, my delivery to Rama had been signed and sealed.

That night, on the same day he tried to drown me, Rama came back. Of course, he had to work fast. I might just be able to get a little rest and that would make me stronger. I was on my bed drifting off when the exhaustion just hit me all at once and I fell into a deep sleep.

"Deborah wake up," Rama said. I opened my eyes to his evil. He put his hand over my mouth so I could not scream.

"What you did today was very bad. You must be punished severely," he said with anticipation of receiving my soul.

"Never!" I yelled.

"Never say never. I shall make you eat your words," he said laughing.

I pulled away and said, "And I shall make you see the face of the God Force."

He drew himself up like I was some virgin that was worth the savoring and backed off a bit. "In time you will see and take me to you," he said with a glitter in his eyes.

"You don't get it do you. I will never take you anywhere except to the God Force," I said.

"We will see about that," he said hitting me and throwing me up against the wall as he departed.

I thought about calling Chris and decided against it. If I went against his master he would only tell him. Chris was very happy that Rama had connected with me. He had no idea that I already knew him. I called an attorney but in order to get some money out of this accident I had to stay with the original attending physician. Did that mean I would have to see more of Chris? Yes and I had to keep the appointments coming. I kept saying no, but the attorney said that doctors that leave in the middle of things often threaten the case. Out of all of the time in my life, this was more traumatic than anything I had ever experienced.

Athena was right, all was not as it appeared, it was worse. Chris was destroying my life, my ability to help people, my mission. He blew everything off, as if I had asked for it. It was one of those twisted Zen principles, all things come to you that you ask for. Like I had asked for Rama? It was all worse than a movie. No one could believe what Rama was getting away with. Those that tried to intervene were hit as well. He kept coming back and within a week he had worked me over so badly that he almost broke me. Although he did not hit my head, he did pound me in the stomach again and again. He said I had a chakra there that controlled my will power. After pounding me out, he would part my hair and rub my head trying to show me how nice it could be if only I would surrender. I kept saying never but he insisted that the day would come that I would join him. Do you know how creepy all of this was? He was so Dark my skin crawled.

I do not believe in free will because I see the cost of all things. I do believe that depending on how strong we are in the Dark or Light, determines the will to stay there and how strongly we put forth that energy. We do the journey, no matter what. There are only two choices, do it in Light or do it in Dark. Your mind only tells you that you are making choices and you fall for this one big time. How can you possibly cope with choices when you can barely stand on your own two feet. Thank the God Force for looking out for all of us.

This was hard to see where I was concerned though. The set up was more than even I could ever have imagined. Was I set up, of course, it was very apparent. The one time I tried not to listen to my soul, I got it big time. I never thought in a million years that my own Soulmate would not be there to help with such Darkness.

Oh God Force, take me from all of this, I pleaded silently. You cannot imagine how this one event affected everything. It devastated thousands of people. It rewrote history and unless it could be corrected, it would continue to destroy forever. Such waves of sadness hit me. Everything I had ever done was now all for nothing. What was even more devastating, was Chris and his evil attitude. He certainly came across so nice in the public but oh, did he switch to his true self when few were looking. Rama wanted me so vulnerable and this accident put me right where he needed me to be. Did Chris do the medical care? No, he used Rama's cult teaching on me. The most dangerous thing he could have done, he did to me. The connections were too much. Chris could have kept everything about me to himself if he had been following his medical ethics. My guard kept going down as I could not get past what Chris had done. I would no longer be able to rescue anyone. How could I ever get back on my feet? You do not get out of Rama's hold, you just buy time for yourself. The question was, how much time was I paying for and just what was the price?

I knew that the sexual thing was going to eventually surface. His theory was, the greater the will, the stronger the orgasm, the more power he got. Talk about sick, it could not get any Darker. What was I going to do? I decided to talk to Lois and Joan about him. Another shock to hit me. They had hundreds of his tapes and plenty of five by seven glossies. They not only knew him, they knew him well.

"Chris comes in here all of the time to have Rama's tapes copied," Lois said. Picture the expression on my face because I cannot. Picture the size of my headache. I should have done a great deal of denial right then and there but I'm also sure I would have received another big impact. I would never love this man. He had such a controlled environment. Throw in a little Zen and you come up with, you are, therefore you are not, zazen. In a moment's notice he would change the program and pity on those that didn't get it. He made sure that no one ever got it, except for me, who continued to baffle him. Rama and I had played this before in other lifetimes. The ignorance of people kept him in business.

There is a way to see the Dark that you cannot see but it continues to be hopeless because most cannot even see the Dark you can see. It was clear that I was in for the battle of the millenniums. Everyone kept saying I could do it but what was it I was supposed to do? Do you know how disgusting a man is who is obsessed with orgasms? It is equivalent to an assembly line in some factory. The more he could twist their minds the better. He got off on setting up the females and then slamming them when they were too stupid to play his game. As I said, he made the games and rules. No one else could understand it but I could. You were marked once he acknowledged you. He would walk right by someone or just think about them and they were marked. I, on the other hand, was a big problem for him. He knew that he would never have me totally, no matter what. I would die before I would ever let him take my soul.

Here I was with a head injury. The one tape in the whole entire world that Rama used to take souls, Chris gives me, knowing that that is what it would do and he had no regard for me what so ever. What did I tell you about doctors like this? I never did go into details about attorneys but I will. There was nothing I could do about these people calling me from all over but I still had my soul energies and some very strong ones who were not going to put up with Rama. Nighttime was his favorite time, especially with me. He stayed with me for hours, night upon night. It was always the same ritual. It was only a short time after the accident that he had pounded me so hard that I did not bounce back to battle him and he left quite sure he would be picking up my pieces the next day. I just came completely apart. Everything came apart and I became hysterical.

"Deborah?" a voice said. I opened my eyes trying to dry them. Always someone calling my name.

"Who is it?" I asked.

"Look at me. You will recognize me," a deep and gentle voice spoke.

"Jesus, my brother Jesus? The God Force had heard me," I said trying to come together, "I need help Jesus. I cannot take it. He is killing me," I cried.

"We all know what he is trying to do. He is very dangerous and he will try to trick you. We are all there watching out for you, my sister, Deborah. Never believe that you are alone. We are next to you so strongly that all you have to do is call out," Jesus said with that gentle voice I had grown to know so well.

"Doesn't he know that all of you are there?" I asked.

"Deborah, he knows only that some great power surrounds you. He craves to have you. He also feels that if he gets you he will also get all of the power," Jesus said.

"Why me? He is not my Soulmate. He's not anything to me," I told Jesus. Then like all the rest, Jesus would not respond. It was in this silence I knew that they were all keeping something from me. It had to be big and very dangerous. Why wouldn't anyone tell me?

It was at this time, Jimmy called me very concerned. He said that he could not get me off his mind and he felt like something was wrong. I saw his call as a way to get out of this Rama thing so I tried to reconnect. I should have known that would be impossible. Rama fried him big time, so much so that Jimmy never reconnected again. Rama was obsessed with the sexual thoughts and there was no way that he was going to allow a potential contact from someone who was as sensual as Jimmy. Everyone was calling me, picking up great danger with my life.

Do not even try to tell me that none of you has the ability to tune in. All of you have it but continue to deny it. Try getting very close to someone and telling me that you cannot tune in on them. You know that you can. Of course, you denying types will say that you sort of have a feeling or sense. Wake up and be enlightened.

I had to go to my appointments with Chris. It was worse each time. He had to touch me and I cringed just like when Rama touched me. And with Chris, there was always the sarcasm. He wanted me to say how great Rama was. Both of them repulsed me. He was so identical to Rama that if I closed my eyes I could not tell the difference. My headaches were so bad that I had to lie down most of the day. I had dizzy spells too. Chris always power tripped me with every appointment. He was obsessed to make me see life through his eyes, which of course meant, Rama's eyes.

It came as a sort of rapture and then quickly changed. Yes it was Rama concluding his own orgasm that he was trying to send to me. I was repulsed by his vulgarity. He tried to project images in my mind of the vivid details of his act. He knew that it would not be well received but he kept it up day after day. There was nowhere to go. He found me no matter where I went. There was not one situation that he did not know about. It was an invasion of privacy at all levels.

I released him constantly to the God Force. I needed my Soulmate so in this situation. It didn't mean that he wasn't there on some level but oh I needed him next to me. It continued to conclude that Rama was my Soulmate instead of Chris. I must say the head injury made everything harder but there was one thing that separated Chris from Rama. Rama was insanely jealous of this energy he thought was between Chris and me. There was a strong chemistry between us that Rama of course interpreted as sexual. He did not want me to be involved with any man and he certainly did not want me sharing my bed. Who marched in and anointed him god?

Every time I had to see Chris he'd demand that I look into his eyes and demand that I turn my life over to Rama. Again, I'd like to say perhaps he was brainwashed but he knew exactly what he was doing. Chris would toy with me and tease me knowing I was in pain. He wanted me to perform in his office and he screamed at a nurse one day for walking in on us. He was so mad he forbad her right in front of me to ever open the door again. He was in control and then out of control. I decided to get another doctor against my attorney's wishes and predictably, he quickly dropped me. I was forced to go back to Chris. Here is Chris telling me how great Rama was while his precious Rama was pounding me out at night and trying to seduce me.

Some of my students started to see major changes in me and some began to flip out. "He is killing you Deborah," Michele said. She was right and the more Chris came at me the more Rama came down on me. I knew that I could not break or he'd destroy me. He knew that I was repulsed by him sexually as well and that was the one thing that made him crazy more than anything else. He tried everything to make me love him but I could not. All I kept doing was releasing him to the White Light of the God Force. I knew all of it was the mission but still he would stay in the Force less than one second and be twice as mad for me sending him there when he came back out.

Although Athena was with me, great concern came one night when Rama showed up and she was there. He went ballistic over her being with me and he started pounding me again. I yelled to Athena to help me but the look on her face was terrifying.

"Mother, do something!" I cried.

"I cannot, Daughter," she said very sadly.

"What do you mean you cannot?" I yelled.

"I cannot defend you against him," she said very nervous.

"Why are you saying this, Mother? It is as if you are on his side. What is this? Are you connected to him?" I insisted on knowing.

Just then Rama yelled at her, "Get out of here at once woman. I command you. Remove yourself or else!"

"Or else what?" I said holding my tone of voice as he had.

He lifted his hand to hit her and Athena stepped back. Now Athena never stepped back to anyone, even Zeus. I was nearly lost for words.

"Mother, you act as if he is your son," I stated. That was it. As soon as the words left my mouth the truth was out. This was an awful blow to me. I felt as if she had been informing him all along. Rama looked at me and stormed out. Athena held her head down in shame.

"Mother, how could you keep such a thing from me? I am broken in my heart and my love for you is shattered. I want you to leave me forever and never come back," I said weeping.

"Daughter, listen to me," she pleaded.

"For what, Mother, for excuses? Or Deborah couldn't handle it?" I said coldly to her. I was numb and speechless from that point on.

"I will leave, Daughter but I will be close by if you need me," she said so sad and bewildered. Here Athena told me she would be there for years. Now what was I to do?

I needed to sleep. I could not cope. Chris was intolerant of my lack of progress with Rama so I decided to let him know what his star mentor was doing to me. I knew I would be disbelieved but shocked?

"Rama says we cannot marry unless you think the same as I do," he said quite upset.

"Marry?" I responded thinking that I must have been out to lunch when this so-called relationship started. I was totally unaware of his thinking about this. Could I ever stop being floored?

"Chris, where does this idea of marriage come from?" I asked, waiting for something good like a logical response.

"Why Rama of course," he said as if he thought I would know this.

"So Rama determines who belongs in what relationship?" I asked him.

"Why of course. He determines everything," he said.

"Do you actually believe this?" I asked him.

"Somewhat." He replied.

I could see my affect on him because he went from a definite to a somewhat. Then he got angry at me and blamed me for trying to make him doubt Rama. Once again I got the brunt of it all. I knew Rama did not want Chris, of all people, with me. He became so hostile if the name even came up. He had apparently been scripting Chris about being with me. It was all unreal. What I refused to tell Rama, which by the way was nearly everything, he just turned around and got it from Chris. Rama was not all that capable where I was concerned. Without even trying I was a major pull on Chris and I needed to stay clear of him. I felt terrible about Athena and sending her away but I could no longer trust her. I felt so betrayed by her. My students were slipping away, including the ones that had been there for a long time. I was not able to teach in such pain and our get-togethers were mainly to stay in touch.

Rob was a beautiful soul energy that I loved dearly. My heart smiled when he came by. I totally adored him and we had talked often about our Atlantis a past life. I could not get enough of his conversation. It truly was a relationship of kindred souls. Oh how I loved him and so looked forward to each visit. He hated Rama. All did, except the robots Rama was able to brain delete. All of my students recognized who he was. In my whole life, Rob was one of the ones I loved the most and could never forget.

Then there was Rene who was one of those rare and special kind of people. She had a heart and soul bonded so to the God Force. She desired her Soulmate so much and had waited so long to find him. I loved her so and would never forget her.

I could go on and on about all of the others because the bonding with these soul energies was so connected. Of course Rama couldn't stand it and threatened to get rid of them all. I had more problems with Chris coming on to me one minute and trying to deep freeze me the next.

There was one thing Rama knew never to mess around with and that was my son. There seemed to be a mutual understanding in this area. He did not cross that line. He was elated that Athena was gone. He would often hit me and then say, "Let's see how that God of yours takes care of you now."

Always the tests, morning, noon and night. The level of detesting him grew and just when I thought that I could detest him no more, he would do something else to increase it. You do not feel well with this kind of evil around. It gets on your nerves and irritates everything. I was always tired because he kept bothering me and I could not get enough sleep. He could go for hours without any. He expected everyone else to copy this regiment. It was more than insane. Those who could not keep up, got fried. Go two steps forward and be knocked ten back.

For the potential female next in line to sleep with him, there was a special initiation. I did tell you some of it but the graphic parts are so beyond me to say, I just can't go into such details and still be able to go on. I suppose in time, perhaps I will be able to tell you more. Now you may be thinking why didn't I go to the police. I did but as the story goes, without a witness there was nothing they could do. I went several times and actually managed to block that from him for a while. When he found out, he took it out on one of my students, nearly killing her and her two sons in a car accident. They were not hurt very badly but Rama's point was made. Of course he took credit for it. The lady he had tried to eliminate saw the word Rama written on the stop sign. It was her warning from him to never go near me again and she did not.

Rama found everyone's deepest fear and brought it forward. Get out of line and get fried. He had been working me over for this initiation thing for sex but I was not budging. I was able to focus too good and so he began major programs of distraction. He taught a twisted version of Zen which was not Zen but he tried it on me. He had people chanting at me and watching me. Nothing worked and so he would become angrier.

I had a lot of students and so one by one he began the process of elimination. Whatever their greatest fear was, he set it up. I have to tell you my students were warriors because most did not surrender quickly or easily. He would grab them and demand to know what was it I was teaching them that they should dare to come up against him. He pounded them out too for what he called their smart mouths.

"Oh she's good," he would rant and rave.

"She's the best," they would say and he would hit them again.

"Where are these things written? What book?" he would demand.

"They are in no book. She has them inside her," the students would say.

Rama could not get past this trickery. "Oh you're clever," he would say again and again to me.

"If you say so," I would answer back. He could not really get me to react as I knew that was what he wanted. "You're just a primitive," I would conclude.

"Oh we'll see how primitive I am," he would state in that pompous voice.

For me, I had no fears, so whatever he tried on others did not work on me. My students were not as strong as I was and they did not have the systems I had either. In the end, one by one they started to break away, usually fleeing for their lives. You cannot say that Rama wasn't good. Where he was concerned there was no mission impossible. He promised to find my weakness and promised that the day would come when he would win. Chris was his sounding board and he definitely used him. Chris on the other hand loved all of the attention. He was even more superior than before he had met me. Notice how he concluded that I must have asked to meet him on some level but never him asking to meet me. Their pms prevents them from being able to admit this.

You may ask why didn't the God Force intervene. It did intervene as much as possible. I kept hearing, show him nothing but love. He was looking for my weakness when in actuality he had told me what his was by his obsession with me.

Where was the Light in this man? He obviously felt that he was beyond it. He kept looking for the Dark in me and that was definitely beyond me. It was more and more Soulmate related than I even wanted to look at. Where was I supposed to go with all of this? The only place I have ever known was to the God Force. As the students fled in great fear of Rama every time he got someone else, my soul energies became stronger. Soul energies are used to laying down their lives for you in other lifetimes.

Oh, he laughed at me and power tripped me but he could not make me leave the Light. He was exerting more energy on me than he had ever used on anyone. I would not budge. How could I? I had been raised by the Angels to do just that, stay fixed in the God Force.

It became more and more ridiculous with Chris. Rama noticed this more and more too. He began to use things with Chris to try to annoy me. I must admit that Chris was a very big distraction. He would call me at my apartment many times each day. Half of the time he would not know what to say. It was awkward and very strange. It was unreal the way he behaved. During one of my appointments, Chris told me that I was going to make him lose his medical license. I looked at him and once again, I was wondering where in the world this was coming from. He went on and on about how it would be my fault if he did. What in the world did I have to do with Chris and his medical license? He kept saying that I would drive him to do things that would get him in trouble. He was already doing things that were unprofessional. I knew that Rama was filling his mind with these things.

I could not even have this injury and get any peace. I was getting more annoyed with Chris and unable to cope. I decided to cut back on my appointments and stay clear of him. When I canceled my appointment, Chris called me demanding to know why I had done this. I told him I did not need as many appointments. He told me that Rama insisted that I see him. I could not believe it. Then he got good and mad at me. Once again, I would have liked to have said he was brainwashed but he was too deliberate in his behaviors. He had too many controlling situations and knew exactly what he was doing. I would go over that same old sentence to him, stop saying Rama's the greatest.

"You have no idea what he is really like." He would always reply. "You just have to convert over to him. Once you do this he will tell you what to do and how to live."

All I kept thinking to myself was how Chris had just turned me over to Rama after I had fought for years. Chris enjoyed power tripping me. He did this same ritual to hundreds of patients that then affected thousands of lives. He was recruiting for Rama. One of the interesting things about Chris was that he could not stand being a doctor. He hated it when people called him this. He would say to me how much he could not stand his patients and their constant complaining. "These people have all manifested their sicknesses. They have asked for it and I have to deal with their chronic complaining. I hate it. I absolutely hate it," he would yell out. What a horrible man, a Dark man without an ounce of love in him. I doubt he ever loved in his life. It certainly was not love that Rama got from him. I could feel his bitterness.

I thought at moments his turning me over to Rama could end up with it not being all for nothing. I knew that there were things that I had not experienced sexually. What I would like to say is passionately but it is easier to understand if I put it in the way Rama was presenting it. I knew he was going to eventually get around to these things. It is something a woman just knows. I would never consent, never. I looked at it and realized too, that I was outnumbered, outmaneuvered. There is always that one thing that pushes you over the edge. He had to own me, conquer me, and take my soul. Yes indeed, it was looking as though Rama was playing Soulmate more and more. It seemed as though he put Chris in the path to make me believe that it was him instead. Having a head injury made nothing easy. There were constant floods of emotional trauma between Chris and me. There was this intense sexual pulling between us, so much so we were exchanging visual acts in each other's minds constantly. Then there was the touch at the office. We would battle and then in a moment's notice we could bed and breakfast each other. The man was no fool. He knew exactly what he was doing. Rama was constantly on the rampage carrying on about everything Chris and I did.

I kept thinking that when the headaches ended and I got better I'd be able to get away from all of this. I was not a pushover. No one just slammed me around. My vision slowly came back. The months continued to go by and the boys just kept it up. The number of students dwindled down to near nothing. Only my soul energies remained by my side. If a student missed me and called, Rama went after them. How did Rama know? It is called tuning in, the same way I could tune in. Remember what I said about what you cannot see? Rama always knew, always, just like I did. What was the ultimate challenge was trying to read each other. With Chris, I could always expect the same old negative attitude. With Rama, everything was always a surprise. They were both Dark but they both wanted me. I knew that I would die before I would ever surrender to either one. I did not do the human race level, man's level. I did not understand it and had no reason to because it was way too low, filled with traps, violence, and great levels of Darkness.

Athena had mothered Rama in another time. Chris and Rama were on many levels similar to twins. I was too brilliant to be fooled. My life had little challenge to start with and now there was an overdose of it. Both of them knew I would have fried them if I had not had the accident and become impaired by the swelling and pain and Rama's treatment of me.

Oh Athena, how I missed her but what could she base the reason for betrayal on? Whose side was she on? A mother can't divide between her children so the answer was probably both of our sides. I know it was as if she was stuck in an Olympian lifetime but whatever life, the problems needed to be re-enacted. I could not trust it any more. I knew that she was close by and watching because I could feel it.

Angel of Silk was still there but our conversations had pretty much ended. I knew that the Angels were on guard for the next step whatever that might be. I really did not want to know. What were they expecting? No thank you, I never thought that it would go like this. I sat by myself and just poured it all out to the God Force. Look what happened from meeting Chris. The violator, the evil, evil man he was. What hurt was how he just nonchalantly tucked it under the carpet because he did not want to hear it. I was, after all, nothing.

I spent so much time with the God Force trying to understand what was going on. I knew that whatever was being kept from me had to be so big that they were afraid I would not do it if I found out. I trusted that I was being well looked after even though it did not appear that way.

I recalled Athena telling me that I needed to convince Rama that I was his Soulmate. Who was there to convince me that I was not? Why did she use the word convince? It almost seemed as though she was deliberately turning it around on me. Rama and I were total opposites one hundred percent. The God Force was slowly preparing me for something and it was definitely about the two of us. Even Jesus did not respond when I questioned all of this. He must have known it would have been more than I could deal with if I knew.

All of my soul energies and I got together trying to figure out a way to fry Rama. Now I would have normally intervened but soul energies see things differently. Perhaps they are blindly optimistic, Vikings from the past or just plain warriors who will not quit. We were not just going to let him get away with it all without a battle.

So we started to put a plan together. One of the things Rama forbid me to do was eat meat. He said that it would ground me and he warned me that if I was caught eating it he would hurt me badly. What else was new? So I started eating meat. If you have ever had a large steak dinner, you do feel full, heavy and sometimes sleepy.

Things had been so sad that we all decided to have a party. Rama could take a hike. We started to talk about the good old days before Rombo. Then, we feasted on hamburgers, steaks, chickens, and any and all heavy foods. We were laughing so hard and eating so much that it was all worth it, no matter what Rama did next. It was wonderful. We could not stop eating or laughing. It was as if we had so much bottled up inside that it just poured out of us. Oh how I loved these people. Oh how they loved me. Things were wonderful for that brief time. We had had so many lifetimes together. We were all grounded big time and laughing so loudly that we never heard the car pull into the driveway.

All of a sudden, intense energy started to hit me and I yelled that we all needed to turn out the lights and duck down. Someone was close by, I told everyone. It was so hard to calm down and stop laughing. Everyone had eaten so much that they were bulging through their seams. As they all started to duck down, their clothes were so tight that the laughter turned into horrible moans. I tried to be serious but I was as contagious as the rest between the groans and the laughter.

Someone looked out the window and saw a shadow of a man standing there. Then we all started whispering that it was probably Rama and we were all going to be fried. We all came to a halt when the door blew open. You could hear everyone's heart beating it was so quiet. I stepped forward and looked at the shadow. Whoever it was, stood still. By now we were all completely spooked. I stepped out and walked in this man's direction. Oh no, I said softly. I recognized the car. It was Chris and his blue Saab. I stopped and tiptoed back into the apartment. What was Chris doing in the driveway? He was scaring me something awful. Here we were expecting Rama and his wicked ways and it was Chris instead. It came to me that I had seen this before and that Chris was spying on me. He was such a sneak and I am sure I had been unaware of just how much he was sneaking around. I was livid because he had just wrecked our party. At least Rama would have had a grand entrance for all of us. Everyone waited until Chris left, which was about a half an hour later.

After everyone left, I sat down and started to piece things together. All of those strange phone calls and gifts that came from nowhere came to my mind. I kept wondering who was doing this. No! Chris would make phone calls but never give a gift to anyone or at least not to me. He was too selfish. Besides, I knew he was calling. There had been many things that did not make sense. From that point on I saw Chris many times in my driveway late at night just sitting in his car. I wondered how often he had been there before I ever noticed. I was now getting over one hundred phone calls a week, weird ones, hang ups, Chris talking, Rama talking. Rama did find out about our little party and he raged big time. He hated to not have total control over all situations. He went after all of us and all it did was bring us together again for another party.

The less I saw Chris, the more he pursued me. I was so tired of his negative and nasty ways. After months I finally quit going to him and I lost the case because of what Chris wrote about me. After I made these changes, Rama decided to change the program and set me up with Chris in a new way. He did not want me with Chris but he also saw things in me that for some reason only Chris was able to bring out. I cannot imagine why. There is so much I cannot write. It seemed as soon as I came even close to happiness, Rama was there to destroy it. He was so deep in misery but he loved to portray this altogether totally successful person. I knew that deep down inside Rama had never been loved. Oh, people bonded to themselves could give that artificial love but when I speak of love I mean the God Force Love. I had triggered so much that Rama was beginning to change.

Rama needed Chris in the picture in order to observe me. In reference to the accident, when Chris told the insurance agent that I was fine and could go back to work, he lied. He had no idea what I did for a living. Because of what he did, handing me over to Rama, it was impossible to be okay, to work or do anything. Did he care? No! For the rest of my life I would regret ever having met him.

He destroyed my students, my purpose, and the reason I existed. Sure I had the mission but that could have gone on with my still having control of my life. How was I to win these battles constantly with Rama? I knew on a soul level how dangerous he was years back that is why I made sure he never got a hold of me. Even if it was in the journey to meet up with him, I did not need an accident to do it. I also would have been better prepared to battle him. When it came to different degrees of evil, Chris did to me the Darkest violation. All that happened, day in and day out, was Rama. He was even in the shower, clothes drawers, and everywhere that you could imagine. It was horrible and he went beyond obsession. He moved in on my territory and stayed. Now the new plan with Chris was to send him things.

"You are out of your mind," I told him.

"You will do it," he said.

"Why? This is beyond insane. I don't care about Chris," I told him.

"But you see, Chris cares about you," he said.

"No he doesn't. Chris does not even care about himself. I will not do it. I won't play your sick games," I yelled at him.

"Oh you'll play. I can guarantee you that you'll play," he said smiling.

"What do you think you can do to me now?" I asked him.

"How about your friend Rob? How would you like to see him have his worst nightmare?" Rama said very confidently.

"Leave me alone and everyone else. We mean you no harm. We do not want to be involved or deal with you on any level. Why can't you leave me alone?" I pleaded with him.

"Oh Deborah you really don't get it. I am bored and have no challenges here. You have a spirit that just will not quit. You challenge me. You amuse me but most of all you must surrender to me," he said so sure of himself.

"Didn't you get it, low life, I will never surrender to you, never!" I yelled at him.

"Well, let's start with Rob then. If you refuse what I tell you to send Chris, Rob gets it," he concluded as he left.

Oh I loved Rob in a way you would love the best brother in the world. Rob was so sensitive and beautiful. He was especially triggered by Rama. It would not take much to put Rob over the edge. I knew Rama would do more than hurt him. Why, because I loved Rob so, and Rama hated anything that I loved. He had to destroy it. He wanted me to love him no matter what he did to me. It was always let's see how your God takes care of you now. Yes, Rama wanted my love with all of the conditions he made. His levels of jealousy grew month after month. Oh I battled him but in the end I knew that he would take Rob so I gave in and Rama gave me what he wanted Chris to get. I had no other choice. I cried my heart out but everywhere I turned everyone was terrified of this man. I thought about Athena and the Angel of Silk. I knew everyone was watching out for me and I hung on to them. Someday I would go back home to all of them. I thought about Zeus, nothing like a good lightning bolt to wake someone up. Good old Zeus, how about a lightning bolt for Rama? Perhaps we could work a deal?

CHAPTER FOURTEEN

It was gifts to Chris. That is what Rama had me doing. Lots of cards, love cards, sense of humor cards, get well cards and so on. Well, Rama was right about the get well cards. Chris was as sick as he was. I was wondering if the two of them had a thing for each other on some level. My mind kept trying to adjust to the sick thing Rama had me doing. At least Rob was all right and I needed him to be okay. He did not deserve what Rama was going to do to him if I had not cooperated. Rob, being that soul energy, had plenty of battle in him already but no one could out do Rama. The Family kept telling me that I could but it certainly did not look that way. I suppose I would have lost great hope if I did not know that the Family was there. It gave me a confidence Rama could not understand.

You see, there is the Light that you can see and the Light that you cannot see. The same techniques are used, just different sides. I was doing the same thing he was but I was doing it in the Light. I embraced people with a full volume of Love. My love for the human race came from the Light I saw in them, from their souls. Even if I did not see any Light, I knew it was within everyone. It was only a matter of time before it came to the surface, especially if they remained around me. Oh, what had I just come upon? Rama was around me almost constantly. I was not embracing him, no way. He was the only one I could not embrace. I heard the words come out of my mouth and I knew right, then and there, I would have to embrace him somehow, someday. Oh never, I just could not!

"He needs you to embrace him," I heard a voice say.

Great, who was this? Then with such a grand entrance, there stood Zeus. "Well, someone had to intervene," he said so stately.

192

"Oh great! The great lord and master himself. I suppose you've come to strike me too!" I said putting my hands on my hips.

"No. We have collided enough for one lifetime. It's just that you frustrate me so," he said, somewhat puzzled as to why.

"I am like my Mother. What else would you expect?" I said standing even straighter.

"Be that of your Mother, not of your Father?" Zeus asked.

"Since when are you laying claim to me? Haven't I been something you would have rather forgotten about?" I said sarcastically.

"Daughter, I have not been the best of fathers," he told me.

"Tell me of this Rama, Zeus. Tell me all you can as I am shielded so and the Force keeps things from me," I pleaded with him.

Now if anyone would talk I thought it would be Zeus. Something in me wanted to charm him into it. Good heavens, where had that come from? I could not even understand what charm was. He was so much like Rama or was Rama so much like him. Zeus would tell me just to make amends with me. There was a great pause and then nothing.

"Well, are you going to tell me, because I know that you know?" I said.

The look on his face was of great disappointment. "Divine Order holds itself above me," he answered. Well, that was a definite no. "However, I could give you some clues," he said looking like jolly old St. Nicholas with a Christmas present for me.

"Okay, that will do," I said smiling.

Zeus and I were really having a very good time. I really missed this big old entity. He put his hands around my forehead and projected the knowledge into my mind. "Even I have compassion for you where this man is concerned," he said trying to convince me that he was truly concerned.

"Oh come on Zeus! You could care less about me. I do not need your pity. Be gone with you. Stay clear of me," I yelled out. He just ignored me.

"It was a battle so long ago. So very, very long ago," he said. "Sit and listen to me, Deborah," he continued. I sat down not quite sure why but what was there to lose? I knew he would not hurt me this time,

I just knew it. There was something kind in his voice, something familiar to me from another time. I momentarily recalled being very small and sitting next to him in another time. He was telling me a story then as he was telling me one now.

"Oh, so very long ago in Olympus there was a great turn of events. I loved your Mother so greatly that it angered me the effect that she had on me. It was similar to you and this one that you battle," he said, but then stopped. "Daughter, sit next to me. I will not conclude danger your way," as he went on with the story. I slowly nudged over to him, not really sure why but I just did it. It was really okay for the first time in a very long time. "Daughter, search your soul for this story, you know it so well. Remember the horses?" he asked me.

"I kind of remember. You mean your fleet of golden horses?" I asked.

"Yes! Oh how I loved them so and how they danced and raced," he went on.

I became so relaxed almost instantly because Zeus and I had one thing in common now. Our love for horses connected us. "Do go on Zeus," I said.

"There were many battles in Olympus way back then and I was so mesmerized by your Mother. She had such a hypnotic effect on me. I often lost much control because of it. I would anger myself and storm from her but I would always come back quite humbled," he said.

"You, humbled?" I chuckled.

"Oh, you may not believe it but the right woman owns the man without even knowing it. Her gracious turns and beautiful gowns enchanted me so. You cannot imagine how much she was worth waiting for. Oh she had such a smile and oh the scorn. When she angered, it made me smile. That would anger her further. That would make me love her further. It is much like this one that battles you," he said.

"Zeus, nothing wonderful like you're speaking of could ever happen with this one," I said quite sure of myself.

"Oh but you do not see what comes next," he continued. "You must understand that a man does not show so much anger unless he feels a great deal for a woman. It is your effect on him, like your Mother's effect on me."

"Do you still have that for her?" I asked.

"I shall love her more than eternity but I lost her love because of Darkness. I fell Daughter, so far did I fall. Like this one who pursues you," he stated.

"This one who pursues me doesn't want me. He wants to bed women left and right," I told him.

"No! He only wants you and just does these other things," Zeus said.

"I cannot believe this because he strikes me," I said.

"Daughter, he is angry as I was with your Mother," he told me.

"Did you ever strike Athena?" I asked him.

"No, but most close did I come," he said. "I was driven with madness over her. I am still driven with madness over her. She parades herself around in such elegance. She fires my very soul," he said.

"You know I can't believe, that out of everyone, you of all entities are here sitting next to me. Why do you dislike me so much?" I asked him.

"You so remind me of your Mother when she was of fewer years. It brought up many battles with Athena as well. Your Mother always won. I had to surrender to her beauty in her most angered states," he said smiling.

"This is incredible. You really do love her. I am so glad that you have told me this. Tell me, how do you feel about this one who pursues me," I asked him.

"There is much Darkness, more than you see. He is like me Daughter, very temperamental," Zeus said.

"Promise to tell me right now that which weighs heavily on my heart," I stated. "Is he, Zeus?"

"Yes Daughter, he is," Zeus said, knowing that I could not deal with hearing this answer. He then embraced me, which was very awkward. "I am an old fool. Can you tell?" he said laughing.

"Yes," I said, bursting into my own laughter.

"You are so beautiful, Daughter. So much your Mother but so strong in determination like me. You are a fighter as strong as if the blaze is right there in front of you," he said proudly.

Instead of getting clues from Zeus I got the lifetime of distress and players that were all here in this life. One big show from the team up above. Do you know without their constant sense of humor, I would have folded. It is the human body that has a problem coping with such intensity in missions. When a Dark Force field is put up around you, the body starts to crumble. Sure it takes plenty of Force fields from the Dark Force but it is like sitting in pollution, eventually you fold. You should know this by now but for you slower and more sleepy ones I need to repeat things. Right now you should be trying to visualize Zeus and you're probably right, he's monstrous in size and very much like the Greek figures done of him. If you have been reading along you are probably seeing Soulmate energies between Zeus and Athena. No, she was not his daughter. Once again the human race has no clarity. If this were the case, we would all be begotten from each other. What a tight Family. Can you imagine having Zeus for your Pops, especially on one of his rampages? As powerful as they are, is as temperamental as they are. To go on, Zeus told me of this one very bad lifetime. My skin had goose bumps all over. Goose bumps are really truth bumps, by the way.

Rama was horrible once again, but Chris was there too. Good old Chris, always hanging around somewhere. Of course drill sergeant Rama couldn't miss an opportunity to grab some soul. As Zeus went on to tell me, it was worse than you can imagine. Athena and Zeus did do that relationship thing and Rama was the first offspring in that lifetime. He was Dark in features like Athena but Zeus wanted a son that looked like him. Then thirteen years later I was born, fair in features like Zeus, and he was angry again. He wanted a daughter that looked like Athena. There was another boy born the same time I was, a twin who was weak and sickly, so Athena hid him away with a nursing woman. My twin brother was Chris. Zeus would have thrown him to the serpents because here was the second son born with Athena's features again but sickly. Sickness was a sign of a defect and defects were not allowed in Olympus. If you could not manifest to the full stature of what you were, then be gone with you. Zeus had to have a superior race.

Each one of us had our own unique powers yet I doubt that Chris ever really found his. So no one knew of my twin brother. Zeus had decided to give the key to Olympus to his only true acknowledged children. Any child from Athena was the keeper of his domain. Only three children were ever born to her and Zeus.

As my brother was hidden I grew until the age of four when Rama challenged Zeus one day. They always battled and caused a great disturbance but Rama was impatient to obtain Olympus. Zeus saw the Dark in him and the evil he would cast upon all of Olympus. The battle was great on this day as Rama cornered Zeus. They played an Olympian game in which Zeus said the winner would get all but when Rama won Zeus changed his mind. Now Athena was holding onto me in front of all of this and Rama stormed out past us swearing to return for what was rightfully his. The years went by with some peace and then when I was twelve Rama came back for war. Zeus was away that day but Athena stood firm in protection of me.

"Mother, to a game I shall challenge you," he said.

Athena had never lost at archery and everyone knew this. "What do you want," she asked him.

"If I win, I will take my sister," he said smiling.

"Mother, you will never lose. Do it!" I pleaded.

Athena responded by saying, "If I win, will you go and leave us in peace?"

"Oh I will leave, Mother. Do not concern further for me," he promised.

They took their bows and prepared for the challenge. It was easy. Athena gathered her bow and arrows. Rama went first hitting the target. Then Athena stepped forward. Just as she released her arrow, Rama yelled, "Mother, let's invite my brother to play." Athena flinched and missed.

"No," I screamed as Rama raced at me, picked me up and ran off. Athena fell to her knees screaming so loud it woke the universes.

"Let me go, brother," I yelled but he squeezed me tighter hurting me so.

Zeus was telling this story so vividly that I forgot myself and spoke, "Father? Oh how it must have pained you to hear Athena." He looked long and deep into my eyes and tears fell from his eyes.

"I shall never forget that sound," he said.

We all play so many roles when we come back lifetime after lifetime. What may have been your uncle may very well be your brother in this life. This can help explain why you have a strong connection or a strong dislike without reason where certain people are concerned. Very evolved entities do not analyze good or bad. They already know what is going on. The human race is so hung up on the age that someone is. You place expectations on this as well. If someone can commit a crime at thirty, they can do it at ten. Man and his stupid stupidity designed a system to keep his pms priority, always laying claim that all is for the good of the woman, child, or human race. Don't be fooled. He is doing what he is doing to power trip the planet. If you cannot deal with this, then put it down. Chances are your pms has reached its max anyway. It is never going to be all right until the female reclaims her power. The male and female must find the balance. Nothing is going to work with such discrepancies between the two. Can't you see the large spell that the planet is under? You have pounded yourself into the ground trying to find the answers and justify it by claiming that you must have needed the challenge. I look at you and say, wake up!

Zeus continued on with this story. "Rama took you to his coliseum, a place where he did much magic and set all kinds of traps. The goal was to see how many idiots would collect within these confines. He professed to be a great wizard. He was good at this kind of thing. Of course he was good, he had been doing this for a very long time. Zeus went on to say, "Oh Daughter, what he did to you then is no longer among my memories as it so brought shame upon all of us that I could not keep such Dark amongst my thoughts."

I looked at him and our memories met and I knew that Rama had violated me beyond endurance. The same feeling in this lifetime came upon me and I stood naked in my thoughts. He had shamed me and destroyed my innocence. He had marked me for many lifetimes.

I turned from Zeus for as much as he had erased these memories my mere presence had brought them forward once again.

"Daughter I will help you battle him in this life. He is no longer my son. He will never inherit Olympus," Zeus said grabbing me.

I fell into his strong arms and cried like never before. "I'm marked Father forever. I will never be free. Oh Father I'll never be free," I said trembling.

"Daughter I will not tell you that which won't be. He has been cast out from everywhere. You are our only hope," he said so kind to me.

"Hope for what?" I asked as if I thought there was really any hope.

"Hope to get him back to the Light," Zeus said holding me so tightly.

"Father you are just like all of the rest," I told him.

"Daughter you must love him. Love is the only way back. I should know. Trust this old fool, love this old fool," he said as tears fell from both of our eyes.

"Do you know how much I have missed you?" I said flooding his heart with the much needed love he so craved.

I don't know who cried the most that day. I don't know who felt the most but a part of me was able to go forward which had been missing. You must understand how much I fought to be free of this tangled mess. As much as I denied all of this, the Truth surpassed in whatever form it presented itself. Everywhere I turned it was there, in my face, waiting to be taken on.

This was all ridiculous, this card sending to Chris, the notes, letters, cards, and phone calls. Rama was obsessed to force a confrontation with Chris.

"He is the one, not me!" he would say storming all over the place.

"Get a life. He is the one? What?" I'd say back. What in this world was he talking about? Chris could not stand me. That was always very clear. I certainly could not stand Chris. Look at what he had done to me. It was doomed the minute Chris violated his medical license. Sure Rama had played Chris but Chris got off on his own pms. There was never anything naive about Chris. Chris even had the same sexual desires and sexual acts as Rama had in his mind. Some of the conversations I had had with Chris had been just that, always his eyes going to certain places on the body. You could see the mind working overtime. Did I want to deal with this? No, but did I have a choice?

Zeus had realized that I was a star in the universe struggling to shine on. I felt confident that he would come to my rescue if I called out. Both Zeus and Rama had denied each other but guess what, Zeus had to love Rama for his own Light to shine again. It would right the wrong with Athena as well. A mother has a very hard time denying her own offspring and Athena still had love in her for her son.

Oh how the Soulmate thing does not leave you once you know about it. Such illusions are thrown out in these relationships. Lives are destroyed unless the alignment is ready. The pulling can be so tremendous that you can lose your entire self to it. Knowing full well about all of this I was not about to lose myself over my own Soulmate. Rama was a charlatan. He had managed to trick everyone but he had met his match with me. He would never be able to trick me. Again and again he came upon me with great desires only to be emotionally slammed by my denial. Waves of Jimmy would come to me from time to time. Now that was bed and breakfast, not Rama. He had managed to destroy Jimmy completely. I cringed at the thought of Rama touching me. It would never be, it could not be. I would force myself to astroproject out and he would not be able to find me. He so disgusted me.

Chris was now going ballistic over this new attention from me. He did not know what to make of it and he got good and angry. I would have been angry too. Rama, though, was so excited and having a wonderful time gauging behaviors off of the both of us. This whole thing was so sick that I decided to tell Chris what Rama was doing. That was one big mistake. He defended Rama to eternity telling me that I was a liar. Oh Rama would never do something like that, he'd say again and again. When I explained to Chris how his evil had put Rama and I together he even denied that. How do you handle the great denial? You let it sit on the pity plate. Sooner or later the main course will be ready for the meal. Oh Rama did the main course just wonderfully. You cannot imagine how angry he got when Chris told him what I had said.

What raced through my mind was, who was he going to hurt because of this. Someone was definitely going to get it because that was Rama's style. He boasted about how he controlled the whole planet. I would watch how he would target an entire town, putting a Force field around it. Everyone would wake to a bad feeling, energy and mood. Yes the good old Dark that you cannot see. Of course, no one could explain their feelings but if there was even one familiar with Rama they would recognize it right away. He saw nothing wrong with this. In fact, he would laugh and mock everyone for being so stupid. No one really even had a running chance.

The one thing that definitely had a hold on him was Chris. He would drop everything if I even so much as thought the name. The hold that this had on Rama was incredible. He would rage if it interrupted something important but he was sharp and on it immediately. Of course, there was always the punishment, yet he was forcing me to activate things by all of these cards. That old saying, you are damned if you do, you are damned if you don't, had to have been started by Rama. The whole planet was doomed by someone this powerful.

I realized that I needed to kick in my sense of humor, so it was time for another one of our grounding parties. It was so great when everyone got together. We would always pick up right where we had left off. Oh could we laugh and eat. We could also talk about any lifetime we wanted to and always the connections would re-link. We all loved each other so much. People would bring their friends and the parties just grew. Chris would pull into the driveway and just observe. I knew that he was not observing me because Rama had told him to but because he wanted to.

We would pull our resources together to try and help each other at our parties. Rama was wreaking havoc on all of our lives. Roadblocks were put up all over in the direction of financial success. No one paid me for putting up with Rama and his Dark cruel ways. I was the pawn, the player, the taker for everyone's refusal to get into the Light. I took the blows left and right. My mere existence had to be eliminated safely leaving no witnesses. Rama knew one blow too many could do it but he wanted total control over me with the option to do me in if I could not be broken. Often I would sit so deep in thought over this whole thing that hours would go by with my losing track of time.

Zeus said I had to love Rama and so I kept releasing him to the Love and Light of the God Force. Somehow I felt that Zeus meant something a little more on the mortal level. No way, I would never be able to cope. Rama would brag about all of the females he had conquered hoping that I would respond to this. My empty stare would reaffirm once again my rejection and lack of jealousy he so tried to stir in me. I was not stuck in the human race so I was not doing jealousy now or ever. I never realized then how bad it would become as Rama was put to his full tolerance level with me. I was the complete and total opposite of him. Every time he moved I knew it would be bad. Every time I moved he knew it would be good. Where was Chris in all of this? Chris was just wondering who in the world he was.

None of us really knew where it was really going but the pulling just became stronger as everyone stood firm in their beliefs. Chris reacted, Rama reacted, and I reacted. Rama would wear these silk robes and all I wanted to do was look the other way. He was a total embarrassment. The trip he presented was the master slave scenario.

In spite of all of this, my students kept trying to get classes. Of course I tried to give them but it was very hard. I couldn't say no, as I saw the Light in all that came. Even disgusting Chris had moments of Light but Rama, never. They questioned who my Soulmate was but it went to the wayside as both kept denying it but acting it. There is nothing worse than twisting a lot of religions together. If you have to do religion then you should keep it within its boundaries. Rama twisted everything including this. If he could not get enough people to buy his sale, he would change it. For believing he was a master, it was clear that the master had many flaws. Of course I definitely pointed them all out to him and yes he would slam me again and again for it.

The time for his sexual initiation of me was arriving because he was making it clear that he was losing his patience. My return on this was that if he crossed that line, Divine Order would prevail and he would sign and seal his fate for eternity. He said that the whole point of life was to gain power and dominate the human race.

"Fine," I said. "Go do dominance but leave me out of it all."

He laughed at me saying, "Never Deborah, you are my prize."

The thought of him putting his hands on me made me sick to my stomach. He bragged that there was not a female that he could not alter their level of consciousness during sex. To be more specific, he was talking about during their orgasm. Rama projected heavily into Chris's consciousness the sexual act with me and I kept picking it up. Chris did not want to be responsible for anything when Rama could do it all. Chris and I had carried on enough in the office. There was chemistry between us but nothing that I could not live without.

The parties continued and more and more people came. Of course Rama had a fit and none of us ever knew who would get it next. He was worse than an electrical storm. He would take his students out in the desert and do his magic. They would be so worn out from lack of sleep that to get them to hallucinate was easy. It had to be all Rama and his way. People lived in a perpetual state of fear. All was not going well. It kept coming back all of what Chris had done. It did not seem that any wrong would ever be set right. Chris was Rama's Achilles' heel. I was the one that had to be conquered. Every waking day was hell with Rama. His whole day was designed around ruining people's lives. I would always hear about it. He loved blowing up relationships, planting doubt in people and lying nonstop. You could see him playing with people's minds. If anyone was happy, he had to destroy it. He projected enough evil to break the strongest of people. It never mattered what it cost. Rama had this undying belief that he was exempt from Divine Order. He actually was convinced one hundred percent of this. He saw how people heard Truth from me and he knew if I talked that people would believe me.

The only one who seemed unaffected by my Truth was Chris. The more I spoke Truth the more he lied. Back to the yin and yang of it all. He remained totally unfazed by turning me over to Rama. He justified it by concluding that I had asked for it on some level. Always an answer in this twisted Zen Rama thought. Rama was trying to create a superior race of androids. He kept trying to present himself as the nice guy, but behind closed doors the evil would be bursting to come out. When it did, all that had gone against him that day would get it. No one was spared, no one. What was sad was others that were in the way without even being connected got it too. It did not matter what age or circumstances. You must understand that no one could control him and being threatened by him always resulted in his following through with his threats. Even if you backed off, he would not stop. He put no one ahead of himself but he did react to me unlike anyone else. I knew that he was watching Chris, gauging Chris's reactions to me. The more he made me send these cards the more Chris became angry. When Chris raged, Rama could tap into his mind easier and set him up more. What in the world was the reasoning behind this? It could not all be over Soulmate issues. Was Chris the scorned brother in another life? Or was Chris up in line for the power Rama had been disowned from in Olympus? I could not forget the evil Chris did to me, so Rama being jealous served nothing. Actually, Rama had no reason whatsoever to feel I would ever even tolerate Chris. As far as I was concerned, Chris needed to be sued. It was clear that his habitual lying would be a permanent thing along with his sneaking around. As far as I was concerned, Chris should have gone to jail and lost his medical license permanently. I decided to make a plan to sever this mail sending with Chris. I would just tell Rama that I had mailed something and leave it at that. I should have figured he would find out and when he did, he fractured my right hand. I screamed in pain as he stormed out.

"Zeus," I cried, "Come to me." I sat down and watched my hand swell. Zeus came within seconds and he raged big time.

"Take him Father. Get him off this planet. He'll kill me," I wept.

"Daughter," Zeus said as he knelt down in front of me. "You must listen to me. There is a way to change this and I will help you but you must listen."

"How do I listen when you will tell me to love him. I can't!" I said nearly screaming in his face.

"You cannot imagine the effect that you have on him. There is no other way. Daughter, I would not tell you something that was not so. Oh, the years that I have gone without you in my life have left such a void within me. I cannot even catch up to fill this void for it lies so deep. Imagine Daughter, the void that this one I have disowned feels. He has no one to console this but you. I want you to look beyond all of us and see the way to come," he said trying to express the seriousness of it all.

I started to laugh. "You are not this old fool you claim," I said. "How about a deal Father," I continued to say. "You and Mother need to reconnect and you need to love this wayward son of yours as well. If you will do this then I will try with all of my heart to do the same."

"He will not trust you, Daughter. You will have to win his trust among other things. Can you do it?" Zeus asked.

"I can do whatever I set my mind to, Father. Can you?" I asked him. He laughed and I laughed. "Perhaps Father, we are both a pair of fools," I said joking with him.

"Now you are that of your Father," he said holding me. He was so warm and loving and so needed in my heart. There is nothing greater than the reconnecting of love. Good old Zeus convinced me and so I decided to change and give it a try. Really, what did I have to lose? What did the planet have to lose? I knew that being nice to Rama would appear to look like a set up, a trap or whatever his mind could make it to appear. The shock of my being nice was more than Rama could handle. He raged louder than I had ever heard.

"So you play games with me?" he yelled in my face.

"No! I have come to see things differently. It has taken me a long time to come to this conclusion," I said calmly.

"You lie! You are clever!" he screamed. He started shaking and trembling.

I could not believe that finally I was doing what he wanted and he couldn't stand it. Zeus was right. Athena was right. They were all right. Finally, I had won a victory. Perhaps it was a tiny one but I had won. From this point on I had something to work with and so to the best of my ability I was going to try to turn things around.

CHAPTER FIFTEEN

The change in me drove Rama to levels of despair. He did not know if he was coming or going. He did not know what to expect from me. It was all I could do to behave nicely, show gentleness and kindness. He kept telling me that it was a trap or a game and he wasn't buying it. His levels of being cruel to me increased as he thought I was now playing him. Instead of becoming more calm he was more hostile than ever, not only to me, but also to everyone else. Interesting, how he could not handle the very thing he was so determined to make sure no one else had, that was, any kind of happiness. The bottom line was that anyone in the Light coming at him made him Darker than I even thought that he could get.

I called to Zeus in a short moment of peace. "Father what do I do now?" I asked.

"Keep doing it, love him and no matter what, don't stop," he said.

"No matter what?" I asked.

"What did you say years ago? You would do whatever it took to accomplish this mission. Remember, no matter what and whatever it takes?" he reminded me.

"Yes but I didn't know I'd have to live with nearly being killed every day. How do I know when he will go too far?" I asked Zeus.

"You don't but you are the only one," he replied.

"Oh that makes me feel just wonderful!" I said, as Zeus smiled and left.

If I had any acting abilities I was hoping that they would now come to the forefront. I could see that I had my work cut out for me. I was hoping that it would be over with shortly. I had known Chris for a year now and had dismissed any further acknowledgment but Rama, behind my back, was still actively playing the game making it look as if I was.

One of my students who was jealous of me decided to do something so evil that it would alter the future of many. He went and told Rama I had secretly married Chris. Rama was so upset that he terminated the medical practice Chris was in, making him move immediately. He was going to make sure that there would never be contact with me again. He came storming in slamming me up against the wall demanding to know if it was true. I had no idea what he was talking about and he kept slamming me harder and harder until I broke down. I started crying and he backed off.

"Did you secretly marry him?" he asked me.

"What? I am not married. Do you mean Chris?" I asked.

"Don't you lie to me!" he growled at me.

"I am not married to anyone," I said.

"I will see to the future now," he yelled at me, and he left promising me that he would kill me if I went near Chris.

As soon as he left I ran to the phone and called Chris. Amazingly, he came to the phone. I told him I needed to leave right away because Rama was going to take me and I knew I had no time left. I told Chris that I thought Rama was coming after him and that we needed to leave right away. I told Chris that I would just move on and that he needed to hide. Chris, of course, said I was lying and told me to leave him alone. He said that he lost his office because of me. I yelled at Chris for all that he had done to me and I fell apart on the phone begging him to listen. He got good and nasty and hung up. I started to pack as fast as possible. I knew that Rama had snapped and that he was definitely about to do something big time. Whatever plan Rama had, it would be big. The faster I packed the faster my mind went. As I was doing this, a knock came on the door. As I opened it a student of mine named Sherry asked what was wrong. I told her I had to go right away. She looked in total amazement. She asked why and I told her Rama had snapped. I told her a student had gone and spread this horrible rumor and told Rama I had married Chris.

"Oh Sherry, he's gone crazy," I told her. "I've got to leave before he comes back. You know how jealous he is over Chris."

She looked at me and was speechless for a moment. "My goodness Deborah, that has been Rama's Achilles heel for how long? What must he have been thinking when he heard this?" she said.

"Do you know how angry he was? I've got pain all through me where he threw me up against the wall again and again," I told her. "Oh you've got to get away or he'll kill you. How many times had he scared all of us? I can't even count them all," she said helping me pack.

"Sherry where am I to go so fast?" I asked her.

"You can come and stay with me," she offered.

"Yes but he'll come after you! I can't move fast enough," I said.

"Deborah, I have a very bad feeling about tonight. He is going to do something bad, I know it," Sherry said.

"I know it too and I'm so afraid for the first time ever," I told her.

"What do we do?" she asked.

"Sherry you don't have to be involved. I can see what he'll do to you if you even try to help," I told her.

"Screw him," she said.

We both burst into laughter. She knew the second she had said it that we were hoping on some level that Rama had not heard it. "Chris is pure trouble. He has been all along," Sherry said.

"He is Darker than Rama," I said.

"We need a plan, Deborah. I want to go with you," Sherry said.

"Go with me? Sherry, do you know what you are asking here?" I asked her.

"Yes but I'll miss you something awful and my life has been so boring until I met you," she said coming across very sincere.

"It will be so dangerous!" I said making it real clear.

"Screw him. I'm going with you if you'll have me," she said.

"Of course I'll have you," I told her, giving her a hug. Now Sherry knew that Rama was going to come after her but she didn't care. I knew he would do his best to try and stop her. She rushed out with plans to pack and I raced around trying to get ready. I ran past my window only to see Chris sitting in his car staring in. He told me off on the phone and then showed up. I couldn't deal with Chris and kept packing. I later went to bed and finally fell asleep around one in the morning. All of a sudden Rama came in and saw that I had been packing.

"Going somewhere Deborah, with Chris?" he asked snidely.

I woke up startled. "Screw you stupid!" I said remembering Sherry's words. He backhanded me so hard I was thrown clear across the room. He had knocked the wind out of me and I could not get up. I had landed so hard I was dazed.

"Get up," he demanded again.

"No. Go to hell," I said. "That's where you come from."

He walked over and hit me again and I blacked out. When I finally woke up I had been undressed and I was under my covers on my bed. I felt like I had been drugged. "Now I will touch you," he said as he came from the other room. The features of his face were blurry and I felt like I was going to faint.

"You drugged me," I said in a whisper. I barely had the strength to speak.

"Now why would I do that, Deborah?" he said laughing.

"Because you are evil," I said, very weak.

"Now, now, let's see if we can get you into the Dark," he concluded. He pulled back the covers and he began to tell me how women lose their levels of consciousness when they have an orgasm. He said he could alter all female's levels of consciousness.

"And who alters yours?" I whispered.

"Why no one, no one knows how," he said quite confident.

"I can," I whispered as I passed out. He was mad because he needed me to be awake but he had drugged me so that I went into such a deep sleep that he could not wake me for hours. He stayed there not sure what to do with me. As I woke, I could not move my arms or legs. The drug had made me so impaired that I could no longer speak either. My mouth would not move. I lay there paralyzed by this drug. I could not stop him and he could not stop himself. What came next shocked even him. He started to lose himself in the ritualistic program he had created during sex. He didn't want intercourse with me, he wanted something else. I couldn't even react. I had to lie there and take it. It was beyond degradation. I was so drugged that I couldn't even astroproject out. I had never experienced this kind of sex before and it so badly violated me. He said that he could have intercourse with any female but I was different and he wanted to savor every moment of me. It was beyond rape and I couldn't even fight him. My mind went dead and my heavy eyelids finally closed. I wanted to go beyond death. In my mind I heard Chris saying that I must have asked for it on some level. Rama went on to do this for hours. What he was not aware of until it was over was that I had altered his level of consciousness during my degradation.

Rama finally left but I was falling all over the place trying to get to the shower to get the stench of him off me. I fell on the floor and blacked out again. I wanted to stay out forever. How could anything ever be the same. I hated Chris if you could call it hate. He had given me over to this evil. What I had held sacred, that which was mine alone, he had put the violator there to take.

I was so ashamed and embarrassed I could not leave my apartment and there was no one there to hear this from me. I know I cried until I could no longer. I sank to the depths of despair alone and shattered. There are some things you never get over and for me this was one of them. To write this I must relive it and I still cry years later. I never had a chance, I was so badly drugged. A part of my heart left me and a part of my soul shut down. I became numb and I stayed numb. My smile left me.

"Someone hold me," I cried out, "Don't abandon me now," I cried even louder. It was Athena who came and I could not send her away. I had no energy within me to do it. I knelt down and cried until I fell asleep again. Athena said nothing, she just held me and stayed with me. What was there to say anyway? The levels of devastation so overwhelmed me that I kept sleeping day in, day out. I didn't even care that Athena had come. I didn't care about anything. I knew Rama was coming back and he would do this all over again. I was determined to leave so I pulled myself together and continued to pack.

Days had passed and he had not come back. Chris continued to go by and I knew that he knew what had happened. I looked in the mirror and I could not erase it from my face. More days passed and Rama still did not return. Chris started calling me and hanging up all day and all hours of the night. I would never stomach him ever. It was his evil again and again that had destroyed me now.

Sherry started packing too since we had planned to leave together. I didn't tell Sherry what had happened. One late night while I was asleep Rama showed up again. You just could not lock the man out because he opened the door, locks and all. I woke to a strange smell and his hand waving something across my face. He was drugging me again. I saw his face but he was not laughing. He brushed his hand through my hair. I felt myself losing consciousness but I pulled away.

"No matter what you do you will never have me," I mumbled.

"You are mine and always will be. If you do not fight me I will not hurt you," he said trying to make me understand how he was justifying things.

"You're so evil you have to drug me so I cannot move. Fight you? Oh you will see, I promise you. If I die doing it, you will see the Light," I stated.

"Let's see how your God takes care of you now," he said.

Again, he violated me repeatedly. The ritual, the violation, and I blacked out. I pretended that it was not my body. I flew from my body and flew to the Angels. I looked down and saw this lifeless body that was supposed to be me. How else was I to cope? I looked upon the face of the God Force and they said he must come back home or the planet was doomed. It is only a body. Let go of it and remember Love. Fill yourself with Love and never let go. I reentered my body flooding myself with Love.

"What are you doing?" Rama tried to say as he stopped.

I did not speak as he had drugged me so badly, I was too impaired to speak. The word Love played out in my mind again and again. My body had succumbed to it. I began to glow I was so flooded by Light. The Angels came forward and stood by his side and my side.

"What are you doing to me?" he demanded to know.

I had nothing to say. It was as if the sun had gone down for me never to come back up. Rama began to lose his balance and everything started spinning on him. Where the words came from I do not know but when I spoke he was held in place unable to move himself.

"Even you cannot violate Divine Order," I said, but not from my mouth. It was spoken through vibration language from my soul. Rama and I did not need the human aspects to communicate, we were both very evolved. Instead of gaining power from me he had actually lost some. He had a conscience for the first time ever. He was now being held accountable for his actions. Pangs of guilt, remorse and regret hit him. I was turning things around on him. Now you would have thought that he might have started to change. Oh, he was bothered by me but not enough to stop, and change, that was something Rama did very slowly.

Now you may be thinking that Rama deserved to be put away but you have to see that it was Chris who was responsible for all of this. He even stood by watching, knowing all along that he could have stopped it. His evil surpassed Rama by millenniums. I do not know how anyone could have stood by watching without stepping in. This level of evil was far beyond my mind's abilities. Rama had a reputation for being Dark and evil. All you had to do was ask his students, the ones not too petrified to talk.

I kept hearing the words from Zeus. I thought of Angel of Silk standing guard. A lifetime of standing is only a moment to an Angel. It was clear that Athena was being affected greatly and Dark evil Chris stood by watching, getting off on all of it.

Sherry and I continued to pack. I knew that we were going somewhere. Most everything I had went into storage. Rama was forcing me out. I had no idea if I would ever have another home. Rama did not want me grounded in any area of my life. Before Sherry and I left he came back many more times. Of course he pleasured himself without realizing the magnitude of what was happening to him. He was stealing the flesh in hopes of taking the soul. In reality, he was losing his power very slowly. You cannot imagine to what degree evil can go but it can be so good at deception that it can lay out a plan for you many years down the road. Then when it hits you all at once, you end up hitting the bottom, to paralyzed beyond belief to even crawl back out. It sneaks up with absolutely no warning whatsoever. It is meant to destroy you with no witnesses to blame it on. Oh believe me, you have got to wake up to the reality here. The Dark you cannot see must be called on its action.

I must give you a quick story here of someone I knew for about a year. He was a doctor, of course, who had cheated on his wife. She knew on a soul level and started treating him badly but couldn't explain why to anyone. As the record later showed, all of his events coincided with her behaviors. Now this doctor came to me expecting pity to be passed out on him. Why does she treat me so badly he would carry on. Because you are a liar and cheat on her. I told him but his comeback was that she did not know about it. Yes, one more moron on the planet. To make it all worse he was cheating with a blacker than pitch female who was casting spells on him. When I made him aware of this he said that he would break up with her. He then moaned later that this evil female was lying and manipulating him. I told him for the last time to end it with her and to stop putting his personal life on me as he was being paid to treat me. I finally did not go back as I was sick of it all. Today he lives with this evil female and he is Dark too. The only reason he is with her is because of his pms.

I certainly would not want to go to a doctor this Dark. All doctors have always felt the need to confide in me without my even bringing this forward. Why would I, of all people, want to deal with any doctors? So you see how even when you yourself can recognize evil and you deliberately stay in it, you deserve to be miserable. This doctor had a promising future coming after his divorce but this female fed his own Darkness and he got off on it. The truth is that many people crave the Dark. It excites them, turns them on but oh, how they try to get out of the price it hangs on their heads. You will pay, I guarantee you will pay and it will be presented in the most elusive ways. You cannot imagine the magnitude of the Dark you will activate and in the long run you will be unable to get out. How much will it cost you? I guarantee plenty. You see there are some things consistent in Dark also, then again you probably know this.

It took Sherry and me what seemed like forever to be packed and be ready to go. Rama kept throwing roadblocks at everything yet he was planning to take me away anyway. Nothing ever made sense with this man. All I could say was that nothing seemed to be lining up when Rama wanted it to. Whatever was not in his timing, the whole world had to stop and wait until it was. Once again I remind you that it was Chris all along who had the power to stop it all. He knew he could too. In his opinion it was all too messy to deal with. Chris had major female issues anyway. He would carry on that all women were after him for his money.

The traps that Rama put in our way were unreal. The departure kept changing and all of the plans kept falling through but we did eventually pull everything together. Rene was such a wonderful soul energy. She was the kind of person who packed fabulous lunches to take on trips. She was so kind, loving and special. Oh, how she was dear to my soul. Before I left I tried to have a direction but Rama had fixed my car so he could keep track of me. He told me that he would take me to California or I could go myself if I did not resist. But, if I didn't arrive when he told me to, he would come looking for me. What do you do? You do what the master says or you get fried.

I never ever thought that things could get any worse than they were. I guess because I had been optimistic my whole life. You also need to recognize the real evil here was Chris. When someone attacks you that is evil and when the person responsible for bringing the actual assault on you stands by and watches doing nothing, this is the ultimate evil. Chris stood by all right, year after year, after year.

It was all because of the lie this student had told that Rama decided once I got to California, he would marry me, ensuring Chris could never. How do you just marry someone without their consent? Wake up people. It is easy, especially when you are Rama. He was obsessed with Chris. He was obsessed with me. What would ever make him think that Chris wanted to marry me? He knew that I would have never agreed to it. What was between these two was unreal. It was sick to start with but it grew into something evil beyond words.

Rama had fixed it so that Chris moved from Colorado to Virginia to put more distance between us. Meanwhile, the long distance separation between Chris and me drove Rama crazy. That emotional up and down, between us blew apart and died down but Rama kept up with the mail sending. He thought by separating us by distance, he could get a better grip on me, but only the opposite happened.

He married me all right, with a gun to my head on board a large sailboat. He told me that I could never sue him, as if I had ever thought of it. He told me that he could control me better and if he chose, he could take everything of mine. Then to finalize it all, he said that the day would come when I would take his name because my name would be gone, dead and buried. What a strange conclusion he drafted. I would never be Deborah Lenz, he was Lenz, just demeaning, Dark Lenz. I personally did not deal with two things, people's last names or birth dates. Of course, you know what the human race does with this. All in all, I told Rama that he could take his marriage and shove it. It was a very bad joke that I would never buy. He shoved it all right. Right into the places it would do the most harm.

It started with a bank transaction that rejected because all of the funds had been taken out of the account. At the time I didn't catch on that it was Rama. It was very baffling to me but I couldn't hold still long enough to battle it, fill out the paper work, etc. and he knew it. Other things began to happen which made no sense, things that could only be done by one having private personal information. I was tired of the roadblocks, the abductions and general grief from everything. No one would listen, they just wanted me to make everything right with their own personal lives.

Students now came to me in California and they were more programmed than those in other states. A haze, a Rama haze, held all of them in place. Just try and plow through invisible concrete. In nearly every case it was a lost cause. The strange thing about California was that everyone kept asking me if I was the Angel sent to rescue them. Such strange terminology.

Rama was more at peace here in many ways, more than any other place. He seemed to feel that he had full control of everyone. I am sad to say that he did and still does. Oh, you can argue forever but I know different. Yes, your name is on the rolodex of departure. His techniques are very clean. It will always appear that your death was either self-inflicted, accidental or of natural causes. Again people, this is the Dark you cannot see. How do you get out of it? Do you need to ask me again? Haven't I told you again and again?

The months went on and Sherry and I kept intense journals. I refused Rama nonstop but in the end, he always got his own way. The real trauma had not started and this California move took its toll on my son, Sherry and me. There was no peace or harmony. Everywhere we turned we were hit by Rama. He wanted me at his California house and I said no. No meant being slammed again and again.

I became deathly sick and one day blacked out behind the wheel. Sherry took me to the hospital. I had no blood sugar readings whatsoever. Rama was chanting his sick meditations at me and we were so worn out. We went from Malibu to Newport Beach only to be followed and found again and again.

No one would listen or snap out of it. I guess people enjoyed being messed around with by Rama especially if it involved money and sex. I saw right through the whole thing but he wasn't threatened by me in California. He referred to everyone there as androids willing to sell their souls for a free and good life.

When I challenged many they would say, who cares about tomorrow as long as I can live today. It did not matter from what walks of life these people were from. It was so dangerous and Dark here that it wasn't any wonder that people had predicted California falling off into the ocean. There was a sick thrill in many enjoying the danger of the big quake. There was never anything good or positive such as, what can we do to heal Mother Nature. There were so many Dark and evil souls all lining up for Rama. He didn't really have to work to get people here either. He didn't even have to fry them as examples to others. All he had to do was send out the twisted thoughts of sex and he could grab hundreds in a night.

I bothered him greatly when it came to my surrender, you know that big surrender that he was so sure I was going to do. What would it take? You got me, because as far as I was concerned, nothing could do it, ever!

It was more than I could bear to see the hundreds of brain gone people wandering around completely drained of the substance of life.

You would probably say street people or homeless but their souls were homeless long before their bodies became so. So badly broken were they that their energy even gave off that of the dying. It was too late for most. Only a handful here and there were still salvageable. Many had found peace in living out a certain role from another life. Some of these people were very talented and had been very successful before the blows hit them. Remember this, your house houses you. You do not house the house. In other words, do not let anything own you. The less you are attached, the better you will handle the roller coasters of life. If you are attached, you will play out devastation. Once the button on devastation is hit, it starts a domino effect and is very hard to stop and harder still to recover from. Attach yourself to the White Light and enjoy your house or houses. If you own things, enjoy them but remember to recognize that only the White Light is where you put your power and your investment. You will not bottom out or ever do devastation there. Now, I can hear some of you moaning that it is all too much for you to do. Maybe someday, but guess what, you don't have someday because the second you read all this, you are at the crossroad. Which way are you going?

With Chris out of range it was boring for Rama. Oh, sure he had the marriage license and control over many areas of my life with it but I never surrendered my name or acknowledged his. Just in case I did get away though, he warned me, that if I got married elsewhere, it would be illegal and he could prove it. What a sick man. I really just blew it all off not giving it any merit whatsoever. He was good, very good, especially at hacking into things and rearranging everything. If you are brilliant enough you can bypass all of the human race and its small thinking levels. To the fools who even thought they could compete with Rama, great anguish and pain would hit them from every direction. You did not mess around with the Zen Master. You know it was funny because as much as he wanted to be a master, he was actually a slave to me on many levels. I would hold Chris over my head and oh, he would just come undone and go ballistic on me.

Sherry became sick from stress and her main point for coming on this trip was to find her Soulmate. I already knew where he was and who he was. I also knew that he was going to strike her the wrong way. They had had a heavy past life in Boston. She was pulled to go there something fierce. We kept up with the journals and she did meet her Soulmate. She could not stand him but she led him on. She was so disappointed that he was not upper class. He finally found a reason to clean up his act but Sherry wanted that all to be done before she had ever arrived. In the end, we drove away and for a whole year later, he called at all hours of the night waking me constantly. He begged to know where she was. He finally said that he was going to kill himself. Here is a perfect example of someone, once again, being irresponsible.

Every time Rama decided the females were too boring in California, he would hunt me down and demand I perform. He wanted the fight. He said these idiot females were so stupid that you could get them to believe anything. This was true. Rama was so Dark, how could you not see it? They did but they also thought that they could control him on some level or they would not have done it. Of course, I speak of the cheap version. He would always speak badly about them when it was over. Truly it was a using situation and this kind of females never clean up their acts. They are Dark through and through. All of the other ones that were truly brainwashed were a completely different story. Rama's ego was so big that he actually pleasured himself with it all day long.

The man never had anything I wanted and I do mean anything. In fact, he was the total opposite to what I would have ever desired. Here we go again with the total opposite thing, the Soulmate thing. I supposed that that is what bothered me most of all. What was creepy was that Rama had the same eyes I did. Right down to the same exact color. It was like looking right into a mirror. He enjoyed this because it was one more connection.

Dread continued to fill me over Rama. Too much dread can be a very bad thing. Even too much Soulmate can be a very bad thing if you are not ready to line up. This is why I have told you not to drop everything and go hunting for the Soulmate. They love to show up and wreck marriages, lovers, friends and the likes of all relationships. If you want to give your power away right here to me, then by all means do so and listen to what I've just said. They will ruin everything and then walk away because the game is over. Believe me, I know. There are some things you must consider here because they can pull on your soul so badly that it can drive you insane.

There are many traps with the Soulmate. Once they have wrecked a relationship that you had with someone else, seldom can you ever get it back. The only relationships that rekindle after the Soulmate has trampled all over everything are the ones with the partner who has the same Soulmate scenario. Their Soulmate trampled them. Be careful what you are willing to give up. Never ever sacrifice anyone or anything for the Soulmate if they begin to tug on you. The second you find yourself using this word sacrifice stop everything because they have you big time. What do you do? Recognize it and release it only to the Awesome White Light and Love of the Creator. You should know this by now but I could never tell you this too many times. Bravo, to the one who does this often for it is the very best thing you could ever do.

Now, when Dark and Light battle it continues until it is finally done. Although there are no grudges for the hierarchy, the much smaller levels cling to the constant continuations of battle like a thirst they cannot quench. Whoever said the Light does not battle? You can't imagine how they step in front of fatal situations. If it were left up to me, I would send the whole human race back to the Light, literally. I could tell you many places you should not be going but the human race does not want to listen. If they do not fall into traps, they canot play the pity plate.

We were camping in Newport Beach when we heard chimes and a fragrance of perfume, which filled the tent. It was Athena and she began to speak poetry to us. Mother and I had our differences but my love for her was too deep to send her away. Of course, I understood her connection to Rama but there was so much to this picture that no one was telling me. Did it make sense? Yes, a lot of it did but a lot was still to come. What was I to do, rattle it out of the clouds? Athena was awesome and Sherry felt honored.

Sherry was also torn apart by her Soulmate. I could see it but she needed to give him a chance to change. I knew she would not. They were in two different classes and while a lower class doesn't have a problem climbing up, the upper class just hates to go down.

Sherry and I looked so much alike that when Rama sent his hit men they thought they had me when it was actually Sherry. There was nothing more hysterical than Rama sending a bunch of muscular beefy types, we called them beefers, to pick us up and all I had to do was tell them where their Soulmates were. I knew

Sherry could not accept her other half, they were too far apart. He did love her instantly but he also wanted to control her too. It was clear to her that Rama was driving us into the ground. It was also clear that Chris could have stopped it at any given moment. We were constantly chased and living on the edge of danger. At night while we were asleep, Rama would come and summon me to wake and meet him. Sherry said that she could always tell when he had taken me because I would look different and be somewhat in a trance. He was trying to drain me so that I would surrender.

We were chased by a helicopter one night and it landed nearly on top of our tent and tried to pick us up. We fled in terror completely hysterical as to what we should do. Sure Rama needed to be caught in the act but when you are dealing with idiots like police officers, they won't come near something like this. That does not mean that all police are idiots but most are. I called the police many times only to hear that they did not deal with Rama because he was too dangerous. To quote one officer, "We don't go near him." You are on your own, they would all conclude. Again and again he would be in our faces. It was like being in a cage, like mice being probed, waiting for the experiment. He would always say, let's see how your God takes care of you now, Deborah.

Athena tried to help as she began to stand guard by our tent. What was strange is the trip to California somehow caused the loss of Angel of Silk. He was there and then gone. This in itself alerted me to greater danger. We kept hearing wind chimes and smelling Athena's fragrance. We were hungry a great deal of the time as Rama took every cent. Whenever we would try to save anything, he would blow out one of our tires or do something horrible to force us to spend our money. You may say to me that it would all need to be proven that he had done these things. Would you like me to give him your address? For those that dispute any of this, stop right now. Guess what, he already has you. Did any of you bother to get clarity from the God Force? It was so bad that we all got very sick and almost died. We tried to get out and head back to Colorado but he would not let us go.

I knew that it would take something drastic and the only thing I knew to do was contact Chris. This of course, was the unmentionable but it put Rama on to a new focus. I sent Chris a letter telling him to do something. After I mailed it, we were feeling so tired, so we all stretched out in the tent and started to anticipate Rama's reaction when he finally tuned into things. I was forbidden, as you know, to ever go near Chris. It had been Chris all along that made Rama so driven to despair. As you can imagine, the worst was on its way. As soon as Chris alerted Rama, he dropped everything and raced to get to me. Of course, Chris turned me in and how many times had he done this all along.

Athena came rushing in so fast that the tent nearly blew over. "Daughter, oh Daughter, quick, he is coming and he may kill you he is so raging" she said so upset.

"Mother! What shall I do? Where can we go? He will find us!" I said as upset as she was.

"Oh Daughter, I have never seen him so angry. He cannot deal with the threat of losing you!" she said.

"Losing me? He does not have me or own me. Mother, it must end, he is killing us," I told her so bewildered.

"Daughter, there are many more years to come," she said.

"More years of this," I shrieked. She did not respond and of course I knew that she was right. Athena paced around the tent waiting for his arrival.

"Mother, why are you helping us?" I asked her because the last time she had turned away from me.

"Daughter, I do not know what I can do but I will try my best to stop him," she said almost in tears. We finally drifted off into a deep, deep sleep. Athena stood guard until a thick Dark energy with almost a black color headed our way.

"Daughter," Athena whispered "He is coming quickly. Wake Daughter, wake!" I shook Sherry and both of us held perfectly still. The energy was so thick that the tent started to fold in on us.

"How dare you!" Rama yelled as he stood there pointing his hand at me. Before I even had a chance to speak, he snapped my wrist in making it buckle back and forth.

Athena stepped in and when he saw her, he took off. The wrist started swelling fast. Rama yelled to me that that would fix me for writing that letter. I could not write with a broken wrist. I cannot tell you how I cried it hurt so badly. We all huddled together crying. It would never stop, never! We went to the hospital and cried most of the night. Of course, I made a police report but what good was it, like all of the others, nothing ever came about from speaking of such things.

CHAPTER SIXTEEN

I could not cope anymore and Athena said I had years more to go. The pain in my wrist was so severe I would scream when I moved it even the slightest. Rama meant to teach me a good lesson and he did his best to stop any handwriting abilities.

It was impossible to stay in California so we went to the beach to talk everything out and try to come up with a plan to leave without Rama knowing. Sherry and my son walked ahead of me as I often walked alone contemplating what I should do. I looked up to the road momentarily and saw Rama standing there. Oh no, we had been followed! I turned to see where Sherry and my son were. It had only been a few seconds and they were nearly out of sight. I realized I was in a time warp and needed to run as fast as I could. I saw men closing in on them up ahead. As I started to run, Rama came towards me raising his hands. All of a sudden I ran right into an invisible wall as hard as a real concrete wall. I hit it so hard it knocked me on my back. I got up, turning to another direction only to hit another wall, falling again. I crawled in the sand on my hands and knees trying to find a way out. Rama got closer and closer. As he nearly reached me, the walls all of a sudden closed in on me tighter and tighter. I tried to get up and I started banging on these invisible walls. Sherry and my son turned around and realized that something was terribly wrong and started running back towards me.

"Now," Rama said, "When I tell you not to contact Chris, you will not contact Chris."

I was crying and banging on these walls when all of a sudden a vacuum of energy took all of the air out of this encasement and sealed up. The air was gone and I started gasping for every breath. I fell down unable to hang on. I was turning blue, losing consciousness. Sherry and my son were running faster and faster trying to get to me. Then all of a sudden my prison blew apart and I was thrown out, hitting the sand with my feet in front of me. My heart was pounding so hard as I stood up and started running. Rama slammed me causing me to fall again and again. My knees and elbows were skinned and burning.

"You will never contact him again. Do you understand me?" Rama yelled.

"I will never do what you say, never! I release you to the White Light and Love of the God Force!" I screamed as tears poured from my eyes so much so that I had blurry vision. I landed for the last time on the cold wet sand as he threw me and walked off. I got up, tripping over myself trying to get my balance. I started running again towards Sherry and my son. I landed in their arms and we all fell to the ground.

"We have to leave now, right now! Next time I may not be so able to get away," I said.

We ran to the car and went back to pack up the tent. The sun was setting and we decided to wait until morning to go. We huddled together and decided that it would be safer to stay in the car all night. We kept trying to doze off but we would wake up, startled as if someone were watching us or listening. I could not shake this feeling. My wrist was causing me excruciating pain and it would be months before it would be healed and strong again.

It was not over with Rama and I was beginning to believe that it would be forever that it would all go on. There is so much that I cannot say. He never stopped, never and his levels of evil only increased. Rama was determined to own me no matter what the price was. He was determined also to make sure that Chris and I never saw each other again. How stupid this was. Why would I ever want to see Chris? He would remain the evil, ugly man he was. You can see the power that Chris had in this whole thing. Why was Rama obsessed to keep the two of us separated? Chris was told constantly what was happening. He did nothing. He was the only one who could get me out of this. He was the one who got me into it. Chris knew what Rama would do to me. He was disgusted that I could not beat Rama at his game. Like I said, the evil far greater is the one that is responsible and sits back and watches.

It wasn't until we were on the road that I was alerted to a strange sound coming from under the car. Sherry could not hear it but I could. I could hear things that no one else could. We stopped and as I got out to locate this sound, it hit me what it was. Rama had put a tracking mechanism under the car and he knew exactly where we were. We stopped at a truck stop, I took it off and put it on a truck going east. We went on and as we drove I thought to call out to Zeus. Athena was unable to really help but she was a reason why. I began to see that it was more than just her being Rama's mother in another life. There was so much that the Allegiance was not telling me.

I once again underestimated Rama as he was onto my act of removing his device. We were plowing through all of this thick energy when we noticed a problem with the tires. We stopped at an inn and decided to go on the next day after trying to fix the tire problems. We were somewhere on Wilshire Boulevard in Santa Monica, California. I went into the bathroom to draw water for a bath. I sat on the edge of the bathtub when all of a sudden Rama came charging through the door grabbing my shaver and cutting into my shins from my knee down to my foot. It was so deep that it took off a layer of the bone. The whole front of my leg was bleeding something awful. I screamed so loud and he hit me.

"Don't ever remove anything I put on, around or in you. Do you understand me?" Rama said pulling my hair back and forcing my head back.

"I will never do anything you say, low life!" I responded.

Sherry yelled out to me and I told her to come quickly. Rama sped off and by now the bathtub was filling up with blood. Poor Sherry had no idea what had happened. The burning pain was unreal. She applied pressure for nearly an hour and still it would not stop bleeding. Finally, nearly two hours later, it stopped. I cried so and Sherry did too. To this day I have a scar that runs all the way down my right shin. I felt us all losing and I felt powerless to change it. I was barely able to breathe and he'd hit me again and again. We were so stressed out but what could I do? I called out to Zeus and he came very quickly.

"Father please help me. I cannot understand anymore. I cannot stop him," I cried out.

"Daughter, you must stop him. You are the only one who can," he said so convinced that he had the right answers.

"I cannot! It is an impossible situation. How can Chris just sit there knowing what is going on and do nothing?" I asked Zeus.

"He is Darker than all others. It fulfills a sick fantasy of his. He is greatly jealous of you and blames you for taking his mentor from him. He wants you to suffer, be humiliated and disgraced. If you were crawling in the dirt, he would walk up and kick dirt in your face. He hates you with such a vengeance that it even eats away at him. He lies to all about you and he tells only the ones who will believe him. He could stop it all in a moment but he chooses to watch and enjoy your pain," Zeus told me.

"He could have stopped it in the very beginning when he turned me over to Rama." I said.

"Most definitely Daughter." he agreed.

"I am right, Father, about the Dark which is most evil. The Dark that Chris does," I said.

"Daughter, you are always right." he spoke.

"I did not think to call to you. Look at the scars all over my body from Rama. Athena says I have years more of this to come." I told him.

"Yes, she is right. Many years to come you shall still battle him and Chris will still watch doing nothing. He will twist things to try to save himself, but Daughter, in the end he will go down all of the way," Zeus said.

"It is beyond hate that which Chris does. He knows he could end it. Thousands of lives are being destroyed because every time I go forward Rama slams me backwards. Not only that, Rama cringes over this Chris thing. He is the only one who makes Rama go ballistic. Chris has power over him, lots of power over him. I have never seen anyone affect Rama so except for myself. Not only that, no matter what I say or do Rama does not believe me. He will still run dreams through Chris to gauge my possible reactions. Where is the sense in all of this, Father? " I asked.

"Daughter, this Soulmate thing has him by surprise. He cannot get clarity because he is so affected by you. He hates being out of control and you put him there. He rages in violence even though you are constantly unaware to what degree you make him doubt himself. He cannot get a grip on things yet he is driven to you at levels that even he has not touched upon. The challenge is unreal and his determination is beyond any level he could ever imagine," Zeus said.

"I am doomed. There is no way in or out. I cannot go forward. I cannot get away. I am more than doomed, Zeus. I am destroyed and going through the motions," I said greatly saddened.

"Daughter, Love him. Shower him in the White Light. Melt him down." Zeus concluded as he left.

Yeah, right, shower him in Love. Oh, I will shower him all right. I will probably break my other hand with such showers. I started thinking that maybe someone would like to come forward and trade places with me. That was impossible of course. Love him, oh please, just let me get out of California first.

We started to leave again but by the time we made it to Tahoe we needed four tires. It was obvious Rama had continued to sabotage our finances. I was surprised that he hadn't put a bomb under the car. I guess that would have ended the game too soon but that thought did run through my mind many times. We made it back to Colorado nearly broke, we were all sick and hugely stressed. Rama knew right where we were. He called telling me that if Chris claimed me he would walk from me. Claimed me, like I'm some pawn you just toss around? What was this? All of a sudden he is walking away if Chris claims me? What in the world was going on to make Rama say this? Chris and I were miles apart. It was all set up that way. Chris fell for it and I just had no other choice.

Sherry had her only chance for her Soulmate and she left it. Her stress was great because for the rest of her life she would never forget this.

I was strongest in Colorado where Rama did not do so well. This should tell you how badly he handled high altitude. I got up and told myself to regain my energy and go forward with total success. A radio station saw my advertisement and had me on the air. It was wonderful and more than forty-six thousand people responded. I was strong in this area and needed to keep up with the radio contracts. I was able to make a great deal of money from all of these responses. Feeling that all was fine, I went forward completely thinking I was safe now.

Then it happened, Rama took every cent and I fell to the bottom again. Many doors had opened though so I went on letting it all be released to the God Force. I did not care anymore, I was determined to go forward. I had so many clients and classes going I did not have time for Lenz. Yes, from this point on, I started to call him Lenz out loud. I was sick of the name Rama, all it was, was a reflection of his overinflated pms.

I did not see Sherry anymore but I did connect to some more soul energies, which Colorado seemed to be full of for me. Talk about warrior types, they were ready to take on the world with me and so we started to have fun again. There were parties, outings, picnics and most of all laughter, plenty of laughter. I cannot tell you how good all of this laughter was. Things were turning around and I had a place to live and my wonderful Spanky was happy. My son made friends and we were all finally fine again. Yes, you are going to say, that it was all too good to be true and you are right.

It was only a few months later when Chris called. Oh, the activation that took place. I told him never to call back because Lenz would go ballistic on me. I cried for him to leave me alone but he could not. He was now obsessed to see me and talk to me, but certainly not to claim me. Oh, well that was another story. I forbid him to come near me. I told him I was trying to build my life and that his Rama would destroy me if I had any contact with him. It did not matter, Chris was on some mission from hell to find me.

I had given everyone my phone number and now to change it would destroy all of my connections. I needed to be left alone. I broke down begging the Allegiance to block him and keep him away. Nothing good could ever come from Chris. I did not realize that Lenz was still sending cards on my behalf to Chris. What was really going on was that Lenz wanted to see Chris and me together so he could activate more things. Every time I had tried to be nice, Lenz would rage at me with great levels of doubt. People were finally beginning to have hope and feel positive. My radio shows started to open the doors to other shows elsewhere.

There was no way that Chris' coming into the picture would ever be successful. He would not stop calling and he was upsetting everything. He could not stand me, that was always the case but what made him think that I ever wanted anything to do with him? Now that some time had passed, maybe all would be forgotten. Lenz was having a field day with Chris and it was so obvious. Chris played out this disbelief that his Rama could ever do anything I was saying he was doing. How about some x-rays and scars all over my body. You would think that that would be proof enough for any doctor. Not Chris though, he was a master in his own right. I knew that nothing good could come from him. No real man could have allowed such horrors to take place and just stand by and watch. The messages on my phone were now up to the hundreds and those from Chris were a fair share of these. He would call at all hours of the night also. Every time he called, it stirred Lenz up. Chris did not care, he kept right on bothering me.

After weeks of this he told me that he was coming to Denver to see me. I knew this connection could never take place. I was finally able to break free of Lenz even though it had not been for that long. I was determined to go forward and now Chris was making this big get together speech. I knew it was a trap but I had to get rid of Chris. I knew that Lenz could not stand him and I to be geographically together now. Chris would not quit and I thought that if we did see each other, he might be able to go on with his life and leave me alone. There would never be any recovery after what he had done to me. He had done everything with such deliberate malice. Why the great interest in me? There was no real interest, it was all one big trap.

I agreed to meet Chris in a park that we both knew about and so I went there and waited. The hours passed and I was thinking that something had happened. Just about the time I was deciding to leave, a car filled with men pulled up.

"Going somewhere?" they all said at once.

"What! Did the moron send you?" I asked. "Or should I ask which moron sent you?"

"Oh, that's funny Deborah!" this biggest beefer said.

"You might as well start laughing because you're more of a moron for listening to your master," I told them. They all got out and approached me swinging their arms my way. Each one took a hit at me and threw me around in a circle.

"Guess what Deborah?" the dumbest one said.

"Rama killed Chris just hours ago. You see, he is not coming, not now or ever." They got in their car and left.

Had I loved Chris somewhere, somehow in another lifetime? I heard the cello and then I heard the flute. Did I keep deep within my heart such private things that I did not even know of this? The tears poured from places I knew not of. Oh how I cried. Oh how my soul bleed from the wells of feeling. Where was the place to turn all of this off? Where was presence? No, he could not be dead! I refused to believe it. It was one more lie. My soul searched frantically for its wholeness, its identity. I was at the deepest wells of despair. Oh God, he could not be dead. The cello ached to be heard, to be embraced. It was cold and struggling to sound. It was trying, as if Chris was taking his last breath. Oh God, I cannot breathe. The flute could not bear the weight. It fell from key barely touching sound. I yelled to him, his name upon every possible cloud. There was nothing I did not reach for.

"Live!" I screamed. "Be that of your Mother, your Father, just be. Don't make me ache, regret, long for your sound." I burst further into blazing tears, tears that refused to stop. Nothing could quench my soul. Nothing. Was he dead? Maybe this time Lenz was telling the truth. Why was I reacting so? Why did it matter? I had concluded a hundred times that Chris did not matter. Oh God Force!

"Father, where are you?" I searched for his substance. Angel of Silk rushed in and a tear fell from his eyes. It was a tear of hope, it was Silk and Silk's way of holding me. "I love you Angel of Silk." I said. I heard the Angels in chorus with the cello and flute.

Zeus appeared. "Daughter, come into my mind, we shall keep him alive."

"Can we? We must. He cannot die," I said bewildered.

"Oh Daughter, how you have held such things in for so long." Zeus said touching my hand to his. "Join, Daughter, our fingertips and think of him. Think harder than you have ever thought. Let your soul take flight to dance around his. Love Daughter, give him Love." Zeus said. It was easy. It was so easy to do. For the first time ever there was no struggle, no despair.

I said it again and again. "I Love you Chris. I release you to the Awesome Love and White Light of the God Force. Bind all things that keep you from such bonding. With all that I am and could ever be, I Love you from the deepest energy that my soul could ever create. I Love you Chris. Angels embrace him. Father, acknowledge your son. Mother, Love your son." I thought that tears had a time of stopping but all that could be was taken from me. It hit me so hard I had to catch more than my breath. I had to catch his.

Athena came and I was breaking apart as Chris was going down quickly. "If he dies, Mother, it will change all. Life will not be the same with him gone." I said shocked beyond everything. I could not conclude how I could be saying such things. I did not even see him or have any kind of relationship with him but I knew what Lenz would do. For the first time ever Lenz had a declared battle with me. I had activated him big time with all of these things for Chris coming forward.

I needed Zeus more than Athena right now. Zeus had much to repair. It was so involved, all of it. I had displayed Soulmate behaviors as well and Lenz was on to it. He had crossed the line once and for all. The music kept playing in my mind. I looked to the heavens and saw Zeus staring into Athena's face. I saw Light coming from both souls to meet and shelter each other. The Angels stood in harmony waiting, as I was. Athena touched Zeus on the side of his face. Zeus held her hand in peace.

"Can you love this old fool my dear?" Zeus asked Athena.

"Let all be as it was and that which is now, begin." Athena replied.

"Go Mother. Go Father. Love awaits you," I yelled up to them.

Then as Soulmates do, both of their energies merged into one. Together, they had fused back together. I stood gazing at all of this as if it were an example for me to follow. I know they were still playing my parents and you might say it is hard to believe but it is all true. I fell to my knees and cried out. Oh Chris, do not die, don't let go. I lay in limbo as I felt my soul being pulled on.

"No, you can't pull me out," I kept whispering. "Only my Soulmate could do this. I will not go with you Chris and we aren't supposed to be like this." It was all so easy to say. It kept surprising me. How could anything with Chris ever be easy? His letting go of life certainly was. "Fight," I kept saying. On a level so private, he did hear me but I could not tell if it was enough. Angel of Silk stood by watching.

"Go to him," I yelled. "Make him live," I screamed in despair.

"I will see to him," Angel of Silk softly spoke as he left.

Can a heart weigh so much that it can break the steps to Olympus? Can a soul be so filled with unexpected Knowingness that it leaves you in such an unconcluded state? Oh can the matters of Soulmate come upon you at such speeds. Chris was like Lenz in so many ways. At times it had been hard to tell the two apart, yet there was a connection and they both thought that I was their Soulmate. None of this would have happened if Chris had not sold out the Light for Dark. He had been unbelievably cruel. I had to focus and get a grip on things. I was just pulled towards him because of the haunting music. It was the same game Lenz was playing. I collected myself as strongly as I could but I could not break free. I had no way of knowing if Chris was indeed in Colorado or New York where Lenz had told me he had put him. I knew nothing other than what I felt. My feelings told that he was in New York and severely depressed. I felt as though some of his Darkness was doing him in. I also felt he was close to death but not dead. I saw the set up and the plan but the wrenching of my soul had never been greater. It was beyond my control and affecting me greatly. Oh, how I was being flipped off and on back and forth until I thought that I would burst. Every thought Chris had, came into me. I thought, analyzed it, and I then returned it back to him. It was the balance, grounding and reflection. It was exhausting and very intense.

Lenz wanted to see all of this because it was validating his idea that I was really not his Soulmate.

Without notice Zeus and Athena came upon me, completely merged together. "He must come home Daughter. You must share this intimacy with him," Athena spoke.

"Here we go again with me having to do all of the work. How about a little help Family!" I said putting in the order for Lenz to return home.

"Daughter, that of your Mother and myself, you have all you need within you. Take command and go with lightning upon him," Zeus said smiling.

"Oh, I'll go upon him with lighting. He will be fried big time now," I concluded as the Lovebirds left.

"Where are you Lenz?" I yelled out. "Come on coward, you want attention? You are going to get it now. I command you forward!"

"You have no music for me," I heard him say. "Chris has music but I have none."

"Oh, grow up! Things are going to change from this point on." I told him. He started laughing and thought I was just speaking words without action. "Go ahead and laugh. Wait until I fry you." I concluded as he left. I knew that Zeus and Athena merging as one in front of me was done to tell me what I had to do with Lenz. How lovely the great merge program.

It did change from that point on. It changed in all areas. I took charge while Lenz stood back and watched. It was pure entertainment for him and for me it was a full time job and then some. I was used to Lenz twenty-four hours a day anyway so add what would be equivalent to seven jobs a day all put together on one person and you had me. The object was to wear me out so badly that I'd go down and Lenz could take me. He lifted the hundreds of roadblocks and the doors blew open so wide that I had to hang onto the hinges, big time. I went morning, noon and night nonstop, week after week. Everyone that had been around me also saw how many things Lenz had a hold on. As he released his grip, people in the way were falling on their faces. I was swept up in a whirlwind, spinning nearly out of control. The ball was in my park now and I had to keep it there.

Although Lenz could not program me, it was truly amazing how many things he had the ability to rearrange while all thought it was something else. No one had a grip on him. I was now in quadruple time.

Students came out of the woodwork and I was flooded with questions from everyone wanting to know about their Soulmates now. Lenz was hoping I would drop from exhaustion but just the opposite happened. I was rejuvenated and stronger than ever. I was constantly reminded by the those around me that I flowed and had super human strength. I just laughed at all of this but Lenz moved back and watched what he called the best performance he had ever seen. What I did not realize at the time was that I had somehow kicked in what Athena had told me I had many years back. I had my systems working and it was one of the most natural things ever for me. I was gliding on what felt like a hovering sphere of energy. I did not have time for Lenz or his garbage. In fact, I warned him greatly not to get into my face. He laughed, big time but he did begin to tread with caution around me.

Things were very busy and people were coming into my space for help by the hundreds. During classes, energies would become so strong that colors could be seen flying around and images of people from the past would take form when spoken about. No one could keep away and it was beyond wonderful. There was never enough room for everyone and our classes would be so full we would have to move outside for more space. My students were being filled with happiness. No one wanted to leave and many classes went on well into the early morning hours.

There is never silence because once the soul is activated it has so much to catch up on. What is sad is those who start to wake up and have no one to share it with. They will trigger those around them and end up dealing with all of the morons threatened by this newfound truth. Of course, you end up closing back up and dying inside unless you pick up and literally cut all ties. It does take such severe measures unless you are strong enough to keep the leaches off of you and most are not. What happens too is that you can no longer stand the people around you. You begin to recognize their laziness and they give their power away. In other words, as the soul tries to wake you, the morons regroup their power because they feel you slipping away. After all, the soul is the true power and so it threatens their mind's power, ego power and illusionary power. Quick, the threat is there so you close up and the soul allows it for a time. Here is where we say I was given the opportunity to change but didn't. So the soul does let you go on until it must force the wake up.

Now, if you are around these morons and you are listening to your soul, take a look at the big threat you present around everyone. You are out-numbered and you are being asked if you want to be a moron any longer. So sorry to be so blunt but if you are not listening to your soul, I cannot find a more suiting word for one than moron. You may say but what if the time to wake up isn't yet? I will say that when the soul speaks it has goodies for you to take along your journey. These goodies or snacks are all part of the waking up. Food for the soul, from the soul and so on

Although I continued to deny the so-called marriage Lenz had pulled off, he was using his power in this especially where finances were concerned. No matter where I put money he took it. Short of an armored truck, he got into everything, everywhere. When I had someone in this area help me, he would always go through their minds to remove them. He was great on the big set up. Lay out a game and watch them fall right for it. I knew Lenz inside and out. People were being blamed constantly for things he had set in motion. This part of Lenz increased, after all he had to push me to the maximum trying to make me break. Don't get me wrong, he might have changed how he was with me, but for others he became more cruel and vicious. Let us test Deborah. He was always testing and then the sudden halt if Chris surfaced. He could not stand Chris but he could not stand the lack of cause and effect.

Chris, on the other hand, needed this undying eternal love from Lenz and he needed to eliminate me. Chris loved to see Lenz put the pressure on me and try to make me fall. At the same time though, he was intensely jealous of any attention my way by Lenz. Every time the name of Chris came up, everyone immediately showed a major dislike of him. Chris was a very active player. Now you have probably felt that

Lenz has been the major evil. Again, I tell you it was Chris. Lenz and he had so many heavy things in this picture but all it would have taken was Chris stepping forward to put an end to all of it.

You may say to me, how could this be, but let me say that Lenz needed Chris to be present in front of me. He said that he needed to see our eyes meet to finally put to rest the question of who was who with the Soulmate. Yes, Lenz may have known many things but he did not know for sure and every minute of every day it haunted him. There are so many things than can only be revealed in their time. When it became close to seeing Chris, Lenz would buckle under and prevent the contact. Then he would rant and rave that he had to know once and for all and start the scenario all over again.

The public on the other hand, heard a whole different story. They heard a bunch of twisted religion from Lenz but never the mention of Soulmate as this was never to be revealed. Lenz was a very private man. Chris was a very vindictive man. Students tried so hard to stay in the White Light. They had tremendous hope and love so strongly activated by the Teachings. They would practice affirmations around the clock. Just as many made leaps and bounds towards enlightenment, Lenz would come crashing into the picture up heaving everything. No one lasted and nothing stayed put.

By now you should understand why. Everything was overtime, overbooked, over loaded but I had no problems keeping up. One of the reasons I could do this was because I did not give my power away to anything. I was not tired or drained from endless classes and sessions of a more private matter. I even went and rescued people in between everything else. Was it impossible to do? In the mortal realm, yes, but to my realm, no.

From time to time Athena would visit and oh, the time with her became more and more precious. My love for her was deep and well planted. There was always Chris in the background watching and sneaking around. After a time I just accepted that he would do this forever. The only thing that moved me his way was the sound of that cello. I would literally become paralyzed in my thoughts of him and a deep longing would begin to exit my soul, seeking his soul out. It had such a haunting effect and opened the doors to such intense emotions and traumas. The mystery of Chris would continue and of that I was sure. I had endless conversations with Lenz about Chris. He would go into this deep withdrawal and his mood would change greatly. I felt that there was a great plan that, from time to time, became close to collapsing from some invasion of some kind. He would tell me how Chris felt and his purpose on the planet. He told me that Chris came to him on many levels, sharing his intense desires for me. The slightest thoughts going towards Chris would make Lenz go off the deep end, as I have said.

It was all growing so old. There was great joy seeing Zeus again. We would laugh and talk so. His soul was flooded with Love once again and of course it was due to his beautiful Athena. I was so elated that they had re-bonded. Zeus spoke of Lenz and how he would interject if it was needed. All I had to do was call his name and he promised to be there. This gave me great comfort. Looking back on all of it, whoever would have thought that it would have changed so with him?

"Are you sure Father, that you shall hear me if indeed I should come upon the need?" I asked.

"No matter where I am Daughter, I shall come upon you at once and protect you from my fallen son," he said with a chuckle.

"Oh, how long shall he be fallen?" I asked not really expecting an answer.

"Until his heart remembers." He said, all of a sudden his eyes filling with tears.

"You mean Father that of your memory is that of his?" I spoke as he nodded to me. "Oh Father, there is no in with this man or out. It is not that I find no reason of it all, it is that it is all so unreasonable. I trigger him so without even a trigger. He is so irritated and hostile, yet I cannot put up with it and will not," I told him.

"Daughter, you must Love him as I have said and I will be there if he shows the rage he and I have within us. Oh, your Mother has calmed it some but it is most difficult to control at times," Zeus said now very sad.

"You look so sad. What pains you so Father?" I asked him.

"Oh Daughter," he said embracing me so, "there is such danger ahead for you, so much danger. I feel for you and all that you must do. My love is with you." he said as tears fell from his large deep eyes.

"Father, do not concern yourself so for all that I must do. You said if I ever needed you, you would be there. For this I come upon you with love as well. What can any of us do? What will be, will be," I concluded.

Zeus and I sat in silence for awhile as the birds flew by us and the clouds moved on. He and I were together in such silence. Then Athena smiled calling upon Zeus and he departed leaving me feeling the void of my own Soulmate. Oh, how I was happy for my Mother and Father. In spite of it all, oh what a life.

CHAPTER SEVENTEEN

I was firm with Lenz, very firm and he did stand back and view everything. I would get very little sleep but then, I did not need it. Lenz did not realize that he was getting closer to me in areas he had never allowed before. He saw many similarities with me and he was beginning to merge my way. I was using systems full time and it was matching his. I realized too how unbearably lonely it all was having such powers and no one to share them with. I recalled moments in my childhood when I would hear his soul scream for validation, connection and bonding. It haunted me as much as that cello did.

Lenz began to let his guard down and I began to let him in a little bit at a time. There certainly was no trust and we were as opposite as we were the same. You should understand by now it was Soulmate energy that both of us were displaying. Picture the way though, that others viewed us. They really did not have a clue as to what was going on.

Like the sun setting and coming up, all of a sudden Lenz changed and came storming in. I knew by now that only Chris could trigger such a rage. What had he thought or done now? I knew I was in for it immediately. I put my guard back up and threw Lenz out of my space. He felt the jolt and the closing up of my energy. It was like being slammed in the face. He did not take it well.

"I will not put up with your rage, Lenz." I said with a force that he knew to respect.

"How dare you display power in front of and toward me?" he yelled.

"Get a clue, Lenz. I will display that which I please when and where and how I please," I stated very confidently. He came within inches of my face and stopped.

"Don't even try it," I ordered him. In a moment's time he felt his strength slipping away and a melting down coming forward. At this moment I spoke, "You always rage about this situation which does not exist. You conclude that I am validating mere thoughts that Chris is thinking."

"You do validate it," he yelled out at me.

"Oh nor nor! I have better things to do than tune into him. Don't you understand that it is Chris who is trying to tap into us? " As soon as I used the word us, Lenz calmed down and I had control again.

"Us?" he asked.

"Well, we may not tolerate each other well but we are very much alike in systems," I said.

"If you loved me you would use your systems on me," he said.

"I love myself," I concluded as he left.

Now, you need to understand that everything I've written has been done deliberately. Those of you who have had a hard time understanding all of this are merely just asleep and those who have understood it are awake. You must realize the importance of staying awake and you must go with great speed to the White Light. The more you know, the greater the Dark Force pursues this knowledge, however they cannot tap into the White Light. If you are secured there, then you are fine, unless it is matters of the Soulmate. The pulling they present is incredible. Remember, one is always in Dark so they will automatically attempt to pull you there. They see nothing wrong with the Dark because they have been void of Light.

Remember, if you are not consciously aware, you have nothing to base negativity on. As Light approaches, you begin to recognize what you are in and thus a conscious level begins to stir. All of a sudden, what never bothered you begins to and you start to feel so unsettled. Most will attempt to bury this immediately and do the great denial. More people have their Soulmates pulling on them than you can imagine but it is being blamed on everything else. Once you can call something on its actions, you also begin to regain your power over it again. A good term for this is, caught you. A lie will travel a long way and so will the blame system. Are not they both related? As you read on, I must tell you that there are many messages that I have given you. You will not find these until you are ready to wake up further. Each chapter has been designed to allow you a different access.

For me, having such Knowledge had required me to deal with the big boys and so far, there was really only one on the planet. Chris was the want-to-be big boy but it was really Lenz. As the years progressed, the hate people felt for Chris just grew. It was clear to all that he was the one tied to Lenz and kept trying to eliminate me. Although it seemed impossible, Lenz and I were very much in a relationship. Whatever I told him to do he did. It was a game and he loved games. He had underestimated me again and again. I was so into my systems that I realized that no one could handle them, certainly not any mortal realm. For the first time ever I related with Lenz on a level I had never felt before. Oh, how it had been such a lonely walk for him. It had been for me as well but I had never really stopped to notice it until now.

I did not sleep that much but when I did it was deep. The summer breeze flooded my room so that I completely relaxed. Sometime into this sleep there was a nudging of me to wake me.

"Father?" I whispered in surprise.

"He has come to you, Daughter, like never before. Wake and meet him," Zeus said rushing out.

I sat up and there was only a little moonlight coming through my window. Lenz stood outside waiting. What in the world was he waiting for? I went to the window and in silence I welcomed him. He then sent energy towards me and I did the same to him. Colors began to pass between us and I laughed. Imagine me laughing with this man. He wanted to play and for the first time ever, I did too. He sent colors and I sent colors and with delight I absolutely adored this game. We had done this before in another time and slowly I began to recall this past life. Music had come to us and it was there again. Then I stopped and held my hand over my mouth so that I could not speak. Oh my God, he was that cello, not Chris! He had sent Chris in his place to see my reaction. I tried desperately to hold back the tears but I could not. I stood there asking myself how could I have not known this. Oh God Force, help me. The pain of the cello began to play and I struggled to find the flute to answer him back. Oh God Force help me, I cannot let him down but I could not present the sound and he turned and walked away.

"She does not love me." I heard him sadly say.

I tried frantically to get out of my room and out the door to reach him. He was gone and had carried with him lifetimes of rejection from me all in a moment of time. I cried out his name and heard no response. I yelled to the wind that he had tricked me and that no one could have unveiled such a thing. I kept yelling to the stars that I needed to be loved and that all of the years pounding me about certainly was not love. I kept yelling until exhaustion hit me. Oh God Force what a shock. I felt stripped of all Knowingness. I wanted to die and be born in a moment's notice all over again. Everything crashed in on me and yet everything lifted. There was no purpose, yet there was now a great direction.

The pain of the cello had taken my love to the wrong man. No, he had set me up and that was all there was to it. I was getting angry because it had been such a waste of time when we could have done other things, productive things, positive things. Then the reality hit me that I had activated my own Soulmate and there was no return. Oh God, I was in trouble and I was in a heap of it. No wonder Lenz had pointed out that he had had no music and Chris did. Everything began to point itself out to me. I definitely did not want to see what was becoming quite visual. I should have seen it but I did not want to. I mean, who wants to be hit with someone being as black as pitch? I am sure it was as bad as his being hit with this purer than thou Victorian innocence. How many times had I told him to take a hike? I had rejected him since day one and made sure I had every defense up to keep him out. Look at all he had done to me but to him it was viewed differently. Surely I required a gentleman. I had to take a break from life here because it all was rushing upon me so.

It had to have been crucial for Zeus to have shown up to wake me. How could I have not seen it? It was impossible to see without a constant open line of communication. I sat for hours and days alone contemplating what I should do next. Nothing had even jolted me so, not in this life anyway. The first thing that hit me was that finally he would terminate this Chris thing but he did just the opposite. He went away for the first time on all levels and I did not see him, feel him or have any contact of any kind. The void was tremendous. The weather went crazy and it was as if there was a constant funeral passing by.

All of my students started calling me, telling me that they all felt that their Soulmates were in trouble. Big trouble and they were all in such a desperate state about it all. Even my soul energies were all in a panic attack. What in the world was Lenz doing now? Revenge was the first thing that hit me. Everyone would have to pay big time for my not remembering that the cello belonged to him. So what else was new? He always had a pay back. What surprised me most was the lack of awareness as to how bad it could get and oh, it dove even deeper to the pits of hell. Everyone I knew became out of control and kept flipping out all over the place. I was genuinely disgusted in this whole Soulmate thing.

I could not call Lenz primitive, that is for sure but some of his actions were most primitive. I got hit with "I'm pouting and it's your fault." Oh yes, let us do the blame system. If anyone was to blame, it was Chris, evil Chris who got his thrill during his orgasms, trying in those moments to free himself from his body to merge with Lenz. Of course, Lenz could take Chris and do things with him because he had sold his soul to his master. It fed Chris to such degrees of gluttony. He would lay for hours after these sexual experiences totally lacking for memory of where and what he had actually done. He was addicted to Lenz and even wanted to merge with him as one being. Of course Chris could deny everything because he would never claim responsibility of any kind. Chris was a pig, a disgusting sexual pervert. He was so addicted to Lenz that he wanted to extend his male anatomy to merge with his master's. Lenz had a will as strong as mine. Oh, we were opposites all right but what we did have the same wills was as strong for the both of us.

I thought about Jimmy for the first time in years. He was so much like Lenz in ways that only now I could see. Lenz had this smile, this intensity and charisma that Jimmy had had. I thought about other men that I had connected with and all of these revelations where coming forward. I even recalled childhood flashes when I could have sworn that Lenz had been there. Had I been taken in by all of this lack of realization? I had not given Lenz credit for being as good at throwing things in my face as he deserved. Thank you very much, honey! It felt like an invasion hitting me for all of those private times, which now turned out to be not so private. Was he good? Oh, was he good but I was too and there had to be an in on all of this. I knew that all of my years of denying him would come back sooner or later by his denying me. He now was setting it up to force Chris to be my Soulmate, to trash me and get rid of me. I was in a corner and I would have to win him back. With dread, I was forced into this direction.

The words of Zeus and Athena hit me hard. "Daughter, you have to get him back to the White Light. You have to," they would both say again and again. All of my going forward stopped. This whole picture of Chris and the cello so unsettled me to levels of despair, that I could not get it out of my mind. It was so private and intimate and I was so violated. Who would send another in place of their own self? I am sure that Lenz was standing right there watching it all. Now he was angry and going to make Chris my Soulmate? Did he actually think that I was going to hold still for all of this? How could he do this? So all of these years he had been putting Chris in the way as the player of Soulmate so that he did not have to deal with me? How dare he! I was livid now and behaving just like him. The more I put things together, the more livid I became.

I had never behaved like Lenz, never! I had never needed him, desired him or wanted him. If he was thinking that that was going to change now, he was in for a shock, a big shock. How about a shock so big it sends him back to Olympus. Wouldn't it be entertaining to see Zeus and him together? I was floored something awful and I kept telling myself to calm down that I was reacting and that is exactly what Lenz wanted me to do. I had never been out of control and now I felt myself bouncing off the walls. How dare he!

It was time for a big gathering of my soul energies and so we feasted and talked for so many hours. We had all decided to forget the

Soulmates and run off with a good Soul Energy. Yeah, right. Oh, how we all loved each other and how open we all were to things. I tell you all that there is nothing as refreshing to the soul as a good soul energy. How wonderful these parties always were. We would laugh and laugh until we were all so silly. We were all quite the handful for anyone viewing us.

Lenz stayed clear of this now and had new plans for me. More trouble was really the bottom line. He had been wounded in spite of his trap. Oh, for the love of all of us, we were destined to pay. No one made fun of the master and got away with it. Who was making fun though? We were not, it was merely his interpretation of these parties we had. I am the one that was devastated but what mattered was he being wounded. Well, if all of us females had no power, what was all of the fuss?

I realized again that Lenz needed to see Chris face to face with me as it had been this way all along. He was not sure of anything because of my misguided awareness of the cello. I knew that he would never forgive me for not having clarity but it was all right for him to not have clarity. Either he knew or didn't know. Chris was so much like Lenz that at times it was hard to tell them apart.

Now you may be thinking, what if your Soulmate sent another in his or her place? Do not think too long on this. It is rare and not so easy to do. When you are on a mission, many things happen of an unusual nature. Chris was the puppet and Lenz put on the show. I did prefer to ask for a rain ticket rather than be in the audience. Lenz was an entertainer though and full to the maximum with shows like you could not imagine. He really did fabulous magic. In fact, that was his forte. Cross the line though and it became lethal. His strength was something best left unchallenged. I knew that all of these Soulmate matters were connected to this mission and that all was playing out as it needed to be, leaving little clarity for all. One thing Lenz knew for sure, he had met his match in me. I would never buckle under, surrender or give up on the challenge and oh, did I present this. Chris remained the clinging leash that awaited the next command. If for any reason he felt that I had interfered, he would go ballistic and become vindictive towards me, but what else was new?

I needed all of my Family right now. What would be better than having everyone surrounding me? I went to a place where I knew I had privacy and the beauty of outside. Then I sat down and was ready to receive them all.

"Zeus," I called out, somehow needing to see him more than anyone else. I loved him and adored him so. The memory of this so stubborn, towering sized man having come to tears before me never left my memory. It reminded me of the mortal male ego when you see it come down all of the way and all at once. It brought to mind a man I once met who came upon such news that he gasped for air as he cupped his hands into his face and fell to his knees in tears. He was finally to the full circle of all of the denial and disaster he had caused. All of the souls he had affected and bought to better himself. It was not until the realization that he was using himself, that there was any hope for change. So many had to suffer while he got off power tripping the world. It was his pms that cost so much. Zeus smiled as much as one could smile being so content. I could not help but smile back as I knew how deep his love was.

"Father that was and is and probably always will be, that which has fallen to such a mess. I cannot do such mission things. Chris has played such a Dark game with Lenz. They have merged somewhere in time and attached themselves to each other. They are still attached and have exchanged parts of each other's soul. Chris wanted Lenz to be his Soulmate and agreed to have me eliminated. They did magic together and other things. They exchanged blood and did a sacrifice. They were very clear as to what they were doing. It was never a question of unawareness. With malice and evil they laughed and carried on."

Zeus looked at me. "Daughter this is correct. You have concluded to great truth."

"So?" I asked.

"Can you conclude further?" he asked me. "Yes Father, they are both lower than low," I said.

Zeus burst into a jolly voice, "Oh you are most brilliant but, Daughter, do you see more of that which we cannot tell you?" he asked me.

"Sure, I see the whole plan. I just send them both to the White Light and Love of the God Force and be gone with them. Yes Father, I conclude now to the last and final level," I stated. It was impossible to keep a straight face with such a jolly face glaring at me but I fell into the silence of no speech. "Be gone with you, Zeus. Go love your mate" and as I thought these thoughts, Zeus nodded his head and departed. We all spoke vibration language.

Maybe I did not need anyone in such matters but as I turned my head, there stood in his majestic glory, Angel of Silk. "Oh, it's you," I spoke.

"Am I not welcome?" he asked.

"Oh Angel of Silk, come and entertain me with speech."

"Descendent from Olympus, are you not troubled?" he asked treading gently as if he sensed it all.

"Troubled? You have been there for so long of course you know what is going on. I cannot talk of it." I told him.

He reached for me and stopped. Then I reached for him. "Do not conclude, gentle entity. All shall be fine," I told him as he embraced me. "You are friend, you are Love, you are Light. I love you," I said as he left. Oh Angel of Silk was precious and he had often been such an inspiration to me. It was as if he was sent for only one thing and to get involved elsewhere was nearly impossible. He was often awkward but oh, could he battle if it was warranted. He had come to protect me, it was that simple.

To those of you who could never fathom Angels, how sad and unenlightened you all are. There really is nothing familiar in this earth realm. You keep trying to force familiarity here. Only the souls are familiar and that is the true natural state of things. Why do so many of you deny your natural state? Why do you deny your Knowingness? Oh sleepy heads, you have to reclaim Truth. Athena was right that it was all going to go on for such a long, long time. In Soulmate matters, Lenz and Chris were both counting on me not having clarity as to who was who. They could play these roles but the Truth was the Truth. In my silence I knew and they knew I knew. It is the unspoken word that has so much power. Quite frankly, why would I want to claim either one?

Lenz was a complicated man to the world yet it was so clear to me seeing right through him. My lack of clarity about the cello now concluded nonstop energy on me. He worked double time sending thoughts of Chris and then some. My mind was so flooded with thoughts of Chris that I would accidentally call out his name when I knew the person I was talking to was not named Chris.

Oh Lenz was having a wonderful time. In one given day I would say Chris maybe twenty or thirty times but once I was onto the full energy of this game, I was able to override this program. Lenz would then do something else and so back and forth we continued. No matter what he threw at me, I outmaneuvered or bypassed it. He was so angry and so intrigued all at the same time. It was playtime with Deborah and at last the planet had been kind to him and given him a playmate. I did keep him busy and as long as he was busy, he was not going after so many people.

Chris, the jerk, thought that I was now tuning into him and started coming after me. He would call and call and call and I would hang up on him. It was bad enough dealing with Lenz but both of them on me was too much. As much as I kept trying to stay on top of things, I could not take the harassment of both. My soul energies all came together to try to intervene and for a while it did work but one night I woke alone and startled with Lenz at my bedside. He was being affected by what he was doing to me and his whole being was changed. I was half asleep and my guard was not only down but I was too exhausted to put it up.

"Why don't you love me?" he asked.

"Hello Lenz. What? You don't get it? You do all of these Dark things to me and what is it about this picture you don't get? "

"It is my way or nothing." He said back to me.

"I will not surrender to you. You should know this. Never, means never and this is the end of the conversation," I concluded lying back down and turning away.

"Wait," he said.

"For what?" I asked.

"Maybe we can work it out." he said so low I was barely able to hear him. I started laughing and laughing and oh, how I could not stop.

"What is so funny?" he demanded to know.

"Why don't you be that of your Father? Admit that you are a fool, an old fool," I said laughing much like Zeus.

Lenz was angered and got up. "I come to you and attempt to bring peace and you laugh at me?" he said, changing his tone of voice back to his usual way.

"Are you just plain stupid? You hurt me and everyone else. You violate and control and play this sick, sick game with Chris. You want to make peace and not only that, you want to make it all on your terms. What is this, more sneaking and untruths, more traps? Do you still think that I am not onto you? Now be gone with you. No one invited you!" I said jumping into his face, pointing to the door.

"Just wait!" he growled at me.

"Oh, for what, more of your evil? No thank you. Let us see, Lenz. Now we all have to pay again for my not surrendering to you? So long," I said holding my own. He slammed the door and I fell back on my bed. I didn't care anymore. We would all get fried no matter what, so what did it matter? He would find another excuse to hit us all.

Can you imagine the ego of Lenz? It could not even be contained in the whole United States. Imagine being born a god and ruling the earth. Imagine being viewed as one celled entities only waiting for the big vacuum Lenz was plugging in and getting ready with glee to point it in your direction. There was nowhere to run or hide. If you thought there was, then you were fooling yourself. You may say how could this be? Easy. Once again I tell you of the Dark you cannot see. If you are ever going to get it, you must remember that this Force does exist.

Nothing is going to really evolve if you leave parts out. I realize that many of you have been so traumatized that you have shut down, big time. Well, what do you want to do about it? Here we are at the crossroads again. Now, I tell you that I shall give you more Teachings along the way but every time you come to a crossroad, you will stop in all of this if you have not decided to awake. Those awaking will not even bother with stopping, they will just read on. So remember this, those of you who stop in certain places in this story need to hear it perhaps even more than once. There are so many hidden messages all throughout my writing.

Recognize one thing here. All has been put to you in a way to keep you safe and secure. This is one of the reasons you will only receive part of the Teachings. Note too that as you grow, you will reread and see something else completely different. It is your spirit grabbing hold of Truth.

By now we should all know that males have pms and females have been severely repressed. The ego should be nothing more than the bridge to what the soul is trying to get to the mind. What kind of bridge do you have? The bridge of expression has been grossly blown up as time has gone by. You are probably thinking this very moment about someone you know with a really big bridge. Remember this, the bigger the bridge the longer it take to get the thought from the soul to the mind, thus we have the big egos. The threat of losing their knowledge makes one blow up their bridge to a bigger size

Okay, you will say to me but enlightened people would know better. Yes, they would but I said knowledge not Knowingness. Knowledge is located through someone else's ideas, expressions, experiences and so on. Knowingness comes from the God Force only. That is enlightenment. We will always have to come back to terminologies as long as we are on the earth. It helps each other identify where they are. Are you stuck in the human race level? I will know it by what you speak. Are you stuck in Soulmate? I will know it by what you speak. I will know it regardless of speech, however, in this example I give you, you too can know of these things. If you ever desire vibration language, then it is there for you too. First though, you must be able to identify the spoken language. How fast can you evolve, only as fast as you are able to remember that Awesome Love that floods your soul, leaving you at such levels of peace that you may be brought to tears or smiles. You may have to feel the shrinking of your bridge somewhat but at least your chest will be lighter.

Some terminologies here would be, what a relief, I needed to get that off of my chest and the weight has been lifted, just to list a few.

Whenever anyone says these things, I laugh and hear the reconstruction of their bridge, their ego. Thank the God Force that there is no charge for that huge reconstruction bill. I can promise if you go back and forth, you will blow up the seams of the construction and your bridge will constantly be in a state of weak structure. Do you want to drive over a bridge with such bad conditions? No and you certainly do not want this kind of ego coming at you either.

Oh, how the Love of the God Force can entertain us. We are all down here playing out egos, bridges, pms, repression, yet I tell you our bungee cords are never gone. The God Force can pull on them at any given moment and you will go back. I see your Light, you feel the fog, the sleepy states, the confusion. You hesitate on claiming Knowingness for fear of the human race. It is in a deep, deep sleep and if you try to stir it, it will grab you and say to you, go back to sleep now. Give it up you'll never make it. I could go on about ego forever but you only need to recognize that bridge. It is not a long lengthy study to open up the doors to Truth. It needs to be given to you easy, simple and in a light manner so that you can see it. Complications are human race levels.

Don't doctors use that word complications a lot? Do not worry, I told you that I would get into attorneys too but that is still to come. Females do not have such big egos. Only when their Soulmates have ego problems might the female have a bigger ego. Then the males would be unexpressive and have a really hard time getting things out. I must move on here and not stay too long on these matters.

There are five basic elements we use all of the time. Spiritual is the most important if you are bonding to the White Light. Physical is the least important only because it is temporary and not the natural state for the soul. Emotional would be next to spiritual and intellect would be after that. Mental would be next to the physical plane. When you bond to the White Light, you must be able to feel this and express yourself. The last thing you need to do is sit and think about it all. This becomes a trap if you apply the mental.

You certainly need all five of these elements to function every day but there are times when one element comes to the forefront more so than the rest. If you take a shower, the physical comes to the forefront. If you take a test, the mental comes to the forefront and so on. All day long we use these five basic elements unless we are head on with Soulmate. They blow all concepts of everything. With them all five elements charge you and race you at such a rapid speed that you will bounce around unless you are well fixed in the White Light. The Soulmate can change tracks faster than you can even imagine. Oh but you change tracks just as fast. How many buttons do you have? They will push those and then some. Anything private is exposed.

Even though I have explained some of these things already, it is important to keep bringing certain things to the forefront. You may not understand it right now but you will eventually.

As time went by, as you can imagine, things only grew more desperate for all. Chris was so evil and Lenz kept it going with him. He would send Chris intense sexual energy with the focus that I was doing it. Do you think that there was even one ray of Light in Chris to stop it? No and it was the sickest thoughts of sex ever. Sure Lenz laughed as he knew it stimulated Chris big time and he also knew Chris didn't have a clue as to who was doing this to him. It went on morning, noon and night. Both men combined had nothing in this department, no class, no style, no abilities. Neither one of them ever had a clue that they were beyond functional in this area. A real man who is in his own presence does not have to show, prove or try. Chris and Lenz were like pms with the first letter missing. The arrival of class had somehow missed their addresses. Chris kept focusing on me and Lenz kept focusing on Chris. As for me, it was the eternal manashatwa with someone standing in for me. I was never going to validate this or take it on.

Wouldn't you know it, Chris perceived it as a catch me if you can game. "She's just teasing me," he would say. "How could she reject someone as great as me? I'm drop dead gorgeous," he would continue. Can you believe it? No matter what, Lenz had an in on everything and he would bounce games off of everyone. He was counting on that chemistry he thought Chris and I had but it was never anything.

Meanwhile, I had my thoughts on another man who was slowly getting closer without actually activating any energy to alert Lenz or Chris. He was wonderful and very much a Soul Energy. He was also aware of what was going on and used great caution in all matters connected with me. We had had many lifetimes before. Stepping cautiously seemed to be natural for him. His name was John and there was great love between us. There were many things we wanted to do but somehow we knew our time would be short; so we eliminated many desires and focused on the immediate one. He was adorable and the kind of man you could cuddle up next to and talk to for hours. He would interject passion by touch, all along staying focused on the conversation. We did touch greatly and deeply and loved each other as best as we could with the situation as such. Only in memory of other times could we have seen the future. He was so well scripted for his role that when the time came, he kissed me and held me only momentarily before he departed for good. He went on his journey and no one ever knew. I had several wonderful Soul Energies as the years went by. Seldom did anyone ever suspect. Lenz was so busy power tripping the planet that he did not know either. Then there was sick Chris clinging to his Rama and blaming me for his miserable life. I needed my soul energies to help deal with such intense Darkness but more than that, we truly needed each other.

From time to time I thought of Jimmy and how, if it had not been for him, I probably would not have ever gone this way but let me tell you to notice what I just wrote. I wrote the word probably and you should have caught that word. Of course I would have gone this way. Jimmy was the button that pushed the movie to begin. In spite of everything he did, I still loved him dearly and greatly.

Part of recognizing Knowingness is being responsible for participating in all of the events that come your way. Remember, the human race hates the void of the blame system. If they have to be even the slightest responsible for anything, including a mere thought, they all go ballistic. Religion can show this again and again. Let someone else carry the weight. The human race always needs a villain and a hero. It's a turn on, a high, a thrill. What they are really saying on a soul level is that this is once again a Soulmate scenario each playing off the other like Light and Dark, hero and villain. Do you want me to say everyone down deep is searching for his or her Soulmate? Hello sleepyheads, I will let you draw your own conclusion here. Now for some of you, you are too stirred up and need to take a great break from all of this. My purpose too, is to touch all of you, no matter where you are in your enlightenment. If you have become angry in some of what I've written, good. I don't care how you feel because all I will give you is a constant affirmation back to the Awesome White Light and Love of the God Force. You are loved, gentle entities. You are loved radical entities. All of you are loved and it will never end. For those of you who want control, guess what? You have no control in this kind of power. Bravo, because the human race would even destroy this if they could.

CHAPTER EIGHTEEN

There are many states of being. The desire state is the highest. I was desiring to be left alone but Lenz had other desires. Getting rid of him was impossible. I couldn't tolerate him, put up with him or anything else. At times he was like a child getting caught with his hand in the cookie jar. To say he drove me nuts would not even come close to it. He was always in my face, my paperwork, my students, clients, my personal belongings and he helped himself nonstop as any money passed by me. He even entertained himself at my classes driving my students into an unsettling state of being. He knew that he would never be invited, so he just helped himself.

Again and again we all had our soul energy parties and for most it was the rejuvenation all of us needed. Things began to change and as you can guess, Lenz was focusing on my dear friends hard and long. I realized that if they could not hang on, he would eventually single them all out and do each one of them in. He saw how close we all were and how much love passed through all of us. He was jealous and demanded attention from me. It did not matter what he had to do. What he did was cruel and violent but it still did not make me leave the White Light. How far would he go? Would he go all of the way? What had happened so far was nothing next to what was coming. There was nothing I could do because he literally went right through people. He destroyed one life after another and then would joke about it in front of me.

"Oh, these morons," he would say. "They are so stupid. You can do anything to them. They cannott catch me because I program them to blame someone else. Oh Deborah, you are the only one onto me." He would laugh and laugh no matter how cruel it was. He would stare at me trying so hard to read my mind but he could not. I was cloaked and that fascinated him to no end. I was the toy, the trinket, the pawn and the ultimate challenge. He did not belong on earth. No one was safe from such power.

Now you will probably say, what if you are in the White Light, wouldn't you be safe? Yes, unless Soulmate is activated. If you are walking around with clarity but those around you are not in the White Light there is a big threat with your presence. Your loyalty to the White Light must be as such that you would let go of, this very moment, everything and everyone. If you could not do this then you would not be in the Light. What I say here is that the White Light must be a priority before all other things. How many can do this right this very moment? Okay, so plenty of you are in Darkness but Light is there for you to take. Now for those of you in the White Light there is a constant price to pay. You must make sure that Darkness knows exactly where you are.

If you do not use the terminologies, it will not recognize where you are. Let me give you an example. A good, kind, loving person who became connected to me kept saying that he was talking to god and praying for me. I said to him, why do you stay in Darkness as you are using terminologies that Darkness can identify with? Why aren't you saying God Force and affirmations? I told him he was only thinking he was hearing god. He then said to me that he thought, as long as he was talking only to me, that I would understand where he was. You cannot hide your terminologies or vibrations. I did know where he was and told him.

"But, but," he said, "can't we talk privately among ourselves with both knowing that we are talking about the same god?" No, because we were not talking about the same god. Why? Because Darkness recognizes these words, god, prayers, etc. and tries to put it together to locate where you are. He did not realize that even I must use the terminologies that I taught. He also thought that what I told people I myself did not have to do. Excuse me, I am not exempt, none of us are. It was sad to watch all of the people falling apart and suffering all because Lenz was bored. I could not bear it but I could not let him know this. I kept trying to reach as many people as I could.

Now, you may say that you have said all of the affirmations possible and you have followed every word to the exact letter but you still do not progress forward. First, you cannot always expect to see forward in the way you believe it should go. If you lack, though, in that internal peace, you are deep in Soulmate. Please do not say something like you don't even know who your Soulmate is. Have I told you again and again about the Dark that you cannot see as well as the Light you cannot see? As long as you remain in that tunnel vision, hitting the concrete wall head on, you will continue to have injury and lack clarity. How many head-on collisions have you come close to and here all along you were thinking some idiot just got in your way. Hello brain dead sleepyhead, or are you just plain forgetful. Wake up! There is always someone who will live in the denial state no matter what you do. They are what I call an atom bomb going through life spewing out gaseous forms of dangerous matter. Hooray to the gas bomb who finally disintegrates somewhere in life and has the chance to breath fresh air.

Of course you know who your Soulmate is. There are levels of being in Soulmate. Try this for a description. First, you have the onset of a small cold. Next, you find every possible bodily avenue clogged up, nose, ears, eyes and so on. You are now laying claim that something big time has you but take a look at the picture. Did you not have symptoms of something coming earlier? Well, here it comes, the full-blown cold going into the flu, aches, pains and misery.

Hello! Soulmate has now arrived. It is a mess, you are a mess, life is a mess or should I ask, what life. The one advantage for you is that you are contagious and guess who is coming to share your fever? Everyone lives in the illusion that Soulmates are standing on the top of mountains seeing each other, the music plays and they go rushing into each other's arms. This will never happen because true Soulmate bonding have severe levels of resisting each other. The phrase is so loosely used, "Oh, he's my Soulmate or she's my Soulmate." I can tell you right now that ninety-nine percent of you have the wrong word for your relationship. Soulmates are extremists, from one extreme to the other. They try to slide past each other ever so carefully as to not infringe on each other's space. Then in the next moment, they crash into each other to claim the full experience of both ends of the spectrum. If all you have is one side of the picture, how can you see the other side if only one person, your match, has it? You may say, "No, this cannot be."

You may argue that you have met others who can give you this. They can only give you a fragment next to what the Soulmate can give you. Soulmates are in a perpetual state of passion and they can stop anywhere to accomplish that which the body desires. Their desires are as strong as their resistance. Imagine that kind of bonding. Do either one of them know what they want? No, and then they both agree, yes. They can do as they please. They can make it up as they go along. You do not have plans anymore. They have all gone out the window. Your future? You now have this person so opposite to you that you can finally see both sides of things. Hey, this person is not so bad after all. Your blinders are lifting. You are even sharing that box of tissues now and without real direction, you even have a place to go. Does anything matter? Only what the two of you decide on. Even without a decision, things will just pour into you. All of a sudden one thing will set one of you off and the discord will be magnified so that your souls will be pulled on. Search, you will think, and a peace treaty will come about again. Are you in this? You are in Soulmate.

Let me explain some of this. Picture a big ball of White Light. If you go to the right of this ball and head out it will take you deep into Darkness. Let us say that you go all the way to the end. This would put you all the way into the deepest of all Darkness. Now let's say, just for the purpose of an example, that your Soulmate goes in the other direction, all the way into the deepest of White Light clear to the end as if both of you would each come up against a wall. Soulmates would be at their greatest separation. Now, the problem for one of you is that your mate would be so deep in Darkness that they would have lost their direction. It is clear that they cannot find their way back. You on the other end would be filled so with Light that you could locate them. Again I say that the one in Light is responsible for the one in Dark. They cannot see.

There is a ball of Light that you first left, let us call that the God Force. While you have been out in the sunshine, your other half has been frozen in their Dark space. Can you understand how Darkness is lost, dangerous and ready for war? You have to stop blaming or saying Darkness could change if it wanted to. How, without Light it cannot see. The more Darkness the more problems Soulmates are having. It is a mess but it can be resolved. You are waiting for more but for now I will let this settle.

Lenz came rushing in and stopped short. He was upset and for him not to be ranting and raving it must have been greatly serious. I did not want to ask him what it was but at the same time he stood right in my face. I looked at him and read his mind.

"You've been up to no good and it's all backfired on you. Your conscience is bothering you. I do not believe it. What do you want me to do about it?" I said looking away. "Oh, so how many years later have you finally realized this? And what does it mean? You'll never change," I said walking away.

"Wait," he said, "I'm trying to talk of it all."

"Talk of it all? You? Why don't we sign a contract right here and now? You can confirm that from time to time you will talk of it all. Get it all clear, I will never want you. I will never need you. I will never put up with you. End of conversation." I said flaring up with energy.

He looked at me. "I have no music." he said finally leaving.

"So what?" I echoed in his direction. "You don't deserve any." I fell asleep and into a sort of magical dream. This was a well dream, not filled with distress or anything. There was a game and many men who came to court me all had hoods upon their faces so that I could not recognize them. The game was wonderful. They would hold a certain fragrance and rush past me. I was blindfolded as well but they could see through their hoods to keep them from falling. There seemed to be a strong desire to cheat and take a peek at who might be in front of me. The music played in the background. It was light and somewhat of a high renaissance flute sound. Each would put a grape up to my mouth. I would then bite into it and if it were sour, they would be disqualified. Whoever won with the sweetest grape got to kiss me.

I woke suddenly, blindly and my bedroom was dark. I felt a rush of energy, which had worked its way below my waist. He was here trying to use magic on me to seduce me again.

"How dare you Lenz?" I demanded.

"I am lonely and want to pleasure myself upon you," he said acting as if there was absolutely nothing wrong with his actions.

"And who said I'd be pleasured allowing you your pleasure?" I concluded. I would never agree or admit to being married to him and that was final. How dare he? I knew his magic was powerful and he could create illusions so good that they could be fully acted out without anyone ever suspecting any wrongdoing. Mr. Pro could pick up and rearrange a whole room in a matter of seconds.

Are you all in the Dark even when you see the Dark working? Who is going to speak up and say the chair just moved? None of you wants to appear crazy. Guess what, you are Dark because cowards are a low vibration. This is just another form of Darkness. You are below crazy.

If I see a chair move, not only will I say I saw it, I can even tell you who did it. I can also move it myself. Why don't you try impressing yourself from time to time and see what you come up with. The minute you are concerned by what others think, you have gone and done it again, stepped into speaking the human terminologies giving your power away, big time. More Darkness? The second you are concerned by what others think, you have lost the full power of whatever you are trying to do.

Lenz continued to show up with this guilty look. Of course Chris remained in the background watching, always the upset, the greed for attention, the Rama want-to-be. It was a really old scene and quite sickening. In Chris' mind he thought I wanted him. He also felt jealous that I had such an effect on Lenz. As long as Lenz kept projecting certain things, it kept him in the picture. He saw Lenz go through things, which he had never seen before, such as the chain reactions the three of us triggered. It had been going on for years but Chris was so caught up in the game he really had not sorted out with clarity the magnitude of this connection.

For me, I had a job to do. When it was done, I would get onto other things. As time went by, the dread of Chris became so repulsive that I began to think of ways to get him out of the picture all together. He constantly upset what I was doing. He wanted me removed so he could get his Rama back. There was also the power he felt he had over the whole situation.

Lenz began to change slowly but not with other people. We were thrown together on many levels into a special place, a level no one understood but us. Chris somewhat knew about this place but had been there and violated so much and although it was still within his energy fields he was powerless to access it. Whenever I occupied Lenz, I noticed roadblocks lifted on everyone. As much as he denied the word love and spoke how it made one weak, he was heading in that direction. I saw that undeniable curiosity that kept taking him to that place. At times he was naïve to things I would say. I was naïve to his reaction to me. It was like coming upon something so unexpected and pure that it was an invitation of great desire. When this presented itself, Lenz was wonderful to be around. It did not last long though and he would become angry, blaming me for being so clever and trying to trick him.

In a strange way I understood him more than I wanted to. He was temperamental, moody, raging but in between everything, this naïve side would come forward without any warning. If I could locate this place in him, I could at least keep some peace during his ranting times. He wanted to know that I would be there just in case loneliness set in, and it did more and more as the years went by.

My times with Athena were always special but when Lenz was around, she refused to come near. Zeus kept a good distance but unlike Athena, he kept an eye out for me. I longed for Olympus so deeply. So much had been set in motion there. How warm the presence of Zeus was. He laughed at how primitive the earth people were. We spoke at great length about how human beings constantly gave their power away to everything. What was amusing was all of these idiots that worshipped gurus, masters and the likes of these so called leaders. He had no respect for one this stupid. He did however admire the fighters, the ones who, in spite of and regardless of, kept on going. The greatest insult was the idiots who portrayed the same name or claimed to channel the Gods and Goddesses. Truly only an idiot could believe such nonsense. We spoke of how these people did religion, the great divider of Light.

"Oh, to the little man who had a god after him," Zeus would say. He truly was a wise and gentle entity until provoked. Now he had come to speak of Lenz but somehow his words always remained the same. "You must love him Daughter," he said.

Here it comes again. I had heard this so much that it was useless to respond. I gave Zeus this look and he knew to say no more.

Angel of Silk had been with me for so long that he blended with me. He would watch intensely everything and was constantly ready for some big battle. So much time had passed that I really gave up on anything coming in the form of a battle. At the most I expected some small disputes, but battle? Angels are on a different time than people. They do not have the solid mass of the human body. The timer has started for the life cycle of the human body and it counts down. What amazed me is how something so important like your Soulmate was so badly erased from the human memory.

Now you are probably coming up with all kinds of theories about life and your beliefs, which is fine but I ask you how complete is your soul? The second you are settling for less or tolerating your situation, you are out of the Light. By now you should be saying, except in the situation of Soulmate. Now, someone is going to say that most of the people in the world are tolerating. I will say most of the world is asleep. Are there no exceptions or other possibilities? No. As long as it is on the human level, there will never be Light. You cannot have it halfway because that is like saying you are in the grey zone. The grey zone is Darkness.

The classes increased and many students from years back started to return. If Lenz decided that he wanted attention all day, he would cause problems for people so that they would be blocked from me. Since when do two hundred people all have right front flat tires on their cars or all their cars will not start and so on. Mr. Joker and his bionics on the planet had to do grand things in a grand style. He also had to make it so obvious that all eyes turned to him. Oh, how he loved the attention. People could not look too long his way though because the wrath would be on its way moments later. Then everyone would get fried. A good fry job from Lenz was equivalent to touching a high voltage wire, except you were forced to live through it all. He was good with telephones and major blackouts in one mood swing. It was unreal to the mortal eye but so familiar to me. If you didn't believe what he could do, he would give you a show that would render you so helpless you'd be speechless big time. No one or anything could quite scare you like he could. The problem was that once he touched your life, he never left it. Even if you thought he was done with you he'd show back up years later. I cannot tell you quite how one could be so powerful because there is so much I cannot tell you but this kind of power was not of this world.

When Athena came to see me, I cried with happiness. She brought me volumes of love and great remembrance of my soul. Being with Zeus had done her well and she glowed from such entertainment. We could not talk of Lenz because it so badly upset her but we could talk of matters elsewhere. We walked and held each other within our energy fields for hours. We spoke of many things until her purpose came forward.

"Mother, you once told me of troubles taking a very long time. Be this the same as before?" I asked her.

"Daughter, representing that of our Family, there is much I must tell you now and shall. It will bring great sadness perhaps to that of all of our futures. Son that I gave to Zeus, that being of your Father and that being of your brother has only one direction. It must be intervened at all costs. Whatever that which you, Daughter, can do you must. He absorbed that with the one you call Chris to give him part of his soul to retain your presence in hopes that you would be drawn to Chris instead. That which he gave to Chris was the essence of the sexual realm."

I started laughing. "You mean a severe case of pms?" I asked her.

"Yes Daughter," she said, both of us laughing so. It reminded me of years ago when Athena spoke of Zeus and that lightening rod. She became serious and continued on. "Oh Daughter, great disaster applies to all of us. In giving Chris the sexual realm, he that disturbs me did not realize how much he gave up." Athena put her head down. She could not speak his name. "You were there Daughter and in attempting to avoid it all, it hit upon you too."

"So we have to untangle the mess?" I asked her.

"Yes but it is upon you with great difficulty," she said. "They don't see it, do they?" I asked her.

"Yes and no. Daughter, you are the key to all of their realizations," she stated.

"I do not want to be involved. I do not care about either one of them and never did. Mother, it is clear that sooner or later it shall be revealed, my true feelings," I told her.

"Daughter, it is already revealed and obvious to he who is of great distress to me." Athena stated.

"Lenz." I responded.

"Yes" she confirmed turning from the name again. I tried to stop this entanglement. Lenz had Chris and Chris had Lenz. I was in the middle.

"Daughter," Athena continued, "all three of you must come together face to face to put things back as they are supposed to be. Unless this happens, all destinies are doomed. We have kept these things and more from you until it was necessary to bring it forward."

"Mother, you told me that things would be of great upset for a long, long time. Lenz pursues me, Chris pursues Lenz and I have so tried to be kept away from it all. Chris thinks that I pursue him but these are all illusions that Lenz gives him. It stirs things up constantly but when I look at those two I do not see a whole man in either one of them. Why in the world would I want half a man?"

"Daughter, you are courageous and curious with matters of the heart. Love so comes from you that it even surprises you with great levels. You leave such an impression, disappear and leave everyone in wonderment," Athena said so stately.

"Oh Mother, you will always give to me great praises. When would you say that which is not kind to me? Never!" I smiled as I returned to my stately manner. I thought to myself how wonderful it was to be so loved by such a Mother.

Athena read my thoughts and spoke further. "It is all that you know Daughter. Love just pours from your soul. Nothing but hatred pours from theirs."

Athena was right. Entities of her magnitude were sworn to the Allegiance and Sacred Law was never violated. Sacred Law was that which was designed to bring all things to the highest level. This does not just apply to human beings but to all life forms, be it wherever they are. Whenever you threaten the direction of one going towards the White Light, you are attempting to break this law.

Attorneys constantly break this law, through their legal lies. They are the deepest caught in man's levels. They are the Darkest of all careers and the very last on the list for enlightenment. Great fears go to the attorney who attempts to represent me. Now, there will be attorneys yelling that this is not true. Once again, there are some in Light but it is as rare as finding doctors in Light. Remember, I said it cost to be in Light. It also cost to be in Dark. Attorneys hide behind the laws to play the grey zone. Those attorneys being forced to give up their Darkness end up collapsing from going against the grain of how man thinks things are supposed to go. It isn't luck that wins the case it is ego. Where I come from there are no laws created by the human race. Perhaps attorneys should visit this place to see how small their knowingness really is. Where I come from, we deal strictly with Truth. It is easy to see Truth because it is connected to Light. You cannot see Truth in Dark because there is not any. Notice how the presentation from attorneys to all is let us find the truth and justice can be served?

I came upon a woman called Diane. She was that of Light substance such as myself. It was as if we had thirsted for water for many incarnations and came upon a great well providing water with Knowingness in it. She drank for thirst but she spoke as a kindred soul. There was acknowledgement and validation finally. Oh, to come upon a soul energy as I have said again and again. I drank of the water but not for Knowingness but for the rejuvenation of the body. As Diane drank, she spoke of great things as often entities in Light do. She knew of what was to come. I found her in a place one could almost visualize as a black hole. Her Light repelled many but it stood firm and strong among the others. She towered with brilliance and yet she was small in stature. Our time of sharing was brief but of quality time. I had known her in Olympus and Atlantis. Our Lights together had temporarily put the black hole into a rather grey color. There was much evil seated next to her but when I came upon her, she glowed greatly. Yes, we drank of much water and spoke of such magnificent things. I missed her as I left.

Probably the biggest of all programs Lenz could get you into was the financial one. He believed money was it and without it, your word meant nothing. The less you had, the smaller you became. He said that love made you weak and money made you strong. To summarize it all, as long as he had a constant increase of money and enough orgasms, he was flying high in the fast lane. It never mattered where you were in the picture. Who died and made Lenz god? He was so sick and perverted that my stomach turned when any thoughts of him came forward. He was ruthless and vulgar all in the illusion of being Mr. Prince Charming filled with charisma and mystical powers. I heard Zeus tell me how I had to love him and it was harder to do every day that went by. I heard the Angels say the same thing. I heard Athena tell me how much harder things would get. Most of all I heard the God Force tell me that I had to accomplish the mission, no matter what it took or I would be pulled out if I failed.

Lenz was a total embarrassment. He displayed too many old ways of the war lords of long ago. This violation of women was proof of this. The ritual of taking orgasms not only was severely out—dated, it was the ultimate destruction of the female. Chris knew all about this and Lenz did not keep quiet about it either. How either one of them could have thought I would want anything to do with them tells you how their egos were.

Little by little people started to struggle with health problems that made no sense at all. Everyone started crying that Rama was doing them in, they just knew it. I knew it too but I could not carry the weight of the whole world. They did wonderfully with me but fell apart when they left. It was important for everyone to stay close with someone on the same path. I began to pair people up and it did help. Constantly, Lenz used his tactics to sabotage whatever I did. It was growing old and so unnecessary. There were millions of people on the planet. Why me? Yes, the good old illusion of Soulmate scenario. I was so tired of it all. For a moment I wandered off to thoughts of yesterday, many yesterdays ago. Even as a baby Lenz was there. It had all been planned out so well. Not one thing was ever off or out of sync.

I was in awe of the magnitude of the Allegiance. I searched well into my soul and found more rejuvenation to go on and accomplish that which I had to. I stood strong and I was so well Loved by the God Force but I also had to hold greatly onto it.

Everything I did was designed to protect people. Everything was also coded so that private information could never be accessed by anyone or anything. I was involved with people from every walk of life all on their journey, be it of celebrity levels or just regular life styles. No one was ever placed higher than another but some situations were more urgent than the others were. Many of the mid western states were very high in abductions such as North and South Dakota and Nebraska. The western states of Idaho, Utah had high numbers as well. Of course if you look at this picture, for many they still live in the frame of those kinds of things just don't happen in places like this. Oh but they do and little is ever done to make a big fuss about it all.

To give you a good example as to why little fuss is ever made, let us just say your daughter disappears and it is made to look like she ran off with her boyfriend. For many months she has been in love and here the boyfriend was a plant, a set up. You are all thinking she will be back when the relationship ends. Wake up. There is nothing more frustrating than knowing what is going on and you have to deal with a mind as thick as lead refusing to believe you. Somehow this lead head will maybe believe you if enough time goes by. This should tell you that idiots gauge their stupidity on a timeframe. I can stand in front of you and read your soul, which is saying I think she is been taken, abducted but will the acknowledgement come out of your mouth? Not until the human beings around you do their stupid levels of trying to figure the situation out. By now, the little chance of any rescue is lost. Then you have those who know for sure what has happened but no one will believe them. Why, because it has to go the way human beings see things. Are you beginning to recognize how many idiots are around you? Mother Nature needs to clean up the planet.

It came upon me quite quickly and with great surprise as it often did. I was hit by such a blinding light it could have only been Zeus on some warpath.

"Daughter rise and come with me," he said terribly upset.

"Come with you where?" I asked him as I tried to get myself adjusted to his overwhelming presence.

"To Olympus Daughter," he demanded.

"What? I cannot go there." I said to him trying to make sense of his unusual behavior.

"Of course you can go there. I command it Daughter," he said raging by now.

"You command it? Father, be still with certain terminologies. I am not to be commanded by any entity. What is it that has you so out of order? " I asked him.

"It is your Mother. She dares to fancy herself to another," he said now pacing back and forth.

"What? Mother? Never," I declared.

"She has come upon an old desire. It is one I had thought was long and silent. Can you believe such things? I am raged by this. It is not allowed," he stammered.

"Father I can barely come upon such knowledge. Mother? With that of another desire? Father she desires you. I know this. Who is the Entity that makes such noise? " I asked needing so to know now.

"Him!" Zeus said. "Who?" I asked.

"Thor," Zeus said with every bit of energy he could to say such a name. I turned my head to keep from all of this. I smiled and Zeus was floored.

"Daughter, you conspire in this?" he said to me so upset.

"Father, Thor is of no threat to you. So you have made war with each other for millenniums but Mother's soul is that of your soul. Am I sensing a little jealousy? Father, a manashatwa? Mother loves you." I told him trying to calm him down. It was clear that Zeus was deeply in love and devoted to Athena. I wondered what Mother was stirring up. Zeus left me as he could find no comfort with my presence. I sat down and the strangest thought came to me. Athena. Had she been caught in the same thing as I was in now with Chris and enemies and oh, how they had battled over her. I so welcomed Athena as she arrived looking as though she had just changed the journeys of a couple of men.

"Mother?" I greeted her.

"Do not concern yourself Daughter but take upon yourself that which I have done. It is well for the male not to be so sure of himself. Your Father needed to come a bit down to receive that which was necessary. Take it upon yourself, precious one, for I have given you that which will help you greatly."

I looked at her and a grin came upon my face. I got it and I got it big time. Oh Athena, she had given me the best of clues yet.

CHAPTER NINETEEN

I kept trying to get out of this sick thing between Lenz and Chris. They actually thought they could continue, no one would know and I would just buckle under and quietly go away. I had an effect on people and it was taking away power from the both of them. I made plans to move to a private place where I would be left alone but Lenz kept up with my public and private business. My soul energies decided to intervene so that we could outsmart him but he had people all over keeping track of my every move. It felt constantly like being in a trap and watched. I could not get it out of my mind how Chris had just opened the door to his Rama and threw me in. The violation from a doctor who knew beyond all doubts what he was doing was the unforgivable act. Had my mind been clear I still would have had to battle but I had had a head injury way back then.

Chris and his great reassurance, he had said to me "You have a head injury. What kind of clarity can you possibly get now?" He would say.

He was right. I was without clarity, in dreadful pain with swelling in my head. This one event changed my whole life and there was no way to end it. I sat and cried for a long time. How could Chris have done this? He knew you did not get out once Lenz had you. How nasty and ugly Chris treated me, for what? Oh, could the man lie. He knew how to lie so well that he could actually refine a lie to be as believable as the truth. You see, these types did not deal well with messy things. You followed everything to the letter. Even your evil had a format. I need to speak to you again about the evil you cannot see. Remember how I have said it is the most powerful kind of Darkness?

Another form of evil that you cannot see is what Chris did to me. It took a head injury to land me with Lenz. I never would have been anywhere near him considering all of the students I had taken from him. As with levels of Light and Dark, here is another example of the Dark you cannot see. You need to protect the vulnerable more so from this form of evil and not say something stupid like, "Oh, I'm a good person and that kind of thing doesn't affect me." Hello? You are the number one target when you live in that illusion. People that are injured are incredibly vulnerable.

My Soul Energies tried everything they could do but nothing worked. Rene was such a good friend and she so did hang on against the battle. Rob never came back after Lenz fried him but I did speak to him a few more times. My relationship with Rob resulted in nothing but upset and devastation. Why? Because Rob cared about me and it was forbidden by Lenz? I knew deep inside he would do them all in eventually. Whenever we all laughed and shared our love, Lenz went ballistic and punished someone or everyone. You see, we had real Love. The God Force Love. He could not end it, kill it or even put a dent in it. Rarely do you find such friends but they will weather with you through the greatest of storms. Even as I last spoke with Rob, that Love was still there. I will always love him and I know he will always love me. We all knew too that none of us were from here, the earth and that we were from God, the God Force and the Allegiance. Some will tell you that you asked for whatever is in your life. I will tell you that Darkness will give you great illusions about all of this. Why is it that Darkness never has to account for what is in its life? Oh, how it does the blame system so well. People in Light will give you the facts. Almost as if they are laying it out in front of them to review it all, standing apart from it.

Back to the Dark you cannot see. Lenz was counting on this one hundred percent and he knew I could take this form of Darkness and show the human race how to recognize it, catch it in the act and have it all validated on the human level. What uglier way to mess up the planet than with a technique only known to one. Oh, what a threat I was to him. I do not really think years back that I was even fully aware of it all. Understand, I never wanted to do this mission. Maybe Lenz thought that he could fool the whole planet but he could not fool me. He knew how easy it was to grab the innocent, naive and vulnerable and he took great advantage of this situation.

I know that parents have continued to watch their children just go off the deep end for no apparent reason and I have watched Lenz do this again and again to these children. Even in my attempts to tell some of these parents they would flatly refuse to believe any of this. It is not my job to inform everyone about their own situations because they refuse to wake up. It excited Lenz to no end to watch people fold and become so bewildered, caught up in their own disasters without the slightest clue as to what, why and how could this all be happening to them. After all, if he could not create disastrous results, then he had not accomplished his job. I must not forget to tell you of the morons that responded, "Oh give the man a break. No one has that much power." Right, as I stood there for his response,

"Do you see, Deborah, why I am so bored? Man is an idiot. They make my job so easy." Lenz was like a great white shark or should I say great black shark. He craved the frenzy and upset. He would just glide by watching and waiting while everyone was upset and dreadfully nervous. Then the attack with few ever knowing what hit them. Even the greatest of ships could not endure the bite of this great white. Lenz had days where he needed a bigger high and just ruining a few hundred lives a day was not enough. With very little effort he could cause a chain reaction. To help you understand this better, imagine a heavy traffic situation and one person going ballistic on the freeway. Everyone is affected. The more ballistic the person goes, the greater the chaos. People are wrecking their vehicles and being hurt badly but it is all in a morning's break for Lenz to create mostly because he can.

Everything would be fine as long as I kept my mouth shut and did not tell anyone. He could even program someone's mind to not believe a word I said but those in the White Light knew better. Imagine all of this hell because Chris turned me over to him. Lenz had no idea what I was really all about until he finally had me. To think that year after year, with Chris and his sick perverted thinking, how he thought that I was obsessed with him. He knew better but you see, he turned his evil around to justify his behavior. Lenz had taught people a twisted sick religion making irresponsibility a priority. Must I say to all of the idiots that sat there and bought it, you asked for it.

I kept moving but in spite of all the attempts to get rid of Lenz and his goons, I could not get free. I could only buy a little time and that was about it. Everywhere I turned, Lenz set traps. I was watched, stalked and constantly hassled by people paid to do so. Then there was the triggering caused by Chris; he was the constant factor that made Lenz violent and raging.

All I ever wanted was peace but I could not find it. It was no surprise that Athena and Zeus had made up and peace was at least restored in Olympus once again. Oh, for the love of both of them because without that, being of Soulmate, I do not know what I would have done. When they came upon me, I was contemplating many things.

"Oh Daughter, you are tired," Athena said.

"You do not know of such a volume of tiredness Mother. It is stifling in the human body," I said sadly.

"All of us uphold you and watch over you. Know of this. The battle is great but designed to change the journeys of all," she responded.

"Mother, I desire one who can share a great amount of energy with me. It is unbearably lonely. My soul cannot deal with these two. I must have sharing or I shall perish," I told both of them.

"Daughter, listen to your Father now. I shall send a demigod," Zeus said.

"What? Are you still of such a silly nature?" I commented.

"Zeus, our Daughter wants a functional man." Athena told him.

"Excuse me the both of you. I burn up a regular man, a functional man but can a demigod perform great deeds Father?" I asked.

"I shall command it," he stated. Oh, great! These two are in such heavy Olympian energy they cannot get out, I thought to myself.

"Daughter, be that of your Mother, you can put an energy field around your demigod and command his performance." Athena said so matriarch like. You two need to go visit the stars, I said to myself. This is ludicrous.

With smiles they departed and I sat there left up in the air. A demigod? Get real. I did let them go on about it all, realizing that it was all just a game. It was a game, wasn't it? I released Chris and Lenz to the White Light, after all, someone had to do it. Later that evening I ended up at an emergency room over nothing that big, but my soul energy, Judy, took me because she thought it was serious. I will tell you, soul energies do not want to lose you when they finally do find you so they take great precautions.

In walks this doctor and he immediately says to me that he knows Rama. "He is all over you and I can feel it." he said. "He believes that he was the chosen one way up there with that level of being god." Then he laughed and whispered in my ear that he was only just a demigod. I needed him to lean over again and repeat what he had just said. His energy was so wonderful and I was hit head on with the words of Zeus.

What was this immortal's name? "Dr. Scott," he said as if he read my mind. It had to be that sense of humor from Zeus doing demigod doctors. No pun intended, right Pops? Talk about a man. He was so gorgeous that I could not believe it. He forgot that he was a doctor and I forgot I was the patient. We talked about Lenz and he referred to him as Rama. Where was this instant connection going with Scott? Apparently, it was to go all the way? We had our hands on each other, cuddled up together on the gurney. When we touched it was clear that there was energy of a great magnitude coming from both our bodies. He literally walked out of the hospital with me and we found our way to passion, great passion that consumed several days.

After that, many things changed and I had a renewed determination to make this relationship work. Scott had to hide everything but knowing Rama so well, he also had a constant inside knowledge of what he was up to. We could not stay together constantly but the times when we could were fulfilling beyond any earthly experience. Oh, how I could relate to Athena and Zeus on their levels, especially when it came to etheric energy.

Scott was loyal and determined to please me no matter what the cost. He was adorable to me and we had endless encounters so intense we had to tear ourselves away from each other. I must tell you that having a demigod was every woman's dream. Scott became a rock for me and entered avenues that I had never let any man in on before. He entered with respect, strength, gentleness and sensitivity. He was confident and brilliant and absolutely nothing like Chris or Lenz. Those two were bottom-of-the-rung low lives. I had never been attracted to Lenz on any level. In fact, he was repulsive to me. As for Chris, who thought that he was some Adonis, he was embarrassing. It was sick the way he worshipped his Rama. Scott did not have pms. What can I say, he was the ultimate in all areas. Scott was a student of Rama's and a doctor next to Chris. For being a student, he was nothing like Rama's other androids. He told me that Rama had black mailed him, threatening to pull his medical license if he didn't cooperate. He detested him but he did take responsibility for ever getting involved.

"That man is the Darkest person ever. I saw what he did to thousands. I knew little about you. He tried to keep you hidden from everyone. What he did to people was criminal," Scott quietly said.

"What he's done to me has been beyond criminal," I whispered. "And he is not done yet either."

A new part of me bloomed and I took on a strength that no one seemed to know where it was coming from. Lenz, of course, concluded that I was being clever and Chris could not even get a clue. I continued to teach and help as much as I could but Lenz continued his ritual of taking, destroying and ruining every direction I went in. I realized that if he found out about Scott, he would hurt him badly. I told no one about Scott for the reason that Lenz could read someone's mind. Many of his students, in extreme despair, were telling me that his mother had died of a mysterious death and that they all believed that Lenz had killed her. I never concluded this but so many blamed him. Everyone was breathing fear, living in fear and sleeping in fear. If

Lenz was awake, he wanted everyone awake. There were great levels of punishment for disobedience.

Scott spoke about Chris and how obsessed he was, inducting everyone he could rope in and handing them over, no matter what medical condition they were in. Rama knew how vulnerable they all were and grabbling their souls was so easy. He hardly met with any real challenge. Scott told me about hundreds of doctors doing this constantly.

Chris was well aware of the damage that Rama did but he loved messing up people. It gave him this illusion of power. When someone is truly brainwashed, they do not present a hard time staying that way. Chris battled to stay mind controlled but his ego was so big he would not let all of him be consumed. Once again, he knew exactly what he was doing.

While teaching a class one day, a woman came all the way from the projects in New York City. She had come very far and she told me someone had told her that I could help her with her son. Although the class was on another topic, she became the focus of interest. She told us of her ten year old who carried a gun and had shot several boys. Why did he not have a conscience?

What was nice about having Knowingness was the access to immediate answers. First, when a soul cannot progress forward, it tries to locate a comfort zone. What forces the soul to seek a comfort zone is when one begins to lose hope. Children that live in unbearable situations are unable to believe that there is a future. Remember what I said about children. The only thing vulnerable about them is their size. The number one problem nearly all parents have is their lack of awareness to how evolved their children really are. Most will not allow this contact because it forces the parents to look at how asleep they are. Many children cannot respect their parents because they are battling to hold onto their enlightenment. Children are being stripped of their Knowingness so they start to plummet in a downhill spiral. They cannot go forward and are too evolved to go backwards. They become trapped and their conscious level becomes numb and shuts down. The soul allows this to keep you safe.

What happens next? These children are told that they have no conscience, that they are evil, monstrous, demon-possessed and that small ray of hope that they have been clinging to is finally closed up for good. Children continue to be born more and more enlightened while the parents continue to stay in their shut down sleep states. Do you think that children because of their size merely stay shut down until they are bigger? Their souls are just as powerful and capable the second they are born.

So why was this woman's son killing other children? He had completely shut down and lost all hope, thus putting him down into a place that voided him of a conscience. All awareness of even life was gone. Can this child recover? Recovery is possible but they would have to listen and most of you do not want to.

One woman concluded that if Angels were supposed to help us then why weren't they. She had a fit when I told her to invite them in. She then blurted out a bunch of swear words concluding that if Angels were supposed to help and that that was their job, then they were responsible to do what was expected of them. Can you imagine such an attitude? Many people are like this. They feel that the world owes them yet they refuse to collect the Knowingness of the Light so that they can manifest total success.

To go back one moment, I hope that many of you recognize that there are Angels in the Light and Angels in the Dark. What kind of Angels are we talking about? Once again, I tell you that you must recognize that which you speak. When someone says that they didn't mean what they said, that is not true. There are no mistakes. One will only disclaim what they have said if it means they are losing their power over it. People do not like to be found out. People also like the partial truths. It allows them the partial lie theory. This puts you in the position of only partial responsibility. This is the grey zone. It is so hard to get people to admit to what they know. They all have to fall back on phrases like, I am not sure, I do not know, or I could be wrong. How can you speak this way in the White Light? You cannot and never will. When you are in the White Light you do know and if you deny it, then you are right back in the Dark. You have to be straight and strong in the Truth. There can be no partial truths. The

God Force gives you the Truth and Clarity you need. Great troubles can only come your way if you deny that which the God Force gives you. No one is exempt from this, no one.

As long as children are without hope, they will have no conscience and do each other in. They are caught in a sort of time warp between two worlds. The one thing that you must do is to relocate as soon as possible. The child must have new surroundings and untainted space to regroup trust. Your battle is great but not impossible. Impossible means no change, stuck, no hope. Please do not say these words in front of such troubled children. If I could embrace these children I could help them but where do they end up after me? Release all things to the White Light of the God Force. You force your children into war when their hope is gone. They battle desperately to find hope.

My time with Scott was wonderful and the fact that he was a doctor never entered our relationship. It was as if he had been sent just for the purpose of me. Scott could keep track of where Lenz was but had no sense of Chris. Other colleagues could do that for him. We had to watch everything and we were so discreet that all of my Soul Energies never even knew. Scott and I knew that we could never have a future.

All Lenz did was steal from everyone and put them into a holding pattern. He had built an empire on this format. You paid to be inducted, messed up and programmed. Anyone crossing the line was horribly taken apart, brought to ruin and destroyed. Those who defended him were left with few choices. Lenz continued to violate women and was quite proud of his accomplishments. He loved setting them up and watching them fall. He would even have sex with them while their boyfriends were in the next room. After all, Lenz needed to feed himself by pulling out their souls through their orgasms. Why would it be so hard for him to understand that he made me sick and disgusted me so? The kind of love Zeus and Athena spoke of was the God Force Love not the low vibration love of the human level.

I had not talked to Angel of Silk in a long time but he still stood by on guard watching me constantly. He loved me dearly and that love was clear when we did speak.

"Deity Deborah, I wish to speak of something which is forbidden. I have held myself in place for so long but I wish to have another sent to take my place," Angel of Silk said.

"What? You cannot leave me. I love you. I have let you in places I have let no one else. You cannot leave me now," I yelled out to him nearing a state of desperation.

Then he turned from me choking as he spoke further. "I love you too but being with you has opened me to things I had long forgotten. I don't want to be an Angel anymore."

"Angel of Silk, this is not so. You do not mean it. You cannot give up being that which is so close to the God Force," I told him with great concern.

"I want to be with you. I do not want to stand in the summer breeze or winter storm watching you and loving you so. I want to hold you and touch you. I want to be in a body too," he said so sadly.

"I love you so much but it cannot be. I must do the mission. If you leave, I shall not trust another. Please don't go," I pleaded.

If Angels can cry then Silk was crying. I tried to comfort him. I had no idea that he had feelings like this. I was shocked to have not recognized it. I began to cry myself as the realization brought me to great levels of feelings for him. He had remained loyal through all of it.

"I must leave you. I am torn apart now." He said sadly.

"Who will guard my bed at night? You cannot leave me now. I shall be lost without you," I cried out to him. He collected his Light and burst into the air. He was gone. Just like that. What was I to do? I finally cried myself to sleep but some time during the night my sleep became calm and familiar again.

When I awoke, Angel of Silk was back guarding me again. "I could not stay away," he said very simply to me.

I rushed from my covers to embrace him. I did love him greatly. "I need you so," I told him. I knew that Angels guarded people. I also knew that many could see their Angels and even speak to them.

Now here comes the Light you cannot see or hear. How many of you want to believe your Angels are speaking to you and want to believe that they truly are guarding you? For those of you wanting, there is the trap. What is the word "want"? This is not a God Force word. This word needs to be changed to the word "desire". Then you must make sure that you are calling upon Angels in the White Light.

Oh, did you forget we have both kinds of Angels, those in the Light and those in the Dark? You need to be aware of what you call into your space. Stop assuming that you automatically call in only good. Darkness is counting on you doing things like this. If you have had Darkness around you for a very long time, when you do recognize it and attempt to send it back to the White Light, it will battle you. How hard will this battle be? It just depends on how long you have been in it. Remember, what god are you talking to? Who is listening in on your conversations? If you are protected in the White Light, you get results. If you are bonded to the God Force, you have it all.

I woke from a deep sleep and could not locate Scott. He was dead, gone, no longer. I sat up and a cold chill hit me. I was in pre-cognition of his future. He would be found out by Lenz and terminated. This could not take place, it just could not. Often I would get flashes of the things to come. Did these flashes mean these things would happen? Not necessarily, but I could not see exactly when they would or would not. It was horrible to not able to have any kind of future with anyone knowing that Lenz would remove them. Why did he do this? His only purpose was to hang onto any relationship, so why should anyone else be able to. He had an even greater reason for his constant destruction of all relationships where I was concerned. He hated distractions of any kind. He wanted me to submit, surrender, give up and he knew it would not be easy. I would never surrender. We did have communications but the second that he felt that he did not have full control anyone in his path got it. He actually thought that he was evolved beyond everyone, especially the law. He controlled everyone, paid people off and scared the life out of them.

When Chris realized that things were not going to go the way he thought, he then started blaming his Rama for everything. It was all Rama's fault for all of Chris' upsets. It was my fault for merely existing. If I had never come into the picture he would not have been forced to do the things he did. Imagine this, Chris is not responsible for anything. He portrayed this image now to all with whom he came in contact. Did he stop stalking me? No, nothing changed except the illusion he gave to everyone that I had an obsession with him. You see, evil will turn anything around if it begins to lose power. Its levels of lying are so great that one caught up in this can actually make you believe what they are saying. It takes on a kind of illusionary power and after all to the human race, power is power. You do not think that anyone stops to get clarity, do you? No, well, all of you enlightened ones do.

Angel of Silk remained but it was no longer the same. He had shown part of his soul and nothing would ever be the same again. I loved him dearly but no matter what I said or did, there was never a comfortable place for us to be ever again. I felt a separation from him and I saw him leaving in the near future.

So many people had come and gone and their lives were never the same. I had not realized to what magnitude I had ever touched them. To Lenz it was merely bait to force people to do what he commanded. No one could put you in a state of confusion quicker than he could. I would watch this replay again and again. If he was in a good mood he would find it amusing but if he was in a bad mood all hell would break out.

There is so much I cannot say and so much I must repeat to you again and again. You may not understand these reasons not, but in time you will. Many of you are wondering where you are going, how will your life be, what will happen to you. Some of you are thinking that your lives are so far gone that you have no future. Be still and be calm. I speak of these things now. Those of you in such trauma must speak words and not count upon feelings. The words you must speak are, I *release myself to the Awesome White Light and Love of the God Force.* Say these words and do not expect anything. Just listen and say these words. Say them several times. Then say, *I release all Darkness to the Awesome White Light and Love of the God Force.* Say these words several times. Then say, *I am whole and complete and perfectly on schedule. I was created Perfect by the God Force. There are no flaws in Divine Order.*

That which I have been put into by the God Force, I am secured in and cannot leave. This is just the beginning. When talking to the

God Force, there are times when you do not get answers. Be still and listen. If you are not hearing the answers, leave it be. It is not that you are being ignored. Ignoring is the human level. You are not hearing an answer because one, there may be Forces trying to tap in; two, there is still more into the making of your answer; and three, you may try to blow your journey if you know too much too soon.

You must stop thinking that the God Force does not hear you, see you or know what is happening. Every thought that comes into your mind has a place to go. Nothing is just coming into your mind without reason. This is one of the biggest oversights the human being does. Some of you are so downhearted that if you could, you would tell me that you cannot speak such words. I would say then, know these words well and take them from your soul into your mind. Hold them there as long as you can. Remember that your ego is only the bridge that carries what your soul is sending to your mind. More repeating? Of course, you need it or I would not be bringing it back up again.

An ego that is wounded, devastated to the point of being unable to even get the message from the soul is just as traumatized as the ego that is so big, it can't comprehend what the soul is sending. Devastated and destroyed beings usually are battling from not enough ego. Blindly, arrogant know-it-alls have too much ego. When you draw on knowledge of the soul but you power trip the knowledge, you will go in one direction or the other. Your bridge is no good if it cannot carry the load. If the soul gives it to you, you can handle it. It is your shut down human level which tells you that you cannot handle something. Where is your Trust in the God Force? Clarity cannot be received if the ego is not in balance. As you have been reading, your ego may have been going up and down, being triggered to one degree or the other by what I have written. Some of you may have even tried to power trip me as well. Should I say I know many of you have tried this avenue? It is well that I am bonded so to the White Light so that I can release you all there. All that power tripping does is delay your Knowingness.

Now for those of you really desiring to have that balance with your ego but you have been too long in an extreme of it, balance is achieved by the following. Stop everything and go only into the God

Force terminologies. The fact that you desire the balance will take you right there. In order to rebalance, you need only to stay in the terminologies. Remember, the second you doubt, you are back in the human level terminologies. Doubt belongs to the human level not the God Force.

I guess you could conclude that there are plenty of severe ego problems. Why does it happen? Man wants to be god. He somehow feels he is entitled to this position. Sure, when asked he will deny it but it is true. It also goes back to his pms and that seed. Oh yes, that great seed that means absolutely nothing if the carrier of that seed, the female, cannot carry it.

No matter how many times I sent people on their way they would still eventually come back for more. A lot of it was that intense loneliness of being awake while the ones around them were asleep. I loved the ones who came to put me down and tried to trick me. You cannot power trip the Truth. Everyone who tries is always turned around. Picture Lenz sending his goons to spy on me and all I had to do was tell them where their Soulmates were. They were not going to be loyal to Lenz after that. If you do not think everyone is looking for the ultimate relationship, then you are asleep. Few of you have it but those of you who do know exactly what I am talking about. Now, some of you will say that the Soulmate relationship is horrible, just look at me but you do not know the whole story yet. You are not really sure who my Soulmate really is, are you?

Athena, wonderful, beautiful Athena came upon me picking wild flowers. I loved flowers deeper than any other form of mother earth. The two of us could bask in the sun and go on forever about matters of the immortal nature. I could lose myself so quickly and desire to leave the earth just as fast. The human race is forever fascinated by its so-called roots but who ever came from earth?

"Oh Mother, be that of myself." I said. She laughed claiming that I would never lose the Olympian dialect. Leave it to Athena to instill that which was most like her. "What of the mission?" I asked.

"Great disaster is coming Daughter," Athena answered.

"What great disaster? Is that not what I have already been experiencing? Are you saying it gets worse?" I asked in total amazement. How could I be amazed at this point.

"Daughter, it will be that of disaster to even wake up the mighty Kraken. The Angels will war. The Soulmates will battle. The earth will spew out great anger. All of those who have lied will lose their tongues. All evil will turn from side to side looking for a way out. Mighty clouds shall fill and rain upon the mortals." Leave it to Mom to be dramatic but I knew she was right. She spoke often of science destroying life by cloning mortals. Thus, how shall the Soulmates be able to find one another if there are duplicates of the DNA? It was hard enough to locate them as it was. Coming from the levels of the heavens, I knew one could see much further.

Even Zeus had come upon us speaking of man's continual falsehoods, misinterpretations, all along trying to reclaim the power of god. As Zeus put it, man was evil by nature and had never gotten over the necessity of the female to carry life. You do not argue with the likes of this realm. It reminded me of how the human beings believed that all Greek Mythology was left for them to power trip. Never once did anyone get a clue that none of it was anything like what really happened. What can I say? The Gods and Goddesses were good and will always be.

"In order for man to feel that he is progressing, he has to disregard this realm. You see, how can he fit in or ever really feel competent? " Zeus would say while polishing his lightning bolt.

Don't get me wrong, there was a time when Zeus had a terrible case of pms and if it weren't for the charm of Athena, he'd probably still have it. Oh, sad and sorrowful soul, recognize the level you are at. There is no sadness or sorrow in the God Force. Those of you with that of Soulmate sorrow, read on. I shall show you greater beauties than you have ever imagined.

Lenz never stopped and for me there was never the chance of anything else permanent. Moving had a tendency to buy me more time but his energy tainting everything eventually made everyone sick. The drive in him was beyond anything he himself could even control. He made it a living hell but he could not kill the Teachings no matter what he did. I thought of Chris and from time to time I'd confront him to do something because Lenz needed to see Chris and I together long enough to determine for sure if he was my Soulmate or not. Their sick little ritual had so badly messed up things that part of Chris was Lenz and vice versa. I could have cared less but perhaps there could have been a switching back of things with the two together while I stood by.

It was so disgusting while Chris buckled under as a coward and liar but boy, could he blame and slander me. He grew to greatly hate his Rama, yet he never once felt remorse for the hell he put me through. This hell would never end, never. Oh, but with glee he did this hoping to win points with his master. He justified, as Rama had taught him, that I somehow had asked him to do this to me. So Chris continued on with his attitude, bad attitude, superior attitude, sarcastic attitude until he felt secure again that no one would ever find out what he had done to me.

CHAPTER TWENTY

It was clear that everyone was getting sicker even though I had been pairing them to stay bonded and enlightened together. The physical ailments were everything from headaches, stomachaches, to fevers and other types of aches and pains. They would increase as the classes went on and when everyone left the symptoms remained. Of course, it was Lenz but it had more of a purpose than just his messing around. It was strikingly familiar as a Soulmate thing, a Soulmate thing on a grander scale. Now everyone I taught kept falling into Soulmate behaviors and this was a little more than what Lenz was doing. I knew he had a very large plan in mind for the human race but I had to literally sit down when I realized that Lenz had all of the Soulmates to the students I was teaching. He had a two-for-one scenario guaranteed to get the Soulmate by taking the other one.

Oh Athena, you were right. It was getting worse. Whenever I had asked Athena to intervene, she would back off if it were in reference to Lenz. There was something I was not being told. Athena was always the holding back things. Zeus though, had no problem stepping in and taking on the challenge of Lenz.

I must warn all of you of one of the greatest violations you can ever do. I have said this before but it is important to remind all of you again. Do not slander those in the White Light. If you do I promise you that you will be denied all Knowingness. Your speech will become slurred, vague and inconsistent. You will lose your ability to transfer thoughts to speech. The more you power trip those in the Light, the more you will sound ridiculous and ignorant. For those of you who continue to lie about people in the Light, the greater your ruin will be. It will also be quick and taken care of by the Allegiance immediately.

I can give you many examples of this but it brings to mind a certain attorney who continued to slander and his life was turned upside down as a result. His credibility was removed permanently. We do not violate Divine Order or Sacred Law. Slandering those in the White Light falls under violation of Sacred Law. Do you think that the Allegiance will just sit back and allow this? Oh, so you didn't notice all of that White Light that you cannot see? No wonder I have only given you partial Teachings. Perhaps you have been so wrapped up in that Dark you cannot see. Believe me, it is a dreadful place to be. Now release yourself to the God Force and get out of that Dark.

How about the Light you cannot see? Would you classify Angels in this department? What about the White Light completely embracing you? What about that positive knowing that all is right on schedule? You can probably accept the Angel possibility but you probably doubt that Light embracing you. There is that word, probably. Most of you really doubt that everything is right on schedule. Did you catch that word doubt and possibility? What is that terminology? You are stuck in the human level terminology, big time. You must remember how powerful terminologies are. They identify where you are. I know that I have told you this before but you need to hear it again. How quick you are to slide out of the Light and start you rattling on again in the Dark.

No man is attractive who violates. No man is attractive who violates a woman sexually. Lenz was not attractive and never would be. He had violated too many people for too many years with such a deliberate malice towards it all. It was a form of ritualistic punishment. Did it have anything to do with his childhood? No, it came from millenniums of travel. The human beings will always try to pin it on their family and so on.

Have I not told you that the biological family is only for the purpose of DNA? You say that you cannot believe this? Oh sleepyheads, wake to the splendor of the God Force. You cannot hold your parents responsible for all of your existence. Children pick their parents as much as the parents allow these children to be born to them. Oh, to the soul who loses his way and comes upon a mother that does not want him. For you, great Knowingness is within you. Your battle is great but you can make it with the God Force. You will not fall into the traps of clinging to human beings, giving your power away so easily or buying all of these idiot programs designed to ruin your life. Of course, everyone is already telling you your life is ruined. Stay strong and fixed, you are awesome. The only things at ruin are these idiots and their ideas based on their stupidity.

I know that there are plenty of you out there thinking that youare losing your Knowingness because the struggle is great. Remember, struggle is a human level, not God Force level. There is no struggle with the God Force. Try as much as you can to stay bonded. Just remember too, I am here on this earth to help you and I am releasing you to the Light this very moment. Be sure of one more thing. You cannot lose your Knowingness but it may close down briefly if the threat is too great. It does not mean you have lost it. It automatically does this to keep you safe. Relax it will reactivate when it is safe to do so.

I woke in tears and from above I felt the presence of a soul. It was baby James. He wanted to be born again so desperately. I was like the forever mother he craved but could never have. It brought to memory Jimmy and how I had once loved him so. For a moment, I felt baby James in the memory of him. I felt his soul try to bond with mine. In the aching of his energy, I heard him speak.

"Please, oh please let me come back. I will be in the Light this time."

Tears flooded my eyes. "Oh baby James, you are in the Light," I spoke softly to him. "I will always love you, precious soul. You cannot come back. I will forever miss you." He was gone again and it would be years before he would try to come back again. If it could have been different I would have done anything to have him. I could not get such an unsettled feeling from me for many days.

Angel of Silk seemed so distant now and I knew that he would be departing. This would be very sad as I was never able to fully describe him. He stood so majestic year after year moving with my every move constantly showing great concern. I never saw just how much love he had had for me. To give up wanting to be an Angel for me was a very noble thing. He would truly break my heart. When you are so used to something that reinforces such beauty day after day, such Love and Light, how do you say goodbye?

I tried so to talk to him but he kept turning away after he had revealed his true feelings. I then yelled at him, claiming him to be the dearest to my heart and that I held him to my most private of thoughts. He stood there crying, never once flinching or drying a tear. He was nothing but pure Light in almost transparent form. Some of my students did see him from time to time guarding me. He was not only brilliant but also gorgeous. Then it came, I cried out from a dream and Angel of Silk was gone.

"Oh, don't leave me. Oh, come back to me," I cried out to him but he was nowhere to be found. "Mother," I cried out "Come to me." Athena was there quickly and I was afraid and did not want her to go.

"It is Soulmate that carries fear," she said holding me.

"I do not care of such things. I love you and I want to go home with you. No more, no more Mother. I cannot take anymore," I cried out to her.

"Oh Daughter, I have come upon such a place as you are now. It was like being between two steps. I wanted so to go to the next step but I wanted too to step to the last step. I found great sanctuary in my womanhood, in the innocence of peace. It was my own essence that carried me to the next step. I did not falter once it returned upon me," she spoke so filled with wisdom.

"How did it take flight from you?" I asked her understanding exactly what she was saying.

"It was the heart of another that came upon me most unexpectedly. I was on a particular mission and he was needed. The unfolding of desire came upon the both of us and there were great pleasures to be had yet something held me back and I accepted this holding without question. His presence took hold of my space and we shared energy alone. Was it Love? It could not be and when he left, a part of me momentarily tried to leave with him. I so wanted to go but could not. I had to step forward," she said.

"So things came upon you unexpected as well?" I responded.

"When you are out of your own realm the unexpected is most common." she told me. I could listen to her forever but forever was not to be had. She gently put my head from her shoulder to my pillow and she gently moved her hand in a circular motion over my head. I could not stay awake and so I fell into a very deep sleep.

Again and again I have repeated certain things but as I tune into you, some of you need to hear all of this many times. For you more evolved types, you will just have to bear with us. After all, the more evolved types who believe that they have this all down pat are using those badly constructed bridges again. What I speak is of a full-time, minute-to-minute awareness. No one can totally conquer what I teach or share. You do not read souls and are affected by what I write and speak. Get back to the Light, Truth, Love and Protection. Remember, if you cut yourself short or settle for less you are back in the Dark again. Perhaps now you are aware that you are not all as evolved as you thought. Would you like to trade positions with me?

There were big problems now with my students having their Soulmates with Lenz. It was unreal that something like this was happening. I do not even think that Lenz was even aware of it. No wonder everyone was getting sick. Were my students really sick or were they taking on their Soulmate's sicknesses? It was clear that this was not present years back. Things were lining up now. It was total disaster and it required a meeting of the Allegiance. I knew that it was possible to have had a student and Lenz might have been teaching the Soulmate to that student but to have hundreds of students in this scenario was unbelievable. Now, in all of my knowing I could have never come to such a conclusion. It was the mission at full activation. I took a good look at all of the parallels and it was astounding how perfectly everything fit. Sure Lenz was a pain and most of the time unreal but I could not help but wonder how much had been held from him the way it had been held from me.

I closed my eyes and visualized peace coming to me when I could permanently bask in the sun with Athena. Hello God Force, what millennium might that be? There were too many unspoken words, which brought me to such places as this. All along things were held from me.

"Daughter," I heard Athena say, "You must collect all of your power."

Now on one of my travels I came upon some American Indians selling very exquisite jewelry on a reservation. One woman approached me and said that I had very powerful medicine. I looked at her and smiled but she became impatient with me and sat me down.

"You have great owl medicine," she said.

What was interesting was my ability to see owls even in the daylight and I would point this out to everyone. They are nearly impossible to locate day or night. I had always had some connection to this bird but I was able to sense them as well. This was also Athena's bird.

This Indian woman had never met someone with owl medicine but she recognized it right away. She could not contain her energy and spoke in great detail about this kind of medicine. There was truth in what she said. The animal kingdom was something the human beings could not grasp to such levels as they wanted to. For those who have had pets in their lives and the closeness was great, it was just one more connection to the White Light. I do not care how Dark someone is, if they can love their animal they are more in Light than they can see. Good old Spanky was the best cat I could have ever had. Every night she would curl up in her chosen space and carry on with grooming for hours.

I missed Angel of Silk something awful but the way things came and went, I was sure the Allegiance had more surprises for me. Athena was right about things arriving most unexpectedly when you were out of your realm. Who would have told me of such things if it had not been for her?

How could I let my students out of Soulmate behaviors? They were all bouncing around, out of control, being triggered all over the place. As I have told you, Soulmate surpasses every program, every trap, everyone and everything. It is exempt from all combinations. It is terrifying and wonderful. You are suffocating and breathing. As you pull on each other your emotions switch back and forth. You love him, no, you hate him, no, you love him. All along he is saying he hates you the second you are claiming you love him. Then he loves you when you are claiming you hate him. Where is the happy medium? Can this illusive happy medium be found? You will continue to seesaw until the one in the Light stays fixed in the God Force. Do you know how hard it is to stay fixed anywhere in this situation?

I needed to call everyone from the Allegiance to help me solve this mystery. In the presence of Angels I felt right at home. It only took a second though, to realize that I was going to get nowhere with any of them. Do you honestly think this late in the mission anyone was going to talk? Just knowing that they were all there was a great comfort. It came upon me to go to Zeus. I could probably get something out of him. Why did they all think that I could do everything? Now, Zeus was willing at times to go right to the edge of things, almost tipping over the balance but always pulling back just in time. He already knew what I wanted when I called upon him. Believe me, you cannot pull anything over on these entities.

"Zeus, you were not that of the Father that you should have been, many times over. I come upon you now with partial wisdom needed for the wholeness of it all," I declared as if it was my birthright and he had to tell me.

Zeus laughed so and said, "Oh you are good Daughter, to the point of causing some surrender upon me."

"Then surrender Father," I stated. He laughed harder and shook his head.

"No wonder he pursues you," he said.

"Look, nothing matters except getting this whole thing over with. Speak of only that," I ordered him. I was expecting him to become angry but he came upon such compassion that I had to view it.

"Daughter, have we not all come upon you with wisdom?" He spoke.

"Yes, yes, yes! You must love him you have all said again and again! All right, so I have been forcing myself to stomach him in pretense of concern," I cried out finding much frustration.

"You cannot pretend. Can you not have compassion for the old fool? " he said.

"Oh, I am sure Lenz would love to hear you call him an old fool," I responded quickly.

"Well, in matters of love he is most definitely an old fool," he stated.

"And he is an idiot as well. So what!" I said.

"Has he not charged upon you for coming to such conclusions?" Zeus asked me.

"All right Father, you sound as though you defend such behaviors." I said, calming somewhat.

You of all people should refrain from such speech." I told him. Zeus looked at me long and silent. Perhaps I had gone a bit too far. Perhaps it would be best to leave this for another time.

"I love you Daughter," Zeus said as he left.

One of my students asked me, how you could tell if you had settled for less or if it was a Soulmate thing. This seemed to bother many people. Had they settled for less, meaning that they were right back in Darkness or was it an illusion sent by their Soulmates? Once again, terminologies, what kind of terminologies were they using? You are either in the human terminology, God Force terminology or Soulmate terminology. There are three different behaviors associated with each. I can hear someone saying this is ludicrous and that there are many different behaviors. I will tell you that there are three with many categories fitting into these three. When you are in Soulmate terminologies, you cannot be in the human terminology. It is all you can do to deal with Soulmate let alone anything else. While in Soulmate, every inch of you is being pulled upon. You are reacting all over the place. Now I have already told you this but I will get deeper into this now. If you have made it this far, you can take some more.

While in Soulmate your body temperature changes as does your heart rate and pulse. You literally go into an altered state. It depends on how strong the pull is as to how altered you become. You are feeling good, you are feeling bad and you are feeling excited and afraid. You need to remember one thing, you do not have to even know who your Soulmate is yet. What is activated is an internal furnace, a fire, the lifeline to a wholeness you must have. It is this wholeness that you may not even be aware of consciously, that pulls you and as if in a trance, you go.

As I have said, there is only one match that vibrates the same vibration that your soul does. It is as if you are an instrument and there is only one sound that your mate has as well. So you play this instrument, calling upon the mate to come to you. Your Soulmate hears the sound and begins to go in that direction. Both of you may have no conscious awareness as to why you are behaving as such. This is a private, intimate journey back to the ultimate Love and Light. Only in this reunion is there beauty in Light, beauty in Dark. Are you surprised? Yes, there is beauty in Dark. You become one, with neither one in Dark. What is the matter? Some of you are so surprised. You cannot believe this. Haven't I told you again and again to release the Darkness back to the Light? Some of you want to hear more and I will continue in a while. For now, realize the beauty of all of this.

Scott and I had wonderful times as brief as they were. Lenz never caught on to any of it. Chris? Well after all, he was now hating Rama and telling all that I was obsessed with him still. He was a doctor and his work would always hold strength over mine. Must I tell you all again to get rid of the Dark doctors? At least doctors only thought that they were god. Attorneys believed that they actually were god. These are such interesting viewpoints on the human race. The one thing that Scott counted on was my making him laugh. We loved each other deeply but knew that there was no future for us. Often we spoke of all of the devastation Lenz was causing. So many times I thought of all that had happened and for what? Every day was more devastation, more trauma and always wondering who was going to get it next.

Zeus, without saying, told me that which I needed to know. Everything I had Lenz destroyed. I had to keep moving and he would take what I would put in storage for safe keeping. My whole life I had always kept journals and I thought that he was searching for them. I took great caution to hide them very well. When I wrote, I coded everything. No one could have taken this code apart but all my journals represented one more irritation to Lenz.

Oh, to all of you still on the Soulmate note. I want you to realize that I am in Soulmate which is why I can explain this so well. I have always concluded that music was created by all of the souls calling out to their mates. Each having their own sound and the sound echoed into the minds of great musicians. If indeed all souls have their own sound, music would be endless. Is music endless? Look at all of the combinations. Look at all of the souls. I was born being able to hear the sound of souls yet I am considered deaf by the medical world. What sounds are you attracted to? Can you understand that sound is the key to waking up the Soulmates? Music also groups people together. It tells me by the type of music, you are going to wonder about all of this.

As I write, there is much that I cannot tell. I can only give you part of my Teachings at a time. You may be asking why do I keep coming back to so many things? As your soul begins to wake, the realization of what I am saying needs to be reinforced. Some of you will begin to wake and then quickly try to go back to sleep again. Many things surface as you try to wake. Many of you have already felt the impact of this as you have been reading along.

How many of you thought that music was just music? Did any of you stop to consider the desperation the human race must have felt being voided of their other halves? Where do you think that the orchestra came from? If you have been sending sound to your mate and to no avail, you cannot wake him, perhaps it is necessary to go to a concert. If only you could hear what I hear in a room full of people. It is never quiet to me. Did you ever find yourself next to someone and you couldn't stand them? Maybe their sound was off beat colliding with yours.

I needed to draw upon all of my powers and so I had owl medicine. I found this to be most pleasant and so much Athena-like. I kept seeing her with Zeus and Thor. I kept seeing Lenz and Chris and this horrible entanglement. I kept thinking about all of the secret behaviors they were giving me. It had to have been a big deal to carry on so. Oh, did Athena know and with great discretion she remained so mysterious yet ever so gracefully dropping clues. I guess I must have looked like I was in such a big hurry. I was actually. I wanted the two morons out of my life. I wanted to settle down and have some peace. I must have asked myself a hundred times, why me? Every time Chris played out one of his sick scenarios I would get it again and again from Lenz. Usually it seemed to be related to sexual thoughts or actions Chris had experienced.

Then it would escalate into a full-scale battle. In that switch the two had made, the sexual energy of both men had been changed. There was always the same picture played out in my mind. It was Chris and this certain conversation. Then the advancement of the sexual attempt but always the pulling back by me and the termination of the picture. I truly felt as if Chris was doing this deliberately to make Lenz jealous. Picture the picture. These two went through life playing out what they pleased regardless of any consent from anywhere. Both could continually justify their actions by laying claim that that person had asked for it. I never asked either one into my life. I thought about all of the thousands of people messed up severely by Chris doing the zazen. How cruel and inhumane. How did the man sleep at night? He would do that justification technique that Lenz taught all of his students and sleep easy. Can you understand how this gave them all permission to violate without any responsibility or conscience?

I wanted to go back in time to Jimmy, when we had first met. Oh, did we love each other. I could have stayed right there forever. It was Darkness that destroyed that relationship. It was Darkness that did the blame system. Wake up! Darkness is destroying everything. The human race is always thinking that it is stumbling upon something and wants to take credit for all of its newfound information. Just because you have lacked awareness does not mean it's new. Notice too how human beings have a system of the highest you can be and the lowest you can be with no regard for the soul or its journey. Anything that is set up by the human race, based on the human level, is Darkness. How could you leave out the God Force? It is interesting how one can deny not really knowing about this yet it is so easy to claim you know all about yourself. Who do you think you are?

As much as I tried to get doctors out of my life, they continued to show up. I was not sick but they were certainly trying to make me sick. Every time a doctor tried to become a student of mine, they really had no idea why they were really there. I didn't either because I saw them as plants sent by Chris and Lenz. Considering how most of their minds worked, it was a great waste of time. Still I did tell them where their

Soulmates were and they would flee as fast as they could. How silly, all of this was because they all looked like total morons. Doctors always lost control around me. I could see right through them. Do you know how many people give their power away to doctors? People listen to a doctor's every word. Interesting, wouldn't you say? Now how many people give their power away to the God Force and listen to every word the Force tells them? I suppose that is different, though.

During one of our classes the question of UFOs came up. If I ask you if we are alone, please do not tell me you do not know. You can answer yes or no but saying you do not know is the grey zone. You might be used to telling everyone else that you do not know but do not try saying this to me. I can see right through it all. I will know if you know. When you say I do not know, it is a cop out. The only time it is acceptable is in Soulmate. Someone asked me if you could fool someone and act like you were in Soulmate. Never, because it is apparent to all that something has a hold of you and you cannot fake something of this magnitude. Sometimes you can even activate your own Soulmate by just being around someone who is already in it. You cannot, I repeat, fake Soulmate behavior. This behavior comes only from the soul.

Rene was wonderful but little by little I saw Lenz taking control of her. Then the day came when he commanded her out of my life or else. Make sure she does not come back or her job as a flight attendant might end in an airliner crash. She came to see me at my new apartment with a big beautiful spider plant that she had had for years. Rene usually called first before stopping by but this time she just showed up with this housewarming gift. Although she was warm and sensitive, her strengths had been tested to the maximum and she was worn out. I had watched in horror what Lenz had done to Rob. Whoever was closest to me was a great threat and had to be removed, permanently. Lenz commanded that I get rid of Rene no matter what it took. I could not tell her what he was doing. She would have put up a fight as Soul Energies do. Remember what I said about them laying down their lives for you?

When the knock came on the door, I knew I had to do something. "Rene," I said opening the door. "don't ever come by without calling first. I can't believe you'd just show up like this!" The tone of my voice told her all she needed to hear to ensure that she would never come back again. I hurt her horribly and she could barely stand there and take it. I cried when she left. I cried for hours and on into weeks whenever I thought of her. Lenz was delighted but she would be safe as long as she kept away. I never forgot her, Rob and all of the others.

The years went by, and one by one everyone was removed from me. Lenz took friends, students, personal property and every cent I made. He maimed and disabled all he could and delighted in seeing things crippled around me. There are so many things that I cannot even mention. It is so horrifying. I had to witness so much and yet if I tried to intervene, he would do more people in. He was as driven to destroy as I was to heal. We both were vulnerable in certain areas and once in awhile he would collapse from the exhaustion of it all. If I was strong enough at that moment, I could take charge during his weakened states. It was the God Force that kept me focused and oh, did I begin to even battle that, but always the Family came rushing in to hold me together. Let us make it over one more hurdle, one more broken bone, cracked hand or bruised rib. Keep going, Deborah, with nothing to work with.

Whenever possible I would tell Chris again and again to do something because always the moods or quick violent acts were an extension of what Chris did to make Lenz go off the deep end. I told him what he was doing not only to me but also to everyone else. All Chris would do was discredit and disown any responsibility to all of it. He was complaining about how he hated his Rama and had lost his mentor. Of course, this was all my fault. Oh, how quick I was to remind him of the three days into my head injury, bad enough for him to admit me to a hospital and that he had me on my way to Rama because he was sending me to the best doctor ever. Then again, how about that twisted Zen principle, you are because you are not, therefore you don't. Everything about Lenz was twisted but Chris was playing a game where he could sit on the king's throne. He had the best view ever. He could watch me buckle under while he sent Rama into rages. Chris had the ultimate revenge and why would he give up something this evil? As he played doctor he could also play Rama. My value was only as the pawn, which ignited Lenz. After all, when necessary I could just be pounded on or kicked to the wayside.

Chris was violating Sacred Law and I knew that no one gets away with this. He was playing the grey zone. pretending to be in the Light but setting you up for the Dark. Anyone playing grey zone is violating Sacred Law. Trust me, no one gets away with this. Divine Order will prevail and no one can upset the order of this. I don't care how Dark you are. If you break Sacred Law you pay. The cost will be multiplied because the price is high. It will not take you one life to pay it back, it will take you many life times.

Some of you will jump with excitement and tell me that you did not know about this. Do not tell such lies. We all know what is Light verses Dark. Are you trying to tell me that the soul is an idiot or the God Force is? Excuse me, you are in the grey zone with thoughts like that. Now to conclude this, is not the grey zone Darkness? Some of you have actually thought that that the grey zone was a timeout place where you did not have to claim either. Many became very angry with me because I was triggering too much. They wanted what I was offering as long as they could keep their Dark, take their time to pick and choose what they did and didn't want.

Many yuppies sat in this reservoir. They believed that they could have it all regardless of what I said. To give you an update on all of them, they went from the reservoir to the cesspool. Picture a canal with about eight feet of mud at the bottom. You are sitting deep in this mud and all of a sudden here comes Soulmate trudging the bottom of the canal. Yes, it can feel that bad but if you remember to release them to the White Light, all of that mud can begin to feel like one big body mask. Why just do a facial, why not all of you. In other words, it is all or nothing. Most have this feeling that they will lose total control. First, you have only been in the illusion that you've had control. Soulmate makes you wake up to the Truth about this real fast. Did you ever stop to think that the reason they have to drudge that canal is because you've had a control issue. It is your other half and they always know what you are doing. To think you have actually thought you've been alone all of this time.

Spanky the warrior cat did her best to fight the Force. No one ever forgot about her once they met her. I loved her incredibly. She could rocket from one corner to the next in a split second with her long hair puffed up and the show off forced you to laugh. It was more than Lenz could take. Someone or something actually knew more than he did.

People were willing to pay a great deal to find out where their Soulmates were and Lenz was willing to take his share, which was all of it. Being a husband can be very convenient when it serves a purpose. You walk into a bank and tell them that someone just wiped out your account and they tell you that just is not impossible. They then tell you that you must have taken the money out yourself or given out your access code to someone. How many access codes can you get before you finally give up on that avenue? How many addresses do you get before you no longer bother to unpack? Lenz was counting on everyone being stupid. Whoever announced anything could be foolproof? Look around and watch how stupid people really are.

I had been working with a lady for many months who was deathly sick and dying a very slow and torturous death. In her whole life all she ever wanted was to see an Angel. She had such a desire for this that when she met me she finally let all of her years of silence break. She had lived her whole life locked away in a world that made sure she would never have her Knowingness. I knew that if she were ever going to see an Angel she would have to wake up. In her presence she definitely had many Angels but the lines of communication were severely blocked. Day in, day out I stayed with her as much as I could. She was in her sixties and once again, it was clear that her soul knew, regardless of anything, any place or any interference. She craved to wake up before it was too late. My heart went out to her because she was so sick but so determined to do this. I taught her all of the Teachings and she consumed each word as if it were the heart of an Angel speaking to her heart. As the days went on, she grew so weak and her soul began to start its separation from her body. I was concerned about the time as it was coming up much faster than it had first appeared. I spoke to the God Force and the Family told me she would see many Angels moments before her last breath. As I taught her of my Knowingness she became very alert and told me that her Soulmate was calling out to her. He was with the Angels already. Tears came to my eyes and to her eyes too.

"It has been a very long time since we have been together. I cannot wait to tell him that I have remembered the God Force," she said. As she tried to take my hand she was unable to pull enough strength together. Within moments she glowed and the room glowed.

"They are here!" she cried out. "I can see them. They are beautiful. Oh, Deborah, no wonder you know them so well. What is it I can do for you before I leave? You have been with me for so long."

"I need nothing," I told her.

"Oh, that's not what the Angels are telling me. You need a vessel of Light to carry many people. You need a sanctuary that protects you and holds all of these Angels. There are many rescues to come. Where shall you fit all of these people? All I have is money. Let me see to an amount so you can buy a bigger car. Make sure it is worthy of the Allegiance," she said smiling as she began to fall asleep. "Thank you Deborah. I love you."

"I love you too," I said.

CHAPTER TWENTYONE

This woman died a short time later and oh, was she happy as she took her last breath. She left me a very large sum of money, which I knew Lenz would take if he found out about it. I decided to leave and go to California. I could settle somewhere, have some time out and eventually help all of the thousands stuck in the California area. As I started out late at night going through the Utah desert, I was feeling some very strong direction. The Volvo I drove was named Black Beauty, was running fine and I was feeling that, for the first time in years. I could finally relax and have some of that peace I so badly craved. Of course it was coming, that big voice in the sky right on into me from the sunroof, which was wide open for the viewing of the stars.

"Deborah where are you going?" a voice called to me.

"Oh no! I am not listening to this," I yelled out. "It is my time, however short it may be." There was a long silence. "Announce yourself entity," I called out. The silence remained.

"Mother," I called out. "Come at once upon such nonsense." I pulled the car over and turned it off. Oh, for the dread of what was coming, I knew it would be great. Athena came and behind her hundreds of Angels stood guard.

"Oh Mother, I am in great fear," I said reaching out to her.

"Daughter, it is time for a greater purpose to show itself," she said holding me closely in her Light.

"And I suppose I am a big part of this greater purpose? Let me guess. Things are going to get worse," I responded back to her. She nodded and I began to cry. "Oh Mother, I cannot go on any more. I am getting nowhere with this mission. I am going under so quickly," I said as tears kept falling down my face.

"Daughter, there is so much to do and I will always be upon you the moment you call," she said trying so to reassure me.

"He has taken everything and everyone. How do I stop this?" I asked her.

"He, one that I cannot speak well of, has done this many times. It is not new to any of us. Daughter, you are doing as it is written," she said.

"Written? Written where Mother?" I asked her as if there might be a scroll around somewhere that I could read.

"It is written on the sheets of music. The one I cannot speak well of is searching for the sound," she told me.

"You mean the sound of his soul, the cello?" I asked.

"It is not that easy and the vibration must be as such," she responded.

I knew that all Darkness was started by the void of sound and returned to Light by the beginning of sound. Lenz was looking for his sound. I was not about to give him mine. There was no way that it would match up and I stood in the denial of this. Be gone with him, I thought.

"Daughter, you cannot say be gone with him," Athena said reading my mind.

"Mother, even if I say it you don't honestly think that he will be gone do you? I will not share my sound with him. Never! It would be most dreadful to come upon such a match." I told her.

"And what would that mean if the match made itself present?" she asked me.

"Mother, do not tempt me with conversation that is displeasing. You know what it would mean. It need not come upon me, now or ever. Let him go upon space and find his own match," I said to her but I saw that I was backing myself into a corner.

"Daughter, look at all of the grief your Father put me through. His sleep was that of the Kraken and stubbornness as that of the animal called the bull. No one of this temperament could have been tolerated. I had to come upon Thor to ignite many possibilities," Athena said to me once again giving me clues I could not see.

"Mother, you have always adored Thor, though. You could stand him and experience him," I reminded her.

"No, Daughter always does not fit. Your Father raged and Thor raged. Each of their sounds were so close it took great pains to come upon which was which at times. There were many mergings and separations," she told me.

"Why can I not see what you are telling me? Why am I shielded from such view? Help me Mother. I am greatly burdened in my heart," I said as I started to cry.

"Daughter, you must look upon all things. Compare one to the other. That which is the same and that which is nearly the same." Athena said holding me. I felt so small among the audience above me but definitely not small enough to hide. Oh yes, Mom with her great clues. Somehow, I knew that it was all right in front of me but for the life of me, I could not see it. I walked around with all of this Knowingness, yet I could not get the missing pieces of this puzzle. Athena stayed with me for a long time. It seemed as though she could not leave until she saw me through something that was about to happen. I looked up to the sky adorned with so many stars.

"Mother, it is so overwhelming. I wish that I could just go home with all of you. I know I don't belong here," I spoke to her almost in a whisper.

"But Daughter, you do belong here for right now. We are all locked in time for what Chris did. Do you see how he violated Sacred Law?" she said so firm.

"Then come down all of you and fry him," I said.

"Oh, he will pay, do not concern yourself with that. He knew exactly what he was doing and still does. It will be many eternities that he will be paying and what he has to pay will be great, I promise you Daughter," Athena spoke with great confirmation of all of this.

Again I sensed more clues but kept it to myself. I seemed so at home out here in this beautiful desert. What a place to have so much activity. Then Athena spoke that which she should not have said. "You must, Daughter, give way for your sound to touch his. It is something that will eventually have to happen. I tell you this not to upset you but to prepare you."

"Oh Mother, I can't. I will never give to him something of mine that is so intimate and private," I told her.

"Daughter, it is not upon you to have choice. It is as it is. When it comes about, you will have great peace," she continued. "Remember, all is not as it appears."

"In other words, his sound and my sound may not be the same? There is hope of that, right? " I asked.

"You are that of your Father now. He always wants to do that which cannot be done. Be calm and much will reveal itself to you," she finished saying and then departed.

"Go back and buy the vehicle of light as we have opened the doors to this," I heard an Angel say.

"You mean go back to the city I just left? And buy what?" I asked very curious.

"It is upon me to tell you the location of this vessel. It is white and very big. You will buy it and your travels will be great," this Angel said.

I held my own and told this Angel that I could buy any vehicle when I got to my destination. All of a sudden there was a great wind upon me as if I had displeased every one of them. I tried to start my car and it would not start. Oh great, I thought. I have been fried. It didn't take much to convince me of what direction I was going to be going. As I sat there in the silence, I heard a faint sound. It was the soul of one of the Angels, then another and another. The next thing I knew, within a matter of seconds, all were making known their sounds and from the kettledrums to the harp all instruments were heard in an orchestra of great music. I was in the middle of the desert with a concert before me. You cannot image the beauty of it all and I cannot even explain it, even today but I shall never forget this. It so moved me and took hold of me that I was never the same. To share something so intimate and private had no words. The sounds all interlocked so perfectly and knew when to present their notes, creating the most awesome performance ever. I was brought to tears and then some. How could I carry on about my situation after hearing all of this?

I started my car and turned around, heading back to the city I had just left to buy this vessel of light. I had even been given the actual address of where it was. I was tired from so much driving and being up all night. It was early in the morning and I got a very bad case of the giggles. I thought that perhaps I was going to a car dealer but this address was right in the middle of downtown. Perhaps it was a private residence. As I finally turned the last corner I could see no address where I could buy anything. I pulled over and parked, thinking that I would have to go door to door to find this place. It was like being on a treasure hunt. All of a sudden, a large door opened to an underground garage. I could barely make out the cars but I saw many, which appeared to be all the same. They were Lincolns and I started laughing that the God Force would probably pick a Lincoln if they were down here.

"Hello," I yelled to a man walking out. "I'm looking for this address. Do you know where it is?" He looked at my paper and said that I was at the right place.

"Sir, I'm here to buy a big car," I told him.

"A what?" he said, as he walked on past me.

I stuck my head into the garage and all of the Lincolns were black or white. Some of the cars were limousines. I looked for the office and walked in. A girl in a chauffeur's uniform greeted me and took me to the owner.

"Hello, I'm here to buy a big car," I told the owner.

"The only big car I have that I could consider selling is only if the price were right," he said.

"And what might that be?" I asked. When he told me I could see that I would be left with only a few dollars after I bought this.

"I'd like to see the car," I told him as he took me to the far back of the garage. I was floored at the sight of a white, ultra stretch limousine that looked to be two cars long. I thought that there must be some mistake. There had to be. I told the owner to give me a moment and that I had to step out. I nearly ran into several things trying to get out of that garage as fast as I could.

"You are all out of your minds," I started whispering. "Get down here all of you this very moment. Athena, Zeus, get down here immediately."

"Sorry Daughter but your Mother and I are indisposed of," Zeus said.

"Oh no you're not. This has all been a set up. What am I supposed to do with a car this big? You've all had some kind of breakdown up there," I said but my voice was getting louder and I did not want anyone to hear me. "How dare you all ignore me?" It was useless, I was talking to the wind.

I walked back in and bought the car. I had no idea what I was doing but apparently the Family did. Talk about a sense of humor. What in the world was I supposed to do with a limousine? Do you know what I could have done with all of that money? I was right about only having a few dollars left but I trusted the Allegiance. All I wanted was privacy and peace. Where would my privacy be with a car this big? Where would the peace and quiet be? It was more than obvious that this would be denied me. At the time I could not see the bigger picture of it all but I accepted it and went on.

Athena was right. Chris would get it and dread upon anyone around him when it all began to hit. He had been given endless opportunities to put an end to all of it. Athena had no problems stating the facts.

Things shifted greatly with this car and I rightfully named it White Allegiance. I knew nothing about driving something this big and I needed a chauffeur as fast as possible.

Now, all of this was unreal the way Lenz had all of the Soulmates to my students. It was like teaching kindergarten classes. I would finally get everyone calm and someone would burst into a temper tantrum, yelling he is not going to do this to me. If, for some reason the Allegiance felt that I was bored and needed a challenge, this was definitely one big challenge. Knowing how Soulmates behaved I could also gauge my students' behaviors off of what Lenz was teaching his. According to my calculations, the world was in big trouble. As he taught, it pulled on my students and the pull was great. Everything I validated, he would invalidate. The yo-yo effect was similar to bobbing for apples. Lenz made an image of himself right before me during one of these classes. It was as if he had come in on a magic carpet holding in place like a hologram projection. Keep it up Lenz and I will pull the rug out from under you, I said through vibration language. All he did was laugh and laugh. It was kind of funny. It was funny all right but not to my students who were deep in Soulmate problems. Their hearts and souls were breaking into these programs of heavy abandonment. Things like, how could you do this to me, how could you have left me like this. I loved you and you tore my heart out. I trusted you and you betrayed me. Oh, how I searched for you. These were all heavy past life issues that all of these students were sending each other. We did not have to ask where the source of this was because the answer was obvious to all. When Lenz's students felt all of this, he was just telling them that it was their issues. You do not think that he was going to tell them the truth do you? At the time, I do believe that he was not fully aware of all of this but some of it was greatly familiar to him.

As well as being the great denier, Lenz could be the great charmer. Yes, the charmer with the cobra down his shirt or the likes of other places. Notice too, that Athena referred to him as the one she could not speak well of, which told me that somewhere in time she must have held him in high regard. She had no problems speaking Chris' name, he was well hated by many. I tried to not think of him and attended to everything else. Deep inside I actually thought that Chris would just curl up in a hole somewhere and that would be the end of him. I tried to stay away from the radical types that wanted Lenz dead but from time to time, they would show up wanting to take it all out on me for what he had done to them. Here we are again with the Dark you cannot see. How far back was it that a counsel of men with the worse case of pms decided that sight would be the key to determine how the human race would be held accountable. After all, if you could not see it, it couldn't be validated. These men had pms all right, with the letters m and s missing.

Let us say something happens and you see it. If it suits you, you can claim it but if it does not you can deny it. So why would sight become man's way of proving things? The liar will always be there. Believe me, you are not going to see some things even with your eyes open if you are not bonded to the God Force. You should know by now too, that Soulmate is always the exception to the rule. How do you know if you are in that exception? Terminologies. There are still many hidden messages that I have put throughout these pages. For many, you will have to read and reread to find them.

It had not fully come upon me that I had such a big car yet. I just thought I could go on and somehow it would be ignored. My main concern was the progress of my students and the intense techniques needed to keep them from being pulled to Lenz's students. A small group of us were at a restaurant and the class went from breakfast on into lunch. My classes never ended on time. The restaurant owner came over and complained that my car was taking up four parking places and that I had to move it. We were right in the middle of some very important Conclusions and it was not the right time to end.

I decided that we had been thrown out of one too many restaurants and that there had to be a better way to hold classes. The six of us got up. I put everyone in White Allegiance and told my driver to take us on a long ride. The minute everyone was in the car, the intense turmoil stopped and the energy changed. It was gorgeous inside and so comfortable. The struggles and fights turned into understanding and gentleness. As I watched, right before me, my students transformed into beautiful enlightened souls.

Again and again I could watch everyone trying to claim Knowingness while society continued to disclaim everything that was being said. To give you an example, let us start with near death experiences. Leave it to the scientists to cut down, invalidate or completely disclaim any such experience. Again and again people are forced to give up their Knowingness because they rely on others to help keep them validated. When you have had a near death experience and no one will really believe you, what do you do? Most stop talking about it. Here we go with giving up your Knowingness. The God Force cannot do anything without idiots trying to discredit it. Yes, there are out-of-body experiences along with near death experiences. What is the difference? You can have an out-of-body experience without being near death. It is amazing to watch people attack someone who fights to hang onto what they know. Can you see why most give up and let it go because they cannot stand so much negativity coming at them?

It was something else the way sitting in this great big car changed everyone. That intense Soulmate war took on an understanding and everyone was stronger and able to recollect their own power again. All seemed to be so mesmerized by such elegance. Everyone kept saying how safe they felt. I felt incredibly safe too.

What came next shocked even me. I heard a sort of giggling and so did everyone else. One of my students then said that she knew that we were not alone, that the Angels were with us. Can you see how Angels are so necessary? Now, you need to remember that all you have to do is ask for one. If you doubt what I am saying then let me remind you that the word doubt is a human level word. Maybe you need an Angel in Darkness.

I kept getting so many messages that people were in trouble and the source of their trouble always traced back to Lenz. I saw no end to any of it. Everyone began to wonder just how far back had all of this been going on. Perhaps as far back as when I was a child. It was so interesting to see this transformation take place when people were in White Allegiance. Oh, how the Family was now up to something with all of this. I was now glad that I had bought it because Lenz would have only taken the money anyway. I am not sure when he quite found out about this but he was not a happy person. How many times had he said, "Let's see how your God takes care of you now". I guess they were taking care of me just fine.

Once again, the classes were out of control and I ended up in White Allegiance with the same effects each time. One day, after everyone had left, I went back into this vessel of Light and just sat there trying to take it all in. I heard the giggling again and demanded some visual on this sound. Right before my very eyes, hundreds of differently shaped lights burst into rainbows and danced all around me. The shapes would run up and tag me, then collect into one large shape and burst apart again. Then without even calling her, Athena was next to me.

"Mother, is this the most awesome show ever?" I asked her.

"Oh Daughter, you are so loved by the Family. Do you collect your understanding better now?" she asked me.

"Oh, I am collecting something and it is well that all does not appear to be as it is. Can you believe all of this? " I said as these great waves of peace wrapped me in a blanket of rainbows.

"Daughter, you are safe here. No one of Darkness can get in. All that you desire to know shall come upon you quickly while you are inside. You can see out but no one can see in. White Allegiance is well cloaked and will give many illusions. Nowhere on this earth will you find safety of this magnitude. You must remember one thing, if Darkness comes at a magnitude of great volume, you must get in here as fast as you can. You have great power now and the Dark Force knows it very well," she told me so stern to ensure I would absorb to the highest degree the full meaning of it all.

"When did they get a clue Mother?" I asked her.

"When they saw the effect you were having on the one I cannot speak well of," she stated.

"Will you ever speak well of him?" I asked her.

"Unless he does well by you, that being of title, I shall turn from such discord," she said.

"What title? Mother, I do not know of this," I asked her.

"All that is his is yours and you must come upon it and receive it," she told me.

I felt anger come to my mouth. "I am disgusted by his presence and do not want to even touch that which is his. Never shall I touch such Darkness," I declared.

"Oh Daughter, that of the temper of Zeus is upon you. You need the wisdom of that of your Mother," she said laughing.

"Well, I shall collect myself and release the one that you do not speak well of back to the White Light of the God Force." I concluded as I then added silently, be gone with you Lenz.

"Daughter!" Athena declared. We both laughed and such a peace could not leave me. I could not believe it. I actually had that kind of peace that was there before Dark Chris and Lenz made their entrances into my life. I was content for the first time in years. When the God Force delivers, it is always what you least expect. How many of you are in something so big that you ca not even begin to recognize the magnitude of it all? I can tell you that many of you are. The God Force that I know is all Positive, all Love and all Truth. Once again, the level of deprogramming people from their twisted beliefs of god was unreal. There is no negativity in the White Light, God Force and Allegiance of the God Force. There is no negativity, period! That means no hell or brimstone, suffering, denial, taking away of things or pain.

Disease is of the human race and not the God Force. Being forced to live in a Dark environment causes diseases. Since all of us are on the planet we will all encounter disease, sickness, and suffering. Will it strike any of us? Yes, many but it may not be so easily detected. It has nothing to do with bad or good. This is a Soulmate terminology. The great opposites, as you should know by now. The greatest sickness is the detached, unemotional, clinical types who wake every day spreading their diseased minds around. No disease could be greater than the unfeeling. The Soulmates to these types are severely emotional.

As I have told you already, we have five basic elements that we use constantly. They are spiritual, emotional, mental, intellectual and physical. If you deliberately refuse to deal with one of these, you severely unbalance all of the rest. Did you ever notice how the unfeeling are repulsed by the emotional types? I was not someone who would put up with these cold personalities.

Chris especially had to stay away from me. He lost all control and became very emotional around me. What can I say, Truth prevails around liars. Of course, it was my fault because I made him show his true side. Doctors are taught that behaviors determine mental health. So far, the clever ones who could fool doctors and put holes through these theories, the truly sick, could walk. Chris really needed to stop walking. Once again, how did this man sleep at night? What is funny here is how these types really believe that being in control gives them power. They teach others to look down on anyone who shows the slightest emotions. Believe me, you need to feel the God Force, touch the God Force, see the God Force and know the God Force. This is as clear as I can put this to you, the unfeeling have no god. Their pms is based on scientific fact and their performance is done clinically. For these types, do make sure you have all of the cleaning products nearby. After all, you have to be scrubbed, disinfected and bacteria free to even interact with them.

To me, I have always desired privacy and it was one more violation of Sacred Law to violate privacy. I knew too many people in places that privacy was mandatory. The level of trust that was required of me was so important that one thought that it could be broken, would have chain-reacted great disaster. I was dealing with such intimate things and after all, one's soul was about as intimate as one could ever get. People trusted me beyond anything you could have ever imagined. Nothing could ever bring upon me such disaster that I would ever reveal anything. Some of these cult types even tried some of their primitive tactics on me and it did not work. I came so close to putting my life on the line so many times.

Scott came with some very disturbing news. He had to move to California because Lenz was moving people around. This would mean that we would not be able to see each other anymore.

"I will call you as often as I can and I'll let you know what he is up to," he said kissing me good bye. What a wonderful demigod he had been. Now, how do you settle for less after something like that?

Everywhere I turned people hated Lenz. The hate grew so strong that people wanted him dead. They hid behind me as if they were sure I could handle everything. I was somehow the beacon of light, protector and perhaps the Soulmate.

Since there is so much I cannot tell you, I have left all of this up to the Allegiance to tell me what I should and should not say. I have also kept all of this very simple so that all can read and understand it regardless of how far they went in their earthly education. The last thing you need to do is stop and look up the meaning of a word.

I must come back to the young people who are being born feeling either as if they have arrived too late or too soon. If you were here right now, I could tell you that there are no accidents and you have a purpose that probably most around you can't even begin to understand. Remember, if I am to help you at all, you must be bonded to the God Force. I am filled with knowledge but to give all of the Teachings through this book would be to expose them to violation.

All that I have said so far is such a small part of what there is, yet for many this is abundant.

All Truth comes from the God Force and not religion. If you are in religion, it must be part of your journey for now but it will not give you Knowingness. Remember, partial truth is not Truth. You need the whole answer. The God Force is not some mysterious entity that makes you wait years for answers. The God Force does not have only one son or chosen one who will rescue you if you give your power away to this. This is not the God Force I know and believe me, I know my God Force very well. If this very moment I could teach you, I would show you, tell you and you would know beyond all things that this God Force I speak of is what you have always needed all along.

Beware of the Dark you cannot see, for it tries hard to have you. Speak to it without it knowing for sure if you know it is there. Speak to it by saying, *I release all Darkness to the Love and White Light of the God Force.* Already by doing this, you begin your bonding to the Force. Watch the energy shift and change. You will feel this if you are speaking the words I have given you.

Now release yourself to the Awesome Love and White Light of the God Force. Oh, just do it. You will feel it, you will want it and then it will just happen upon you that your desires will begin to come back to you. You are not alone. If I am not alone, you are not and although you may be thinking no one can tune into everyone, I can. I know right where you are this very moment. You had better smile or I will have to send you one. Is it all really that bad? Yes, it is. I also know where your Soulmate is. I certainly cannot help you on this adventure if you are not bonded. So get there, stay there and let us go on. I promise to give you many clues to open the doors to everyone's journey. I will make you look at yourself, whether you want to or not but I will tell you where your change lies and eventually you will even go there. Forget what these morons are doing around you.

Truth was lost on the earth because the justice system, filled with great evils, has decided that since they are god, they can change Sacred Law and Divine Order. You feel that you are forced to hold truth inside and let it be there until the world changes. You share your truth with those of the same. You are forced to wear your armor for times of war. Do you see the battle between Dark and Light yet? Oh, hang on the discouraged and broken hearted.

You must remain for the victory. You are now the unheard heroes and I know that you are out there feeling that nothing and no one can have an effect. Not only do I have an effect but I change things and I need you to be there in this. Darkness believes that it has won with you but I know better. Get up this very moment and talk to me. I will hear your voice, your heart and I will hear your soul. Stand tall and speak. You, gentle soul are part of the Force, the God Force and nothing will ever take this from you. Do it, stand up and touch the White Light, which is right there in front of you. Take a hold of your Angel and call upon your Knowingness now. Dry those tears and try again, do not quit.

What will you do if your Soulmate is seeking you out and you have exhausted yourself in Darkness? Wake, sleepy heads and go on. You can touch the God Force and it will only waken you to realize that it has always been there all along. Do not let these foolish types tell you anything. Listen and let the Knowingness you have always had tell you what is and what is not.

It was clear where all of my students went if they could not stay out of Soulmate discord. Into White Allegiance and instantly, things became strong and clear. At least there, they could really hold onto their own power while releasing their other half into the Light. One needs as much help as possible in these areas. Was it enough? It is never enough with Soulmate but having a break from their Soulmate's clutch was always nice, especially if they were really acting up. After finding all this, White Allegiance became my office. It was the only place I could find peace and get things accomplished. The best part of all of this was that I was cloaked from Lenz and he could not tap in. It seemed that my clients became more important and discretion was the number one priority.

I had always told everyone, no matter where they were in their journeys, that Sacred Law was the one thing that no one violated. Again and again I told everyone that if they broke this, all Knowingness would be taken from them. I had seen the instant results of such violations. With Sacred Law you honored Love, Light and Truth. As much as you are Protected by the God Force, you also protect that which is given to you by the Light. When you violate Sacred Law you immediately activate termination. You may still exist but no production will ever come from you again. You will feel haunted and you will know, without a doubt, that your most precious desire will forever be denied you. It is as if it comes to the forefront constantly. Even the Darkest of criminals are given notice by their soul, sometimes seconds before the crime. When one has bad intentions, the soul sounds an alarm and gives you plenty of notice not to take action. Of course, you are born with everything, yet you continue to give yourself over to systems that try to undo your Knowingness.

With Scott gone it was lonely. He was so loving and brilliant. From time to time my soul energies from the past would call but our relationships had been so severely strained by Lenz that we could not reconnect. It all served nothing but his evil. He craved for me to be in isolation. Again my thoughts kept flashing back to what Chris had done to me. Lenz always counted on impaired people being easy targets. I never had a chance and Chris knew it. He turned me over to his Rama, severely impaired by that accident. That would have been the only way that Lenz could have gained control of me. Chris resented that Rama had never given him enough recognition or attention.

Let me tell you something about all of this. Masters of Darkness have their plans all laid out long before you arrive. When you do show up, they activate the programs to give you whatever illusions they want you to have. Time had now turned Chris bitter and nasty towards his Rama. He did not have the courage to confront him but he knew that coming after me would be his best revenge on him.

The violence with Lenz continued. It would end briefly when he thought that he had disabled me. It took tremendous energy to battle him and always, in the midst of battle, he had to make some reference to Chris. He continued to warn me not to go near him. What came to me again and again was how much I wanted nothing to do with Chris, yet Lenz could not see this. A great missing link had to do with Chris seeing me. Some kind of contact with him had to be the key to setting things right.

Again, I must tell you to be aware of weaknesses, especially physical ones. The Dark Force will use this against you if it can locate it. I can look at someone proclaiming perfect health and I can see cancer. Just because you have a physical weakness does not mean that you are not bonded to the God Force enough. The soul will always be without flaws but the second you take the physical body it has to run its life cycle. How many of you have said god did this to me or god is punishing me. God did this to me is the blame system which is not the God Force. God does not punish you, which means god does not reward you either. This is not the God Force. Once your life begins, it is not suddenly changed because you swore to a better life or whatever you did to believe this. Perhaps you have finally opened your eyes to something but I pity the one who thinks that god does favoritism. Why must the human race continue to battle who is bigger, better and more important? You are all a bunch of primitives.

The male pms is the reason for all of this discord on the planet. Oh, you didn't want to hear this? Then stop right here and go check your pms out. How important is it to you? Will it always be more important than the God Force? I rest my case. Make haste, Mother Nature, to clean up such evil on the planet. Notice that, as the females fight to reclaim their power, the male pms minus the m and the s, means less and less to them but more and more to the males. Now, I can see all of the males reacting to this but if you do react, you are deep into your pms. If all is well with you and the God Force, I am sure all is well with your pms.

White Allegiance had many people come into her and all seemed to be instantly stabilized. Everyone knew Angels were present and that was just the way it was. When things are, they are. It is the human race that continues to plant evil. They love the word doubt. These types never came near the car because they were greatly afraid. White Allegiance could go everywhere. Even the Darkest of Dark left the car alone. They all knew business was business and whatever kind of business was going on inside this vessel of Light, they wanted nothing to do with it. The car projected the strangest ideas out of people. Finally, here was a place that I could be, where I could collect myself against the Forces. I must have needed it greatly for it was such a strange way to me.

I also did not realize at the time, how much traveling I would have to do. The issues with Lenz increased but my ability for teaching became easier. Just put them in White Allegiance. I do believe the privacy and safety factors accounted for a lot of progress. Everyone did not just think that they were safe, they knew they were safe. All doubt left their minds.

I now had to battle Lenz at several levels, which rendered me to exhaustion well beyond the word tired. He was still intolerant of things all over the place and took it out on everyone. Of course he saved the biggest attacks for me because I was many things besides the biggest threat. If it was necessary to activate Chris, he would. Of course, Chris would go into this euphoric walk down memory lane and feel guilty over the hate he felt for Rama. There was nowhere to go to get away and every move was followed by one of his moves. I stood up to Lenz and looked deeply into his eyes. They were cold and lifeless. They were eyes that had looked upon souls and had determined the fate of many. Sad to say, their fates were not of any well ending. The more I looked, the more I saw. Yes, these eyes were ancient and from so much cruelty, they had collapsed somewhere on flight, only to come upon my eyes, which validated their Darkness. These eyes had seen wars and heard endless souls crying out for help but shunned them and trampled them going on. He held the scepter and the hourglass of time determining the conclusion of many, always the ending for all, never the beginning. I stood before him knowing at full volume that I was the only one that could stop him. I was the only one that could break the horrible Dark curse laid upon mankind. I heard the growling of his soul, the loneliness of time. No one could violate forever and forever was running out so fast. Such horrible eyes that I had to turn away and search for the answers, to put an end to all of this evil.

I cried out to the Family to embrace me, take me that I could not complete what this evil one had started. There was my own Soulmate but somehow it was upon both of these men because of this horrible merge. They knew not of this and for some reason it was kept from them. Chris was frustrated with all of this growing hatred for Rama and he blamed me more for all of these emotions. I was tired of this whole thing. Nothing broke the threesome. I would struggle to break free and the pursuit would begin again. One continued to trigger the other. Rather than facing each other, they needed to validate their pms. This entire thing came down to the pms and millenniums of abuse with it. No matter what lifetime or situation anyone is in, it is based on the male pms that has caused it to travel in the direction it has. Many ancient vibrations have come from this male energy in constant violation. The biggest crime on this planet is the slavery of women, not what color they are. If we could have harmony among the discordant males and their pms, the big divisions among all of us would leave.

There was only so much of me to go around and so many people were left waiting. Time was precious and I knew some would die in their wait. It was heart breaking because many had exhausted all resources to recovery. You must understand the power Lenz had was not of this world and was not magic, meaning a reasonable explanation for it. The resources he had could not be explained by the human race. They could not be found out, caught, understood or even imagined by the majority. To me though, I understood him completely because we both knew about the soul. I kept trying to keep souls where they were, in the body, safe and protected and he kept trying with great success to pull them out and endanger them.

My voice mail was filled with messages of a different nature now. Lenz had moved to another phase and people were desperate beyond the ability to keep listening to them. They counted on me for nearly everything and trusted me but I was unable to keep up with all of the upset Lenz kept causing. I sat in the back of White Allegiance crying as I came to the full realization of how big this job had become.

I was tapped out in so many areas. I had to hear horror stories of these so-called professionals, claiming to be deprogrammers when they knew nothing. You do not use cult practices to rescue people. You do not take people against their will. It is not Light that does this. The public can read their books and get a false presentation of it all. When the soul has had enough, it will know it. There are no professionals or experts. The human race will never be an expert in anything. Only the soul is the expert. It is unreal how you just give your power away believing whatever you hear or read. How easy it all comes to you to do this but do you ever think to do this with the God Force? I know, you're going to say, that's a different story. It is a wake-up call here and either get with it or you are going to continue to do deep sleep and it will get worse.

Now to the few brave, bold and undying, you are the heroes and your battle with the villains is constant. Remember the chain reaction effect. You do not have to be the CEO to have power. One person of any size can cause a chain reaction.

What comes to mind is a daycare and a three-year old named Tim. Everything would be calm until he started in. Right before he did his chain reaction, he would look around as if he knew when the time was right. All of a sudden he would start to cry for no apparent reason and every child would start crying too. When the chorus of screams and fits finally kicked into full volume, he would sit back and watch it all. Like I said, anyone can cause a chain reaction no matter what their position in life or their size. Love him was all that kept coming into my mind. How many times had I been told this? More than I wanted to hear.

It couldn't get worse, it just couldn't. So many times I tried to walk, run, hide, forget and start again to get away from Chris and Lenz. Zeus came to give me one of those gentle lectures of course and I suppose if I'd had this whole story ahead of time, I would have cancelled. If I could best describe Zeus, he was a gentle giant with a kind of intense power always on the verge of coming forward. I so missed Angel of Silk and although there were other Angels about, it was not the same. Dr. Scott being gone was the end for many feelings now going back to the Allegiance only.

I sensed a battle coming and went to White Allegiance for clarity. When I opened the back door there was Spanky who was sound asleep curled up among the pillows as if she were home. For all of you pet lovers there is nothing quite like greeting your pet and relaxing next to them. A war was coming and much was about to change, but Spanky gave me a sense of peace even though it was only temporary.

Oh, God Force, give me the strength to carry on. I tried to smile but for today, the tears fell and that was okay too.

CHAPTER TWENTYTWO

Was there hope for stopping such a war? No and so the Allegiance lined up and held in their place that which was needed. I wanted to hide somewhere from all of this. I did not want to hear the name Lenz or Chris. I did not want to hear one more crying soul or one more plan to help another impossible situation. I knew deep in my soul the war would be a horrible situation. The Soulmate situation was growing bigger with so many out-of-control people and my ability to help so limited.

Chris continued to make threatening phone calls and stalked my every move. The back and forth of these two only increased. Chris was telling more lies and slandering me. Lenz was doing his usual raging. What is hard to understand, even now as I write this, is how Chris could be so evil when I had never done anything to this man. He knew from the beginning and he was well informed all along, yet he continued to scheme and try to destroy me.

I knew that White Allegiance was in the picture for safety and security but there were other reasons I could not see it or understand at the time. Never could I have ever believed what direction everything was going and to what degrees Chris would pursue. From the beginning, I was intolerant of Lenz but at least there was a part of me that could understand what he was about. People did want him dead and these were the kinds of people that would have stood up for evil Chris. The only kind of people Chris could lie well to and be believed by were the yuppie types. You know the kind that sweep messy things under the carpet. It is all right for these types to make the mess, deny it, be irresponsible to it and then get out the broom.

I did not do domestics and neither did Lenz. Chris had said many times that Rama commanded that everything be neat, folded and in order in case it was your last day. Everything had to be spotless and perfect. If one speck of dirt was found, you would be reprimanded. After all, there was always the possibility that the master might call you to come to him. What Chris wanted was to make Rama responsible for him one hundred per cent. By making Rama responsible, Chris could do anything. When he came up against a block that he could not resolve, it was Rama who created the block and Rama's fault. You know what I have said about the blame system.

I was deeply touched by so many and there was always that one who could touch your heart a little bit more than the others. Many of you have experienced this. Sometimes their impact does not hit you until they are gone. The woman who had raised me after I left the stepmother situation ended up to be one of these people to me. As the years passed, she kept reconnecting to me trying to make up for the things that had happened to me as a teenager. We had slowly but strongly come together as friends. She wrote me letters, signing them Mom. I wrote to her and so as time went by she truly became that human type Mom role. We would exchange presents on holidays and I would visit her whenever I was in town. It was funny how it turned out because she told me one day that I had taught her so much. I did not realize that I had really much of an influence on her. We so closely connected that she started to use the techniques that I did. She would love to predict the future in what she called a small way. Then when what she predicted came true, she was elated. Years later she had a ruptured appendix and later, due to medical negligence, she ended up with pancreatic cancer.

She never told me how sick she was and oh, would she lie to me about it. I knew better. About a year later, I had just mailed out Christmas presents to her and the next few days boxes of gifts began to arrive for me. On Christmas Eve, my living room was filled with all of these surprises from her. I must tell you it was wonderful. Christmas morning the call came that told me of her death during the night. The day after Christmas a letter came, her last one to me. She told me that she was concerned about her son and that she thought that he would kill himself if anything ever happened to her. She was in that precognition again. A year later, on Christmas, her son shot himself in the head and died.

I still have her last letter and from time to time I remember how much love she gave. In the end, she told me that she had never met anyone who could just love and love, never expecting anything in return. Of course, I could love because of the God Force. Many from my past did similar things years later. I gave what I had received and from the very beginning of my life, I was dearly loved. Love was familiar to me, hate was not. Light was familiar to me. Dark? I knew it well from my Soulmate.

I kept releasing Chris and Lenz to the White Light, hoping that the two of them could work out whatever it was that they needed to. If all I had to do was love Lenz, I would try to do what the Allegiance told me to do. This love would be the kind that would come from the White Light, not a human level love. Even the Angels in Darkness recognized this kind of Love. When they battled, Angels always ended in the honor system. How many battles on the human level end in the honor system? Remember the chain reaction effect, it only takes one to create this. How many of you still think that they have to be someone or something big to really be effective?

What I have said all along is that you have to be bonded to the God Force and if you are, you get Clarity, Truth and Protection. Your journey may require things like religion, certain careers and a life style which may make your bonding to the God Force harder then someone else's life. If things are in your life that you must go through for whatever reason, you will never have clarity enough to come through it with total success and no Light. If you read a book, you will have clarity in the Light to take what you need from it along the way. Even in the Darkest situation, with clarity, you open the doors to Light. Is not the whole purpose of your journey to return to Light? It is automatic to the soul. You can go through anything bonded to the God Force. You must be bonded to go through Soulmate or you will continue to be pulled back into their Darkness, if they can do it.

Some old patients that had seen Chris told me that he had done the same thing to them and that this horrible black cloud still hung over their lives. They described what he had done as a spiritual violation as well as a medical one. They were all from successful lives, which had overnight turned into total poverty. None of them had ever heard of zazen and to this day, still claim that Chris used some Dark demonic magic on them. When they refused to follow the tapes Chris had given them, all at once their lives were in ruins overnight. I wasn't any threat to Chris and I had never done anything to Lenz. Why would I, of all people, want anything to do with either one of them? Like I said, you do not have to know the man to see what he did to people.

If I had to love Lenz, then I was determined to find one spark of Light in him. I still thought I could do my job and be free to go on and have a life. As Athena had told me, it was much more complicated than that. I still thought that maybe someone else would come forward and take my place. I thought about Lenz for a very long time and there was absolutely nothing that I was attached to. Chris? He was a total embarrassment and low life. I could not compare him to the lowest of all thoughts because he was an insult to even that. He was not doing well at all but it was my fault, of course. Stalking made no sense either but he did this constantly. I was tired of it all. The constant moving, threats, danger, confrontations and financial devastation that both participated in. It was done so cleverly that it would have been so hard to ever prove. The same patterns played out on others as well. Chris was counting on no one believing me. He could just use his medical license to override those messy little situations. Lenz was counting on his money to buy people or pay them off when necessary. He had to make sure they were silent forever. All he would have to do was scare them nearly to death to guarantee their silence. Did people die because of what he did? Of course they did, and he knew they did. It is similar to the doctor doing surgery. If the patient is still alive when the surgery is over, the doctor is exempt from all responsibility. It does not matter that something was done or forgotten during surgery that causes the patient to later die due to his negligence. If you move out of the way fast enough someone else can take the blame. Of course, it seems to always end up back on the patient. Why do I say these things about doctors? Due to confidentiality I will not divulge the names of all of the doctors who I personally knew who told me one horror story after another. Few are the doctors in Light but they exist and can be found.

The students along the way who were very involved would watch Chris and what he did. Many even went to him as a patient only to be horrified at his treatment of them. Still, he would sit for hours and hours watching me through windows. There were so many near misses that I knew he wanted me dead. It was as if he had put a contract out on me.

It is truly amazing when you redo your life from the human level to the God Force level. Many students wanted to express this major change in their lives. You cannot imagine what reading a book on the human level looks like when read from the God Force level. The words just literally jump right out at you. Everything takes on a new meaning and interpretation. As gentle as I could put it, things were falling quickly and only the strongest were hanging on. Lenz would devastate the Soulmates to my students and they would go completely out of control, losing everything. No one had a profit from either side of this except Lenz. You paid him to destroy your life. If you could not make the grade, you even lost your life. Yes, I just said lost your life. Many just froze and remained quiet because they knew no one would believe them. Lenz was counting on this too. Since the idiots on the planet have been allowed higher positions, they have also been allowed to cast more doubt. Doesn't it come down to proving yourself? Lenz was a perfectionist. Did you honestly think he would leave proof lying around?

Then came my poof, the proof collected from the Dark you cannot see. It was very easy for me to transfer it into the Dark you could see. Lenz did what he knew best and this had a consistent pattern. It is similar to math. If you continue to add the same numbers you will come up with the same total. This is true for behaviors and so on. Certain actions will result in the same conclusions if played out over and again.

Even though I cannot tell you many things, I have left many clues for you to ponder on. Remember, all thoughts that are not sought for that immediate answer will remain in the mind, giving you vacillating and inconsistent answers. The soul is immediate, the answer is immediate. The soul will not remain open to continue with repeats. Vulnerability becomes the reason for this. As long as the soul is in the human body, you have this vulnerability. Remember, Darkness needs to know and if you are stumbling around anywhere in life, you alert it to a weakness. Stumbling around for answers is perceived as Darkness. If you seek answers, you are with clarity already with the direction of it all. Seek out the answer and you have direction, stumble for it and you continue to relapse in it. Even in giving you examples I must hold back better examples because of the need to keep the human race from trying to violate this.

Chris continued his lies about me. Never once did he tell anyone that this whole situation could have been worked out. Everything that Lenz had done to me could have been stopped if Chris had come forward. All that needed to be recognized was that neither one was my Soulmate. Coming forward would have forced their separation from the merge Chris and Lenz had done and each would have become a whole person again. The ripping me apart would have ended and things would have changed greatly. The violations Chris had done would cost greatly.

Now Lenz was an entirely different matter. He knew he was violating big time and as far as he saw it, a god can do whatever they please. Coming upon these thoughts, Zeus arrived and we both sat in White Allegiance.

"It shall do Daughter but it is not that of Pegasus," Zeus said quite oversized for even the biggest of limousines.

"Father, do you see what is upon me now?" I told him.

"What is upon you Daughter is what is required. Do you not see further to that which must be? " he asked me.

"Oh, I see all right, much disaster as you and Mother have spoken of. Lenz believes he is a god, Chris is a coward and I want out." I tiredly said.

"The one named Chris has come very close to death. He teases the other and tempts him greatly," Zeus said with great concern for me.

"Chris is no match for him, although he could be if he had not made a pact with the . . ." I said pausing.

"Daughter, say the word," Zeus commanded.

"Okay, he made a pact with the devil. It frightens me Father, for there really is no way out," I said sadly.

"Yes, there is," Zeus responded to me very confidently and with a smirk on his face. "The way out is the way you came in."

"Here we go again! Father be straight with me at once," I said firmly. He smiled, oh so big and strongly as if I was going to be told more but as usual, he stopped.

"Oh great, the way out is the way I came in," I stated with great thinking upon me. Riddles, riddles, I had no patience or time for more of his riddles

"Take this, Daughter, for in all of life, the very breath of life is this. Walk in the beginning and you will never have an end. Stay in the beginning and the end will never come," he said leaving me.

The beginning was and always will be the White Light. I came in, in the Light. In the Light there is no end, it is forever. Zeus knew I was fixed in the White Light and could not get out but I had plenty of Light to give.

Can Soulmates violate Sacred Law? No, but they must be in Soulmate with each other for this to apply. In other words, their actions must be held accountable. Are they doing what they do to help their reconnecting? Are they in a karmic lesson with another? Only in Soulmate does this apply. Since one mate is in the Light, of course there may be attacks from the other. Remember, one of the violations of Sacred Law is trying to pull someone in Light out of it. In Soulmates, the one in Dark will definitely try to pull. This is required and so it is not a violation of Sacred Law.

Please know that the levels at which you are held accountable are great. I walk well in this knowledge. Lenz was counting on getting away before the planet found out how much he had done. Chris knew what was going on was dangerous but he had that added element of thrill watching me being slammed and thrown around. Who was releasing Chris to the God Force? No one. Who was releasing Lenz there as well? No one. So I did and I continued to do this. If someone had to lose, it was not going to be me. The beginning is at the start. Let the generator of the Awesome God Force shower all of us with the White Light. I jumped out of White Allegiance and started jumping up and down.

"Yes, yes, yes! Come on boys. You want a connection, come and get it!" I said yelling at the top of my lungs. "You will both go to the White Light because I will not put you anywhere else."

There were so many people messed up over religion. As much as you do not want to wake up to it, when you disagree with these religious types they display cult behaviors. Any god that is claiming only one way, one son, is a god with ego, who is self-appointed. Where is the one way, one daughter theory? Once again, I will tell you that I do not know of your god.

People came to me asking where they could go to get help because I could not help all of these people. Many young people were struggling horribly to hang onto their Knowingness but could not. The God of the God Force does not do ego, favoritism and negativity. What kind of God has one son and no daughter? Do you know that only the female is below the male? When asked how you could believe this, all you would hear is, "that's the way it is".

When I was asked if Jesus had a Soulmate, these religious types nearly dropped over. Of course, Jesus had a Soulmate. A further shocker came when they applied what they called my theory of one in the Light and one in the Dark. If Jesus was in Light then his Soulmate was in Dark. They could not fathom Jesus having any Dark so closely related, after all he was perfect, the only one. By having this, it could validate their theory that man was not perfect. Mind you, I said man because the woman, after all, is below the man.

Where is the only daughter of god? You do not want me to tell you what the name of this god is. Anything that man has touched is Dark. If you cannot deal with what I am saying, stop because there is plenty more. You do not want me to tell you how Dark religion is. It is similar to cities that make up their own rules and regulations. It is also amazing that we have designated certain property as holy land.

There is that favoritism again. Can you wonder why Jesus left? He was in Light and did all he could. Wake up. These religious types were even further floored when they asked me if God had a Soulmate. Yes, of course! This meant that they did not know if God was a male and that was more than their sorry minds could handle. If you have found all of what I have written very intense, realize that I have not uncovered very much.

I had to feel the loneliness that Lenz projected and it was overwhelming. He would not allow love anywhere near him and his obsession for cleanliness was to ensure that his vibration was not available for anyone to tap into. What a cold and isolated projection this was. Do not get close to anyone or anything. Do not under any circumstances feel past the brief interpretation point. This was the so-called healthy point of return unlike those feeling types that got emotional and really felt. That was considered the point of no return. Somewhere deep in his soul Lenz knew his other half was completely in Light. Sure, he denied the very word Soulmate. If he ever acknowledged that, it would mean he did not have total control. He was really in his own illusion to ever think that he had any control. These types shudder the second they feel it slipping away. It is pms that drives the males to such ridged behaviors. Just think of all of the energy it takes to play god while in a human body. It is a horrible program with double standards all over the place.

I did not want to deal with Lenz on any level. These types are total losers. The levels of which they hold themselves important is unreal. The bottom line is based on blackmail, sellouts and violations. Chris was just like Lenz, craving his pms to levels of perversions. They were bonded this way to every detail. The level of high that Lenz got on violating the female was better than pms. He liked to taint things and leave no evidence that he was ever there. Chris was constantly informed as Lenz needed this to keep the show on the edge. They had the same perverted sexual acts, mainly on themselves. What turned them on was the isolation, which forced the fantasy to work overtime. Both could be hundreds of miles away performing the same identical motion and thought. Then the violent jerking away of the fantasy causing one to have to scurry to gain control again. You cannot imagine the levels of anger and frustration this created. Lenz would then have to go stalking for another victim to take it out on. You had to strip down, sterilize your body and soak in the right fragrance. Then wear the right clothes and changing constantly if there was the slightest stain of some kind.

What was so cruel was the way Lenz would destroy a life slowly by the violations of the most intimate of things. By the time he was finished, his victims were torn apart everywhere, so devastated and traumatized. Then he would turn around and cut then apart for all of the flaws they had. Of course he tore you apart and created these flaws but you were supposed to hold your own no matter what. If you lost your job, you were a failure even though he made sure you lost it.

One of the things that drives someone from the Light to Dark is the Soulmate however, along the way other things may interrupt this connection. If the interruptions are great enough it may drive someone to great despair. Oh, the journeys of the Soulmates are deep.

White Allegiance was my only sanctuary, there wasn't anywhere else that I could find such peace and serenity. There was something wonderfully warm about being encased in this vessel of Light. You must realize that you are exactly where you need to be right this very moment. How do I know this? It is Divine Order that maintains where you are. You may break Sacred Law but you will never upset Divine Order. It is impossible to rearrange and even the Darkest of entities stays clear of this. Light will prevail, no matter how Dark it looks. Can too much Light blind you, shock you and throw you further back into the sleepy state? No, and you cannot control this, so stop trying. I will remind you of many things again and again. You will never be able to power trip the Light so do not even try for believe me, you not only will lose all of your direction but you will become a babbling idiot. Your Darkness will be so multiplied you will never recover. You cannot say you did not know because you do. Your days of pulling the wool over someone's eyes are ended, now. What you are reading is Light. If you cannot take this, stop reading. If you tend to lie, you will be cured of this, if you make it through this journey. In fact, you will be cured of many things if you complete the journey.

Remember, you are exactly where you need to be at this very moment. You must also accept where you are and if you do not, you are asleep still. As long as you play like and dislike, you fail to see the bigger picture. Your ability to do this must be there because you will jump your precognition if it isn't. Your journey is intact by Divine Order. Do not worry, you will not upset this. Everyone has the capability to see the bigger picture but never the whole picture. Do not put your energy into trying to see it all. You will exhaust yourself and get nowhere. Could it be that you've been a little tired trying to figure it all out? All you little mini gods lighten up. Remember, once again, in the situation of Soulmates this is exempt. The pulling of their soul to each other and then pushing away from each other is incredibly intense. Soulmates can see the bigger picture and then see no picture at all. Soulmates are also the ultimate enlightenment. Why? Soulmate is the merge of Light and Dark. Many of you pms males out there hate the thought of a female having so much power and connection. That is just too bad because it is as it is. Women have been denied long enough. How many places have they been banned throughout history?

There was always time for Athena and me, always. She was back to staying close to me almost as if she had taken Angel of Silk's place. There was alarm when Lenz was nearby. Something deep and silent would come upon her. How dreadful could it have been? I wanted to know what it was. I knew that it was from a long time ago. Was not all of this from so long ago? I did not know if she would ever tell me or if I would just come upon it. I had always said what was on my mind and the last thing I was, was a coward, weak or afraid. I had more courage than anyone. I had so much protection and my Family was only a moment away. I never had to deal with gaps or voids in my life where Knowingness was concerned. What I was involved with was a Soulmate who apparently was well into this mission with me and yet completely unaware of it.

My days went on and Lenz continued to badger me with his constant power trips but I released it all to the White Light. Yes, he tried to break me and control me but I held firm and although it was all taking its toll on the body, the spirit was as solid as it had always been. It is amazing the power of no reaction. It has immense power. Be careful what you react to, it holds you somewhere if you do.

With Lenz you were never good enough. You either sold him your soul or regretted it the rest of your life. You did not have any other options. In the process of selling your soul, you had to sell your personal items, property and anything dear to you. You had to starve, freeze and suffer with all of your bare necessities gone. Lenz could work you over better than anyone. He could break down your personality, reality and any functions you had as a human being. If you bought his program any other way, you were sealed off as one who could sell beyond their soul.

His students came to me starving and broken. The fear he put in them froze them in time and they knew that no one would believe what they would say. Wake up people! It is only in your stupid minds that you are thinking, even right now, that no one could have such power. What I speak about here does not even touch upon it. If he did things like this to mere students and people that got in his way, what do you think he did to major corporations? Remember the ease of the chain reaction. Stop thinking one person cannot upset everything. Where do all of you grasp your realities? They come from Darkness, the one power producing such power. Must someone bulldoze your mind just to clean up your collapsing bridge?

How could I describe the wrath of Lenz? For one who proclaimed control, he was majorly out of control. He used many eastern philosophies mixed up and twisted. Even one of his teachers claimed the man had to learn humility, among many other things. Although he continued to destroy through his illusions, whatever he did to me came back on him. Each test he did on me resulted in disaster for him. This made him angry and the tests became more and more complicated. Sooner or later he would find what would break me and I would surrender to him. As I have told you, this would never happen. For the longest time he could not get it that Chris was not the one I cherished. Once again we must go back to that twisted ritual the two of them had done, creating broken down bits and pieces of each other getting all mixed up. Can you make a pact with whoever you choose and be held accountable? Yes!

Two males cannot be Soulmates no matter how hard they try. Your Soulmate cannot be your child or baby. What you speak of is Soul Energies here. Yes, your baby can be a soul energy but never Soulmate. Soulmates must connect within a certain time and space. The soul will not allow too much of a space, not even in biological years unless they are on missions. It is hard enough to get them together. They need as much in common as possible. Those on missions may have to be cloaked for many years because their power together has a tremendous impact on the world. In an example such as this, their ages may vary.

The questions from my students were great but the answers filled in all of the gaps Lenz had created. All of them began to say that I was his Soulmate and they wanted me to get him for what he had done to them. I had much difficulty trying to get them to let this go and release this to the White Light. Here is an example of holding onto the Dark you can and cannot see. You must let go of revenge, hatred and all negativity. The amount of energy you use up holding on allows Darkness to grab hold of you even greater. Honor Divine Order because it knows what it is doing far better than all of us. If you cannot release the negative that you hold onto with all of the power it contains, just say the words, I release all to the White Light and Love of the God Force. In time you will be able to speak and identify each thing individually as you release it. In all things remember one thing, it is the Light that will give you sight.

Now Zeus came upon me most rapidly in great distress for Athena. I sensed a little Soulmate discord and even after all of this time they still battled over Soulmate things. I had seen these two at their closest and their furthest.

"Father, such noise emerging from you is not pleasant," I announced.

"Oh, it is your Mother and this display of nonchalant behaviors," he stated very sadly.

"She loves you and you know of this. Her love is of the magnitude of the universe, Father," I said trying to reassure him. "What is it really?" I asked gently.

"It pains me greatly that I ever rejected her. It is catching up upon me that I did things I would not myself even respect," he said. I knew immediately what was wrong here and confronted Zeus.

"Father, it is this repulsive energy she has for Lenz. It is connected to him and I want to know what it is. It is the only thing that comes upon me. What is Mother going to do? Will she try to intervene? She cannot and what holds such separation must come together," I said.

"She will never look upon him. The more she is with you the more it comes to the surface of the earth. She is used to taking flight quickly and it is beginning to weigh upon her." He said softly

"What can I do? I know not what it is," I asked him.

"It is heavy. It is explosive. Most of all, it is devastating," he said.

"Devastating for whom?" I asked.

He pulled away and then turned to me so serious. "For all of us," he said leaving me.

Zeus had changed as this mission went on and I sensed a great alarm on him. There was great trickery and thievery taking place. Zeus saw this magic and without great speech had conveyed this to me in vibration language. Lenz may have thought he had power but he did not want to step into the path of Zeus. What a power game that would be as Zeus could use great Darkness on Lenz, especially the Darkness you cannot see. Remember, I told you that we all have something that we run from and run to? I must tell you that there was a great love upon Zeus regardless of how ornery he could be. I could see the similarity that Lenz and Zeus had. The same was true for Athena and me.

Everyone was a witness to my speech and when someone violated Sacred Law, their payback began immediately. People were able to see this and the stress of waiting forever ended. What most did not realize is that, once you are in the Light, you are aware of things you never saw before. When someone does something, you begin to have clarity of her or her actions because you are in the Light. When you become a babbling idiot, the only ones that you can communicate with are other babbling idiots. As soon as a violation takes place, Divine Order begins your restitution states. For those of you who think payback takes years and years, it is one more Dark concept something or someone has told you. It brings to mind attorneys who slander constantly. They brutally, with a vicious tongue slander their own clients left and right. Do not you love how they charge you while they break Sacred Law, the only law they cannot manipulate. For those who use statements like, someday you'll get yours or what goes around comes around, it has already arrived. The days of basking in the sun had come to an end. I was basking in White Allegiance because the level of danger was so high.

It was on one such basking that I became acutely alert and Spanky went on full alert. As the sun was setting, three very tall and Dark entities approached White Allegiance. Where had I felt this energy before? I stopped my breath and gasped. It was Kayborg, Seakept and Nawbay, the Angels of Darkness who guarded him. I had been found out now and war was about to begin.

"Athena, come quick. It is I who represents Olympus. Before me stands the seal of Darkness which must be broken," I spoke nearly in a whisper.

"Daughter" Athena said quietly, "I am here. Make haste. We are Protected by the Allegiance."

CHAPTER TWENTYTHREE

The nice thing about White Allegiance is that we could talk freely while the Angels of Darkness crept around the car.

"It is a great spell they are trying to cast, Daughter, and they must not," Athena said with great seriousness. "They will do whatever it takes to keep the one I cannot speak well of right on his course," she further added.

"Mother, you are greatly concerned," I said.

"It will freeze all of time if they put you under this spell," she said.

"This will not happen Mother," I told her.

"Daughter your weakness is the body. If you come upon stress, you must seek your sanctuary with great haste. I see that which has been before. You remained once, long ago in a very deep sleep for many seasons. None could bring you to wake. It was only when your Soulmate tried to join you, were you awakened," Athena told me.

"Good luck in this life because my Soulmate won't be rushing in to save anything, much less me," I said.

"Great pain fills my heart for I see well into this future and this is the last chance we have to see it all the way through," Athena said frowning.

"I swell with great levels of tears which have come upon me with no delay to reason it all. Will I fail Mother? Is it already too late? Is there much I must come upon to prevent this spell?" I asked her.

"Chris sold you to the Dark Force. This injury to you took you from your senses temporarily. During this time he took full control of you. Daughter, you could barely sit no less walk. You had been hit very hard and your injury caused swelling. You were impaired and it was a perfect situation for Chris to easily hand you over. You did not resist because you did not know what was going on. When they made this switch each had the Soulmate energy in connection to you. Chris knew exactly what he was doing, which was the ultimate evil. If you had been just a commoner, it would have still been dreadful but he betrayed the Light, broke Sacred Law and tried to steal your soul. As long as he does not come forward you are unable to change what lies ahead," Mother said.

"I am feeling doomed, Mother. Chris is evil beyond all that I have ever known. I do not want him anywhere near me. He is not done with his evil to me," I told her.

"You are right, he is not done and he will do all he can to destroy you." She said sadly.

"Wait! Mother, you said he tried to steal my soul? How could he do this? Know that he has given over many," I asked her.

"Yes, handed over many souls but for you? He needed you so impaired that you would just let go. He waited a long, long time for you to walk through his door. That is why he was so nasty to you because he knew exactly what he was doing. He knew your spirit and he wanted you broken and destroyed. When he handed you over to the one I do not speak well of, he did not see that he was handing himself over as well. Both having a piece of each other created this horrible confusion," she told me.

"But Mother, who stole whom?" I asked. "Exactly who is who and if your soul attaches can you not un-attach it?"

"Just the opposite occurred. They merged to you. You see how Darkness finally meets its match. Then it begins to trip itself up. Notice how your Mother now speaks more like the mortals," Athena said laughing.

"Their speech will always be foreign to me. I crave to have such a place unless one can come upon me as Scott did. Every day I think of home with you and the Angels. How I miss the spontaneity of it all," I said.

"This planet is in great distress. Great sufferings and traumas must happen and they will because man is more evil now. Those in the Light will stand firm and hold tight. Some are in the Light and do not even know it. The planet reeks of the liar and this cannot be allowed to continue. The justice system must fold completely because it too is evil. They use primitive means to deal with the evil ones. All they need to do is look into their eyes to see guilt to determine truth. They ignore this, though, because they all want to be someone or something big. Watch what happens to the attorneys and their legal systems. They, at all costs, protect Darkness and represent it. Rare is the attorney in Light. Those that are must band together," Athena said.

"They all think that they are invincible. That payback will never show up for them," I said.

"Guess what, Daughter? We have counseled and released the aromas. When they reach their destination, payback begins. Does man actually believe he is it? Oh, do not send the wrath our way. We will trample them in a moment's notice. The violation of Sacred Law will end. It has been written," Athena concluded. Her energy was gone and quite refreshing. She had spoken Truth, and Truth was Truth. It did not matter who was speaking it. Sacred Law broken would be restored, no matter what the cost.

As the years passed, Lenz caused me to change my phone numbers again and again. It was impossible for many who needed me to find me. I would pay a bill and he would cancel it. I would buy something and he would take it. Wherever my mail was, he would go through it. There was never any rest whatsoever. Day in and day out, I had to solve problems created by him. I would make appointments or reservations and he would cancel them. He would sneak around so that he would not get caught but he would always make sure that I knew he did it. When people would find out in their moron levels, they would make comments of disbelief claiming no one did things like that. I would then turn around and tell them what he had already done to their lives. Shocked that I could tune into their intimate secrets, they would silently walk away.

Lenz knew how people thought and their reactions. It was easy to do anything to them. I was still there for those trying to find the God Force but Lenz made it increasingly harder and many lost hope or thought my constant moving was suspicious. No one really knew what was going on. It was too dangerous for them to know too much.

When I connected with anyone, I made sure that they kept what they knew sacred and protected. They were never to exploit Knowingness and by now, you should know that it was not for everyone. When I went out on any rescue, no one was to follow or interfere. Those concerned for me were warned that they could trip up a plan if they did not stay clear of me during this time. Everyone knew too, that if I never came back that meant I did not make it. Since Lenz stole my messages, no matter how many codes or phone systems I used, you were never to leave detailed messages. Everything had to be coded. Do you know how tiring it was to deal with all of this?

Of course Chris was told about this by others who wanted him dead. Many saw this sick game he and Lenz played and their hatred grew for both of them. They would lie claiming all of these obsessions I had for them. I recall Chris really laying it on thickly to some of his friends, if you can call what he associated with friends. He would go on and on about how I was delusional and after him with this obsession and they would all believe him. He would then drive to where I was and stalk me for hours and sometimes days. All he did was slander me nonstop. He searched for a foolproof medical diagnosis that would ensure to others that I was exactly as Chris claimed. This way no one would believe all of his sneaking and stalking of me. Many watched Chris do this and knew for a certainty that anyone that turned their patients over to Lenz was the evil, sick one.

The wonder of Zeus never ended. He was busy making plans for his beloved Athena. He would go off in laughter about the human race. By now you should realize his view of humans was that of a bunch of un-evolved losers. Take a look at how stupid the human race is. One minute it tells you one thing, then it changes it, constantly going back and forth. Of course, it is blamed on lack of knowing. It is like all of the products put out for you to try and then the recalled. Then it is available to do again. Are you going to claim pity for all of this because some idiot did not know? Of course they know, they merely want you to buy their Darkness. Come on, how many times have you said that you don't believe what is being sold to you. You are not the idiot consumer who will buy anything but you end up buying it anyway. You want to make a difference but you retreat thinking that you really cannot have an effect on things. You are just the one who can make that difference. Where is the Light? Do you know?

In all, it has been hard to keep most of the Teachings from you but the way all of this has come about has been designed to keep both you and them safe. No one anywhere can have such effects trying to use them and claim them as their own. All who even try will fall into instant payback. Many will never have all of the Teachings because of reasons like this. What has been such a shock is how much the Truth shows all of the levels of lies one has been telling.

Many continued to ask me about UFOs. Of course there are UFOs. Once again, who told man he was it? It certainly was not woman. The government has to deny it because it would lose all of the power it thinks it has over the people. In reality the government could never match up to a battle of that magnitude if a UFO decided to attack. What would happen to the ego? Science? Well, science is as I have said, a great place for the atheist to be. It is also a great place to permanently seal up the tartar on the soul. Then again, science does not deal well with any of this.

What did the God Force feel like? This turned out to be a class in itself. One person said it felt like swinging in a hammock until you drifted off on a beautiful sunny day. Someone else said that they felt the God Force shining down on them while they floated on a raft in a pool. The God Force felt like the wind blowing through the canyons. The God Force felt like something tickling them from the tip of their toes to the top of their head. Another spoke saying that the God Force felt like rain gently falling on them during a summer shower. It all started out as one question that no one thought they knew the answer to. How quickly they all remembered what the God Force felt like. Each student had a different answer. The God Force felt like the warmth of a fireplace on them. The God Force felt like the crinkling of fall leaves while walking in the woods. It felt like a great peace, a serenity, a sureness of Love. All these answers were correct.

What surprised everyone was how much they knew about the God Force. They realized also how much they had all been denying their Knowingness. When given the chance to actually remember the God Force, many could not stop coming up with what the God

Force felt like. All things are of movement and all movement creates a force. Why is it perceived as Dark when using the word force? It comes from those stuffy religious types who power trip their insecure beliefs. What boring gods they must all have. It came upon many that they really knew the God Force and were feeling as though they weren't all that primitive after all. As I will always say, the God Force is instant, no delays, hesitations or tickets to buy. Could one go from primitive to immensely awesome all at once? Yes! So what are you waiting for? I know you have the excuse that some of you have tried this before. No, you have not because if you had, you would have that immense energy about you. Perhaps I should tell you that what you tried went to some god with heavy religious programs attached to it. By claiming that there is only one son of god, one leader, one special one denies the human race the full bonding to the Creator, the God Force. Who said you are one lower because another is higher, better or more favored? Did you get it from a book because your soul did not tell you that. I can promise you, you will experience the casting out effect if you refuse to follow these beliefs.

Fine then, let yourself be cast out so you can find Truth. Do you see the evil of the human race? Think if your brain must, that Sacred Law and Divine Order will never be fully exposed for people to violate. As long as the human race is left to interpret things, the result will always be false. All Truth, only Truth is from the God Force. You have no Truth and never will. Get this picture clearly. If you do anything other than Truth, you are Dark. You must reach to the God Force for Truth and that is the only way you will have it. It is given to you but you do not own it, you cannot patent it or sell it. Those who seek Truth seek the God Force. Beware of the false truth, man's creation. You should know that the old saying, what is true for one may not be true for another? Do you see the manipulation of this? Is there anything that the human race cannot mess up? All Truth from the God Force is the same for all. There is no division, favoritism or special circumstances. Get a clue, will you? Oh how angry some of this makes you and oh how free some of you now feel. Your soul is seeking Truth.

The devastation of things increased and as usual, it always turned out that Lenz was connected. With a determination set in motion, he would destroy me no matter what. Chris was a sexual pervert and in that sick exchange, took Lenz's sexuality but was denied the ability to a full performance of it. His frustration sexually was unreal and dangerous to me. Lenz on the other hand lacked in his sexuality but had the ability to perform. Without the connection of both, it created unnatural ideas and drives to the obsessive level.

Lenz was denied his ability to create music and so he could not get the full power of it on paper. He could not play it or contain it. Someone else of a mortal level was required, which truly took away from the beauty of sound. Of course, Lenz had problems with sound. I could sit down to a piano and play anything instantly without music in front of me. All you had to do was name the piece and it came out of me fully and completely. I was filled with sound, overwhelming sound and I could hear the sound of everyone's soul so clearly.

Lenz was stingy and tight. His levels of giving never existed. He only gave illusions and led you into dead end streets. Come, take his journey and then get slammed against a wall. Sorry to say, you took journeys with him and he affected your soul. If you were so stupid to do it again, then you must go on with him. You cannot say you did not know. You did and I know you did. It will not get you sympathy any longer. The only one that can get you out is the God Force.

Lenz boasted about all the people he was going to take with him when he left the planet and all of the followers that would continue with his work long after he was gone. Still, the only person that affected him so badly was Chris but he had a hold that Chris just snuggled up to and no one was going to break it. He sat, watched and got off on Lenz being violent and cruel to me. Chris was a time bomb ticking away. He had major problems his whole life with females. Of course, it came back to that switch that the two had performed, that half a man pms problem. There was not one inch of these men I did not know, right down to the male anatomy. To tell you it was disgusting below the waist was putting it mildly. I would watch Lenz ruin lives and then if the public on any level found out, he would turn it around claiming to be some big important star and how he tried to get this person off of him. He would disclaim everything, degrading whoever it was. Oh, he did not know I was watching though. Lenz was never a star. He was as much of a habitual liar as Chris was.

Every time someone special came into my life Lenz would go after them until they would collapse from the pressure. If it was a personal relationship with a man, Lenz would taunt and tease him to such levels that he could not cope. No matter what I did to prevent this, Lenz would set things up leaving doubt, manipulation and deception. Few had enough courage to go up against Lenz and he would disassemble anyone who tried. Even Scott had to leave because his life was in danger. Most would run and hide trying desperately to avoid and forget such evil.

How well Lenz knew these souls? He was best at invading the dreams people had. He would dangle one's desires, especially their hearts' desires and then blow it apart so the person felt the full devastation of hopelessness. I could go into great detail as to how he did all of these things but there is so much to say. I must not lay heavily on these kinds of details for they serve nothing but to give power to his deeds. There was so much that he destroyed that can never again. He often used the chain reaction effect.

Many people reached out to me for answers. They all wanted to hear the God Force and know it as well as they knew I did. For the first time ever, all they would have to do is listen and release themselves to the Awesome White Light and Love of the God Force. They would instantly be filled with such Love and Light that they would begin to cry. Oh, how long it has been since I have been with God, many of them would say. I would cry too for it was the ultimate of all things. Why when they were alone could they not have such effects? It was because they did not believe it and to stand next to someone already there made that belief tangible. Once you have it, you do not forget it.

Many must realize that you cannot be twenty years in the human race and think it will be twenty years to return to the God Force. Where were people to go? If you turned on the television set, you saw the reinforcement of Darkness. Especially Dark were the talk shows and all of the negative old programs of love your family first, see the doctor for help and give up your promiscuous behaviors. All four of these things are Dark. Do not love your biological family. Love the

God Force first and foremost. Do not tell me it is not there to love. Then if there are family members bonded to you spiritually, you will have a family bonded to the God Force. All others need to be released to the God Force in Love and Light. While in this biological family, seek that which the soul desires you to know. Share the God Force Love but remember, unless you are bonded to this Force, you cannot claim love of any kind. You are incapable of any Love. Go ahead and rant and rave but notice your reaction.

So many children craved their Knowingness and their hearts were broken from such devastation. All of this made it easy for the Dark Force to take control and it did. There were so many runaways and abuse of their young bodies and minds. When they met me, they knew that I knew. There was an instant connection. No one wanted to deal with these children. I recall on many occasions, yuppie type parents letting their kids of two or three years of age wander, hands free, in parking lots coming out of stores. The kids came within inches of being hit by cars. Again and again, their parents' comments were "We have to move out of their way. They think that where they are going is more important than us, dear." In reality those little kids were running free from their parents with glee. Always that superior attitude. What is that saying? Do things correctly and you will end up with the correct results. I have yet to meet a yuppie that did not have an attitude and a major messed up life. Did I forget to tell you how these kinds of children grow up? It is from birth that parents mess up their children.

Notice how only those who have some outstanding degree are credible and lie the best. Then you hear things like, we must rely on doctors or attorneys even though they have proven to be liars too. Where does this garbage come from? Why do you allow it? Why aren't you relying on the God Force? What is god going to do for us, many of you may say. For one, go ahead and break Sacred Law and watch what kind of action you get. With attitudes like this, why don't you just dig a hole and bury yourselves? Somewhere along the way you have decided that you are more important than the rest. This type needs to stay clear of me or their Soulmate will be knocking at their door. To you sweeter and kinder souls, do not let the Dark get the better of you. Let the morons separate from you. Remember you are not alone and never will be. I shall send Angels your way to uphold you. Do not despair. Once you claim the God Force everything changes and quite quickly. Remember, unless you know what to look for, you may not be aware of any changes. They will take place though, regardless of what you see. Do not give up or quit because we are not allowed to see every detail of our journeys.

The despair of seeing all of the homeless continued to affect my heart. I saw the same set up from all of them. Do as I say or you are out the door. Many were children so lost and bewildered that they would never recover. Nearly all had been born with great Knowingness, which would not go back to sleep. Parents were losing their abilities to control their children at very young ages. Centuries earlier the need to remain with your Knowingness was not as strong but it was still there for all. Children back then seldom hung onto any Knowingness but when they did, they were cast out, burned, crucified for going against a system that took them from the God Force. I stopped often with White Allegiance and fed the homeless giving what I had even though I myself did not have much. How could I with Lenz constantly taking everything I had. It was such a violation, such devastation. With all of his attempts though, he stayed clear of White Allegiance very much afraid to get even near her, let alone in. He detested the car and wanted to disassemble it.

What is so sick is that both Chris and Lenz would not stop. You would have thought in time that it would have all dissipated but instead it grew larger and larger. They both kept trying to pull me apart. At times it was as if Lenz had my right arm and Chris my left arm. Lenz knew that he was taking a big risk tempting Sacred Law but Chris in his deliberate state believed he could truly do as he pleased, counting on lies and the many sick he associated with to back him up. When I say sick, I do not speak of medical patients but the nuts he associated with. Was Chris so evil that he forgot about Sacred Law? Lenz had a healthy respect for other life forces and the second he felt that he was stirring them up, he quickly retreated. Grant you, what he was doing was evil and with great trickery but in a second's time he could convince you to step into his program. The second you stepped in, you then became responsible, leaving him exempt of all forces. After all you did not have to participate, did you? Little did it matter to him what techniques he used to get you to step in. He must not have realized that there was a Higher Force keeping tabs on his every move. The man had charisma and charm, the two forefronts of his personality. How many times I watched this I cannot tell you because I lost count. I would watch the people walk into his trap feeling all excited and filled with anticipation. For many, when things started feeling strange or bad, they refused to get up and walk out. Why? Let us not make a scene, after all, he was the enlightened one not us.

Lenz was enlightened, believe me and by all accounts a very brilliant man too. I never underestimated his intelligence but I too had a very high intelligence and level of enlightenment. He was brilliant in the Dark as much as I was brilliant in the Light. Nothing gave me greater joy than being with the God Force. The doors constantly opened, outmaneuvering Lenz to levels of further frustration for him. It was a constant statement, let us see how your God takes care of you now, as he would try to sabotage something else. Of course, you may be asking yourself why did all of this happen. You will know in good time. I somehow kept hoping it would all just go away. It did seem to me that there had to be an end to all of this and it would only be a matter of time. The Angels, however, told me different and so did all others in the Allegiance. So much trauma was about to come, something I never realized and at what a magnitude it would show itself. I could not see it because I still could not comprehend to what levels of evil Chris and Lenz would go. I also could not handle it all at once. A terrible wrong had been done and it needed to be set right.

When we are in the human body, it changes everything. Many will gravitate towards their physical needs first. Listen to me. Your soul is not going to fly away or get confused. That lost feeling is there because of programs. I know you and you have never been lost to the God Force. This very moment that you are in, right now, is exactly where you must be. Can you breathe? Can you feel? Feel with your heart. Can you hear? Hear with the energy around you. Do not tell me you cannot. Cannot is the human level. What are you doing there again? Some of you will say because you are human. No! You are a visitor to this body. Your soul is your true form and loyalty is to that first. That is our pager to the God Force. How many times must I tell you of your awesomeness? Stop playing the role of the moron. Claim your awesomeness. Claim it now.

Athena knew what was coming next. They all did but Athena was most familiar to me even as a child. Just when I thought things would go one way they would turn and go another. I swore to Athena with great allegiance that I would never love Lenz. She swore upon such an allegiance that I would. I broke down laughing and the two of us were feeling very strong about our own conclusions.

"Mother, they have all caught a virus along with you!" I said laughing so hard. "You all actually think you know my heart."

"Daughter," Athena said with such a smile and sort of smugness, "we know!"

"Yeah, right," I said laughing even harder. "You mean to tell me that I, Deborah, will love this Dark entity with my heart and you will probably say all of my heart?"

"I did not say that, Daughter. You have concluded that of your heart. I will rest upon all of this now," she said.

"Oh, no you don't, Mother!" I stated but broke down laughing still. I could not believe all of this nonsense. Athena embraced me with her wonderful energy. Oh, she was so magnificent. I adored her so. Be gone with this Lenz thing once and for all, I thought. My guardian Angels were many but Athena stayed very close as the priority keeper of my safety.

Good old Zeus rolled around the clouds with his business deals but still keeping a healthy watch out for his Achilles heel, Thor. People were seeking knowledge in all the wrong places. What they really wanted was their Knowingness deep inside of them. It was a bit hard to find with so much tartar on their souls. Every time they bought someone else's program, giving their power away, on went another layer of tartar. Believe me, going to the dentist is not going to cure this. You may say that you do not know where you are. Listen to your terminologies. Release yourself to the God Force. Stop looking for clarity everywhere else. With defiance, some of you will never do this. So be it and Darkness will remain. All the human race can do is create an ugly god. It is the soul only that knows the Truth. One man told me that he did not like his soul. You mean you have an issue with the God Force? I do not care what you like or dislike. You are not important. Your soul is important and if it houses you, then find the love through your soul not your opinion of yourself.

Oh, can the human race battle Truth. When are you infants going to grow up? The Allegiance had said the human race would do itself in and it was certainly looking that way. Each day more and more evil was allowed. As soon as I named someone who had broken Sacred Law, the restitution state began. Those around me saw this and it gave many hope that all that had been done to them would indeed be paid for by those who had caused such traumas. Trust me, the Allegiance is immediate. What many saw was not what they expected. The most common of acts of restitution, besides becoming a babbling idiot, was the destruction of one's health. This person doing restitution lost their credibility, their children, others their wives, friends and everything. I warn all of you not to defend or stand in the way of restitution. If one has broken Sacred Law, and you wish to help change this state you will end up doing it yourself. For you it will be more devastating because you will be attempting to redirect Divine Order. Without restitution, hope will never be restored for those whose souls have screamed in pain. I can hear many whining that they do not want to lose their friend, husband or wife because they have to do restitution. No one cares what you want. To break Sacred Law is the most devastating of all things. It is that of the God Force you take on directly. Everyone is born knowing Sacred Law and no one is exempt when they have broken it.

I have told you that Soulmates cannot break Sacred Law but separated, they can break it to others. Remember too, that you do not have to know your Soulmate in person. This still applies on all levels of Soulmates, those who have met and those who have not met. When you send thoughts they automatically pick them up and they are registered in their soul. This does not mean that all of your thoughts come to the forefront when you meet your other half. Your thoughts have been put into a sifter and sorted to their proper memory bank. Your Soulmate will only pull upon such information if necessary. True brilliance comes when the Soulmates meet head on. The full activation of opposites colliding has endless possibilities, making this meeting the most challenging and stimulating of all. After all, he is a moron and you are brilliant. Too bad you were so stupid as to not see what a moron he was. He, on the other hand with great brilliance, allows you your thoughts but only for a moment. You have been found out by this moron who, for being so stupid, has now shown his brilliance.

CHAPTER TWENTYFOUR

What I was involved in was so big that it made everything else look small. You could not imagine that it could get worse but it did. The levels that Lenz would go to ruin you or eliminate you were at all levels. He actually thought that he was it. I would witness innocent people being set up and destroyed for no reason at all. It would be test runs for his so-called power shows. I was not impressed. What a cruel approach to not even allow someone to have the chance to defend themselves, especially against someone they had never done anything to. I saw it though, again and again. I saw people blaming innocent people for these vicious acts. Oh, he loved the chain reaction system. Only the brazen and strong held on, trusting something they themselves could not even name. The more he did, the bigger the chain reaction. I was only one person trying desperately to help as many as I could. He counted on two things, one was never getting caught and the other was always being able to convince anyone to believe that he was not doing these things. Everything he touched turned black and the more he demanded Chris be confronted by me, the more angry he became at the possibilities of us ever connecting. He needed to know for sure if he indeed was my Soulmate or if Chris was.

Lenz had been born on a mission and that was to find her, the one and only that belonged to him. There was so much hatred in him that he took it out constantly on females. He often talked of charming them, beguiling them and then slamming them hard physically and emotionally, so they would be permanently dysfunctional. The best way that he would get the female was by degradation, humility and violations so degrading that no one could recover. Remember too, that he had all of the Soulmates to my students. Once again, here was Chris antagonizing Lenz to no end. To Lenz there could only be one other possibility and that was Chris. Of course it was Chris because that ritual had caused each to hold parts of the other. If you can understand the concept of Soulmate, you can understand yourself. You get your clarity from the God Force but you understand opposite polarity from the mate.

The male likes to cloak the truth the way he cloaks his pms. Always giving you a story that things are so much bigger and better than they really are. They were the ones that made size an issue. If they want to give their power away to size, why should not the female take it? I must again repeat that there are only two choices. Go through life in the Light or Dark. Many a male has left the Light for his pms thinking that he had choices to return when he grew tired of the act or bored with it. As if he can turn Light off and on by his own selfish acts of pms indulgence. No one in the God Force is interested in the male organs. No one in the God Force invites violation. If you want to take a quick dip, you will pay the price. Do not cry wolf either. Only Dark will rescue you.

This comes upon a repeated story about a man, a doctor, who also wanted his Soulmate more than anything. He figured he could put his pms anywhere he wanted and when his Soulmate showed up he would stop his other relationships. A very Dark and evil female came into his life. She was close to sixty and this doctor in his late thirties. She was twisted and looking for a meal ticket. She lied nonstop and when he found out, he broke down to me. Of course I was there for him but was never paid for my endless hours of help. Again, I went into the cycle of Soulmate. The sexuality of Soulmate is very fragile. You do not mess around when you have called the Soulmate forward. One of the big traps Darkness will give you is a sexual disease. This doctor kept going back to this evil woman and she hired another girl to perform in a threesome with him. At this point he cancelled his Soulmate out for good the second he went into this perverted act. He had actually said the affirmations to call her into him and turned around and endangered their coming together by knowingly doing what he should not do. Once he did it, she was removed from ever being able to connect to him. The disgust and disbelief of it all terminated her. It was violating Light. It was violating Sacred Law. Do not tell me that a man cannot resist. If you believe this you yourself are still in bondage. Soulmate is the ultimate prevailing force far above this evil the human race has allowed. The betrayal of it all has no words.

What is interesting here is the second I witness something, it is as solid as the Force. Are you so used to believing your desires are not heard or will never come, that you go ahead and step into a greater evil? There was always the sweet soul who would just walk up and bare their thoughts to me. It never failed that all would let me hear the same words, again and again. Isn't it a Dark world? Do not worry people, as long as I am on the planet I will handle this Darkness with a determination that even Darkness cannot grasp. If I had been able to ignore it, all my life would have been easy, comfortable and safe. This is how most want their lives to be and their concept that establishments are looking out for their best interests is one big fog.

Why do you keep looking for more morons to love you, care for you and make you comfortable? Hello primitive, it is the God Force that waits for you. Go ahead and keep giving your power away to everything but this Force. Remain with the brain of a piece of paper. I have plenty of sheets I can hand out to you. What have you got to say? Then speak it. Do not become a radical, become Light because if you are doing sheets of paper you have a lot to say.

Remember the White Light is immediate. When I tell you immediate, it is. Wait, is the human race. In time, is the human race. If you struggle, which is the human race, I will call the Light forward for you but be aware to take hold of it. Right now, this very moment, I release you, gentle reader, to the Awesome White Light and Love of the God Force. Go forward to receive it. If you cannot receive it yet, be calm, there will be a moment it comes upon you permanently. How do I know this? We all go back to the Light. I know this. You know this. Divine Order knows this.

The stress that Lenz put on me increased and it became harder to reach people. Against major roadblocks they still tried to connect. You must understand, there are some men who worship their statue, which of course is their pms. They lay with this, worship this and believe it holds all power to controlling all things. This, in a sense, makes them gods at least in their minds. It is sad to say that there are low vibration women that worship this male pms causing more delays for Light to reach them. These kinds of females are low grade, which went astray lifetimes ago because of Soulmate devastation. They are severely addicted to this ritualistic behavior. They believe too, that it is worth the illusion, the temporary comfort.

Lenz would visit Chris all of the time and then come after me gauging what Chris had said in reference to my reaction. I did not react though, making Lenz more hostile. It was always the same thing, "Let's see how that God of yours takes care of you." Of course, the God Force took care of me the same consistent way. How thick was Lenz to not see this? Apparently, he was thick enough to keep it up. There were more evil places to live on the planet than others. I will not tell you of all of them but Lenz did own certain states for himself. When I tell you that people were androids, they were. It was easier to program them to places as well.

The abusive doctor came into my presence again and again. If one person is damaged, it is one too many. The big plan with doctors in the Dark was to let their damage blow over and hope no one else complained. They could always count on their colleagues to back them up which was the perfect arrangement. Chris had caused a chain reaction as many like him had. Through patronizing behaviors they could silence their patients. Believe me, the planet will not heal until these Dark, evil people leave it. How horrible that you have to pay these evil types for their very bad service. Could one thing cause a chain reaction of devastation? Yes, or course. You cannot restore to the original state that which someone has destroyed. What comes to mind is a stampede and all that is left is destroyed land. Do you think that this is any different from a stampede through your emotions?

As much as I continued to speak about the violation of Sacred Law, there were those who continued to break it. Then the shock of how fast payback was there to collect. Some would complain that they had gone their whole lives doing as they pleased without problems until they encountered me. Excuse me, do I hear the stampede scenario? I stood before the ancient ruins as the sun began to rise. I reached up to the sky with my waist-long mane of hair blowing all over. I thought deeply about direction and how I had made it through all of the traps, losses and trauma. My heart ached for those who could not battle such levels of Darkness. If I could have, I would have healed the whole world for that was as deep as the yearning was. My relationship with the God Force was so bonded, that at times people had to step back. How could anyone Love God so much? Easy!

How could you love anything greater? I knew not of any other love. Sure there were the wonderful earthly loves but nothing could ever compare to the God Force. How often I had heard voices in groups yell out, "Teach me how to Love the God Force as much as you do." Lenz was number one for Lenz. Lenz was number one for Chris but the God Force would always be number one for me. As long as you did not Love the God Force, you would never have a chance for a personal relationship with me. Scott Loved the God Force. Jimmy had too. I had many good loves in my life.

I was always able to understand the so-called complicated male. When you understand things, you travel in a relationship. As I thought, it was Jimmy I had loved the most of these earthly loves. My heart would sometimes ache for his presence. I do not believe he ever realized how much he meant to me. To think that I would have never met him had it not all gone the way it did would have been a great loss. I sat down and watched the colored sky try for blue.

Before me was White Allegiance in all her splendor. Oh, what a sanctuary she had become. The memory of Celtic music came from the swaying branches of the surrounding trees. There were some things I knew for sure. I would never see Jimmy again. I would never carry baby James. What Chris had done would never end. I had to be reminded of some of these things each day. What was evil is how Chris continued to remain blameless, justifying it as something I must have asked for. I had a head injury and absolutely no defense. I was the perfect inductee to give to Lenz. He had no struggle or resistance because I had absolutely no idea what was going on. I knew that for the rest of my life this would never go away from my thoughts. What was done to me in those days as I left the hospital, was more horrifying than you could ever imagine. Chris could not wait either. Sure, he had wanted to keep me longer in the hospital and that also would have given him more time to prepare me for his master. I recalled how he kept yelling at me to obey his orders. The severing of all that was sacred to me was slowly ripped out of me. Chris stood by, feeling like a champion but little did he know he had not scored any points with his master. Do you know how this horrible event changed everything?

Again, students came from all over with major conflicts with religion. The falsehoods, contradictions and unbalanced formats only led to a very unstable god. This was not the god I knew. Try this thought, what happened to the only begotten daughter of god? We are told of a son but no daughter? Once again, we have a male god doing prejudice. Comments? Well that is just the way it is. God can do as god pleases. God is a man and would have a son. You mean god has a severe case of pms? People wake up. How can you embrace a god who is tipped over? As I said, religion is the great divider of Light. God is God. Solid as solid can be. God is Love, Light, Protection. God gives you Clarity and Knowingness. God is God and Goddess. God is whole. You are attached to the bungee cord. Haven't you stretched this cord long enough? Everyone laughed because in less than a minute they all had god back on the bungee cord with them. They all needed an aspirin to calm down the soul ache but since the soul does not do medicine, I told them that the God Force was the best medicine.

Anyone that had ever met me tried to give up that ugly word think and changed it to the word know. Think is giving away your power. Do you know how much power is floating around to be picked up by the junkyard of the Dark Force? Every time you say that word think and you are not in Knowingness, you give your power away. You will say, what if you do not know. Ask the God Force primitive. What have I been telling you all along? You are nothing but an illusion without the God Force. Check this out, in a moment's notice all can dissipate when you release yourself to the God Force. That dear heart is reality.

Then came the group of people who could not let go of the sick interpretation of religion. Somehow they could not see that the God

Force was not religion. When it came to the perspective of having a Soulmate, that however was much easier to grasp. Everyone wanted love and the relationship. It was very hard to watch parents brainwash their children with religion. You could see the indecisiveness in their eyes knowing that it was not Knowingness they were receiving. It was amazing too, that females felt second class to this religion proclaiming one son of god and god being male. Merely further enslavement of women came from this religion. Sure, there are others, which is why I tell you it is not of the god I know. Women are still in slavery all over the world but they are not in slavery with the God Force.

I knew I was being watched now full time by Seakept, Nawbay and Kayborg. They were treacherous Angels of Darkness and they strongly created a very unsettling feeling that even others around me felt. Short of mere shadows, it was brought upon me quite quickly when they came forward. Remember what I said about things coming upon you quickly. There were many tribes of people put here from other places. Yes, I speak of UFO travels. Some of these tribes have had their links return to check on them. In doing so there are claims of UFO abductions. I, along with many others, have seen everything from mere force fields to actual visual fields.

I traveled with White Allegiance and affected many people by the mere conclusions they came up with. No one had any idea what this vehicle was all about. I, myself never really had a full awareness of it either. All I knew was how safe it was and realized that when I was inside, how quick my clarity came and how strong I was in this experience. Lenz had made home an impossible place. He had so badly damaged everything that stopping only meant another fracture or slam. If that did not have what he felt was an impact, he would go after someone I knew. As usual, Chris felt he was not responsible for any of it. Just because he had turned me over to him, gave justification to the arrogant attitude, that I deserved it. Lenz would storm in raging over something Chris had done or thought or was about to do. Lenz demanded more and more attention and I refused to give it. He stripped me down to nothing again and again but somehow I still went on. Everything was based on Chris and to say that all of this was sick, was putting it mildly. He closed every possible exit and left me to battle him. It was exhausting beyond everything. I would make calls and try to stop him with all I could do but you could never catch him in the act. If, by rare chance, someone did witness anything, they were removed or eliminated.

Lenz had no regard for life. He only needed fuel enough to gain control of as many as he could. He needed souls and the power of a locked soul was great for escape. How much will one fight to be free? Much energy is given out in search of the exit.

I want to show you the Dark you cannot see. I want you to realize how much power you give away every minute or hour. The only place you should be giving your power away is to the God Force.

Still there was no stopping people to try to reach me. I bounced right back with an endurance which even surprised me. We were all doomed Athena had said, if this mission failed. Right from my birth I was so attended to, to make sure I was well prepared for all of this. I had been greatly loved and I had heard the God Force right from the time I had been born. Now, there was a real problem with all of this because you are not allowed to hear God. If you do, you are called mentally sick. It is just voices or the total opposite would apply. It must be a saint. Being a female ruled out the saint possibility. The fact that whatever I said would happen and quite quickly at that, only led people to make things up. The more they lied, the more I proclaimed events. Since when do you allow the liars to rule? Hello people, youare losing the battle. You all have allowed a society that forces you to lie. In fact, if you tell the truth, you are usually not believed. Notice how the lie fits right in. Certain careers allow the liar priority treatment too. Yes, doctors lie constantly using terminologies, which keep them in a safe zone.

You know by now, rare is the doctor in Light but oh, so refreshing to meet. I came upon one such person who would say the truth each day keeps the cancer away. How awesome this doctor was because he had an energy around him, which reflected his Light. He was alone because practicing with other doctors had caused such conflicts. His colleagues wanted their patients' loyalty and kept sick, forcing their return. You must wake up to the Truth of this. Until you take your power back, you will remain feeding this evil. The level of their evil is why they rank as one of the three entities that must be stopped. I have seen again and again that what a doctor tells the patient, initiates the disease. Could it be that you have gone to the doctor to get the disease or other afflictions? Truth would have kept disease away but the planet is so far gone that even the strongest of people have something.

You are better to go into holistic medicine. The levels of Truth are great in this area. That is why doctors are against it. It takes power away from them. It tells Truth, plain and simple Truth. Remember, a doctor who cannot do Truth is Dark. Stay away from them. Put an end to this evil. It is hard on your Knowingness when you are physically ill. Where do diseases come from? Some diseases come from emotional organs, some from mental organs.

"Now youare saying, what is all this about? I could go into great detail about this but I will not. I will give you a couple of examples. The heart is an emotional organ. The brain is a mental organ. When we are severely, emotionally bottled up, we trigger certain organs. No emotion is a guarantee to trigger something. The pancreas is an emotional organ. We live in a society that forces you to repress emotions. In other words, we live in a world that forces the closure of the God Force. Once again comes the evil doctor who gauges your emotional state. If you appear calm and sedated, you are manageable. How often have you heard, just go along with it, don't make a scene, someone will lock you away if you express yourself? We have emotional diseases and mental disease. Physical diseases would be bone related.

One last thing, beware of the moron doctor who says you do not look sick. Remember that when you are, you are only allowed a small amount of emotional expression. I know many who have horrible diseases but they force themselves every day to dress and try to look their very best. Tell me if you have always put on makeup or shaved and you get sick, that you aren't going to try to still look your best. There are some women who would rather die than leave the house without make up, no matter how sick they are. Do not forget, if you show emotions, your doctor will be given a reason to refer you to a shrink. Remember me telling you about that little tag game they play with referrals? Is it really that bad? No, it is worse than I can begin to tell you. Stop going to these idiots. Find the Light people. In all that you search for, find the Light.

Those in the Dark were having children in the Dark. No one was even desiring the Light because of selfishness and greed. By the time many had burned out from life in general, they then moved the same Dark habits to go on their quest for knowledge or what they would call enlightenment. Instead of any clarity, they would further add to Darkness by going to gurus, masters and religion that would validate their habits in the illusion of great change. What applies here is that saying, once a low life always a low life. People would now view these types as bettering themselves, that religion was good. If you are Dark, you are Dark. There is only one way to Light. It is immediate with immediate results. Anything else is power tripping the Light. Why do people power trip the Light? In hopes that along the way they might gain more power for themselves. I thought about my childhood and how it was all so planned. When you know what is coming, you are well prepared. It is that which rushes upon you that causes concern. Only those in the Allegiance could rush upon me. Of course, by now you are saying except for the Soulmate who just seems to be exempt from all things. Do you want to add also the cause of all things? Go ahead, I will back you up on that. Are all people here to meet their Soulmates? No, but they are here to understand it. Many will admit that they have one. Many are curious about theirs but are hesitant at the same time. Can you blame them?

My entire life I had never taken drugs of any kind. I was one hundred percent against this and the reactions I had from an occasional antibiotic were deadly on me. I had violent reactions to chemicals and even walking by a factory or shipyard, I would get very sick. Certain laundry products my clothes were washed in would cause a reaction. One major abuse doctors did was give out too many antibiotics and allow refills so casually. Always the years later news alert, that one should not be on these drugs for months. People just give their power away to doctors. Anytime a doctor gives you anything, it is a risk. With a risk, you need to do your best to stay alert to your own body and know it very well. At any given time for all of us, a complication can arise. Again I say, walk away from the doctor in Dark to the ones in Light.

When it came to doctors wanting to check me out, it was a fatal connection. They were completely dysfunctional. Then came someone like Doctor Scott who was in complete Light. You may say to me, then why was he with Rama? In time you will see what role Scott played in saving my life before he lost his. As I tell you this, I cry. Yes, years later, Scott lost his life trying to save mine.

Many lost their lives and you can bet Lenz could not be linked to any of them. It was always one accident after another. They were not accidents, though, and no one ever thought to look in any other direction. Many did not even know him, yet they went with all of the rest. How many people in a chain reaction know what is going on? Most are so busy reacting they are completely unaware. Lenz also knew that no one would believe me because the human race was too ignorant to recognize anything. Even if they had a clue, the legal system was against them.

It should never have come upon me again but it did. This time with great devastation. Oh God Force, spare me this event, I cried out but my speech fell to the earth and my soul soared to the heavens. I gasped for my breath as a Light, a blinding Light covered me. No one came to my side and thus I was alone, alone with the cello. As it approached, I felt the wrenching pain of its sound piercing my soul. No, I whispered, please go away.

The wrenching was as powerful as the pull to physically move me towards him. I heard the Angels in their chorus. I slowly got up and went towards his shadow, dusted by the moonlight. The swelling of tears burst from me and I lost my resistance to him. I cannot do this, I kept repeating to myself, yet the pull, the wrenching, had taken over me. I could not prepare or anticipate. In my innocence I met his and together we revealed our souls. Before us stood an altar of our thoughts, a nakedness penetrating our clothes and we touched deep inside to the core of our creation. Sadness and loneliness came forward from him as the cello wrenched the casing of the flute. He fell before me and held me, bearing upon me tightly. I felt the limits of the ocean, which were none. He, for the first time, felt my acceptance and cried. He cried so, that I bent down to comfort him. Oh he cried and I did too. Our devastations exploded and then dissipated. How could I have not seen such loneliness, sadness, such bewilderment? I knew it was there for him but for me? Our souls had danced and in this dance, had fallen upon each other, touching and momentarily holding in place. I was terrified and then pleasured greatly. I looked at him and he looked at me. The song had ended and with a deep breath, I sat back and relaxed. The moonlight was flooding in from the skylight, touching me when I turned to see the reflection from the mirrors. The crystals were alive with colors and bursting with energy. As I looked, I saw myself turn into him. This I could never accept. I was in that dream still. Of course, that had to be it. I turned and looked into the mirror again. He was gone and I took a deep breath. I was caught up in the experience. I was tired and that was it.

I closed my eyes and when I opened them moments later, the sun was coming up. Where had I been for all of that time? Waves of fatigue hit me as if I had not slept for days. I was completely worn out as if I had run a marathon. I opened the door and stepped out. As it had happened just after I bought White Allegiance, sparks of Light started coming forward and coming within their own sound. As each Angel made their presence known, the orchestra began. The stroke of each sound had a color and the sky was filled with fire reds and pinks. The music was of that of celebration. I heard the kettledrums and violins. I heard the bells and harps.

"Family," I called out. "Be that of before? " I asked.

Then Zeus came forward with great reflection in his face.

"Father?" I asked, "Father?"

"Oh Daughter, you have done well," he said as he dissipated with all of the rest.

I stood still watching the sun climb with a trail of colors sweeping by me. For a moment I heard the cello. For a moment I heard the flute. The birds began to sing, waking from their darkened night. As for me, I would never, never be the same again but then neither would Frederick. We had both walked on the silk carpet of the soul. There had only been one small strand that needed for thread. With the golden honey of dew, we had put it back together, quickly walking from our work, going greatly with denial. Words with funny meanings came into my head. This did not happen. It was time to bargain with the Allegiance. Such levels of denial began to build that I started telling the Family that the mission had been completed and I was going to get on with my life alone and definitely with him out of it for good. Oh, I went on and on that day, pacing about as if I had the full power of the etheric body upon me. I made it clear that I was now going to have a normal, peaceful life with my house, piano, garden and touch as many lives as possible with Love and Light. I talked until I tired myself. Heavily sure of no success, I finally fell asleep. My last words to the Allegiance that day were, "Thank you Family."

Wait, Frederick? I had called him Frederick. Since when did I refer to Lenz as Frederick? From that point on I could no longer call him Lenz. It had nothing to do with what was proper or correct. The part of him that identified him had now been experienced. He was still Dark but perhaps not quite as Dark. Somewhere in the wonder of this experience a close connection, one born from Light, had been created that allowed me to acknowledge him by his first name. Nothing would change all the violations and degradation of the past, but for some reason I now had a new perspective of this man I had spent so long battling. He still lied, manipulated, charmed and showered the mortal race with his undying charisma. His seduction was filled with flaws but only I could see this. I still wanted nothing to do with him. It seemed like the Family saw it as one big game and it would all be played out at any cost. Everyone kept saying he had met his match with me. Like I was supposed to be impressed? He had reached no status with me. He controlled, bought and sold what he wanted the public to have or know. He never gave anyone a choice to pick or choose.

I had power over the media. I never wanted articles, photos or publicity. One of the reasons I had such a success rate is because everyone was safe and protected. You did not share with the unknowing anything. The unknowing were asleep in the Dark, the Dark Force. If you broke Sacred Law, you would lose all of your Knowingness. I never put on display any such information. I, of all people, knew the costs. When the media tried to harass me or any of my students, they concluded that we were hiding something.

Always the Dark terminologies. We were protecting something far more powerful than their small and unimportant show. One reporter chased me once with a great need to conquer me. He darted in and out of traffic, with near misses on a rental car I was driving. Finally, he darted in front of me with everyone in my car bracing for impact. I told everyone to watch as I set him straight. With both hands up upon my head, I sent him a telepathic message, which forced him to look into his rearview mirror. I then stretched both of my arms straight out and forward in his direction. Great energy came out of my hands sending a powerful force to his body. He bucked, jolted and hit the gas pedal. That car reached top speed, breaking new records. Please do not mess with the Force. Please do not break Sacred Law. And last but not least, please do not do this in front of me or behind me.

Frederick needed to deal with Chris. He needed to strip him down of everyone and everything. He needed to take him apart and permanently put him on the street, hungry, homeless, with a stench about him that would keep all away. Chris needed to become the babbling idiot while still being forced to remember why. He needed to walk the earth a long time in his dirtiness. Never could there be an evil as evil as Chris. My mind could not comprehend it.

No one could do Darkness with such grandeur as Frederick. His Darkness had style, class and an undeniable charm. I had to laugh at times when students had been forewarned not to mess with the master and later they would come back totally fried.

I would say to the whole class, "And what don't we do?"

In a full chorus all would say, "We do not mess with the master."

"Did you actually think he would not keep his word?" I said.

I did not forget this night Frederick and I had. I still did not like him, want him, desire him or even care about him. Could any of that change? No, never . . . well, maybe. It was only a small maybe but it would take the title to Olympus to move me. Only then might I even consider it. For a moment I smiled. I could just see Zeus and Athena trying to draft up paperwork on this.

"Don't even think it!" I concluded.

CHAPTER TWENTYFIVE

I could never forget what Chris had done to me years back. My entire life was changed and for what? How vivid those doctor appointments remained in my mind. The way he was so nasty and ugly. How he glowed when he spoke of his Rama and I would sit there trying desperately to hold back the tears. When I could not, he would yell at me to stop crying. Yes, while he sat next to me telling me all about his Rama, I sat there bruised and beaten by his mentor. When I had tried to tell Chris what he was doing to me, he would immediately change the conversation. Chris wanted me to bow down and continue to thank all of these nurses for caring for me. Oh, how they had gone out of their way for me, he would say. Right from this sick beginning he was evil. I was not even allowed to express myself or to receive medical care all because I would not bow down and receive his Rama as my mentor. Do you know how sick all of this was?

You, reader, must seek out only those in Light. This includes doctors. They really do have a license to kill. If you want to view history, man's history, women were not allowed in anything. Women had to die for their rights and beliefs. Laws written by man have never included women. How many long, hard years have women battled for their rights and their freedom? How long was it before there was a woman doctor? How much longer before a woman doctor was accepted?

Now I have repeated many things and some of you may say, why? You are absorbing Knowingness. Many are used to thinking that they have the full meaning of what I am saying. You are used to thinking I am used to knowing. Knowingness cannot be drafted up in a simple form that you fully comprehend on any level but the soul. Have you ever heard something and then heard it again and again and each time it has a new viewpoint to you? Knowingness comes upon you in the degrees of which you can handle it. With me, there are no crutches such as mentors, channelers, psychics, books or other ways to believe you're going towards enlightenment. You stand before the God Force just as you are this very moment. No search, change, battle, efforts or struggle. You are there just as you are. That is where Enlightenment starts, with you! How much have you given your power away? How much have you spent searching for Knowingness? What has been the price that you have paid? I speak here of the price spiritually, emotionally, intellectually, mentally and physically.

People would come to me from all over. Some have been told about me or read something that gave them great interest. Always they had that lost, searching look that no one else around them seemed to ever notice. How refreshing it was to finally meet someone who actually knew them. I had claimed to have never read any books because the second I laid my hand upon them, I had complete insight on all that the books contained. Again and again people would hear about horrible situations with doctors, lawyers, insurance companies and people from all walks of life. Still they would continue to go back into these situations. If someone is Dark, stay away. Stop feeding this evil because you cannot get out, you know better. You will eventually go completely down while they drain you and get stronger in their evil. Sure, they themselves will fall but long after you have.

There are levels of Darkness as well as Light. Stop being in the grey zone. Take action with the direction you are going. Do not just sit there saying silly things like, god will take care of me or in the right time things will happen. How do you know that the God Force has not been touching your soul and it is saying, "Hello, release yourself, protect yourself, get clarity!" You are not one of those fools on the hill, are you? I am quite confident that if enough Darkness scares the life out of you, you will take action. Why wait until then?

Now, let us move on to more exciting things. Remember, you can never release, protect or get clarity enough. Be responsible and realize all of your thoughts go somewhere. If someone is Dark for one person, they are Dark for all. Do not go to someone who has done Darkness. Only a moron will say, "Well he is good for me but not for someone else." Get a clue. Another moron will say, "It is all opinion." Opinion? Let me tell you what opinion is. It is more Darkness.

I had many students that were gay. I need you all to understand that the soul is what I call the true body. If all is well with the soul that does not mean all is well with the body, no matter what you do. I told you a long time back that gay people do not meet their Soulmates while they are gay. It is not required and it is similar to two batteries being forced together. The energy they give off forces the batteries to push away from each other with a great force. Is there a problem? No but gay people have Soul Energies for relationships. You know how wonderful Soul Energies are.

Remember, I told you about that doctor who had made a great commitment to his Soulmate and then went with a very Dark female and did the threesome. The violation was the betrayal to the Soulmate. It was the breaking of Sacred Law. It was devastating to her as she was making her journey towards him. She will never know the awesomeness of any relationship. For her, she will make sure he is constantly reminded of this. Do not call in your Soulmate and then turn on the violation state. You will have more than you know what to do with. Was it worth the violation to him? Sorry to say, no and he later agreed. I point out in all of this that a sexual relationship may be performed by many in different ways. When you add Soulmate to this, it changes everything. An example now would be that this doctor and his Soulmate had a cheating issue. It is magnified now. You may say, but they had never met.

You see, you are doing the same old human level thinking. We are dealing with the Light and Dark you cannot see. We are dealing with matters of the soul. This threesome act was sick and perverted and violating to his Soulmate. The manner of which it was done and the attitude even increased the levels of trauma. She was left with seeing the cheapness of loving this man. In his sick response he said that maybe he could lie to her about it. You do not lie to the Soulmate. They know, believe me, they know.

So many of you speak without regard for the impact of your words on others. If you are not held accountable for your actions, you begin to trample all over everyone. Oh, you are being held accountable all right, you just cannot see it. So many parents are screaming about their children trampling all over them yet no one ever calls it by its correct name, Darkness. Your children are Dark and evil. How many of you are now screaming at me? What moron decided that Darkness does not hit you until you become of age? Now, what about the parents of these Dark children? They are Dark too or things would be called for what they are.

How is the child to go to Light with its sleepiness keeping the Dark there? Who wakes the child? These children going into Light do not need that great divider of Light called religion. These souls know better. In many ways they are brilliant and in their Darkness trying to do the best in what they know best.

The energy that teenagers give off can be very evil. Instead of being called on their deeds they go further into the Dark, trampling right over their parents. Parents then argue with me that no one woke them up. Do you wonder why I call many, morons? What will floor you is that many also blamed me for not telling them.

I love the one about god is free. No one should charge for services related to god. You are lucky I have not charged you for all of the Dark energy you have been spewing out of your mouth. Only the strong will endure these chapters. Only the ones ready for a wake-up call will make it all the way to the end of this. The violators will suffer great trauma. That comes with trying to power trip Divine Order and breaking Sacred Law.

As much as I tried, I still could not stand Frederick. His ego was so large that he could not understand why all women should not be enslaved to him. The most important thing to him was controlling and owning their orgasms. Even in ancient times this was a male power trip. The root of all Darkness fell upon this area. Even today all of this Darkness is always brought back down to the male female battles and abuses of the sexual nature. Often it can be just a sexist remark that fuels the fire and stirs up the Forces. More Soulmates were together years and years ago. The male knew where to keep his pms because he had found the ultimate fulfillment. Picture a man standing in a silk robe trying to collect his herd of females for the orgasm feast. You are picturing a disgusting low life. This is what the God Force kept telling me I had to Love? Never! Can you understand how strong that word never was? I leave the vivid details of it all to your imaginations. I am sure your each and every thought will be exactly correct. Remember what imagination is. Frederick often had articles written about him stating such sick and sexual abuse. Did someone need to give him a clue that this did not impress people?

I knew every detail and thought that he had and I cringed at the awareness. I was not Deborah Lenz and I made this clear to everyone. Where was this casual slip of the tongue coming from? Good heavens, do you know what that would have done to the thousands I had helped? My whole representation to the Light would have appeared invalid. People would have gone crazy thinking I was a fraud, a phony and had lied to them.

No one wanted to be associated with this man, especially me. I thought strongly that that would be the ultimate way to ruin me. He would have one more huge group of souls that I had once helped tell them I was Deborah Lenz and they would go to the deepest levels of devastation. There was little concern though, because I did not marry him, no matter what fraudulent thing he had done to me.

People did not make him angry because he would hurt them. As for me, not only would I make him angry, I kept it up. Frederick had great problems frying me because I had a tremendous strength and would get right back up. I had beautiful legs for running and that had always been my favorite sport. I had beautiful teeth and everyone wanted them. I had many beautiful things, especially this mane of hair to my waist. The most beautiful thing I had though, was my son, who I deliberately did not speak very much about. Up until now, Frederick had only momentarily tried a few things on him but quickly retreated.

I warned him once in a voice he would never forget. "Touch my child and I will end you, here, now, on this spot at this instant."

He knew I would too. The horrible things he was doing to me did affect my son though but I did my best to shield him at all cost.

I was an intensely private person and this was the one thing in my life that was a constant priority. I retreated often to private places and found such pleasure in solitude. I kept waiting for this mission to end so that I could get on. At the time, little did I know that it would never end. That which was ahead would be so devastating that I would never recover and would be in excruciating pain for the rest of my life. This fate that was coming would make me Deborah Lenz and many that believed what I had taught would turn against me, attack me and try to destroy me, all doing so without ever knowing the facts or even wanting to. I say to you, do not go where evil is. If I tell anything that will greatly help your journey in Light, it is this. Would you go to a doctor like Chris? If so, you are Dark or asking for Darkness in your life. If you say to me that you went to him and he was nice, I will tell you that he gave you the illusion of it. If one person is harmed, no one should ever go there. You do have great power in the Light by not going to such places. You will put the likes of these kinds out of business. Stand up and hold your Light strong. Do not tempt your journey. Do not say that Chris went through medical school and deserves his career. He went to medical school at the cost of souls. They paid horribly for his Darkness and the chain reaction caused by each soul will never see its end.

How dare you tell me Darkness should have privileges, make you sick, take your money and destroy your life. If you believe this, then your soul is already gone. You are not worth the time of day. Remember, the Darkness you cannot see? They are experts at this. You may be thinking that it cannot be that bad. Denial is a great retreat for the follower. You have to know too that Darkness does not want you finding out about their sneaky approach.

Someone like me is pure trouble for them. I can dissipate their powers. The reason it has so much power is because you are unable to see it. What I tell you takes you from the visual of the human level to the visual of the spiritual level. It is similar to a hunt. Let us say you are sent out to find a missing coin, which is hidden deep in grass. You cannot possibly see it but it is not impossible to find it. Notice how, when all else fails you will say something like you sense it is over there or you feel it is over here. You are forced to rely on intuition versus visual. This is just part of an example. It gives you some small insight to the Darkness you cannot see. If you can find a coin you cannot see, you can find an entity you cannot see.

There was no way that you could be around me and not have your Knowingness begin to surface. Every word I spoke was constantly a Teaching. If you spent a day with me, you changed. Communications and teaching for me were as natural as breathing. The reason I could help someone, once out of a cult situation, was because I knew where everything was and where it was going. No one could pull the wool over my eyes. I was upon them before the thought even came into their minds. I was so fast with Knowingness I was in a perpetual state of precognition. For me, there was no entertainment and boredom came often.

I always expected the worse from Frederick and on those rare occasions when he was not, I was quite surprised. I knew his gracious moments would never last but all in all, he was slowly beginning to change. Imagine never being loved for millenniums. This is how I felt about Frederick. I am not talking about that fake, human love. There was a great risk for me going near him. It was just as much of a risk for him. Darkness needed him as their leader. If I were even remotely involved with his going towards Light, it would be devastating.

I knew many people who had a great deal to lose and I had logged my information well into my memory bank. If any of it ever got out, it would cost many their lives. It would be a chain reaction that would never be able to end. It would be the biggest of all violations and Darkness would take all it could, without great intervention. Again and again I told all not to violate their own Knowingness by sharing it with Dark. Your relationship with the God Force will always be intimate and private. You cannot talk to Darkness about such things without violating Sacred Law. Your soul will attempt to intervene if you go too far. Thus, one becomes the babbling idiot. There are no limits with your Knowingness where the God Force is concerned. Ask anything and you will be told but I warn you not to try to violate or sell what you hear. There is more danger in this violation than you can imagine. Your whole life will be of dread and all that you desire will be pulled from you. Great sickness will fall on you and you will be destroyed before you are allowed to destroy souls. If you journey with one in the God Force, you must honor it and it is well to share. You will not violate in this situation. You will know your limits between sharing and keeping things intimate. You will activate your soul for discretion.

My travels took me long and far but no matter where I went, Chris was there ahead of me as if he always knew where I was going. I was always naive about this until I saw it. Whatever made me think that the next move would be Chris free? He was always a sneak and stalked you from behind. My trip up the California coastline was treacherous as Frederick had staked this region out many years ago. Each time I made this trip, it was more overcome with his androids.

Frederick's vibration was strong and he had millions of people under his spell. I use this word spell because many had no idea what state they were in.

Three things were always apparent. California had perversion, great evils and illusions unlike New York, which had chilling cold vibrations, acceptance of evil and many leftover warrior energies. California's battles were internal, New York's were external. Thus comes the statement, "Anything goes in California," versus "if you can make it in New York, you can make it anywhere." People quite often speak great truths without even knowing it. In New York you will have to battle to keep your soul. In California you will lose your soul. I can hear the response to all of this. That is too bad because the only exceptions, of course, are those in the Light. Each state or providence has its own energy just like each country.

Visualize a body covering the earth. Are you part of the arm, leg or heart? Now, where would you find the heart of the United States of America? I will give you an example here. Where you live is important. If you have ever traveled a lot, it is amazing when you cross into another state it really feels like it has its own energy. Why are you drawn to one place instead of another?

Chris' stalking was similar to the feeling that someone was undressing you in their mind. It was ugly and evil beyond even my ability to describe it. The only reason he was stalking me was to find out about Frederick and get revenge on him. The more he stalked the worse Frederick became. Frederick definitely had some nice programs that he put Chris into and like a leach clinging, Chris fell right into every one of them. Eventually though, he would squirm out and be in everyone's face again. He was like the irritating fly that you could not seem to kill. Some of the things I caught him doing to himself in his car were disgusting. Once again, that imagination comes in. For many years Chris had sent his orgasms to his Rama. Frederick had a net up to catch as many as he could. It fueled Frederick because it stripped the power of the female and imprisoned the male. What a perfect setup for a master. This ritualistic behavior was by no means a new philosophy. As I have told you, it goes back to ancient times. The battle was great between Chris and Frederick as it was of a sexual nature that caused such conflicts.

It was my job to help people. I did not need courage. I needed to plow through Frederick's blizzards. He would set things up and then sabotage them. Meanwhile everyone was being torn apart from every direction. I could not stand by and watch it. Where were these people supposed to go? Were they to go to the moron psychiatrist or back to the dysfunctional family? They came to me because they knew I knew the God Force and that is exactly where they craved to go. Even without the words spoken, they knew it from the soul. What else was I about? Soulmates and that was it.

I knew nothing about domestics and for the life of me, I could not comprehend them. I could not even boil water right. No matter how hard I tried I could not understand domestics. I would continually burn food, iron holes in clothes, burn up vacuum motors and stand in wonderment as to how primitive it all was. Matters of the soul do not do control. Matters of the human race do total control. I always talked in the third party. Instead of saying my ankle,

I would say, that ankle as if I had just borrowed this strange part to get around on. I found the human body funny and odd. It only had limited pleasures, which really did not last very long. Much time had to be spent attending to it. People would say, take a shower and you will feel better. I would say in return, go to the God Force, you will feel better. Take that shower to cleanse all of the energy fields you encountered that day. Water was always such a wonderful relaxation. Because I encountered so many energies, I took two showers a day. If it were an especially intense day, I would take a late night bath with my English lavender sea salts. What a heavenly scent and very much my favorite.

It was things like that that made the earth such a wonderful place to be. Never could people just have such pleasure without conditions attached to them. I loved English clothes like the Chesterfield Reefer coat from London. I loved tweeds and English patterns. I thought that I was of English blood until the mystery of who my father was, came about so many years later. I had received a strange note from an unknown person, revealing that my father had actually been the doctor my biological mother had seen during her pregnancy with me. Just what I needed, one more doctor in the picture. It would remain an enigma for reasons only the God Force knew. Here is the funny thing. It bothered some people to no end. How can you not know or not be driven to find out, they would ask me. My answer was, how could you waste so much energy on everything? Where was the God Force? How long would it take some to get their priorities straight?

One thing that was disturbing was how people wanted everyone else like themselves. To give you an example, many gay people would always say to me that they would wonder if someone would end up gay. Will that child be gay or a friend of theirs go gay. Is being gay a sexual thing? No, it is a polarity switch, which creates the desire for the same sex. It is devastating to be gay and desire your Soulmate because it cannot happen as long as you have made a polarity switch.

Hoping someone will be gay is not all right. Finding a wonderful soul energy is. There are so many conflicts for Soulmates that any influence can be disastrous. If Soulmates have had a recent past life where they were gay, the residue may still linger in their memories causing confusion in both.

How many prejudice things are all around you? It is not all right to feel that you are of one race and condemn others who search out something different. It is not all right to force yourself onto or into someone's life because they are different. Honor who you are, all of you. Allow each to go their journeys. If they come along your path, honor, respect and allow each one their own ways. Share your love regardless of differences and allow your light to shine on all.

Soulmates must be recognized as a very delicate and sensitive unity needing no influence from others. Of course, I heard comments like you are no good unless you are black or white or gay or whatever. People, you are no good without the God Force. I do not care who you are, you are nothing without that.

I would like to give you an example of the Dark you cannot see. This should be easy for all of you. There was a very important person needed on the planet, a person in Light. They parked their car in a parking lot where it was a proper place to park. A man in Darkness was programmed to wreck their car, so he drove in and parked behind this person. There were five empty places around these cars but he had an attitude and blocked this car instead. Being alert to everything, when this person in Light came out to leave, they could not move. Immediately they saw a set up. Did this person in Darkness deliberately know that they were about to cause a death? No, they had no knowledge of this on the conscious level. In other words, not on the level of Dark you can see. This person in Light gets in their car and is now lined up for the fatal event. Moments before it happens, they get a flash of being hit by a truck just as it hits this car sticking way out. They begin to write down the events of all of this. Quick, I want to say, get out of the car, it is about to be hit. It is too late though as an eighteen—wheeler makes the bend, thinking no one parked in the fifth lane. He never sees the car and hits it with a great force that slams it into this person in Light, crushing them into a concrete wall. The note was found during the crash cleanup, read and I was called. Yes, it was a deliberate set up. It was Darkness you could not see but if you really looked, all of the clues were there. This person in Light sensed it and even began to write it down long enough before the event to have avoided it. Do not say to me that it was some foolish kid or some innocent event. Trust what your soul is telling you. If what you see or sense does not make it to a full manifestation, it does not mean it is not going to happen. It merely means that the Dark you cannot see changed its direction, usually at the last minute. That is why, when the unsettling feeling goes, it is usually very quickly.

I know that you feel powerless in so much but I will continue to tell you how to get your power back. Do not go near people who do Darkness. Do not! Light will always be Light to you but Dark will only do illusional light. Remember, if one person harms another, they are Dark. If they have not harmed you, it is on its way. Do not tell me that it is not. If you went to a dentist and he caused you great harm, would I go to this person? No and if I did I would begin the initiation of allowing Dark in. You regain your power by not feeding these Dark entities. Let us say someone else goes to this dentist swearing by his or her great deeds. I would say they are in Dark because to get the clarity you need, all you have to do is ask the God Force if someone is in Light. How many souls have had to pay to keep this dentist in his life style? I tell you there are no exceptions unless it is the Soulmate, in which case they may be trying to eliminate you altogether.

How do you hear the God Force? That is a very special class and also very sacred so I cannot go into great detail. I will give you a few examples without giving so much that some moron tries to violate it. The first thing you do is release yourself to the Awesome White Light and Love of the God Force. When asking a question, three very strong possibilities will occur. One, you must listen to the very first answer you get. Any delay brings the answer to your mind where you will start to question it then it is too late. You have power tripped the soul. You may say, god did not answer me. The God Force always answers you, you just may not hear it. I love how some religions will tell you god does not always answer your prayers. I am sure that is true because the god they worship would probably do something like that. Go back now and ask the question again. Release and ask. What comes into your soul? Stop right there. Do not listen for what comes into your mind, listen to your soul. Feel the answer in your soul.

That is where the God Force answers you. Did you get an immediate answer? Yes. Someone else asks a question. No, I got somewhat of an answer. You need to fine-tune your question. It is too involved, so ask it with better detail. This is the second type of answer. Third, then you ask a question and hear nothing. Ask if you should know the answer at this time. You will get an answer and if it is a no you are not supposed to know it yet. The more you ask questions, the more you are using the Knowingness. Remember, circumstances change constantly and your answer may change within minutes or hours.

Some religions teach you that god takes care of you. He is the father and you are the child. That is not what the God Force I know is about. The God Force I know does not make you feel smaller, inadequate or childlike. What a difference. Once again, who wrote down these things? Is it that god that is a male and a bunch of men sat down to interpret this male god? It sounds like transference of role-playing. You know that male thing. The God Force always answers you. You do not wait for answers. To wait would be ego, power trip and control. To wait was designed to show inadequacies, upset of one's journey and a god who picked and chose. It left you hanging. Don't you love the one, in god's time? After all, man was created in god's image. Were the women? In other words, god was a prejudiced, self-righteous man god. The woman did the tempting and she was the cause for bringing the Dark side into man's life. How can you morons believe such garbage? How can you women allow it? So take a look at the pms male control issues. Notice how it can all be justified by the male needing to populate the world so he had to extend his sexual organ all over the place. Women were in bondage. All through history there was always an excuse. After all, he just could not help it. Take a look at all of the wars, it has always been the male pms that has started them. Why don't we address the oldest crime in the world if the true reason for all upset is because of it?

Ladies, get a grip on it all. Stop making excuses. It is a world where women cannot and men can. Women have always been closer to the God Force than men by the fact they are the carrier of the seed. It does not mean you have to have children, just the equipment, whether it ever carries anything or not. What good is the seed if the carrier cannot carry it? Have I not told you this before?

I want you to recognize that all through the human history there has always been a female somewhere in all things. Why then do you have a male god and no female god of the same level? There is absolutely no balance in all of this. Look what this has done to those being born female and fed this very Dark falsehood. It is beyond catastrophic in comprehension. What god have you been talking with?

Time was running out and I could feel waves of this more and more. Frederick had a tenseness about him and the Angels on guard seemed jumpy about every move.

"It comes upon us quickly," Athena said.

"It does Mother and I know not what but it is so Dark," I said.

"Oh, Daughter, I tell you great things now," Athena spoke holding me.

"Mother, you are acting as if I am going away somewhere. Am I leaving? " I asked her.

"Yes and no," she responded.

"You mean on your level I am not but on the human level I am," I inquired.

"Yes Daughter, you somewhat get this," she told me. "We must speak of great things now," she went on to say. "First, I tell you that nothing has gone well. The evil one, Chris, shall suffer beyond what anyone can imagine. His lies and trickery will grow to such evil levels that he will try to kill off all in the Light."

"Take him off the planet Mother," I said.

"If I could I would disassemble him, piece by piece so that the likes of him could never reenter. What he has done has upset the balance of life and he has known it all along. His revenge is so great he even wants to kill the God Force. Your life has been in constant danger and the way you have had to live with your child always on the run will cost Chris everything. As long as you had to keep moving, you were vulnerable. Chris loved seeing this and oh, did he watch it. The minute you came to a stop you were slammed, hit, beaten or broken apart. There was never any recovery for you or your son from the minute that evil manipulator touched you. He wanted you hit in the head because he could do all of his evil on you and later claim, "she had a head injury and made things up." I promise you, Daughter, we will see to the destruction of Chris. One should not want us on their trail."

She went on to tell me many things. Her beauty fused with me, making me feel beautiful but it was clear that a lot of these years had taken a toll on me. In order to do something, I had to collect more and more strength. Chris and Frederick always snuck up behind my back, both attacking me again and again. Chris had his plan but not getting caught was his big concern. Frederick could afford to not get caught. He had schemed for so long, he had plenty of wealth. His trampling over people had truly paid off. Without money, invalidation played. Talk about an evil place to live. Does anyone get the picture yet? When I tell you do not go to Darkness, do not. Many knew all along what Chris was doing. All knew what Frederick was doing. Hundreds of thousands all over the world lost their lives. In all, it was millions but always blamed on something else.

Who do you think programs the mind of the chain reactor? Oh, you do not want to hear it or believe such a thing. How many times have I witnessed this and it was minds like yours that kept such events unbelieved. How many hundreds of students witnessed such powers and were taken out or permanently silenced. You, the unimportant nothing who has never experienced anything, dare to conclude it is unbelievable! It is perfectly designed that way because the Dark Force can always count on your ignorance. Remember, any way you prevent Darkness there is a big dent in their power. Make a list of all of those who have inflicted Darkness and I am not talking about a little spat with someone. Do not go back in any way and connect with these people. Ban together and put them out of business. Get out of this religion that tells you to forgive. What is done is done. Release it to the White Light and go on. Forgiveness is a great excuse to give the illusion of wanting to repair what you intentionally did. Oh, many do not want to hear this.

Did I not tell how your soul, even moments before an event, will alert you to not do something? What you fail to see is the instant result of your actions, which leaves you to believe that you got away with it all. No, you did not. Darkness, the kind you cannot see, was immediately brought in by your stupidity and you fell for it. You had better set a few more place settings at the dinner table because now you have permanent guests. Their appetite is great.

The energy Athena had was even stressed and although you may have felt she spoke in riddles, I understood her. When one is in one's realm trying to translate into another, communications may appear lost somehow. I understood her because I was in my realm with her and I was only a visitor to this earth. It was here on earth that communications kept failing but never with the God Force.

One should want greatly to be as bonded to the God Force as I am. All Darkness wanted to silence, one way or another. I had to out-maneuver everyone. If I went flat line for a few days, I still was attacked. I could not get out even when I walked out. You, none of you, can alter that which is in your journey no matter how hard you might try. You will go through it in the Light or Dark. You have no choices but to be pulled or forced back in it if you attempt to leave. You are not lost, you are merely asleep and it is not too late to wake up.

I stood alone holding my dreams so fragile in my hands. Then I looked up and saw my Soulmate as I removed the paper protective sheet from his face. Tears of great length flooded my eyes as I looked more intensely at him. I could not believe that I had actually drawn his portrait so long ago while I had been temporarily blinded from that accident that had led me to Chris. On a soul level I must have needed him so desperately, that I tried with all that was within me to manifest him forward. I needed him so, my warrior, protector and greatest of all loves that could ever be. He did not come, though, leaving me abandoned. I placed my hand on his face and I knew somewhere, somehow he could feel me. Oh precious Love of mine, I so need you now. Please do not abandon me wherever you are. I gently placed the paper back over his face and sealed up again any hope that we would ever be. Little did I know that the portrait I had drawn looked identical to him, done from my soul while my vision had been so impaired.

Little did I know that Thor, that wonderful giant of such peace had been there all along because he was the father of my Soulmate.

Zeus had good reason to be so in need of battle with him because wonderful Athena, precious, beautiful and oh so wise Athena, was the mother of my Soulmate.

With great absolute I knew beyond all knowing that hope was now upon me greater than ever. Maybe, just maybe, I would find my Soulmate after all.